Not In My Back Yard

∞

THE HANDBOOK

by Jane Anne Morris

Silvercat Publications
San Diego, California

For information, contact Silvercat Publications, 4070 Goldfinch St., Suite C, San Diego, CA 92103-1865.

10 9 8 7 6 5 4 3 2 1

Cover design by Earl Storm. Buckminster Duck, featured character from *Such Is Life!* cartoon strip,

Library of Congress Cataloging-in-Publication Data

Morris, Jane Anne, 1953-
Not in my back yard: the handbook / by Jane Anne Morris.
p. cm.
Includes bibliographical references and index
ISBN 0-9624945-7-7
1. Land use—United States—Planning—Citizen participation—
Handbooks, manuals, etc. 2. NIMBY syndrome—United States.
I. Title
HD205.M67 1994 94-8052
333.73'13'0973—dc20 CIP

Printed in the United States of America
on recycled paper using soy-based inks.

Dedication

To The Inhabitants Of The Next Century ...

Who will surely have lots of questions
for the survivors of this one

This book by Jane Anne Morris teaches Americans who practice democracy how to operate in the realistic arenas that are necessary to negotiate for victory. It also keeps your focus on the larger issues of which your own "Project" is a part. If you use this book you're less likely to lose.

Ralph Nader
Consumer Advocate

Table of Contents

Part II

Therefore, it is noways our interest...
to take away the bridge that is already made,
but rather to build another, if it were possible,
that he might make his retreat with the more expedition.

Aristides to Themistocles, as reported by Plutarch

AUTHOR'S FOREWORD

Lois Gibbs, of Love Canal fame, was only one of the most visible of thousands of ordinary citizens who stood up to proclaim *Not In My Back Yard!* and continued standing until the claim was recognized.

Their issues may be different, but NIMBY activists follow in the footsteps of those who in previous decades had to stand up to claim the right to drink at a public drinking fountain or to vote in a public election.

What the history books call social activism is, to its grass-roots practitioners, no more and no less than a sustained claim to rights supposedly belonging to all.

At first, those who will one day be baptized as 'social activists' are usually considered to be somewhat less noble. Criminal, irresponsible, trouble-maker, fanatic, blasphemer, rabble rouser, lunatic fringe, radical, malcontent — these are among the gentler terms that come to mind. People who opposed widespread atomic testing decades ago may be considered prophetic and heroic today, but those opposing today's chemical plants in minority neighborhoods are called obstructionist and short-sighted. Historical distance elevates and enhances the status of those once denounced as hardly human.

For the most part, NIMBY activists have yet to gain the respect usually accorded social activists of the past. NIMBY campaigns are often inconvenient thorns in the side of larger movements that have master plans outlining what is good for other people. The persistence and diversity of NIMBY concerns promise to make them prominent fixtures of everyday life between now and the millennium.

It is no accident that NIMBY groups proliferated in the 1980s. Environmental concerns of the previous decade expanded the scope of 'quality-of-life' issues and added new dimensions to our understanding of community and occupational health at a time when other trends made conflicting priorities inevitable. The energy crisis of the seventies provided the motivation for becoming energy self-sufficient and for exploiting those energy sources, like coal and uranium, which were plentiful in the U.S. At the same time, so-called rust-belt industries headed for the sun belt, lured by the prospect of lower costs, including cheaper energy and less rigorous regulations.

The resulting convergence of aroused environmental concerns, changing energy needs, and a shifting industrial base provided a backdrop against which new development was visible, and vulnerable, as never before. The often haphazard, sometimes desperate attempts to rearrange our economic landscape left a terrain ripe for the flowering of NIMBY activism, and flower it did.

During this period I was a member of two activist organizations: the Austin (Texas) Citizens/Labor Energy Coalition (C/LEC) and the Central Texas Lignite Watch (CTLW). The issues we dealt with centered on energy policy and related development.

By 1980, Austin citizens had become increasingly leery of their share of a cost-overrun-plagued, behind-schedule nuclear project under construction on the hurricane-prone gulf coast. A long campaign to get Austin to sell its fractional share of the new plant eventually succeeded when citizens voted to sell, only to find that no one would buy.

In the meantime, utility officials and mainstream media asked *how could the city replace this 'lost' electricity?* Some rural activists in a nearby county thought they knew. As Austin tried to back out of the nuclear project amid much fanfare and controversy, it was quietly backing into a commitment to strip-mine and burn vast amounts of lignite, a low-grade, dirty, precursor of coal, which was in plentiful supply in several rural counties within an hour's drive of the state capital.

At about the same time, the Central Texas Lignite Watch, a handful of concerned rural and urban citizens, began working to convince everyone affected — the City of Austin, the local utility company pushing for lignite, numerous regulatory agencies, and most importantly, the people of central Texas — that lignite as a power-plant fuel was a very bad idea.

The campaign brought us into direct contact with federal, state, regional, and local authorities, regulatory agencies, and organizations. It involved issues ranging from strip-mining, to surface and ground water quality and supply, to air pollution, to solid waste disposal, to land reclamation, to alternative energy sources such as solar energy and conservation and natural gas. And, jobs.

Our activities ranged from lobbying, to tedious research and preparation for regulatory agency hearings, to press conferences, speaking to groups along the Texas lignite belt, and mounting appeals in court. We also found ourselves managing a city-wide campaign over a $583 million bond package referendum in Austin.

Over a half dozen years the lignite campaign involved several counties and covered a set of linked but ever-changing project proposals. CTLW was not the only group actively opposing one or more aspects of lignite development. And though CTLW is no longer active, it spawned more than one successor group and inspired many others.

Overall, lignite opponents had some rousing victories and some heartbreaking defeats. Along the way, project opponents made countless mistakes. In many cases, they learned from those missteps and became more effective in subsequent actions. At other times, they paid dearly for their errors in judgment. In the end, some lignite strip-mining and use as a power plant fuel did occur, but on a scale far below that envisioned in the original plans.

In 1980, a group of Central Texans had banded together to oppose an unwanted project. They didn't know they were part of a nationwide trend, and they were too busy to care had they known. Being part of that group allowed me to participate in a process that was confusing and raw and technical and exhausting and, above all, mercilessly educational.

This brief handbook is an effort to condense into a few hour's of reading what one NIMBY activist learned over a decade of research and activism. It's about what happens, not what is supposed to happen (you can read about that in a civics textbook). It's about practices followed, even as they are denounced, not about theories illustrated or refuted (you can read about them in academic journals).

The lessons we learned can be applied to wide-ranging issues, from improving public schools to siting nuclear waste facilities to providing for our energy needs — issues that are all linked through the common need of communities to 'take back the hood.'

Your NIMBY campaign will be a little like learning to play the accordion. You'll find yourselves combining simple skills in complex and unexpected ways. You'll become involved with people of all age groups and ethnic backgrounds. It will not always fun for people close to you, and it may be very scary to do in public, especially the first time.

You'll never know what's coming, or what you'll be asked to play next. Sometimes you'll surprise everyone by playing it perfectly, down to the last theme and variation. At other times you'll be unable even to grasp the tune. That's when someone else in your group will step forward and continue the melody...or harmony...or a whole new song.

Playing an accordion changes your wiring forever. So does working in a NIMBY campaign. The world will never look quite the same. And, thanks to the work of NIMBY activists of the past, present, and the future, the world will not be quite the same, either.

I would appreciate receiving any comments about this book or NIMBY issues in general. Please write me in care of the publisher to share your observations and let me know if our successes and failures at playing our 'acordion' have contributed in any way to your NIMBY efforts.

Good luck.

Jane Anne Morris
Hope, New Mexico
January, 1994.

Acknowledgments

In the beginning, the only way for us to learn the stuff in this book was the hard way: we just had to do it. My thanks go out to all those who took on the enormous task of trying to shape their own futures, including those who did so before the Not-In-My-Back-Yard slogan was even invented. Reports of their successes, and their failures, have guided those who later assumed similar tasks.

Members of the Central Texas Lignite Watch (CTLW), the group I worked with, were exceedingly diligent and creative in their efforts to stop an undesirable Project. Without minimizing the work of anyone who contributed to the lignite campaign, I would especially like to thank Margaret Campbell, whose contributions were so varied and lasting that I couldn't even begin to enumerate them. Bill Bishop, editor and publisher of the *Bastrop County Times* in the mid-eighties, added an investigative journalist's perspective to our NIMBY enthusiasm. I learned a tremendous amount from these folks and everyone else who shared our common burden.

I want to thank John Henneberger and Lanny Sinkin for the examples they set; J. M. Baime, C. Baime, K. Batt, and Robert Lawrence for inspiration and conversation; A.G. Hudgens for editorial comments; R. Balkin for just being himself; and DDD for never letting me get away with anything.

These acknowledgments would not be complete without an expression of appreciation for reference librarians everywhere, who behaved as if their goal really was to help people get the information they seek. They helped me pull rabbits out of hats on numerous occasions. Special thanks to the reference librarians at the Jefferson Madison Public Library in Charlottesville, Virginia for their eclectic collection and their assistance in helping me use it.

I want to thank Pam Pettee of Silvercat Publications, who has been direct and enthusiastic while providing constructive criticism and needed perspective.

The hundreds of community college students who marched through my classes during the 1980s persisted in asking the kinds of questions that come from life, not books. In responding to them, I had to revive brain cells left dormant by academic discussions. My thanks to all of those students for the education they gave me.

I have some experience at LULUs (Locally Unwanted Land Uses, facilities that are often opposed by nearby residents). I want to thank the men of the six-digit numbers for allowing me a glimpse into life in their LULU. Thanks to AW for letting me in through the gateway to another, where I had the great privilege of meeting Alan, Broadus, Clarence, Curlie, Dianne, Gordon, Judy, Lillie Mae, Linda, Roger, Sidney, Susie, and Walter. Words fail me, but these people never failed to remind me, even in the darkest of times, of how great, and brave, our species can be.

Veronica Ateaga M. listened to much whining and rambling about NIMBY issues, and took the time to deep-six numerous drafts that she could have more easily ignored. This book isn't the book it once was, and I have her to thank for it.

INTRODUCTION

You haven't been awake for very long, and you are still trying to remember if you took the garbage out last night, when you get a quick, garbled phone call from a neighbor. Have you heard about the *thing* that *they* are going to bring into town? Your neighbor is upset but rushing to work. So, you get a newspaper and read about it for yourself.

The *thing* you read about may be a hazardous waste dump, a new highway loop, an airport, a dam and giant reservoir, a pesticide plant, a race track, a missile practice range, a strip mine, a genetic cloning research facility, a large government building complex, a nuclear fuel reprocessing plant, a coal-fired power plant, a golf course, a super-collider — or any one of the other projects that someone somewhere is always planning.

The *they* behind the thing can be the government (local, state, federal), any of its agencies or subdivisions (the waste water department, a state university, the Army), a small private company, a multinational corporation, or more and more often a combination of some of the above, probably calling itself something like a consortium, a joint venture, or a public-private partnership.

The newspaper article then quotes a few company or government officials promising that all relevant environmental standards will be met or exceeded. Any number of experts will then be cited to the effect that this thing will cause fewer deaths annually than pet hamsters and that there is only one chance in twenty-three zillion of a catastrophic accident.

Finally, the article will quote local politicians, members of women's groups and minorities organizations, Boy Scout troop leaders, Chamber of Commerce members, and labor union officials, all praising the project for the *jobs* it will bring. If the project in question is not very job-intensive, the article will offer impressive numbers for projected tax revenues or tourist income.

You and your neighbor, both opposing the project, don't believe the rosy picture being painted. If you are just going to complain and do nothing, don't read any further unless you're curious about what other, more active doubters in the community will go through. If you want to stop the Project, read on.

This book will greatly improve your chance of winning your battle, because it will tell you what *they* are going to do. If you don't know *their* tactics and game plan, you cannot win. If you do know them, you have a chance.

Not In My Back Yard: The Handbook assumes that you, the reader, are confronting a worst-case situation and tries to prepare you for it. If your predicament is not so drastic, you are a step ahead. But in a NIMBY campaign, especially before you have had a chance to find your sea legs, a splash of paranoia can protect you from many of the mistakes over-confidence can engender. Later on, after you have gotten your bearings, you can fine-tune your strategies.

Before you go on to the rest of the book, some clarification is in order.

First, who are *you* and who are *they?* This book will not define either, but both are very important. *You* and *they* are alike in many ways. And, your ideas about who *they* are will change as you read this book and as you fight your battle. *They* are referred to hereafter simply as *Entity*. And whatever Entity would like to bring into town is called the *Project*.

Second, this book makes no judgments on the merits of individual projects or on the motives of those seeking to stop them or to complete them. The tactics and strategies used against you will be the same whether the Project is an outstanding one or a horrendous one. This book gives you some idea of what to expect and how to respond.

Third, in almost every case, the names of Entities, Projects, and opponents have been changed or otherwise obscured. This book is not written to point a finger at 'guilty' parties or to ridicule those who, in their own minds, are doing the right things. After all, one of the lessons of this book is that your opponents are not necessarily evil people. For our purposes here, it is the example that is important, not the naming of names or the imputation of villainy.

Fourth, most of the people associated with the Project already know this stuff. Planners, bankers, government officials, company vice presidents, politicians, bureaucrats, lawyers, consultants, engineers, public relations people, and others involved with the Project know all about their parts in the process and the tactics that go with them (even though part of their role is to deny that they are using tactics.) Don't expect any of them to agree with characterizations made here. This book is written specifically for members of the public who are at a significant disadvantage because they are not big shots.

One final comment. By the time you even hear about the Project, Entity is already light-years ahead of you. This is not encouraging, nor is it unusual. Entity expects you to be confused, disorganized, and ill-informed. The goal is to play your catch-up game faster and better than expected, so that you may turn your underdog's position into a useful, if temporary, advantage.

Not In My Back Yard: The Handbook consists of two sections. Part I provides an overview of a typical NIMBY campaign. It takes you through each phase of the battle, from the day your group first organizes to the day when there is nothing left to be organized about. Along the way, it discusses the essential things that you need to do — organizing your group, conducting research, educating the public, attending hearings and court appeals, protecting your flanks, countering the sophisticated arsenal of persuasions and appeals that Entity has at its disposal, and, where appropriate, negotiating a successful end to your whole NIMBY campaign.

Part II fills in the necessarily abstract discussion of Part I with additional resources and practical examples of what other NIMBY activists have had to deal with. It is impossible, even for veteran NIMBY activists, to imagine all the things a creative Entity might do to accomplish its strategies. The examples offered in "A Dictionary of Tips and Tricks" illustrate some of the things that Entities have tried to do in the past. These vignettes and anecdotes should help you prepare yourself for both the predictable and the unanticipated maneuvers that spring from the fertile Entity mind.

A bibliography rounds out Part II. This supplements the reference citations which occur throughout the book. It includes works which amplify the more general discussions in the text. It also includes a large number of resources which will help you view your own NIMBY issue in the context of the larger world.

Chapter 1

THE BIG PICTURE

What have you gotten yourselves into? You and some friends decided that you are against the Project and have formed some sort of group. From the very beginning, you need some idea of what to expect. You should also talk about and define your goals.

This book will help you do both. This chapter will give you a preview of what later chapters will cover.

NIMBY! and Proud

As soon as you organize against a Project, the rest of society will declare you to be a NIMBY, a person who fights against a Locally Unwanted Land Use (a LULU) by insisting, *Not In My Back Yard!* The whole NIMBY phenomenon is profoundly irritating to those who are accustomed to planning others' lives.

Once dumped into the NIMBY category, you become the target of abuse and derision. The intent of such attacks is to make you feel ashamed and guilty and to weaken your determination to continue in your NIMBY role. In order to avoid becoming depressed, doubtful, ashamed, or guilty about your NIMBY role, you need to feel comfortable with your active opposition to a Project. Stepping back a moment to survey the NIMBY phenomenon makes this easier.

Everyone is a NIMBY and no one wants a LULU. One might oversimplify a little and say that there are only two kinds of people: public NIMBYs and stealth NIMBYs. Stealth NIMBYs are generally the affluent, the influential, and the well-placed who can the keep LULUs out of their neighborhoods by quietly exerting their influence behind the scenes during the decision making process. Usually, their turf is not even considered as a site. Public NIMBYs, lacking such political clout and effectively excluded from most of the decision making process, have to fight it out in the public domain.

Your group and its members are public NIMBYs. You organized to oppose an unwanted Project in your community. Your emergence was probably announced in the local paper, where prominent members of the community took the opportunity to describe your group and its views as selfish, unscientific, and confused. You will have to fight it out in the public domain of regulatory agencies, city councils, courts, and news media. There is a better than random chance that most of your members are less than affluent, minority, rural, or Southern. Your public NIMBY group is conspicuous partly because of its contrast to stealth NIMBYs.

Stealth NIMBYs are people who *don't* work at dangerous, unhealthy jobs and *don't* live near toxic waste dumps, nuclear weapons factories, or other undesirable facilities. Nor do they want to. They have never had to raise their voices to keep such facilities away, because anyone seeking to site such facilities knows enough not to do so in affluent white suburbs.

These stealth NIMBYs include people like government officials, corporate managers, and professionals and experts of various kinds who make decisions about the location of LULUs. Not surprisingly, most LULUs have been sited in areas where residents had the least chance of successfully opposing the Project.

Stealth NIMBYs have seldom had to speak out because they have rarely been backed into a corner, even when others — the would-be victims — claimed the right to be NIMBYs too. Often these would-be victims are the same people who struggled to ride in the front of the bus, to get paid a decent wage for their labor, or to enjoy equal access to the job market. Now they have to raise their voices once again to maintain the same control over the quality of life in their neighborhoods and communities that stealth NIMBYs have largely enjoyed as a matter of course.

Stealth NIMBYs also include those who have simply never had to face a NIMBY threat. They may have looked the other way when a toxic dump was sited on the opposite side of town, or they may have been honestly unaware of the controversy. They are neither more nor less selfish than public NIMBYs. The community at large may not have heard their voices, but they don't want to live next to a LULU, either. Public and stealth NIMBYs share the desire to avoid being exposed to unpleasant and perhaps dangerous facilities. Having this in common makes them potential allies. Potential allies should be courted, not condemned.

However, public NIMBYs pose two threats to at least some of the stealth NIMBYs and the interests they represent. The first is the possibility that it will become extremely difficult to site any new LULUs. Thus NIMBY gridlock becomes possible, making most current standard operating procedures ineffective. The second threat is that the hitherto voiceless, the newly visible public NIMBYs, will demand to be part of a decision-making process which was once limited to a few government officials and corporate planners.

Public NIMBYs are doing no more than demanding that the privileges and responsibilities of the democratic process be extended to them, too. Welcome to the club!

The Road is Long and Hard

The organization (*Entity*) proposing the Project will be a formidable foe with nearly infinite resources. It has access to the best experts, consultants, lawyers, and public relations specialists that money can buy. These people do this as a job, and are paid well (some would say excessively) for their services. If some quit, or retire, or decide to change careers and become midwives or ski instructors, others are hired to carry on.

Entity is in this for the long haul. You must be, too, though you will certainly be unable to match its resources. Your work opposing the Project will probably never be paid. In fact, the likelihood is that you will be constantly trying to raise money through whatever kinds of donations, memberships, bake sales, or other means that you can devise. Your opposition to the Project may well put a strain on your relationships with friends, family, and perhaps your co-workers and may even involve you in personal risks. Physical, legal, or financial intimidation, while not commonplace, is a possibility as well.

Because it is so easy to lose your perspective in a situation like this, it is especially important for you to be realistic at all times. Over-optimism only leads to depression and despair when you lose a decision of some kind. You will lose many of these battles, but that doesn't mean that you will lose the war. You must be present for some of the battles in order to continue the game. Those losses are not necessarily setbacks.

On the other hand, being pessimistic and cynical doesn't help either. Negative attitudes result in depressed or angry activists who are more likely to make misjudgments and less likely to handle the press well, recruit new members, inspire current members, or get much else done.

Phases of the Battle

Most controversial Projects go through a cycle of stages. Not all of these stages apply to each Project and often several things go on at once. In a typical case, though, you can expect the following stages.

Information Gathering: Shortly after the public discovers the plans for the Project, one or more groups form to oppose it. They then go through an intense period of gathering information on the legal, technical, economic, and political aspects of the Project. This takes time and patience, often involving lawyers and specialists as well. The information-gathering process continues as long as you oppose the Project. There is always information that you have not yet uncovered, while new information is being generated all the time.

In the beginning, Project opponents have a lot of catching up to do. Later, as they become more familiar with the key sources of information, it gets somewhat easier.

Public Education: The task of public education also begins as soon as your group meets, if not before. The appearance of any opposition to the Project is news. The sooner you are able to take advantage of the free media attention surrounding the issue, the more effective your group will be.

Chances are good that the media will perceive the controversy at the outset as David-versus-Goliath. This can work to your advantage. Though the fate of most Projects is not decided by referendum, popular support can be invaluable in gaining the backing of powerful political figures and groups. And, being perceived as serious, honest underdogs will aid in your fundraising efforts.

Sometimes, an election, ballot initiative, or referendum on the Project will be held. Some states make it relatively easy for citizens' groups to get an item on the ballot. In other cases, certain types of Projects require a public vote of approval. A public referendum on the Project should usually be considered as a last resort, not to be embarked upon unless your group is large, well-organized, and well-funded. The amounts of money involved are huge, the attacks vicious, and much of the detailed information you gathered for regulatory hearings and court appeals will be useless.

Like information gathering, public education never stops. Continual public education provides a background of awareness against which certain crises, accompanied by press conferences and pleas for donations, will stand out and be understood.

Regulatory Agencies and Hearings: At some point, you will take all of the information you have gathered and put it to use in a new and very important arena: the regulatory agencies. Entity will be required, by local, state, and/or federal law, to obtain a number of permits before going ahead with the Project. Your group needs to consider challenging every permit that is sought from the time you find out about it.

Before a permit is granted, hearings of one kind or another may be held. Some of these may be required, while some will be held only because they have been requested. Some hearings provide an opportunity for you actually to present arguments, while others are little more than an excuse to hold a press conference and demonstrate broad popular support.

Your NIMBY group will probably spend a great deal of time, effort, and funds preparing both for these regulatory hearings and for the larger process that leads to the granting of a permit. This is where the government can say *no* or much more likely, *yes, but with these conditions.*

Even on a fast-track, most regulatory hearing processes take months, and, on a typical schedule, they can easily last one to two years. During this time, you must keep people's enthusiasm up, go on with your public education, fund raising, and information-gathering. You also need to be preparing for the next step after you've exhausted the regulatory agency procedures: the courts.

The Courts: Under certain conditions, your group may choose to appeal the decisions of a regulatory agency in a regular civil court. If your group feels that your arguments were not handled appropriately by a government agency, you have the option of suing the agency for not carrying out its responsibilities correctly. These court actions can also go on for some time, because there are numerous provisions for delays, re-hearings, and appeals.

Your group will not have the resources to pursue all of the regulatory and court-related possibilities. You will continually have to evaluate the best options — those which give your group the most advantages in terms of media exposure or delays and those which offer the actual possibility of bringing the Project to a halt or at least of throwing substantial obstacles in front of it.

The End Game: Three especially tough issues are likely to surface before you conclude your NIMBY campaign. The first topic is the apparent trade-off between jobs and the environment, a dilemma that is often the centerpiece of a NIMBY controversy. The second involves your response when people begin to agree that the Project is far from ideal but are unable to formulate any convincing alternative courses of action. The third area may be the most difficult and dangerous aspect of the whole NIMBY campaign: what to do when Entity's lawyers approach your group with a settlement proposal.

Nothing Is Final: Whether the arena is the regulatory agencies, the courts, or the voting booth, one thing is certain: nothing is irreversible. Entity can come back in six months, two years, or five years and start again. It has the resources to pay its staff and consultants to do this. All you can do is hope to defeat Entity soundly enough the first time that it doesn't even think of trying again anytime soon. That may be difficult, but it is not impossible.

Goals

Each campaign to stop a Project has its own unique rhythms and paths. Your group can wield some influence, but outside factors will always play a large role. Once you have some idea what the overall campaign might involve, it is time to define your goals, evaluate your options, and set strategies, all in view of the circumstances which make your campaign unique. Consider the following as soon as you can.

Stop It: You may wish to stop the Project altogether. In order for this to happen, either the government or courts must say *No* or the Entity proposing the Project must say *Never mind.* The government rarely issues a clear negative, but conditions, delays, increased costs, or bad publicity can encourage Entity to abandon the Project.

Remember again that nothing is final. Most agency rulings and court decisions are subject to appeal or review, and Entity may pursue one of those options. It is common practice to withdraw a proposal for a few months or years, change it a little, and then bring it up again repackaged or renamed. And the second time around may be tougher. Entity will learn from any mistakes it made the first time around; be sure that you do, too. Entity will be much tougher to deal with in round two.

Move It: You may be willing to accept just forcing the Project to move elsewhere — across town, out of state, or even to another country. Your own consciences and local conditions will affect this choice. If Entity decides to re-propose the Project for another site, you still have the option of sharing your information and experience with those concerned about the second site.

Modify It: Another possibility is that you may be offered something in exchange for withholding your opposition from a modified version of the Project. This modified version will be given an innocent-sounding name, or called 'small scale,' a 'support facility,' or some other phrase suggesting that hardly anything is going on there. Before you agree to Entity's proposal, review "A Foot In The Door," in Part II. It is to Entity's advantage to get both official permission and your group's consent to set up some sort of facility. Within a short time of getting its foot in the door, and usually very quietly, Entity may apply to expand the facility (and expansions of existing facilities generally do not face most of the procedures associated with a new facility).

Alternatively, Entity may agree to accept certain conditions if you agree to accept the Project. These conditions may be promises to live up to this or that standard, to take such-and-such steps so that a particular accident will be less likely, or to accept similar self-imposed constraints.

It is very dangerous to agree to such modifications or conditions. The government or company official who makes the promises may be gone in a matter of weeks. Moreover, because the enforcement branches of most government agencies are underfunded, understaffed, and possibly underenthusiastic, most regulatory agencies get their information from the same people they are supposed to be checking up on.

Just look around the country and remind yourself of how rarely promises are kept.

Delay It: Your most realistic goal may be simply to delay the Project and hope that something happens to stop it. Delays almost always work to the advantage of the opponents. (Elections are frequently but not always an exception to this.) Delays cause Entity to spend more money on lawyers, experts, and other consultants. They also tie up investor money that could be working elsewhere. A delay allows both sides to continue politicking, and this can work in your favor if it permits more people to hear your message.

As delays continue, various facts of life change. The apparent viability of the Project is dependent on a number of factors, many of them economic. Such things as interest rates, the price of a pound of uranium, the exchange rate of the dollar, the unrest in South Africa, the price of a barrel of oil, or a change in the minimum wage all may affect the cost of the Project and Entity's enthusiasm for it.

Meanwhile, political changes following local, state, or national elections may alter the viability of the Project. Sometimes delaying it until conditions change is sufficient to cause the Project to expire on its own. Even if it still breathes after a few years of delays, the data in early studies will be out-of-date, and the whole red-tape cycle must begin again.

Strategies

Though many strategies are offered, this handbook does not recommend any particular overall strategy. The winning strategy or strategies will have to be guided by the realities of each case and emerge out of your group's research and political savvy.

In this contest, Entity is not starting at zero. A great deal of professional expertise, sharpened by a decade of growing NIMBY activism, is poised to thwart any efforts to slow the progress of the Project. Entity has a bag of tricks to draw on in its quest for success. Many are old standards used again and again because they work. Others are brand-new and designed for new situations as they arise.

Conversely, NIMBY groups and other activists have their own arsenal of tactics to increase their chances of success. The difference is that Entity's team has experience, professional resources, and ample funding, whereas the members of a typical NIMBY group have much less experience with organized intrigue and considerably more modest access to resources and funds.

The best protection for your group, and the greatest threat to the Project, is that you begin thinking like Entity, thus learning to anticipate and counter its strategies. The more you know about the Project, its history, and its backers, the closer you come to gaining the insights that enable you to stop it. "A Browser's Dictionary of Tips and Tricks" in Part II offers a selection of anecdotes, examples, and suggestions that will enrich your understanding and bring you closer to making your own NIMBY fight a successful one. Look it over and let it inform your perspective, but don't expect that the Entity you are facing will confine itself to following the scripts outlined there. Each NIMBY campaign is unique. Your group can take advantage of this uniqueness by making the most out of every opportunity that comes your way.

Chapter 2

YOUR NIMBY GROUP

During the first few informal gatherings of people opposed to the Project, you may not even think of yourselves as a group. But, if you are serious about opposing the Project, eventually you will decide that you need to create some sort of organization. This chapter gives a quick survey of some of the issues likely to arise.

Join Up or Start Your Own Group?

One of the first questions that will come up is whether you'd be better off by joining or working through an already-existing group or by forming a new, single-issue group.

Working with an existing organization has numerous advantages. The group is already known, and it has a structure, a membership, a mailing list, and probably some funds. It also has a history of contacts with other organizations and individuals who may share your views or at least be sympathetic and willing to hear you out. There are many examples of church-related organizations, environmental organizations, or social clubs taking on particular issues that arise in a community.

On the other hand, there are disadvantages to plugging into existing groups. They have their own range of interests and priorities which may not match well with the new issue. They may rightfully resent a sudden influx of new members who are fanatical about one issue but show little interest in or understanding of the group's other concerns. Unless the existing groups wholeheartedly embrace your new issue, it may be preferable simply to keep them informed, ask for their support, borrow their mailing lists, and start your own group.

Existing groups can still extend valuable assistance. They are known in the community, and their support can attract attention to and strengthen your cause. Your new group will be taken more seriously if you can draw support from a wide range of groups already recognized in your community. Also, if each of the groups that supports you takes slightly different positions on the Project, Entity will have to respond to a more complex range of issues.

Despite the bad press that single-issue groups, especially NIMBYs, have received in recent years, they have some tremendous advantages. They have a clear, often urgent focus: stopping a Project. In contrast to some well-established organizations, meetings are not taken up discussing the exact duties of the third vice-president or what kind of refreshments to serve at the picnic. People don't go to the meetings so they can be elected honorary chairperson or wear special ceremonial regalia. They are there because they feel that their whole way of life is threatened by someone else's great idea and they want to do something about it.

Your First Few Meetings

During organizing meetings, your informal, single-issue group will probably divide its time haphazardly among three activities. First, people who have picked up bits of information here and there will share it with the group. Don't assume that everything you hear is accurate, but take it seriously enough to check it out. Second, people will be expressing anger and frustration. This is understandable and can inspire and unite the group. After your first few meetings, though, keep this to a minimum. Finally, your group will certainly talk about what to do about the project. Not everyone will agree on tactics.

There may be some who favor pouring sugar into the gas tanks of the construction equipment and others who think that writing letters to their friend in Congress will straighten it all out. Obviously if these people all keep coming to the same meetings, you may never agree on priorities and courses of action. But it is all right, even desirable, to have two or more groups at the outset.

These groups may work closely together or not even know what the others are doing. Some groups will be formally and legally organized and incorporated, while others may have hardly any structure at all. Information can be shared. Of course, any particular individual may choose to belong to more than one group if he or she so chooses.

You, or some of you, will almost certainly want to incorporate as a non-profit, educational group for the purpose of doing research, preparing and sending out newsletters or other notices, and developing other opportunities for public education. If the group follows the rules and regulations of your state and the Internal Revenue Service, limiting its activities as specified, then its tax-exempt status will provide advantages for the group itself and for those making tax-deductible contributions to it.

It is a fine line you will be walking. Anthony Mancuso, in his "Guidelines for Nonprofits," summarizes your situation.

> [N]onprofits must educate themselves about the federal laws that limit lobbying and other political activity. If they don't, they risk paying substantial fines and can even jeopardize their tax-exempt status. On the other hand, if they are too afraid of violating the rules, they may unnecessarily restrict their political activities.

There are several kinds of nonprofit organizations. For up-to-date information about nonprofits, contact the *IRS* and ask for current information and guidelines about nonprofit status.

Some of you may wish to do more than public education, working instead on lobbying appointed or elected officials, seeking to influence the outcome of elections, or initiating legal actions in regulatory agencies and the courts. Pursuing these goals can influence your tax status, obliging you to collect and disburse funds under different conditions than would apply if you were a tax-exempt organization.

Try to insure that all those opposed to the Project find a niche — inside a formal group or not — where they feel comfortable to act as their abilities and consciences dictate. There is no point in listening at each meeting to pointless arguments between the letter-writers and the sugar-pourers.

This book will be most useful for those who want to do more than write letters but want to avoid acts that the legal system would call vandalism. Letter writers can find the addresses of elected officials in the phone book without the aid of this handbook. If you are ready to disable vehicles, you probably already know what's in this book.

When you decide about the kind of group or groups which meet your needs, be sure to take the correct legal steps to formalize the organization. Consult a how-to-incorporate handbook from a local library, borrow the by-laws from similar groups to use as guidelines, or consult an attorney. More specific information on organizing and/or incorporating your group will be found in the bibliography.

Be sure to keep careful records of money which you collect and disburse. Do not mix funds collected for different purposes. Follow the guidelines in handbooks for public non-profit organizations or follow an accountant's advice. Don't complicate your lives by adding the IRS to your problems.

Practice what you preach. If your group demands accountability of the Project and government regulators, you must also be accountable to your members. Failure to do so can give rise to suspicions about your group and its funding sources.

What's In a Name?

Your group needs a name. The name is one more tool in your arsenal. Before you choose one, make sure that your goals are clear, then find a name that matches your goals. If you want the name of your group to be on people's lips, choose a name that they can remember. Sometimes it is important that your group attract attention, and a flashy name or acronym will do this. Names like *ACT UP* and *Earth First!*, for example, are forceful and memorable (and already taken).

If you want to stay in the background or work behind the scenes, choose a more boring, subdued name. It is sometimes an advantage to sound wimpy and forgettable or neutral and faceless. Some private consulting firms and research organizations intentionally choose names that sound similar to government agencies and departments so that their names suggest that they are in some way official or objective.

If you want your name to reflect the fact that you are all strongly opposed to the Project, make it clear by naming your group something like *Citizens Against the Project*. If the group or one of the groups is to be primarily and officially an educational group, the name should imply this. So, while one group may retain the name *Citizens Against the Project*, the educational group should be called something a little milder, like *Project Education Group*. When you or your colleagues make public appearances, have private meetings, or hold news conferences, make sure you state exactly which group you are representing.

Sometimes groups prosper and multiply as the issues become more complex. A splinter group may split off from the main group to focus on an issue that has become especially important, say the health or transportation aspects of the Project. The splinter group can take a name that no one has heard before, produce its own educational materials, circulate petitions, and otherwise pursue its own goals. Splinter groups can maintain contact with the original group.

Your Group At Work

Fortunately, individuals have a variety of different talents, interests, and abilities. Your new group will need to take advantage of many of them. Roughly, the areas a group needs to develop are research, public education, money, and record-keeping. These are applied to specific areas like lobbying, regulatory agencies, the courts, and elections.

Research: If some members of your group have research experience or are good at getting information, they should help with the research. (See Chapters 4-6, below.) The researchers will identify and gather the information that the whole group needs. Some will probably work closely with legal advisors, focusing on especially useful information and, with some luck, saving your group some money in legal fees.

Public Education: Research information will also be used to educate members of your group, the public, the news media, and perhaps even agencies and public officials as well, though both the latter may be much more resistant.

Your group will need information sheets and, later, whole packets or brochures to distribute every chance you get. They don't need to be fancy or clever, but they should be clear and easily understood. Regular newsletters are also excellent ways to educate a public and to raise funds. In order to have a successful public education campaign you'll need more than good researchers. You'll also need people who can write clearly for a general audience.

It is also very helpful to enlist your members' artistic talents when you are designing information sheets, newsletters, or posters. Artistically inclined members of your group can provide valuable help by taking photographs or slides for various public presentations and by preparing illustrations, maps, and diagrams for educational purposes.

The public education function, discussed in Chapter 7, involves not only information sheets, newsletters, and posters, but also other outreach efforts. Some of your members will be interested in public speaking, radio talk shows, and the like. If no one jumps at the chance initially, someone will grow into the role as your members sort themselves out into the areas that utilize their various talents or potentials.

Money: Your group needs to raise money and keep track of where it comes from and where it goes. You will need money for copying, printing, sending letters and newsletters, posters, paper supplies, photography, phone calls, transportation, and legal fees, legal fees, legal fees. You probably will never have as much money as you could use effectively, so be sure that your group agrees generally on its priorities. Don't print expensive brochures if you lack the money to pay for copies of important documents, for example.

Someone in your group may have done fund-raising before. Those who have a natural affinity for this activity should be strongly encouraged. Some people have a genius for organizing fund-raisers. Others can get famous people, musicians, artists, and restaurants to donate goods and services. And still others are adept at managing the whole production, big or small, smoothly from beginning to end. People like this are invaluable, and it should be a high priority to recruit them.

Just as important is the person designated as treasurer. This individual is responsible for keeping your financial records straight. A good treasurer helps your group avoid problems with the IRS, local businesses, attorneys, and anyone else with whom you do business. Incomplete or garbled financial records can cause complicated problems that you may never straighten out and may leave your group liable to legal actions taken against it. That is the last thing you need.

Being the group's treasurer is a heavy responsibility and may become very demanding. Rotating the duties of treasurer among different people each year or so will relieve the personal burden, familiarize other members of the group with the duties of the office, and build trust among members of the group.

One caveat in the financial arena. Do not let your group become dependent on one or two 'sugar daddies,' individuals or businesses that contribute large amounts to your group's treasury. If disagreements or other difficulties arise, these individuals or businesses may seek to exert excessive influence over your group's decisions and actions.

Record-Keeping: While leaving all financial records to the treasurer, someone still needs to keep the rest of the group's paperwork organized. Volunteer lists, addresses, phone numbers, lists of newsletter subscribers and contributors all need to be kept in useful and convenient form. There is no point in collecting sign-up sheets at all public events if you aren't going to use the names and addresses, or worse, if you are not able to locate them when you need them.

Your group will also generate fact sheets, handouts, newsletters and similar literature at a rate more rapid than you might now believe. Copies of all of your literature should be clearly labeled, dated, and kept for reference or future use.

Copies of various official reports, reference books, documents from government agencies, court-related papers, and other useful materials also accumulate quickly. Establishing an informal group library (often in a member's house or apartment) where reference materials are available will make it much easier for the members of your group doing legal and public education work.

Finally, record-keeping involves keeping a detailed calendar of events, past, present, and future. This calendar should include news conferences, speaking engagements, fundraising events, public hearings, group meetings, court appearances, and any deadlines relevant to your group's activities. Outcomes and results of hearings, court cases, and a wide range of other government actions should also be noted.

With all the activities in which your group will participate, it is important that someone keep track of the total picture in order to minimize the problems which result from missed deadlines, missed appointments, and other costly errors. A complete calendar-record of this sort is also extremely helpful when preparing written or oral summaries and histories of the Project controversy.

People are people, and things will not always get done when you want them to. Seemingly simple tasks have a way of ballooning into enormous undertakings. Even when this doesn't happen, some people overestimate their abilities and bite off more than they can chew. Others may simply fail to follow through on what they have agreed to do.

Where possible, try to prevent these situations from occurring. At the first hint that someone is beginning to feel overwhelmed, help him or her out. If you put too much pressure on someone, that person may feel bad about not living up to expectations and drop out of your group. Encourage people to share tasks, and, when something isn't getting done, to help each other accomplish the task. Never get angry at someone who has failed to complete an assignment: anger is a terrible motivator. It takes a while for everyone to figure out how they can be most useful; during this whole process, a little praise goes a long way.

A Word About Outsiders

At this point it is appropriate to insert a cautionary note about various outsiders, especially attorneys, who may work closely with your group.

The task that your group has taken on is complex, immense, and confusing, and will, at times, seem overwhelming. Acronyms, regulations, hearings, agencies, and differing court jurisdictions will at first seem totally impossible to grasp in their entirety. It is when its members feel this way that a group is most vulnerable. When things seem desperate, people look for someone who will say, *I understand what is going on and I know what to do about it.*

This person is often an attorney, perhaps offering his or her services for free, perhaps indicating interest in taking the case for a fee. While the services of an attorney are extremely useful, even essential in many cases, the presence of a willing attorney should never be regarded as heaven-sent deliverance. Many people heave a sigh of relief and just dump their fates into the hands of an attorney who can mumble acronyms, to wits, FONSIs (Findings Of No Significant Impact), or whatever the appropriate jargon may be.

Your group must resist the temptation to abandon itself to an attorney and then to sit back and throw money at him or her. In one case I know of, a highly motivated and diverse group opposed a Project involving thousands of acres and several large facilities. Group members were full of ideas about the politics behind the Project and strategies for stopping it. But unfamiliar with regulatory law, they hired an attorney to help them. His fees were modest, so they agreed to deal with him not as an informal advisor but on a professional basis.

Having found someone with a good grasp of regulatory law and legal procedure, the group began to focus more and more on one or two hearings and failed to pursue many other strategies which they had previously considered. Soon the attorney was holding press conferences at which group members would silently stand around him as he explained the group's position. The group met less and less frequently, its numbers dwindled, and its other activities slowly disappeared. Finally, the group, as such, was reduced to the point where it did little but send out newsletters, the main purpose of which was to raise funds to pay the lawyer. A modified Project was eventually approved, but the modifications were responses mostly to outside factors and not to legal moves at regulatory hearings.

Do not compromise your group's effectiveness by becoming dependent on a lawyer in this manner. Your group should base all of its decisions on information from all sources, including legal information and advice but always as parts of the larger picture. The lawyer should serve but not determine the interests of the group. Total dependence on an attorney's every word can be as harmful as dependence on a single donor for financial viability. Both situations inhibit the full and measured discussion of what the group's priorities and courses of actions should be.

Let there be no misunderstanding here. Knowing your legal rights, options, and possibilities is absolutely necessary to the success of your group. If you are not fully aware of your legal status and vulnerabilities, the other side will use your ignorance against you. But, this does not mean that legal maneuvers are the only answers.

The legal system is far less independent of outside factors than books, lawyers, judges, or the government would have you believe. The most frequently successful strategies combine public education, selective public pressure, and legal smarts. It is plainly foolish to rely on any single method to win your battle. Allowing your group to be led around even by a well-meaning attorney will not improve your chances of success. In fact, it may distract your attention from other promising tactics, giving you the false impressions that you are doing everything that you can do and that you are winning.

Your group's other major worry (after lawyers) is money. Beware of outside fund-raising organizations that come to offer to help your group, promising that they can raise large amounts of money for your cause. What they ask is that you let them take charge of your fundraising in exchange for some form of compensation (often a fee plus a percentage). Keep in mind that, from their perspective, your cause, your group, your problem, the thing that Entity is proposing, all constitute no more than a promising business opportunity.

You got together with friends and neighbors because you perceived an immediate threat to you and your families. You formed your group to address this threat. The outsiders who assist your group — the lawyers, accountants, fund-raisers, technical experts, and others who serve for a price — may be sincere, but their interests do not necessarily coincide wholly with those of your group.

Outsiders such as these may desire credentials and experience to list on a résumé or they may want to become known as good-guy environmental lawyers. Others may be seeking connections or trying to establish a reputation before running for public office. Still others may see your group as a growth industry which will expand over several years, providing them with a source of income, visibility, mailing lists, or simply ego satisfaction. These people are decent and valuable human beings, but do not let them make decisions that should be made by your group as whole. Ask for, listen to, and be thankful for their advice, and consider it as part, but only part, of the larger picture.

When your group starts making waves you will receive other calls, too. In many ways, this is encouraging, because it means that people are hearing about you, know something about your issue, and think you should be taken seriously. Before you get too exhilarated, remind yourself that many of these calls will be from clever salespeople trying to make you a customer. They may offer anything from gummed address labels to highway billboard space; from automated phone-polling to activist computer software; from office space to custom-made key chains.

Whether you are dealing with a high-powered attorney, a nuclear physicist, a fundraising agency, or a bumpersticker manufacturer, follow the same guidelines. Never make a decision on impulse or under pressure; don't lose sight of the purpose of your group; don't allow yourself to be intimidated by anyone; and make sure that your spending is in line with your priorities and your goals.

A Word About Kooks

Especially at the beginning, the meetings of your group will be lively, volatile and unpredictable. Group members will be dedicated, inspired, emotional, perhaps even a little fanatical in their belief that they are battling against a GREAT EVIL. Working with such people can be exciting, a chance to be appreciated and thanked for your contributions, an opportunity to attract attention to yourself.

For whatever reasons, groups and situations of this kind attract kooks. However you define them, their effect on a group can be devastating. If you want to read about their personality characteristics, consult a current psychology textbook. Such individuals can disrupt your group, drive out all but the most tolerant and passive members, and cost your group its credibility by their bizarre public behavior in the name of your group. If your group has made any headway in challenging the economic and political establishment of an area or a major corporation, then you are already a target for attempts to discredit your activities. Don't make it easier by allowing a small number of disruptive and perhaps genuinely ill persons to destroy your group.

This is not to suggest that you suppress dissent or argument about goals, strategies, or tactics or that you impose a rigid hierarchy on your group's operating structure. Nor is it to encourage you to be insensitive, unkind, heavy-handed, or authoritarian in the treatment of fellow human beings. However, while you are sensitive, kind, and tolerant, also be smart. Don't hesitate to ask for professional advice, but whether you seek it or not, deal with the problem before it becomes unmanageable.

Spies

Your group, especially when it begins to have even limited success, may also attract another kind of outsider. For lack of a kinder word and in the interest of clarity, let's call these people *spies*. The federal government has a long history of infiltrating an astonishing variety of U.S. organizations. Your group may not attract the feds, but many persons will be desperate to know what the members of your group are up to, how much they know, whether they have any money, and what they plan to do next, among other things.

Much of this information can be gathered by simply attending an open meeting, slide show, or talk given by your group. It is probably a good idea to keep your legal strategy sessions small and closed, and if you are planning any surprises, don't announce them at a general meeting. Though updates in your general financial situation will probably be announced regularly, it is not a good idea to share financial details or donor lists with general audiences.

Excessive paranoia can tear your group apart, so use secrecy only when absolutely necessary. Just be aware of the fact that you will attract spies, so avoid saying things that might be twisted and used against you (though this may happen anyway).

Surprisingly often, someone who knows that a spy is present (often someone from the same organization) will tip you off. No massive response is necessary, and usually no change in behavior is even appropriate. Just be extra careful. The spy may try to mislead you by signing up for volunteer work, buying a T-shirt with your slogan on it, or taking some other seemingly sympathetic action.

For the most part, there's not much you can do to eliminate spying totally without becoming a secret club. A large part of your group's purpose involves public education and you always need more money, so you will usually want to have a high attendance at meetings and to continue attracting new people to your group. Fortunately, information about what you do in general meetings will not help Entity very much anyway. Entity wants to know if you are serious and if you know what you are doing. It will find this out most directly by your results with the general public and with the regulatory agencies, both of which are public information anyway.

There is another danger from spies when they are sent out not to gather information but to influence the actions of your group. Their main goals are may be:

- to influence your strategies and priorities toward less effective ones;
- to generate internal problems that cause your group either to break apart or to become so divided that it is ineffective in fighting the Project
- to convince your group, or members of it, to do something illegal.

One, two, or all three of these strategies may be pursued. It is not possible to prevent a group from being infiltrated, but your awareness of what to expect can be a very helpful defense.

At some point, individuals from Entity, from government agencies, and/or from law firms will send checks for a subscription to your newsletter. Take this as a compliment. They may refrain from using their official addresses to delay your realization that they are 'the enemy.' A typical tactic is for an official's secretary to subscribe in his or her own name, using a home address.

It is impossible to monitor all attempts to get copies of your newsletter, but you should keep a current list of the various agencies, consultant firms, and companies involved in the Project. If you happen to discover the affiliation of a subscriber, it's up to you to decide whether or not to continue sending your newsletter. (Of course, if you stop sending it, return their money!) One solution might be to charge a higher rate (a common practice among many publications, incidentally) to government agencies and private companies, say fifty or a hundred dollars instead of five or ten.

New Recruits/New Volunteers

Most organizations welcome new recruits. It is important for your group to continue to attract new people as your original members will take vacations, branch off into new issues, focus their interests, or even burn out. As your group expands its range of activities, there will be more research to do, more opportunities to use it, more groups to talk to, more meetings and hearings to attend, longer newsletters to write and mail, and always the need for additional funds.

When a group forms, it is a loose collection of concerned people. The vast needs of the group provide an opportunity for the amazingly diverse talents present in a random assortment of people to emerge.

The day-dreaming bird watcher may turn out to be a great photographer and illustrator. The bake-sale champion may be a fantastic fund-raiser. The head of the bowling team may be a genius for regulations. The stamp collector may turn out to be a superb organizer. The rock musician may be a riveting public speaker. And the closet novelist may help write and edit your newsletter.

This loose collection of people eventually settles into new roles and responsibilities, learning the jargon of government agencies and regulations and talking among themselves about decision dates, FONSIs, Section Elevens, and EIS's, sounding like some kind of specialized S.W.A.T. team. The problem is that these things can seem terribly intimidating to all those who hear about the Project, don't like the sound of it, and come to one of your presentations or meetings, ready to join up and help out.

Nothing can be more discouraging for the newcomer than to be greeted by people speaking a totally unintelligible language. Many talented potential members will be scared away if the old hands forget how specialized and focused they have become.

To avoid losing recruitment opportunities, always be alert for new people at your meetings. Make sure someone greets them and fills them in on general background information. You should hand out basic fact sheets, and give them opportunities to sign up, to indicate their special interests or experience, and to leave you their phone numbers and addresses. A member of your group acting as a volunteer coordinator should call them up, talk about their special interests and abilities, and invite them into the group.

This may seem terribly obvious, but, during the very confusing and intense activities in which your group is participating, many members will become oblivious to outsiders, new members, and, unfortunately, to the news media as well. When your group becomes this introverted, you run the risk of generating interest in your activities and not being able to take advantage of it.

The people in your group are not so different from the people who work for Entity, but your organizations differ greatly. If your group is conscientious and aware of the suggestions and observations offered in this chapter, you will be in a better position to confront Entity in the various contexts that will arise. The next chapter provides a glimpse of Entity designed to prepare you for what is coming your way.

Anthony Mancuso, "Guidelines for nonprofits: legal limits on lobbying." *Nolo News,* Spring 1991. p. 7.; Internal Revenue Service, Publication 557, "Tax-Exempt Status for Your Organization"; J. D. Joseph, *How to Fight City Hall* (Chicago: Contemporary Books, Inc., 1983), which offers guidelines on dealing with the press and explains how to incorporate your group as a non-profit corporation with tax-exempt and non-tax-exempt options. Also offers good basic explanations of what happens in a court of law, and an overview of the Freedom of Information Act; Jeremy Rifkin, *The Green Lifestyle Handbook* (New York: Henry Holt & Co., 1990); Geoffrey Rips, Coordinator, *Un-American Activities: The Campaign Against the Underground Press* (San Francisco: City Lights Press, 1981), which includes reports by Aryeh Neier, Todd Gitlin, Allen Ginsberg, Geoffrey Rips, and Angus Mackenzie explaining why so many stories never make it into the mainstream media. Also includes discussions of surveillance, infiltration, sabotage, and other standard counter-intelligence techniques.

Chapter 3

ENTITY AT A GLANCE

The Entity sponsoring the Project may be a private company or corporation, a public or government Entity, or some mixture of the two (sometimes called a joint venture, a consortium, or a public-private partnership). This chapter discusses some salient characteristics of each type of Entity and then goes on to explore other considerations that will help your group to locate and exploit their vulnerabilities — the cracks in the armor.

Private Entities: Size Isn't Everything

Entities in the private sector may be large or small, and their size will affect their tactics. A huge, multinational corporation has essentially infinite resources at its disposal. However, as numerous plant closings attest, it can also more easily shift its interests elsewhere. If your group seems to present a veritable hornet's nest of problems, the megacorporation may be just as happy to try somewhere else.

A smaller, local company, on the other hand, has more limited resources available to it. Such a private Entity will be able to move its Project elsewhere only with more difficulty. The smaller, local company may fight to the death for its Project, while a larger, more powerful opponent may be more likely to move on.

Small, local companies have many advantages when convincing a community of the merits of their Project. They may have a long history in the area and they may be employing entire families at their facilities. They may have demonstrated their commitment and good will towards the local community on many occasions. They may really believe that their proposed Project will have all of the benefits that they claim for it.

It is never too late to try to convince such an Entity that its Project is not appropriate. But, it is important not to confuse the good deeds of the past or the present with the circumstances of the proposed Project. On the other side of the coin, any broken promises, bad decisions, or ill effects of Entity's past actions are relevant as examples of the company's track record and probable future performance.

Large, multinational companies lack the intimacy and historic community connections of the smaller local companies. Their resources are not to be discounted however. A multinational Entity can use its enormous resources to build community support very quickly. Though its methods may be subtle, its message is transparent: money talks.

A multinational Entity will hire one or more local law firms, often the same ones that represent school boards, local colleges or universities, chambers of commerce, occupational and business groups, governmental bodies, major businesses, and other institutions. Entity will print its public relations brochures at local print shops. It will buy advertising space in local newspapers and other publications. It is often cunning enough to run modest advertisements but pay for full pages not used. It will hire local consultants to advise it and design its public outreach efforts. But this is just the beginning.

Entity can also lend its support to a variety of 'Mom-and-apple-pie' organizations. A rudimentary list includes volunteer fire departments, arts groups, orphanages, historical societies, shelters for battered women, little league clubs, cancer research centers, community schools, drug treatment centers, bird watcher's groups, minority business associations, union halls, veteran's groups, trade schools, police associations, and community colleges. Contributions to these and similar groups may not insure their support of the Project, but this generosity will surely lead many people to think twice before opposing it openly.

An Entity with broad resources can sponsor softball and bowling teams, essay and coloring contests, chili cookoffs, and all of their cousins. In addition, Entity can give out community service and environmental awards, health badges, single-mother-of-the-year awards, and an infinite variety of others. The visibility and good vibes engendered by this sort of activity are powerful. How could an Entity that sponsors The Nature Walk for the Mentally Retarded, gives environmental awards to conscientious recyclers, and presents community service medals to one-armed VFW school crossing guards possibly promote a Project that is anything but wholesome and good? Your group has its work cut out for it.

Private, corporate Entities are inspired by the profit motive. Some need almost immediate results, while others can sustain years of losses before finally seeing black ink. In either case, however, doubts about future profits may be reason enough to abandon, modify, or move the planned Project. Therefore, anything your group can do or suggest to cast doubt on or reduce the projected profits can help your cause. Remember the saying *time is money*. Delays cost money and sow doubts among potential investors or other supporters. Delays can also buy your group time to prepare new strategies.

Private Entities can also have a great effect on the public perception of the Project. Most of what they accomplish is done behind the scenes. Even before you decide on a name for your group, a private Entity will have had numerous contacts with elected officials, community and business leaders, educators, and many other public figures, as well as with powerful individuals and groups with lower profiles.

At private meetings, tours, presentations, and all manner of special gatherings, Entities enlist the support of selected individuals in the target community. People in the affected community will have been treated to private lunches or dinners, often at exclusive restaurants and clubs, during which their support is subtly sought. The information presented will be extremely selective, stressing the advantages of the Project and its supposed economic benefits for the community.

By the time your group forms, many influential members of your community will already be genuinely convinced that the Project is a good idea. These people will have been flattered by being singled out for special attention by rich, powerful, important people. Lacking evidence to the contrary, they may be true believers in the benefits of the Project. This phenomenon is especially effective in sparsely populated rural areas because of the 'big fish in a small pond' phenomenon. A few special meetings for community leaders (selected by Entity) can produce a very impressive and seemingly complete line-up of community supporters.

If possible, get a member of your group invited to one of these special presentations in order to obtain an idea of what Entity's arguments are. Or seek out someone who, despite attending a presentation, is dubious about the Project and willing to share Entity's pitch with you. As soon as possible, prepare an information sheet or brochure answering or countering each of Entity's claims. Send it out with your newsletter, and make it widely available. Try to find out who has been invited to Entity's special meetings. Make sure they get copies of your rejoinders. A good research staff is necessary in order to do this promptly and efficiently.

Keeping your eyes and ears open helps a lot, too. You may hear a local Project supporter, a showcase for Entity, give a speech in which he describes the proposed Project as "an impressive enhancement of our community's tax base" or claims that it will constitute "a bold technological leap into the twenty-first century." These catch-phrases are the sort of vague happythink that public relations firms invent to discourage focused discussion of the actual Project. Keep listening, tune into the local call-in shows on the radio, attend other semi-public dog-and-pony shows, and you will find someone else describing the Project as "a bold technological step into the next century," or "an impressive addition to our community's tax base."

History will indeed repeat itself, as Project supporters (unknown to each other, probably known only to you who have attended numerous Project-related events) parrot nearly identical lines over and over again. As a working hypothesis, you can assume that they all got it from the same source and that the depth of their understanding (and hence their ability to defend the Project intelligently) is very limited.

Before you leap at the chance to humiliate these folks publicly, remember your group's overall goals. Seldom — but not never — will your ends be served by public embarrassment. Get the truth out, but do it in such a way that will encourage people to join you instead of becoming lifelong enemies. Antagonizing possible allies rarely improves your group's chances of success.

Access to information is not particularly easy with private Entities. They are not public, governmental Entities, so existing open meetings and records laws and the federal Freedom of Information Act probably do not apply to them. This gives them a valuable advantage. Even public officials and government agencies may have a difficult time gaining reliable information about Entity or the Project. (Don't give up. There are ways to get information about them. These are discussed in the next two chapters.)

In summary, private Entities have large and sometimes unlimited resources at their disposal while they have much more limited obligations to share information with the public. However, their businesses exist for the purpose of making a profit, and this is where they are vulnerable. Your group's best strategy may be to increase their actual or probable operating costs or to create such a public relations mess that their expected profits from the Project are put in doubt. Meanwhile, be ready to have your group blamed for expectations of imminent economic collapse if the Entity decides not to go ahead with the Project in your area.

Public Entities

In general, public Entities can do most or all of what private Entities can do, and then some. However, there are some important differences.

Like private Entities, public Entities usually have the option of moving, altering, or even abandoning proposed Projects. Their wheelings and dealings involve private sector concerns as well as various governmental bodies and agencies. A major difference, however, is the way in which the profit motive, the bottom line for a private Entity, drives the public Entity.

Projects managed or carried out by public Entities are expected to meet a public need or provide a public service that, for whatever reason, is not or cannot be met by the private sector. But the Project may also be intended to make a profit of sorts — or at least a contribution to the general good and the public coffers. This contribution may occur directly through fees, revenues, or taxes, indirectly through the jobs and spin-off business it creates, or ultimately by the economic growth it can generate for the city or the region.

Because these economic benefits are often indirect, delayed, and intangible, public government Entities can often get away with boondoggles that the private sector would soon abandon or not even take on (unless guaranteed or subsidized by the government). The financial history of numerous public utility companies and convention centers, among other Projects, will attest to this. (Consider the synthetic fuels projects of the 1970s, which were subsidized by the government because oil companies refused to bear the economic risks of a technology that would not be profitable unless oil prices reached and stayed in the astronomical range.) Accordingly, the strategies that work well against a private Entity may be less effective against a public one. A public Entity's Project may well be pursued long after any person seriously believes that the economic benefits outweigh the costs.

Several factors help explain this. First, government Entities in the United States rarely fold, go bankrupt, or go out of business. Other government Entities bail them out with taxpayer money. Another important factor is that economic benefits may not have been the only, or even the main, reason that the Project was proposed in the first place. Government Entities, and the political figures that head them, often act to expand their influence, consolidate their power, return favors, prepare for elections, build résumés, and so on.

With private corporations you can at least assume that they expect to make a profit somewhere down the line. With public Entities it is not safe to assume this. Many private Entities — realtors, engineering and construction firms, restaurant chains, consultants — may themselves profit hugely from a public Entity's Project, while said Project itself loses money steadily. The Project may in effect be little more than an elaborate conduit for the flow of government money into private pockets. If this is the case, the whole noble purpose described by Entity may be only the wishful thinking of a self-interested bureaucracy.

Figuring out how to stop a Project may become a lot easier if you can discover its origins. But with Public-Entity Projects, you may never really know for sure why the Project was proposed. The reasons offered, such as the public welfare, may well be only justifications, rationalizations, or selling points, not the real reasons the Project is being proposed.

In the area of public relations a public Entity, like a private corporation, will have good connections, but these will not be exactly the same. When governmental bodies or agencies get along well with each other, they help each other out, coordinate their activities, make critical information available to each other in a timely manner (sometimes well before anyone else hears it), and try not to air each other's dirty laundry in public.

Governmental agencies can use selective enforcement to gain the support, or avoid the opposition, of private companies. (It can be used just as well with other government departments.) Selective enforcement works in this way. As long as a private company cooperates, routine business goes smoothly. But if the private company becomes too sloppy, or too demanding, or takes the 'wrong' position regarding a certain Project, governmental cooperation may abruptly cease. Previously routine matters of all kinds suddenly become very complicated, time-consuming, and expensive.

In unexceptional times, enforcement of the regulations governing licenses, inspections, permits, and other paperwork is often loose or even lax. There is usually a lot of discretion involving how literally regulations are interpreted and how frequently they are monitored and enforced. But when a private company or rival government organization becomes troublesome — by opposing a pet Project, for instance — enforcement can become very strict. Government Entities can gain the support of numerous powerful private companies and organizations by quietly offering better treatment to those who support the Project and endless red tape and problems to those who do not.

Members of the public will have a slightly easier time getting information from public, governmental agencies than from private companies. Laws to encourage more open government give citizens the right of access to certain kinds of information possessed by their government. While methods of seeking this information will be discussed in greater detail in a later chapter, two points need to be made here.

First, do not assume that the existence of these 'open government laws' means that your group will ever obtain the information that it seeks. Government agencies have learned how to obstruct the release of information and to make the information they do release very difficult to understand. Second, your group can gain a lot from the government's refusal to release information. When you publicize this refusal, the government loses credibility and you gain attention and perhaps increased support. Furthermore, the difficulties caused by your failure to gain access to the information may themselves be reason enough, in the eyes of a court, to delay proceedings concerning the Project. Nothing comes easily, but you will learn to find a silver lining in every cloud.

Projects sponsored by public Entities are much more likely to be influenced by the results of elections. National or state elections may bring about changes in the personnel or policies of the government bodies that manage or regulate Projects. The members of the council, commission, or board that manages a Project may themselves be elected. More often, they are appointed by elected officials. Occasionally (though less and less frequently), the public is allowed to vote *yes* or *no* on a particular Project.

When Entity is a public or governmental body, and sometimes when it is a private concern, elections can be a part of your strategy. Election campaigns are time-consuming and expensive, absorbing much or all of the available time and energy of all volunteers. For this reason, be sure that your group anticipates and prioritizes the possibility of participating in an election as part of an overall strategy.

Public Entities may have more limited financial resources than private Entities, but public Entities are broadly and deeply influential. Though they often have some formal obligation to share information with the public, their great political power sometimes renders this obligation meaningless. Since there is little incentive in the public sector to discourage boondoggles, economic arguments will not be as successful with the public Entities as they are with private ones. However, these same arguments may be very effective when used in an election, referendum, or other public campaign, because taxpayers and voters are increasingly displeased at having to pay for any boondoggles.

It is especially difficult to fight successfully against any part of the military or national security apparatus or even to gain access to information about its plans and activities. This difficulty is not only experienced by citizens' groups. Other branches of government have their difficulties as well. If the Project you are opposing is military-related, you might benefit from trying to involve the legislative branch. Locate and groom a member of Congress who is willing to make inquiries or begin a formal investigation. This will provide you with some of the information you seek and aid in your public education efforts.

Mixed Entities

Some Entities are not quite public and not quite private. They may be created by government bodies but governed by commissions that include representatives of both the public and private sectors. Or, they may be founded but not funded by the government and therefore have to pay their own way through the revenues they collect. Finally, they may be partly or indirectly funded by government money (such as the Tennessee Valley Authority).

Many mixed Entities were created to combine the advantages of private business with the advantages of government bodies. Hence, the hybrid was to be lean and efficient like private business but to serve the public like government.

What has has been just as likely to happen is that the disadvantages of each were combined. The result is an Entity that is like private business, in that it ruthlessly searches for revenues and power while remaining insensitive to community and environment, and like government, in that it is inefficient and arrogant.

The Mixed Entity alternately claims to be more like business or more like government, depending on the particular situation. It wants to withhold information, like private business, but to be non-taxable, like government. On health and safety issues, it follows the absolute minimal standards allowed in order to cut costs, as a private business would. When it comes to acquiring land for the Project, however, it claims the right of eminent domain reserved for government and begins land condemnation proceedings.

A mixed Entity provides an extra challenge to your group. You will have to be alert enough to detect and perhaps even to anticipate when the public mask and when the private mask of Entity is being worn.

If Entity has existed for a number of years, it has a history, a track record, which will be accessible to you in some form. This will help your group understand and counter the way this Entity operates.

If your Entity was created especially for the purpose of building or managing the Project, then it's spanking new, without a track record and probably writing the rules as it proceeds. Even in this case, check for previous incarnations of the Project. It may be that what is being offered as an all-new Project managed by an all-new Entity is really a slightly modified and spiffed-up resurrection of an older Project that failed or was previously rejected.

In the case of a newly created mixed Entity, there is probably some uncertainty regarding the laws and regulations which apply to it. It may be in the interest of your group to challenge it immediately in order to clarify its exact responsibilities and powers. This action will probably attract a lot of attention. It may set precedents for future actions, and it can sometimes cause significant delays as well as unanticipated expenses. Your group should have its priorities clearly in mind before taking on such a task.

Because of the obvious advantages that they have, mixed Entities are becoming increasingly popular. If you think it is difficult to fight the government or a multinational corporation — and it is — then wait until you face an Entity that combines the strengths of both and changes from one to the other and back again to fit the circumstances.

Mixed Entities are especially difficult, but all Entities, public, private, or mixed, have weaknesses. Here are some hints on how to locate them.

Probing for Weak Spots

So far we have emphasized the power, influence, and resources Entity possesses. Any realistic approach begins by recognizing this. However, Entity can be very vulnerable as well. If your group is going to have any success, you must learn to guess what is going on inside of the Entity. If you can do that, you are in a good position to identify some of Entity's weak spots.

Entities are not monolithic. They are not perfectly working, well-oiled machines. They are organizations made up of human beings, with all that implies — just like the place you work, the diner where you eat breakfast, the office where you get your license renewed, and the store where you bought your television. You can probably imagine the inner workings of these places. Now apply that same imagination to the Entity that is proposing the Project.

At some point, probably several years in the past, Entity made a decision to go ahead with the Project and to locate it in your area. How are decisions like this made? After careful study (or at least the appearance of careful study), along with many meetings and lots of internal and external politics. There were probably several reports evaluating this Project as just one possibility among several. Certainly several possible sites for the Project were also considered. Eventually, the Project was selected from among the alternatives and, out of perhaps dozens of sites originally considered, your site was chosen.

During the entire process, alternative Projects and locations were considered, discussed, and finally rejected. That means that there are probably several studies which discuss the disadvantages of doing this Project at this site. You want to get your hands on these studies. There are also various individuals, even some from within Entity, who favored alternative Projects and/or other sites. Some of them might love to say *I told you so*.

Therefore, there are some people at Entity who are displeased with the final outcome. There are also people whose careers may benefit if the Project fails and some who would benefit if another Project or site were chosen. Keep this in mind, and find these people if you can. Few will be openly disloyal, but they can casually point you in the right direction. Listen well.

Constantly be on the lookout for disgruntled employees, consultants, or others who may have formed at most an uneasy alliance with Project backers. Possible allies may appear in unexpected places — learn everything you can from them.

If Entity is a governmental body or a mixed Entity, it may be run by some sort of governing board. If you can learn to read the board the way you read a book, you may find that it is an important source of information, ideas, and maybe even political influence for your group.

The governing board may be called a commission, a board of governors, a board of trustees, a council, a task force, or any of a number of similar names. It may be elected or appointed. Frequently its members are appointed by other government officials or bodies. For example, one state governing board might be a fifteen-member commission, with five of its members selected by the governor, five chosen by mayors of major cities, and five others appointed by the state's legislature.

Find out who these people are, where they live, where they work, what other organizations they belong to, and anything else you can about what makes them tick. Often information is available to the public in the form of brief biographical profiles of each board member. Then go to work on them.

Local members, for example, may be more susceptible to pressure from concerned citizens in their areas. Other members of the board may have quiet skeletons in their closets — business problems, conflicts over state or federal regulations, maybe one even cheated on a Spanish exam at Harvard. Or, some of these people may want to run for elective office some day and will not want to go down in history as supporting an unpopular Project.

The variations are numerous. Do not assume that all board members think alike, that they all favor the Project without reservations, or even that they all really know very much about it. Many times, the governing boards are just showcases — a collection of people who are either familiar public faces or token representatives of different constituencies. Project backers may want the governing board to appear to be broadly based in the community — maybe they need a union member, a woman, a gay person, a black and a brown, an educator, an environmentalist, and a war veteran on the governing board. If this is the case, talk to each one, find out about their interests and expertise, and then return to them with information that speaks to their concerns. Talk their language; don't expect them to learn yours.

In other cases, you get the usual fifteen white male businessmen. But even then, do your background research on them. Businessmen do not all think alike. Some worked their way up from selling sno-cones, others inherited their businesses. They won't see eye-to-eye on how to hire and fire, how to make decisions, or how to run things. Some businessmen would buy from the lowest bidder even if it were the devil himself, while others deal only with those who adhere to certain standards — made in the U.S.A., union only, non-union only, containing or not containing certain materials. Some sell insurance, others think insurance salespeople are the scum of the earth. In short, these governing boards are not homogeneous. They are full of divisions, factions, rivalries, and will seldom agree unanimously about any important issue. Know this, understand this, exploit this.

In many cases the governing board does not do much governing at all. You will need to determine whether or not the board is legally empowered to make major decisions. If it is, make education of these board members a high priority. Even if it is not, don't drop them. They may still be good sources of information and insight for you. Members of a governing board may casually mention something to you, something that, together with other bits of information you have learned, allows you to put two and two together and figure out something important. Even if they have no real power or can be replaced as soon as they utter a syllable of doubt about the Project, you can learn from them. Besides, it will look bad for Project backers if supporters (such as board members) begin to change their minds as a result of your reaching out to them.

Do not assume either that the staff and the governing board of Entity agree on the issues, get along, or have access to the same information. In some cases, the governing board will meet periodically, discuss the Project, and bang a gavel around for a few hours of voting on things (which will be reported by the news media) while the actual decisions will be made by others. These others are the staff of the Entity, those who work full time on the Project, know all the details, and feed information to the governing board in convenient packages. Staff will filter the information presented to the governing board just as carefully as it selects information submitted to the news media.

When nothing controversial is going on, the staff may be able to lead the governing board around for years at a time. Members of governing boards are often treated with much respect, sometimes pomp and circumstance, too. They may not be especially curious about the exact details as long as things seem to be going all right.

Don't be surprised if your group knows far more about Project details than do members of the governing board. Board members are under some pressure to pretend or imply that they know a great deal about the Project. Your group may be able to bring new information to members of the governing board. Don't use this as an opportunity to make them feel stupid or ill-informed. You can even choose to let them take credit for finding the information, if this helps attract attention to it. If they realize that staff is not being fully open about sharing information with them, you may have found an ally.

Apart from the governing board, you will find variation within the staff of Entity. One Entity may have departments for short-term planning, long-term planning, production, and marketing. Another may have legal, engineering, and accounting departments. These departments may have different views of the Project, disagreeing on its merits and how it should be carried forward.

Your group will probably be handled by Entity's public relations department at first. This department is not authorized to give out any real information, nor does it have the authority to make any decisions about what information you receive. As soon as it becomes apparent that you know what you are doing, the legal department will join in. The sooner this happens, the better. Attorneys are notoriously tight-lipped, but at least they won't waste your time by beating about the bush. That's the job of the PR department. Whenever possible, seek information, reports, rumors, or contact with any other departments at Entity.

There is one thing you should never forget about Entity. Most of the people who work there (with the exception of some of the big shots and perhaps a handful of truly evil people) are just like you. They are not looking for problems, controversy, troubles, or added expense. They do not want to be singled out as targets, and they do not want to be hated because of the organization they work for. They just want to live their lives, keep their jobs, and move ahead in their chosen careers. They are just doing their jobs. Some of them know that they would be acting just as you are if the Project were intended for their back yards.

Nothing is to be gained from making personal attacks on any of these people. Some of them will know very little about either the Project or your group's opposition to it. Some of them will be very active in promoting the Project. None of them will be any more likely to help you out, officially or not, if members of your group are calling them liars, murderers, or whatever insult may seem appropriate at the time.

Throughout Entity and among the consultants, lawyers, and others it has hired, there will be people who support your group's position or are at least sympathetic to it. Make it easy for them to find you and help you. Spread your literature all over, even among the 'enemy.' Make sure to include phone numbers and addresses. You will receive in the mail copies of reports and memos that you didn't even know existed or you will receive anonymous tips over the phone.

This does not mean that you should just distribute a few brochures and sit back and wait for the phone to start ringing off the wall with anonymous tips. Those people are out there and they do mean well. But don't expect them to risk life, limb, and livelihood to pass you the latest item of gossip. They need to keep their jobs and can't quite get out of that position. You need to make it convenient for them to contact you. Keep your lines open for them.

This bit of advice also applies when you are in public contact with Entity personnel. It is not always wise to corner them and force them to choose between going ahead with the Project or admitting they are wrong. Sometimes Entity's decision makers will be more likely to abandon the Project if you make it easy for them. Help them manufacture a graceful exit. Find some new information that leads them to re-evaluate the projected economic benefits, for example. Or, formulate some real alternatives that are acceptable to Entity and to your group. A resolution that meets the needs of all parties need not compromise your goals.

Now that you know what to expect from different kinds of Entities, you are ready to go to work on the specific Project Entity is proposing. The next chapter provides an outline of what you need to know.

Chapter 4

INFORMATION YOU'LL NEED

One way or another, you will probably win or lose because of the information you gather. Whether you are fighting a public education battle or a lawsuit, information is critical. Sometimes it is technical facts that make the difference; at other times it is political intelligence; at still others, it is knowledge of procedures and legal technicalities. If you and your supporters have the facts, understand them, and use them effectively, you make formidable opponents.

In this chapter we outline basic kinds of information that your group needs. It falls into four areas: legal, technical, economic, and political. In the next chapter, we'll go over the process of getting this information.

Legal Information

At the outset, there are four kinds of legal information that you need.

Rights to Information: You need to understand the rights you have, as private citizens, to the various documents and reports that Entity has already produced. These rights will differ depending on whether Entity is public, private, or mixed.

Legal Requirements and Procedures Entity Must Follow: You need to know the exact legal requirements which Entity must follow in order to carry out or build the Project. This list is very long and includes many permits and other authorizations to go ahead with various phases of the Project. It may include all aspects of the Project, from zoning, to construction, to waste water discharge permits.

In conjunction with this list of necessary permits, licenses, authorizations, clearances, and waivers, your group needs a precise description of the process that each permit application must go through before a permit may be granted.

Standing and Appeal: The third kind of legal information you need is a description of who may participate in the permit procedure and/or in court challenges of Entity, the Project, or involved government agencies. Certainly Entity and the participating government regulatory agency can take part. But there are rules about who else may participate. In some cases, for example, an individual must be a landowner, or must live within 500 feet of the Project boundary, or must prove that he or she would be affected by the Project. The same applies to groups.

Meeting the particular requirements gives you what is called *standing* in legal language. You need to know if your group as a whole, or any of its members, has standing to participate in the permit process. Rules that specify who has standing vary widely in different kinds of hearings and cases and in different states. For this reason, your group needs to determine early who has or can get standing. Entity may end up spending a lot of time and effort in order to demonstrate that you (or your representative) do not have legal standing. If it is successful, your participation will be seriously limited.

Related to the issue of participation in a permit proceeding is the issue of *appeal*. Often a person or group who participates (called a *party* in legal jargon) in a procedure is unhappy with the outcome. Under certain circumstances the party can register an official legal complaint about the procedure and ask for certain *remedies*. A remedy may require that some or all of the results be reconsidered, changed in some way, thrown out, overturned, or reversed. This complaint is called an appeal. Your group needs to find out who can appeal, under what circumstances they can appeal, and what the appeals process is.

Legal Background of Entity: The fourth kind of legal information that you need to have is the legal background of Entity itself. This information helps your group gain some insight into Entity's tactics and its perceived weak spots. If searches reveal an interesting legal history, you will also have material to use in your public education efforts.

At the basic level, you need to know exactly what Entity is: a corporation, a partnership, a government department or agency, or some sort of hybrid. If Entity seems a little reluctant to discuss this question, it may be feeling somewhat vulnerable in this area.

The importance of understanding Entity's precise legal status can be illustrated by briefly exploring the issue of land acquisition. Many Projects require the acquisition of land. Often, someone has already purchased the needed land at cut-rate prices before any public announcement of the Project is made. However, Entity may also need additional land for things like support facilities, roads, and expansion.

Sometimes, the land must be acquired through normal market-system negotiations. Usually, however, the government has a hand in the Project. This is especially the case when Entity is part of the government, when Entity is a Mixed Entity, or when government agents or bodies (city councils, the governor's office, the Department of Transportation) have promised certain inducements or incentives to Project backers.

If government has a hand in the Project, it is likely that it can exercise its powers of eminent domain. This normally becomes a factor when a proposed Project is defined as being 'in the public good' (an army base, a park, or a highway, for example). Under eminent domain, the government can force you to sell your land, but it must pay you fair market price for it. Your group needs to find out if Entity has, or can get, the power of eminent domain. You should become familiar with existing and recent laws and cases on eminent domain to see exactly how far the power can be extended by whom within the current legal environment.

If Entity was created by the official act or resolution of a government body, you need access to the original act and any amendments or alterations made since its first passage. In some cases the text will be a mere paragraph or a few pages; in others, it may run to many volumes. This is your fundamental clue as to what Entity is exactly and what its responsibilities and powers are. Do not rely on Entity's own public summary of its responsibilities and powers.

Increasingly common are Project developments on reservations or other lands administered by Native Americans. Perhaps even more than water rights law, Native American law is special, tricky, and idiosyncratic. It is a challenge to try to understand, but it may provide unusual possibilities unavailable under other jurisdictions.

Broaden your research to explore some other legal angles. Are there any scandals in Entity's (or its backers' or subsidiaries') past? If so, who was involved, and are they involved in the current Project? How did Entity handle legal challenges in the past? Did it fight in open court or seek to buy off its enemies? Who is Entity's regular law firm? Who else does it represent? Answers to any of these questions may give you useful insights in your fight against the Project.

Technical and Economic Information

Your group also needs technical and financial/economic information. We discuss them together here because they are closely related and because the information in each category is quite similar.

Technical information usually refers to details of the Project that are not directly political, economic, or legal. Biological information, such as whether there are any endangered or threatened species of plants or animals in the area, is one kind of technical information. So is the estimate of how many toilet flushes per hour will occur or how much radiation will be released into the air.

Project costs will be based largely on conclusions drawn from the technical information. If the technical information is accurate and realistic, the economic estimates may also be fairly reliable (although many other factors enter the picture here.) But a small change in the technical data can lead to a large difference in economic estimates. Therefore, you need to pay a lot of attention to the technical data.

At first, it might seem silly for your group to bother with all of the technical stuff. To appreciate the importance of details, however, compare the drama of the Project to a detective novel. Did the bullet enter from the front or the back? Was the victim right-handed or left-handed? Why was the queen of spades missing from the deck? Knowing the answers to these questions, and the significance of the answers, is the key to the identity of the murderer. The same principle holds true in fighting a Project. The following imaginary but realistic example, based on an actual case, gives some idea of how seemingly trivial details can be critically important.

The Pit Story: Imagine a Project that involves moving material in or out of a pit. (Waste dumps and strip mines are two examples.) The expected duration is 24 years, and Entity says that the Project will be cost-effective and environmentally safe. A detailed Project description claims that 4 trucks, each carrying 50 tons of material, will average 20 mph on a 10 percent slope and make one round trip per hour, for 8 hours a day, 5 days a week, 50 weeks a year. According to Entity, the life of the trucks is 8 years, so the fleet of 4 trucks will be replaced 3 times in the Project's estimated 24-year life span.

All of Entity's promises about efficiency, cost savings, and environmental safety rest on the claim that Entity can move about 400,000 tons of material per year at low cost and low risk. (The number of trucks [4] times the tonnage per trip [50] times the trips per truck per work day [8] times 5 days a week times 50 weeks per year works out to 400,000.)

Why should your group care about such details? Because a little research may change the picture drastically. You may learn that at similar Projects, trucks were unable to carry more than 45 tons of material, on average, and that this type of truck averages only about 12 mph on a slope of 10 percent. As a result, Entity will have to build a longer, gentler, but more costly slope or slower trucks (making only 5 round trips per day) will result. You also find, from historic data from the truck manufacturer, that trucks like these are usually out of operation for maintenance at least six weeks per year and that, with heavy workloads like these, their estimated effective life is 6 years, not 8.

Using this comparative data, your group can show that in reality, Entity will be moving only about half the volume it claimed. The same number of trucks (4) moving 45 tons on each of 5 trips per day times 5 days per week and 46 weeks per year equals 207,000 tons per year, not 400,000. In addition, you can point out that the truck fleet will have to be replaced at least four times instead of three given the manufacturer's estimate for the life of a truck under such circumstances.

In this case, a few seemingly minor changes in the numbers halved the estimate of how many tons per year would be moved. Another way of looking at this is to say that it doubled the cost. It may seem like you are counting nuts and bolts, but you are really counting dollars.

The data suggest that it's going to cost a lot more than Entity claims or else that Entity is going to cut corners somewhere. If it is government-supported or tax-supported, increased costs will be paid by the public and show up as higher taxes, lower levels of services, higher costs of services, or all three. If Entity is public or private or mixed, cost-cutting measures will usually end up affecting safety practices, maintenance schedules, environmental protection measures, waste disposal methods, and other functions that affect communities directly.

But don't stop there in your pit analysis. If you look carefully at the maps and diagrams accompanying the Entity's own Project descriptions, you may find that company engineers estimated that the slopes of haul roads were sometimes a 15% grade, much steeper than the 10% used in the company calculations.

Or, you may remember from previous public presentations (where a member of your group took notes or tape-recorded the discussion) that Entity has stated that the Project will be in operation for at least thirty years and implied that the Project will be paying taxes to local authorities for at least that long. Bring this up and expose the discrepancy.

All of Entity's facts and figures are vulnerable to this kind of analysis, and all of their conclusions must be questioned in this manner. This is where the technical data come in, and this is why the technical data and the economic data are so closely linked.

Your group needs the following kinds of information on both technical and economic aspects of the Project.

***A Current Project Description*:** You need a complete, detailed, current description of the Project. Information on every bald eagle, toilet flush, or X-ray should be included, as well as exact cost estimates and information as to exactly how they were calculated.

***Track Record of Similar Projects*:** You need information about the history and success record of similar Projects. If Entity has carried out any similar Projects, these should be analyzed. Whether or not Entity has a track record in this area, other similar Projects should be investigated, both in the U.S. and abroad. You may be able to identify possible problems or weak spots in Entity's analysis of its current Project. (This applies to both technical and economic analyses.)

Independent, critical, outside evaluations: Your group needs to identify alternative sources of information that will give differing points of view on the Project. All of the information that Entity produces or submits to outsiders will be as strongly as possible slanted in favor of the Project. Less positive data, evidence, and examples will be ignored, concealed, or denied. Your group cannot single-handedly evaluate all of the information you receive. The work of outside, disinterested researchers and of avowed critics of similar Projects elsewhere will help your group broaden its perspective on issues concerning the Project.

Political Information

Your group needs political information, the sooner the better and the more the better. Political information is difficult to define. If you have it, though, you may be able to anticipate events, alliances, and crises. If you don't have it, others who do will chuckle as they watch you clumsily make blunder after blunder, or, just as bad, naively miss opportunity after opportunity.

Political information is the intangible knowledge that tells you why two companies usually work together, why so-and-so supports the Project so fiercely, why it was so incredibly difficult to get a copy of a particular document, why two obvious candidates are not even nominated to head a particular commission or agency, why the EIS was delayed for six months ... *ad infinitum*. Politics explains those non-obvious connections that allow you to identify allies and opponents more easily and know whether or when it is worthwhile to try to change their minds. Politics can include information as diverse as where favors are owed, who married whom, who owes money to whom, which law firm always opposes a certain company, and so on.

Partly because political information is so vast, so difficult to define, and so constantly in transformation, it is very difficult to know when you have it. But it is embarrassingly obvious when you don't.

Tips in the next chapter will start you on your way to finding the legal, technical and economic, and political information you will need.

> Philip P. Frickey, "Congressional Intent, Practical Reasoning, and the Dynamic Nature of Federal Indian Law," *California Law Review* (UCB), Vol. 78, No. 5 (Oct. 1990), pp. 1137ff. (An excellent overview of 'Indian' law. Suggests that federal law, Congressional intent, and historical factors are so complex that courts have neither stuck close to the supposed original Congressional intent nor followed a particular deductive theme. Rather, they have been more flexible than the law usually is, drawing upon history, tradition, context, and other factors to produce a legal situation that is very difficult to summarize.)

Chapter 5

FINDING INFORMATION

The good news about finding information is that there is an almost unbelievable amount of information available. All the scientists, researchers, journalists, analysts, government agencies, insurance companies, and investors out there develop and collect an incredible amount of information. Much of it is available to the public.

The bad news is that if you are not selective and well-organized in your quest, it will be easy to get overwhelmed. Think about the previous chapter on the kinds of information you'll need, then read through this chapter to get an overview of what may be available to you. Finally, set information priorities for your group's short- and long-term needs, and research accordingly.

This chapter provides some general guidelines on how and where to find the information you need. Your group needs the skills possessed by a good investigative journalist. Some of the suggestions made here will get you started, but this chapter will not replace the information in those books and articles listed in the bibliography on how to obtain information. Refer to those when you need more focused advice.

An Overview

Your search for information begins in your backyard. Do not neglect the many rich local resources. Many localities have historical societies or informal museums where a variety of artifacts, documents, and other information can be found. Don't be surprised if the archives are disorganized or haphazard. It is time-consuming and expensive to sort through papers and documents professionally, and most local historical groups lack the resources of a large research library. Still, you might be surprised to find that, in many cases, the accessibility of records in a county courthouse compares poorly with what you will find at a local historical society.

In addition, many of the historical society members themselves will be treasure-troves of information about local history. Fascinating to listen to in their own right, they may also drop tidbits of information that will prove invaluable to you later on. Don't hesitate to enlist the local high school classes in gathering oral history. They can enjoy running around interviewing people while your group (and indirectly, the whole community) benefits from the information they uncover.

Whether you are looking for archaeological information, the history of a certain tract of land, the original membership list of a church, or a utility company right-of-way policy, old-timers in the community are great assets. Seemingly trivial bits of information about the history of an area can lead to important insights about who supports a project and why or about why a company is spending so much effort on what seems to be an unimportant issue.

Many of the documents you obtain will seem like gibberish the first time you see them. Don't get discouraged. Remember, even a city telephone book is a very complex, potentially confusing document. It is clear and simple to you only because you have learned how to use it. Once you have learned to use your local phone book, you can usually figure out other phone books as well, even if they are quite different from your own. The same is true with government documents. After you have seen and studied a few, or a few hundred, you'll be able to skim them for important information instead of reading every word.

If your group is serious about stopping the Project, you need access to all kinds of government files. This usually means living near or traveling to the place where relevant documents are kept. In many cases, this is the state capital, where all of the state government regulatory agencies usually have their headquarters. If there is federal involvement in the Project you are fighting (as when federal permits need to be obtained), you may need access to regional headquarters of federal agencies as well.

There is no way around this. There is likely to be tons of paperwork — literally — already generated by the Project backers, much of it on file in government agencies. You cannot expect to ask for and receive copies of appropriate documents in the mail. Plan to spend whole days at these government offices and agencies, first because there is so much material, and second because the important stuff is probably not easy to locate or even recognize. Most of these offices are open only during normal business hours (often with lunch breaks during which offices are closed), so you'll need to do your research there during the day. Your group needs to find someone, or several people, who can spend one or two days during the week at government offices.

You also need access to a large, serious library. This can be a city public library or a university library. Both usually have evening and weekend hours, so it should be a little easier to get there to do research. Many large libraries are repositories for official U.S. government documents; these will be very helpful.

Never hesitate to ask librarians for assistance — they love to help people find information. Part of their funding may depend on their being able to demonstrate that people need them. Many keep tallies of how many times they are asked for assistance. So, each time you ask a question, you get help and they look good. This is not a suggestion that you ask librarians to do your work for you. They can show you how to use a particular index, let you know about particular reference books, and orient you as to where things generally are. Once they have shown you how to get the most out of a library, you can do the rest yourself.

Many people who are not students hesitate to use a university library. Parking problems are common, and the place is overrun with college kids. This may be annoying, but it is easier to get used to them than to the Project in your back yard. Most university libraries make special library cards available to non-students. Usually for a modest fee, you can use most library facilities and borrow most regular library materials. You will be surrounded by eighteen-year-olds hoping to get dates for the weekend while pretending to work on term papers that don't interest them. Just ignore them, and let them envy your sense of purpose.

Legal Information

Rights to Information: If Entity is private, only a limited amount of information has to be made public about it. Much of this will be available in a good library. (Be sure to ask the reference librarian.)

Even a private Entity, however, must file many permit-related documents at government regulatory agencies, where files are generally open to the public. Your rights to information about a private Entity will be largely (but not completely) limited to what it files publicly.

For access to documents filed at or produced by government Entities, mixed Entities, and government regulatory agencies, your legal rights are much clearer. If you are dealing with federal bureaucracies or agencies, using the Freedom of Information Act (FOIA) is one of the most effective ways of gaining information.

FOIA is not perfect. Sometimes years elapse before desired documents see the light of day, it can be difficult and expensive to use, and it doesn't always work. But it does provide the average citizen with some legal rights of access to government documents. FOIA is widely used. (The bibliography contains a few of the numerous guidebooks and articles on how to use it.) If you find something interesting, it certainly does not hurt to pass it on to local newspapers which might be interested in seeking particular information.

For state or local information, your chances, while still good, will differ widely from state to state. Many states have their own versions of FOIA-like laws. These usually differ from FOIA and from each other, but they do spell out a citizen's right of access to government records and often to the public meetings of governmental bodies as well. These laws are sometimes referred to as *open government*, *open meetings*, or *open records* laws or acts.

Handbooks or guidelines on how to take advantage of such state laws are often available through local libraries, legal aid societies, and many citizens action groups. You are more likely to obtain information from government agencies and bodies if you let them know that you are familiar with your legal rights to see certain documents. But the right to access is not the same thing as access, and you should not be misled into thinking that the existence of open government laws automatically provides you with access to information.

These open government laws will outline certain procedures that you must follow in order to obtain the information that you have a right to see. In some cases, agencies will just hand you the documents, while in others, they will maximize the red tape involved and the time and expense it will cost you. Hope for the best, be ready for the worst, and do not lose your temper.

You will be required to identify yourself, often with a driver's license or similar ID and fill out a written request form specifying the documents you would like to see. Some open government laws specifically state that you are not required to explain your reasons for wanting to see public records. Do not let a nosy, aggressive, or very official-looking bureaucrat intimidate you into explaining your business. Be courteous and comply with all formal requirements (search, fingerprinting, whatever), but don't feel that you have tell your life's story. When someone asks whom you are representing, state that you are a private citizen. Civil servants may be more civil and less insulting if they suspect you are a reporter for a big newspaper or a quality-control agent from another bureaucracy.

Often the agency is legally allowed to take a week or ten days to decide whether or not it thinks your request is covered by the open government law. If it wants to delay you as much as possible, it will make you wait the full time period even if it knows immediately that your request is appropriate and in order.

Another way to slow down your access to information is to force you to identify precisely each document that you want to see. If you are too vague, the agency can say that it has two rooms full of documents on Project Costs and cannot possibly bring out all of them. It is always helpful to have the exact name of a particular document or some other clear way of identifying it (a date, author, purchase order number, reference, or similar tag.)

Open government laws may often require an organization to allow you to inspect a document, but they do not require that the organization's personnel do research for you. They may produce particular *documents* but they may not help you locate particular *information*.

Open government legislation is full of loopholes and exceptions, some of which are present to protect members of the public (like you) from unscrupulous outsiders trying to gain access to personal data that is none of their business. Expect to find a whole list of cases where information need not or cannot be made public. Most of these exceptions will be open to interpretation. If the organization does not wish to share certain information with you, it is likely to wait the maximum period of time after receiving your request and then inform you that it believes your request is covered by one or more of the legal exceptions. If you disagree, you must follow the procedures outlined for appealing a decision. If you have reached this point, you definitely need a lawyer to advise you on further steps.

You may wish to follow the appeals procedure and eventually go to court in an attempt to get the documents. If a document is essential for your case, and if you cannot get it anywhere else, and if you do have the time and money for a lawyer and legal costs, then go to court with it. Entity may not want to deal with a well-publicized court case about why it or a government agency is withholding information from the public about the Project.

However, there are at least three reasons why pursuing a lawsuit is not usually the wisest course of action. First, if you have never even seen a document, you have no way of knowing that it will be useful to you. Second, even if you eventually win the case, you may not win it in time for the document to be used in a particular upcoming hearing or other proceeding. Third, your time may be better spent elsewhere. You will lose a few battles, and access to documents may be one of them. Don't allow your group, with its limited resources, to be dragged into long legal battles over trifles.

Ideally, you should obtain a copy of the appropriate open government law, together with some guidelines on how to apply it in actual situations. Sometimes there is a law review article that tells you all you want to know about the law, its history, the intentions of the writers, recent changes in the law, important court cases that may affect its interpretation, and, most importantly, what happens when you actually try to use it.

Legal Requirements and Procedures Entity Must Follow: Your first clues in this area can be found in newspaper articles about the Project. Note any references to regulatory agencies or specific laws. From these begin making phone calls and visiting government offices and libraries.

Two excellent places to find references to laws and regulations that apply are in an Environmental Impact Statement (EIS) and in a bond prospectus. (The bond prospectus is discussed in the next chapter.)

For the exact procedures and regulations, you will need to consult actual books of regulations. Each regulatory agency (like the EPA or the State Water Quality Board) should have a copy of its current regulations available. Your choice is either to pay for a copy of the whole thing or pay to have certain parts copied for you. If you have copies made, use the agency's copy instead of the library's copy, because you need the most current version.

It is likely that the controversy about the Project will drag on for months, perhaps years. During this time, the laws and regulations that apply to it will certainly change. Congress passes laws, state legislatures meet, and courts may essentially invalidate certain parts. These changes will be reflected in updated versions of the regulations. Every once in a while (every couple of months, at least), check with the agency to make sure that the version your group is working from is the most current one.

The Project you are fighting is probably affected by a number of federal regulations, so you will need to keep up with the changes they undergo. There is a way to simplify this task. On every working day that is not a government holiday, an issue of the *Federal Register* is published. The FR is the single most up-to-date source on what is happening now in federal regulations.

The FR publishes all "regulations and legal notices issued by Federal agencies," including the Labor Department, the Bureau of Land Management, the Nuclear Regulatory Commission, the Federal Emergency Management Agency, and the Bureau of Alcohol, Tobacco and Firearms. There is a weekly index as well as information on the status of various environmental impact statement proceedings.

Many libraries receive the FR. Unless you are watching for something in particular and know what to look for, the FR will make no sense to you. But when you get to the point when you know what changes to watch for, it can be invaluable.

In all of your legal research, remember that you are gathering two very different kinds of information. The first kind sets standards that the Project is supposed to meet. This is called *substantive law,* because it deals with matters of substance, (tons per hour, number of toilets, contaminated water, noise).

Make a list of all standards, the agency requiring them, and the regulation that describes them. It will look something like this.

STANDARD	**AGENCY**	**REGULATION**
No more than 3 tons of CO_2 per hour emitted into air	Air Commission	02.02a
At least 4 toilets per 100 employees	Sanitation Agency	12.34b
No leakage of contaminaged water to public water supply	State Water Board	639(d)
Sound levels not to exceed 80 decibels within 500 feet of a school or a church	Health Department	101.3(2)f

A chart like this will help you keep track of the information and evidence your group should focus on. Of course, if the hearing on the Air Commission permit comes up before the Health Department hearing, then focus on that issue first. But keep your eyes open for information that helps you fight any and all permits sought by Entity.

The second kind of information that you seek is not about matters of substance but about process, about the correct procedures to follow in deciding about a matter of substance. This includes the procedures which must be followed in deciding whether or not to give Entity a particular permit or authorization to go ahead with its plans. This second kind of law, called *procedural law*, deals with matters like the following:

- All landowners within five miles of the Project boundary should be informed of a certain hearing about to take place.
- Three copies of the permit application must be submitted to the agency at least two weeks before the public hearings begin.
- Members of the public are allowed thirty days to comment on a particular document before a final decision is made.

You can also make a chart of the procedural law that applies to your case, indicating the agencies involved and the regulations applied.

Once you have determined whether federal or state law applies in a proceeding, you can also refer to administrative law manuals to learn the general procedures that will be followed. Administrative law is pretty rough reading for a beginner. An attorney can tell you in general the procedures that are appropriate and can refer to the specific statutes for details. As you become more familiar with procedures, you too may want to consult such a manual on particular points.

To many people (including myself at first), substantive law seemed to be the real thing, while procedural law seemed boring, even silly, and of secondary importance. As it turns out, however, procedural law may offer the best chance to stop the Project.

In attempting to stop the Project, your group will be using substantive law and procedural law very differently. On the one hand, you will try to convince a regulatory agency or a court that Entity cannot or will not adhere to substantive law in the course of developing or operating the Project. On the other hand, you will hope that a regulatory agency and/or Entity will be careless, arrogant, or lazy enough to violate procedural law repeatedly as the permit process goes forward.

If procedural violations are numerous and serious enough, your group may be able to convince a court (even after an agency has already granted a permit to Entity) that the whole process should be invalidated. This will not work, however, unless you can prove procedural violations. So, be on the lookout and use photographs, notarized documents, tape recorders, and multiple witnesses (not all from your group) to document any suspected procedural violations.

Standing and Appeal: Procedural law should begin to answer questions about standing and appeal. Further information can be found in various handbooks of administrative law. In general, on matters of standing and appeals, you should work closely with an attorney who will make sure that your actions are procedurally sound.

As previously mentioned, you may be able to find a law review article that covers either of these two issues. But whether you consult a law library or an attorney, make sure that your information covers: how to proceed during the original permit procedure; how to file an official complaint (an appeal) about a decision; and how to use the courts if you are not otherwise successful.

Legal Background of Entity: Entity did not simply appear under a cabbage one day. If it is a government entity, it was created by the legal act of a government body. This may be federal or state legislation or city or municipal resolutions or ordinances. The Entity itself should be able to provide you with a copy of the act or law that created it.

However, more thorough documentation is often to be found at the state archives, a large public or university library, or at a law library. Possibly the original law that created Entity has been amended several or many times. You need the most current version, of course. But it may also help your cause immensely to see how Entity's powers and/or responsibilities have been expanded or reduced over the years.

If you examine past controversies over changes to the original legislation, you will see various interest groups lining up pro or con. This is a good place to start making a list of Entity's enemies. For, though the enemies of your opponent may not be your friends, they surely have a lot of information that could prove useful and may share some of your goals as well.

Both libraries and regulatory agencies are a good place to find other information as well. In the library, look up the names of all subsidiaries or parent companies of private or corporate Entities. Ask a librarian to show you the handbooks or directories that contain this information. Each time you check a file thereafter, look under all of these names.

Another source of information is the State Attorney General's Office. Check to see if Entity is registered as itself or as a subsidiary. Then check for *DBA* listings. DBA means *Doing Business As*. A company's real registered name may be Tom's Toxins, Inc., but it may be doing business as (i.e. using the name) Clean Green Transport.

Anyone who owns stock in a publicly held corporation will receive yearly proxy statements. Proxy statements contain basic information about the company's finances, executive compensation, and special arrangements not otherwise apparent to investors. Their purpose is to provide information about issues to be voted on during the company's annual meeting. They are often much more informative than the same company's annual report.

If the Entity you are dealing with is a large company in its industry, then the library may provide you with detailed background information. However, for smaller, less visible companies, some focused research in the offices of state attorneys general, city attorneys, and public court records will be necessary.

Technical and Economic Information

Current Project Description: The best place to start getting information about the Project is in newspaper articles which include the names of reports and regulatory agencies. An EIS, a DEIS (draft EIS), a FEIS (final EIS), a EA (Environmental Assessment), or a bond prospectus will also provide you with a concise general description of the Project.

In an Environmental Impact Statement it is assumed that a proposed activity either does or might have significant effects on the human environment. This is the most thorough of the reviews required by the National Environmental Protection Act (NEPA). An EIS often is several volumes long, including one or more technical volumes. A decision on the issues raised in an EIS is announced in a *Record of Decision*.

An Environmental Assessment is a less extensive Project review that is supposed to determine if a proposed project will have significant effects on the environment. It, too, contains useful information, but it offers fewer opportunities than an EIS. An EA or any version of an EIS is an excellent place to look for a preliminary Project descriptions. The bond prospectus, also a good source, is discussed in the next chapter.

However, for your future use and for more thorough analysis, your group needs a more detailed description of the Project. The best place to look for this will be in the regulatory agencies. Your legal research will have provided you with a list of permits that must be obtained. Often the permit application itself (submitted by Entity) or the supporting documents will include the detailed Project description that you need.

Two caveats should be kept in mind at this point. First, expect that Entity has submitted different plans to different regulatory agencies. This is part of its strategy, which will be discussed more fully in a later chapter. For now, remember that you must ultimately become familiar with each plan filed at each agency.

Second, expect all of these plans to change or be modified as time goes on. This is another part of Entity's strategy and will also be discussed later. Learn whatever you can from what you find on file, but never assume that any of it is final. (This advice is still valid even after a permit has been granted.)

Track Records of Similar Projects: Chances are excellent that other groups around the country have fought against Projects similar to the one you are opposing. These groups will probably be just as eager to make contact with you and to share information, references, insights, and war stories. Early contact with a group that is already ahead of you can save you a lot of time and provide valuable short-cuts.

To locate these groups, visit large public libraries, the offices of various consumer advocate groups, community activists' meeting places, and check all of the newsletters you can find. (The bibliography contains references to directories of organizations and catalogues of newsletters.) These newsletters will be valuable for the information that they contain, but check them as well for names and addresses of groups and references to books, articles, and other references that may be especially helpful.

Another way to find out about groups similar to yours is to read through recent EIS's of similar Projects. The EIS will probably include a list of persons who responded in person or in writing to the original Project proposal. This list will certainly include Project opponents.

For information on similar Projects in your own state or region, regulatory agencies can provide you with complete records on all similar projects. In addition, a large library can provide you with both general background information and perhaps some specific reports, studies, or journal and magazine articles.

Independent Outside Evaluations: The library is probably the best place to find independent outside evaluations. Start with newspapers and magazines, and follow any references to specialized newsletters, university studies, or even government reports.

Political Information

Getting good political information and insights about the Project or about Entity may be more difficult than acquiring the other kinds of information that we have discussed. There is no single best source of political information. Check many sources, keep your eyes and ears open, and you will find yourself better and better informed.

History is always helpful — it may expose origins, past scandals or alliances, old debts, old feuds, continuing prejudices, and lots of other useful information. Public libraries may have special files on local history. These are invaluable. Local newspapers are a great source as well. Many keep files of their own articles, partly so reporters can familiarize themselves with historical background before they write a story. Often these files are open or can be made available to researchers.

Current newspapers and magazines will also let you know who is for or against the Project. You can also follow the memorandum and letter trails at the regulatory agencies to find out who else has supported or opposed the Project. In both cases, be alert for unexpected absences — who would be expected to support the Project, for example, but has not spoken out?

Regulatory agency files on similar projects may reveal supporters and opponents whom you had not thought of or known about. For example, many industries compete with each other. Companies that want to burn hazardous waste on ocean ships may be competing against companies that want to store it in swamps. Or, a realtor's group that wants to rent out a huge facility may be competing with construction companies and unions that want to build one. Building a power plant that burns coal may disappoint the natural gas industry.

Realtors often turn up on interesting sides in controversies over a big Project. In general, any development that fosters, or is believed to foster, growth is usually considered positive by realtors. However, a particular Project right next to a planned subdivision may lower property values and discourage growth in that area. In that case, the realtor community and the various realtor associations may be split regarding the merits of the Project. Those who fear financial losses if the Project goes forward may be willing to help your cause officially or unofficially. Their help might take the form of donations, but even more helpful would be the sharing of maps, specific site information, and specific tips about weaknesses in Project backers' case.

As much as possible, try to understand and anticipate factions that compete on a national or global scale. Where possible, read industry newsletters, trade journals, union magazines, and publications of political parties and consumer groups. Attend public meetings of regulatory agencies, hearings in legislatures or at city councils, and any other political or consumer-oriented meetings open to the public.

If bidding on different parts of the Project has already occurred and some bids have been awarded, there are likely to be unhappy bidders around — companies that did not get the bid and think that they should have. Sometimes they suspect unfair practices, and you may also. At any rate, it never hurts to talk with unhappy bidders, who may offer valuable insights into the behind-the-scenes politics. If rejected bidders (as sometimes occurs) file suit against Entity, you may find their court records helpful as well.

Agencies and companies often have their own official publications, some of which are written for internal consumption but available to outsiders, others of which are specifically designed for customers, libraries, and the news media. These are all very official in the line they take, but they may nevertheless provide insights you can use. An early crisis in the company's history may have exerted much influence on its later direction. Friendships forged among apprentice electricians may become crucial when both have risen to prominent positions in the company, etc. Union publications also can provide insights and perspectives you might otherwise miss.

In general, when attempting to grasp the politics of the Project, Woodward and Bernstein's advice from *All The President's Men* is still useful: "follow the money." Large Projects can easily involve hundreds of millions of dollars, sometimes billions. Every penny spent on the Project goes to someone — for materials, services, loans, land, labor, or certain rights. Those in a position to receive material benefits may find it difficult to oppose the Project. Those who missed out on some of the large financial benefits may be disgruntled but not strongly opposed. However, those who stand to lose money are your likely allies.

Learn as much as you can about the law firms and accounting firms involved as well as other players. Go to meetings, speeches, cocktail parties, and fund-raisers for as many organizations as you can. Read the public notice section of the newspaper, the list of bankruptcies, and the want-ads. In short, hang out as much as possible and read anything you can get your hands on about Entity.

For some reason, people who work at government agencies, and many who work for private companies as well, are often especially open to the requests of students working on term papers or other class projects. Surely there is a student in your group who can go to some of the crustier bureaucracies or corporations and collect information for a research paper.

As a woman, I can testify that the mostly male bureaucrats and managers generally feel less threatened by a female researcher. Frankly, their apparent assumption that the interviewer is mentally deficient allows them to say things to a women researcher that they might not say to an aggressive male reporter. A member of your group may not appreciate someone assuming that she is mentally dim. However, your group is in no position to ignore any useful information that is freely offered. Enough said.

In the next chapter, we'll briefly discuss six sources of information that you should not miss: university and public libraries, law libraries, bond prospectuses, regulatory agencies, site visits, and baseline studies. We'll offer some advice on how to get the most out of each.

A Citizen's Guide on Using the Freedom of Information Act (FOIA) and the Privacy Act of 1974 To Request Government Records, Thirteenth Report by the Committee on Government Operations, House Report 100-19 (Washington, DC: U.S. Government Printing Office, July 1, 1987), a concise fifty-page pamphlet that includes description of applicable exemptions and sample letters for filing requests and appeals (available by writing to your Congressmember and asking for a copy.); *Washington Information Directory 1990-1991*, (Washington, DC: Congressional Quarterly Inc.), an excellent reference source listing information by category and including lists of both governmental and non-governmental organizations, with addresses; also contains brief descriptions of the Freedom of Information and Privacy Acts; Michael J. Ybarra, "Federal Register Chronicles Endless Flow of Regulations," *Washington Post*, Jul. 30, 1990.

Chapter 6

SELECTED SOURCES OF INFORMATION

This chapter discusses six important sources of information which your NIMBY group should not overlook. The time you spend familiarizing yourself with these sources and the best ways to use them will pay for itself many times over.

University and Public Libraries

Look up the general structure and history of the industry involved in the Project you are trying to fight. Learn about the raw materials it needs, the techniques it employs, the equipment it requires. Pay particular attention to input and output: the resources it uses and the waste materials it generates. What happens to these resources while and after they are in Project hands?

Pay attention to personnel issues. How much labor does Entity need, how are its labor relations, does the company have a history of crushing unions or negotiating with them? Are there any particular occupational hazards (safety issues, health problems, etc.) associated with the industry? Would these be confined to the facility itself or would they also affect the community at large? If a particular union represents employees, the union newsletter will be a gold mine of information about many aspects of the company. See if the library has back issues.

Learn to use the library's periodical indexes to general magazines, trade journals, and specialized industry publications. Find out who the industry leaders are in designing, planning, constructing, and operating a facility like the Project you oppose. Look up the records of those chosen for the Project.

Often certain information is widely known within an industry but almost completely unknown in your area. Here is an example, based on my experience. A controversial local Project was the object of much disagreement about its feasibility. Project backers relied heavily on information provided by or commissioned by Entity, particularly a report by a consultant firm that we will call Specter & Co.

The *Specter Report* strongly endorsed the Project, providing masses of data that purportedly confirmed other technical and economic information which overwhelmingly and incontrovertibly favored the project. Though it was possible to question this or that bit of information or this or that interpretation, it was difficult convincingly to refute the report as a whole, at least in the eyes of the uninformed lay public. But then someone thought to check up on Specter & Co.

It turned out that Specter & Co. was well known, infamous even, in that sector of the consulting industry. In the recent past, it had given similar glowing reviews of a Project proposed in another part of the country. Based largely on that Specter evaluation, the Project had gone forward. Within a few years, this project failed spectacularly, its collapse and associated financial ruin making front pages of newspapers nationwide. Specter's evaluations were fallible, to say the least.

In the library, also check any special files on corporations. Many libraries collect the Annual Reports and 10K files of many corporations. These 10K files are reports that the Securities and Exchange Commission (SEC) requires publicly held companies to file. They include much useful information about the company, though you should keep in mind that this information is generated by the company itself. (Note that non-publicly held corporations — companies like Bechtel, a very well-known consulting and construction firm — are not required to file 10K reports with the SEC, nor are they subject to its regulations.)

While you are checking out the resources of area university libraries in particular, do not neglect the theses and dissertations. Usually a university keeps on file all theses and dissertations written by graduates awarded degrees at that institution. Sometimes these are filed in the regular card catalogue, but at other times they may be filed separately, so check carefully or ask.

Much research on topics of local interest, some very detailed, never gets out of the institution. You never know when you are going to be lucky and find a bonanza of information in a long-forgotten thesis. If there is nothing useful there, you are none the worse for trying.

The Law Library

A law library is a specialized library connected to a law school and often housed in the same building. For the uninitiated, and even for experienced researchers, a law library can be very confusing. A lifetime's work with Dewey decimal, the Library of Congress system, or even some fairly arcane archival material will not prepare you for a law library. For those who expect to focus on legal research, I recommend that they begin by reading one of the many books about law libraries first. With names like "How to Use a Law Library," most are easy to locate and absolutely essential if you want to make any headway.

Most of you will not want to devote that much effort to becoming familiar with a law library, choosing instead to use your skills in other ways in the fight the Project. Even in this event, however, you may still want to use the law library for a few specific kinds of information.

You can look up specific codes, regulations, or laws if you copy down references accurately. It is also fairly easy to locate a particular law review article or case. If your need is quite specific, a librarian will be able to direct you to the right place in the library immediately. Someone else (another researcher in your group, an attorney, a sympathetic law student) may have asked you to copy a particular part of the regulations. This is fairly easy to do.

Law dictionaries can also be a big help. To make sure you are not misusing a certain term or concept or to help you understand another reference you are reading, a law dictionary is just what you need.

It will also be worthwhile to browse through the most recent issues of the local or state law review. This is a journal containing articles about current issues of law. These are not as straightforward as *Time* magazine, but they are far easier to understand than regulations, contracts, and case law. Some of these articles may be very useful for your group.

For example, if a federal law has been passed changing the building standards for public buildings, the law review will have an article about the effect this will or will not have on area construction, at least as far as the legal aspects are concerned. Similarly, if the Supreme Court has recently resolved a case regarding toxic waste, the law review will examine the implications of the decision for local, regional, and state law and regulations.

If you browse through the law review, you may even find articles concerning the legal issues underlying the Project you oppose. After all, someone, perhaps many people, has probably already been over the whole proposal in revolting detail.

Finally, check the magazines, periodicals, and especially newsletters that the library subscribes to. These will be chock-full of proper names, references, contacts, current decisions and controversies, and a variety of other useful information that you didn't even know was out there.

The Bond Prospectus

Often overlooked as a source of information, the bond prospectus can be an excellent source of concise data. Surprisingly, it is often quite easy for the layperson to understand, too. But first, what is it?

One way to raise money — and this works for a public agency, a private corporation, or a mixed entity — is to sell bonds. Suppose that Entity needs $1 million to build a treatment plant. Entity offers to sell one million dollars in bonds. An investor loans Entity the money by purchasing the bonds. Entity promises to pay back the investor $10,000 a month until it has paid back the entire amount, plus, say, 12 percent interest, paying back a total of $1.12 million over a ten-year period. (This, by the way, is an extraordinarily low rate of interest.)

Before shelling out a million dollars, the investor is going to want to know about the Project, Entity, the history of both, current financial data, the legal status of the whole thing, and other relevant facts. The bond prospectus provides this information (according to specific legal and financial guidelines) to prospective investors.

Even though it is data generated by Entity with the specific purpose of leaving a favorable impression, it must include certain items of information. Among these are: a review of the legal status of participants (including any unresolved suits or other encumbrances) and a summary of permits and authorizations that must still be obtained before the Project can proceed.

If your group has been around for a while and you think that you have at least given Entity a run for its money, you many be surprised to see how your minor successes are glossed over in the bond prospectus. Or, you may discover that there are others out there also taking legal action against Entity. These are potential allies and information sources.

If Entity is public or mixed, you should have little difficulty obtaining bond prospectuses for current and past bond issues. In that way, you will be able to glimpse the history of Entity and/or the Project through financial and legal eyes. If Entity hesitates to share them with you, either obtain them elsewhere or take legal action immediately.

If Entity is private, however, it may be much more difficult to obtain copies, and your legal rights are less clear. Often, private entities raise needed funds in other ways, avoiding the potential exposure and scrutiny that often accompanies a bond sale.

Regulatory Agencies

Government regulatory agencies (which may be called boards, commissions, departments, offices, bureaus) are excellent sources of information. On your first few visits, you may feel unwanted, out of place, and confused. That is to be expected. After you get used to them, those feelings will be replaced by depression, boredom, frustration...and sometimes exhilaration when you uncover some useful material.

What is a regulatory agency? It is a government body or office that is set up with the official purpose of regulating a particular industry, resource, or activity. It may exist officially to regulate air transportation (an industry), water (a resource), or mining (an activity). In some cases, the regulatory agency is also supposed to plan for the future use of a resource or coordinate activities or industries to safeguard or guarantee the public welfare.

Sometimes it is easy to tell from an agency's name exactly what it is supposed to be doing. Something called the State Water Board, for example, probably regulates water use, planning, wells, dams, and other water uses. Or, on the national level, the Office of Surface Mining regulates surface mining, the bureaucratic euphemism for what everyone else calls strip mining.

However, many times the activities of a particular agency are not clear from its name alone. In Texas, for example, there is a state regulatory agency called the Texas Railroad Commission. It does regulate railroads, but is also responsible for regulating uranium and coal strip mining and oil and (natural) gas exploration.

The vastness of the federal government bureaucracy provides other unexpected combinations. Nuclear weapons research, development, testing, production, and surveillance, as well as the disposal of civilian radioactive wastes, are all responsibilities of the Department of Energy, a circumstance not immediately obvious from its name. Another federal department manages, among other things, the handling, transport, and sale of zoo animals, the provision of electricity to rural communities, and funding for helicopters full of armed men who are shooting at coyotes and wolves on ranches in the West. It should be obvious that this department is the Department of Agriculture.

The annual *United States Government Manual*, found in the reference section of most libraries, will help you to clarify the organization and responsibilities of many federal agencies. Look for state and municipal versions of such a manual to guide your research closer to home. Consult these manuals early and often until you have a clear picture of the bureaucratic terrain.

It is important that your group determine exactly which regulatory agencies have jurisdiction over the various aspects of the Project that you are trying to stop. A particular regulatory agency will be responsible for evaluating particular projects, giving out permits or licenses, monitoring those projects through inspections and/or tests, and enforcing the regulations to make sure that they are being followed.

All information collected during these processes will be kept at the regulatory agency. It will keep on file requests for permits (often called permit applications) along with any material (reports or documents) submitted by Entity to support the permit application. In addition, all proceedings (like permit hearings transcripts), inspection records, enforcement records, and correspondence concerning the permit will also be kept on file. The permit application itself may be several volumes long and contain numerous maps and thousands of pages of charts, lists, and text. By itself, the permit application file may fill several filing drawers, cabinets, or even rooms, so take a big lunch.

Most of the information at a regulatory agency has been provided by the applicant — Entity seeking a permit. Entity may have had its own staff prepare the permit application. More likely, it hired a consulting firm to work with its staff to prepare it. In all cases, it will have used the legal advice of its own staff or an outside law firm to make sure that the document is as close to airtight as possible.

Most Projects are required to keep extensive records and do their own tests, filing copies of the results at regulatory agencies. That means that much of the information used by government inspectors will have been provided by Entity. It also means that regulatory agencies are not a great source of outside, critical information. But most agency files are full of data about standards that have been exceeded or other violations of the regulations. Usually this is not well-known because no one except for Entity and the government agency ever reads the agency files.

When you arrive at a regulatory agency for the first time, you will have to guess where to go. You might try looking for a place with a name like 'Central Records' or 'Central Files.' Some agencies actually have a separate library or reference room, but many do not. When you find the right place, expect a lot of variation in how carefully records are kept, how helpful the staff is, and how long it takes to locate the records that you seek. You will learn a lot about the general attitude of the agency and the amount of money it spends on staff.

There are two extremes. One is a poorly staffed or understaffed regulatory agency that resents outsiders. The filing system in a place like this is supervised by a bureaucrat. It is understaffed, because whoever funds the agency may not really want the agency to do its job well. In this case, the files are disorganized, jumbled, difficult to find, and often unavailable. The few staff working in the records department are suspicious of your interest in the files and not at all helpful if you are not certain about exactly what you want or how to ask for it. They give you a file only after a long wait and leave you standing in the corner of the room trying to examine a huge file without a table or other flat surface to set it on.

The bureaucrats who deal with you this way are not evil people, but they have been trained to be terrified of giving out information that will help you and somehow hurt them. They have learned to be afraid of releasing information and getting into trouble with their bosses later for doing so.

Sometimes, happily, you find the other extreme. These are places that have a separate library set up for filing materials. There is a well-lit room or rooms with many tables to put documents on, often a card catalogue, and helpful, well-organized staff people. There is a filing system organized and run by librarians, who are dedicated to the idea that their job is to help people find the information they seek. The files are arranged for ease in storing them *and* for ease in finding and retrieving them.

Because Entity is often required to obtain multiple permits from several agencies, it may file a particular document at more than one agency. Therefore, do as much of your research as possible at the agency that is organized more like a library. Often a document that has not been available at Entity or at the agency where it was first filed can be found with little trouble at another agency. (Always check around first before you decide that a lawsuit based on applicable open government laws is the only way to get a particular document.)

At these agencies, a group like yours opposing a Project is a rarity. The regulatory agencies are most frequently visited by industry personnel, bureaucrats from other government agencies, and attorneys (or their paralegal assistants) representing everyone. Less often, researchers or reporters will visit the agency. But plain old members of the public are rare birds. Agency records are organized with these other visitors in mind. In fact, many of their requests will take priority over yours. That is perfectly understandable. The people doing research for your group should always be courteous but always know their rights as well.

One of the first things you want to know your rights about is signing in. Most agencies have some sort of guest book like those found in museums and at funerals. A receptionist/gatekeeper will ask you to sign in when you arrive. The guest book usually has places for you to put your name, the date, whom you are representing, and the records you are interested in.

There is no reason to indicate anything that is not legally required. So, write your name and the date. In most cases, unless you are a paid lobbyist for a group or organization, there is no legal requirement for you to identify yourself further. If you want to fill in the blank, put down that you are a private citizen or representing no one. Be as vague as you like, within legal limits, about the records you want to inspect — in bureaucratic parlance, looking at records is called *inspecting* them. If you are at all uncertain, check with an attorney about the information that is legally required in a particular instance. There is no reason to advertise openly to the world exactly what records your group is interested in.

While you are signing in, you might take the opportunity to flip back through the pages to see who else has visited recently. The regulars often do little more than scrawl unreadable initials. If they do sign their names and affiliations, though, you may be able to learn a little about what's in their bullpen.

During your first visits to the agency you will figure out its filing system. It is probable that the name of the Entity, the name of the Project, or the specific location of the Project (especially the county) will be enough to start with. Remember to check parent companies, subsidiaries, and the other names the company may be doing business under. If you have the name of a specific document, ask to see it. If not, a request for the permit application and related correspondence will probably produce enough paper to keep you busy for a week or more.

After you have looked at information on Entity's Project, you may be able to look at documents related to other projects managed by the same Entity or other documents pertaining to similar projects managed by other Entities for comparison. In addition, be sure to ask for the inspection records, enforcement records, and data on any actions (often called enforcement actions) that have been taken regarding Entity.

If the regulatory agency was unhappy with the performance of a particular Project, it may take actions to encourage Entity to improve its behavior and meet standards required by regulations. If the regulatory agency did not receive the response from Entity that it desired, it may have passed the case on to the state attorney general for legal action. If this has happened in a case your group is following, you will have to continue your research in court records.

Once you start inspecting documents, it may take days before you can figure out what they mean. Keep reading, making notes of things that seem important. Slowly a picture will emerge, and you will be able to read more quickly and scan for important information. It helps to talk with your attorney occasionally, informing him or her of what is on file and finding out if there are any specific things you should be keeping an eye out for.

There is almost no end to what might turn up in a regulatory agency file. For example, Entity may want to do something a little differently than it promised in its permit application (usually to save money, cut personnel, speed up operations, or all three). If so, it will hire a consulting firm to do a study that will purport to show that if Entity does *a*, *b*, and *c*, then the Project will be even more efficient, safer, cleaner, and better. The report will contain valuable information that your group will have to respond to.

Or, if Entity and a regulatory agency have a disagreement about whether a certain standard is being followed, agency files will contain the letters and arguments between and among Entity, its law firms, its consultants, and agency personnel.

Agency files will contain detailed plans, down to the last fence post, of what will go where. Do not take these plans to be the final version, but examine them very closely for an insight into Entity's plans.

Copy all references to outside reports, university studies or other outside sources. Entity and its attorneys, consultants, and other hired hands will quote very selectively from all sources in order to strengthen its argument. They may even distort the results of outside studies in order to make it appear that their practices have more widespread support than is really the case. Your group needs to check this and point out any misrepresentations. These outside sources are also good sources of additional information — go right to their bibliographies and follow up on promising-sounding titles.

Finally, sometimes you will want to have copies of material that you find at regulatory agencies. Keep in mind that these will be the most expensive copies that you will ever make in your life. Many government agencies (and this will include Entity if it is a governmental body or a mixed entity) charge two to ten times the usual per-page rates for photocopied material. So, if there is a chance that you can get the material elsewhere, do so.

Sometimes you can borrow a report or a document from a sympathetic official — a mayor, a senator, a clerk — and make your own copies at reasonable rates. If, however, the regulatory agency is the only place that you can find a particular document, then you'll have to get your copies there. Just check around before spending half of your group's treasury on a complete copy of a permit application.

The Site Visit

It is probably well worth your while to make a site visit as soon as you have learned a little about the Project. Depending on circumstances, you may want to make periodic visits to observe and document any changes that may be taking place.

How do you make a site visit? A formal invitation is often unnecessary. The general location and boundaries of the proposed Project site have probably been mentioned in various newspaper accounts. With these as a guide, get as many specifics as possible from site descriptions in official reports. If the information is not forthcoming, call an elected local official or the reporter who wrote the newspaper account, and you will probably have the desired details in short order.

Most sites (unless they are matters of national security or tucked away in truly inaccessible places) will be accessible, at least in part, by public roads. Or, you may want to ask permission from an adjacent private landowner to tramp across his property to get a better look. In any case, be sure that at all times you respect property rights, no trespassing signs, and all other indications that entry or access is prohibited or restricted.

It won't do your group any good to have members arrested for trespassing, so don't leave yourselves open to that possibility.

It is usually preferable to go in a group of two or three people. More than that may attract excessive attention, while a lone visitor will have no witness if any unpleasantness occurs. Feel free to take along binoculars or telescopes, cameras with wide angle and/or telescopic lenses, and video cameras if you have access to any such equipment.

Sunday afternoons are often a great time for unofficial site visits. There is generally less traffic, and fewer people are out and about. You might even want to make a picnic out of it (don't litter), sitting at the side of the road as you toss around ideas and observations.

Many large companies (like utilities) and government entities which are especially security-conscious employ sophisticated (and sometimes overzealous) security systems. Don't be surprised if you are buzzed by a mean-looking unmarked helicopter. If, as advised, you are totally legal, it may do no more than take your pictures with high resolution equipment and run a security check on the license plates of any vehicles nearly. (Make sure that your vehicle's paperwork is up-to-date and that you are not using illegal window tint or anything life-threatening like that.) By all means, take its picture, too.

Obtain as much documentation as possible, and be precise about it. Document the date and time of year by taking a picture of one or more site visitors holding up a daily paper (headlines visible) with the site in the background. If it is spring, work some wildflowers into a picture. Or if someone in your group is pregnant and showing, get her into the picture. These are standard precautions, because you might be surprised how often 'accidents' or acts of nature mysteriously alter a site during a protracted controversy. (See "Accidents Will Happen," in Part II.)

For each photograph, record the date and time, who took the picture, where he or she was standing, and an approximate (but as accurate as possible) compass bearing of the direction the picture was taken in. If possible, also note any special camera settings or filters used (a wide angle lens or a red filter, for example) and what the picture is of. Similar information should be recorded for any video camera tapes. This is easier because you can simply state the data aloud as the camera is rolling.

What should you photograph? You must have some idea from your research of what to look for. Record anything that may affect the Project plans, construction, or track record. Any obvious signs of erosion, piles of suspicious-looking glop, pre-existing structures like barns, streams, or sinkholes should be documented. If you happen to see any endangered or threatened species of birds, flowers, or whatever, document their locations accurately. Do not remove anything from the site, especially things like endangered plant species or archaeological relics.

If you are using a video camera or carrying a tape recorder (though it is difficult with a tape recorder to prove where you were), record sounds as well. In some cases it will be useful to you later to be able to prove that fighter jets fly over, that traffic noise is deafening or nonexistent, or that certain bird calls could be heard.

Finally, if your access to the site is restricted and you feel that a better look would provide valuable information, you may be able to fly over the site. This is much easier than most people realize. There are many people with valid pilot's licenses who own or have access to small aircraft and love to fly. Often their flying time is more limited than they would like because of the high cost of airplane fuel. If your group can get together some money — often under $100 — to pay a pilot's fuel costs, he or she may be very happy to fly you around so that you can do your documentation from the air as well.

To locate your flyer, talk to people at area airports, especially the smaller, rural ones, put up a sign expressing your interest, or run an advertisement in a local newspaper. It is true that in some densely populated urban areas, flight paths are severely restricted. Outside of these, however, a bird's-eye view can give you excellent documentation that may be invaluable for your group.

The Baseline Study

A baseline study can be an excellent source of information, a public education tool, and a basis for future legal action. It can also uncover loose ends that may show you how to tie together all kinds of disparate facts and events into a convincing case.

What is a baseline study? It is a study, often a survey, of the conditions as of right now. The purpose is to have the data later when Entity says, *It was never like that!* or *It was always that way!* Data are Entity's enemy; Project supporters will do almost anything to avoid doing an adequate baseline study. Often your only option is to do your own.

Never trust baseline studies done by others, including big universities, unless you have complete faith in their personnel, methods, and motives. Entity and/or government agencies may conduct their own baseline studies using Entity's own data (an exceedingly common practice), while the consulting firms hired to do the studies may be the pet companies of industry. At any rate, the consulting firm probably derives much or all of its income from projects such as these. If it failed to provide information favorable to the goals of similar entities and government agencies, it would not be hired time after time, would it?

If traffic flow or parking space is an issue, then an adequate baseline study would include these concerns. Health issues relating to a work site, school or neighborhood are very often of major concern. For this reason, we will use a hypothetical health survey as our example of a generic baseline study.

Before beginning your health study, get advice from health professionals sympathetic to your cause. They will help you to focus your concerns, frame basic questions, and identify the useful, accurate data. Try to obtain (with safeguards for confidentiality and privacy, of course) medical records and health data from health clinics, doctors' offices, and hospitals, but do not be surprised if these sources are reluctant to cooperate with you. Accept help from official sources such as these only if you can do so without relinquishing control over the focus of the survey.

Much of your information-gathering will be done through door-to-door visits. By doing this, you will learn, say, what the rate of incidence of respiratory illness seems to be. As you explain why you are collecting this information, you will be performing a public education function. Always carry your group's basic information handout with you and perhaps a second handout which explains the purpose of your baseline study. You may end up recruiting new members for your group or people willing to help you perform your health survey.

In addition to gathering information, educating the public, and recruiting help, you are also providing the groundwork for later legal action. Together with documentation from site visits, the baseline study will be the basis for asserting that the Project has not lived up to standards claimed by its backers. The mere fact that you are attempting to conduct a baseline study will make Entity very nervous as well.

A Last Word on Information

When you first begin to organize your opposition to the Project, Entity and its lawyers and backers will seem like a monolithic, all-powerful, unstoppable steam roller heading your way. And, no doubt about it, they are extremely powerful and have a huge head start.

However, as you learn more about them and their plans, it becomes clear that they are a collection of diverse interests that do not always agree and often distrust one another. In addition, the planned Project will have flaws, often a result of shortcuts introduced to save time and money. Entity thinks that these shortcomings will go unnoticed because no outsider will ever actually read all of the reports.

For the most part, outside events will dictate where to start your information quest. Focus first on information necessary for the earliest Project hearings or other deadlines. If you must formally request hearings, do so as soon as possible. Then, as soon as you have gathered enough information for a newsletter or a fact sheet, distribute it to affected parties, interested groups, public figures, the news media, and anyone else who shows an interest. Before you know it, you will have so many leads to follow up on and tips to pursue that you will never again feel that you don't know where to look.

One of the first places you can put all of your information to work is in public education.

People's Law School (558 Capp St., San Francisco, CA 94110), *How to Use a Law Library*, 1976; *The United States Government Manual* (annual), Office of the Federal Register, National Archives and Records Administration (Lanham, MD: Bernan Press, 1991) lists and briefly describes all agencies, branches, and departments within the federal government.

Chapter 7

PUBLIC EDUCATION

Once you have gathered your information about the Project, you will need to share it with the right people. That's public education. Such efforts by your group are directed toward the general public as well as public officials and other prominent persons. Effective presentations are an important part of your public education campaign.

Your education efforts begins with self-education. Your group must first get the facts and make sure that all of its members are reasonably familiar with them. A few will become specialists, but all should have some grasp of the basic issues. You may then move on to educating the general public, elected and appointed officials, and other big shots.

A caution is in order at this point. Despite the one-sided sound of the term public education, it is a two-way street. If you do not understand this or forget it, your public education efforts will be permanently enfeebled. Like any good teacher, you must listen to the feedback from your audience.

First, pay attention to what interests them, what always perks them up. What issues or examples seem to worry them the most? Make mental notes about questions or comments that are raised. What do they always ask about? What do you always have to explain again? What is never mentioned? What questions or comments are made not publicly but after your talk when people begin to take you aside and have brief private conversations?

It is often in this latter context that you receive some of your best tips: that so-and-so's well was contaminated by leakage from the factory but that the out-of-court settlement prohibited any discussion of it; that Acme Land Company has been quietly going around paying good money for seemingly worthless land...and so on.

Be a good listener. If your message is not informative, not interesting, not clear, not relevant, or not alarming, no one will listen to you. They will just go on with their usual lives. In your literature, speeches, and private talks, hit the points that matter most to your audience. You'll learn what these are only through experience and trial and error.

Educating The Group

No one in your group should feel lost during general discussions of the Project, Entity, or strategies to stop them. If group members feel that they are uninformed or worst, not needed, they may drift off and no longer work with the group. Education is not just for internal cohesion. Uninformed members of your group can make exaggerated or inaccurate claims to the news media and to the public at large. This can cause your group to lose credibility. Once lost, it is nearly impossible to regain.

Everyone in the group should be well-informed enough to handle basic questions about the Project. Each person should carry around a basic handout and some spare newsletters to give to anyone who expresses interest. If questions come up that a particular group member cannot answer, the question should be noted and dealt with later. Options on how to do this include sending more specialized literature or referring the question to a better-informed group member.

Some group members who do technical, legal, and economic research will be able to answer more detailed questions on certain topics. They are probably also the ones who should represent your group at public speaking opportunities and media events, write newsletter articles and information sheets, and help with letters to public officials.

However, there is much more education to be done. Some in your group will learn how to do a bulk mailing, or how to contact TV, radio stations, and print media for an emergency news conference and press release. Others will become adept at setting up and printing a newsletter or getting permission to use a particular facility for public meetings. Still others will handle the complex and often tedious minutiae involved in raising funds through benefit programs, T-shirt sales, or outright pleas.

No single member of your group is capable of understanding the details of all of these diverse activities or even keeping track of them. That's why it's so important that your group meet frequently to share information. Persons responsible for each activity should give brief updates on the progress of research, hearings, public education efforts, fundraising, newsletter production, and other activities.

Those working on research should be encouraged to write brief summaries or fact sheets about what they are working on. This information should first be made available to group members. Then, after it has been understood and discussed by the group, concise, hard-hitting handouts or brochures should be prepared on the various topics.

Group members tend to make fact sheets more and more technical as they learn more. Sometimes this means that ordinary citizens can no longer understand them. To prevent this, always test your newsletters, information sheets, and other literature on outsiders. Seek out people who know nothing about the Project and let them read your stuff. If they hand it back confused, start over. If they want to join the group, then your literature is clear, concise, and effective.

In some cases a new fact sheet will be immediately relevant and therefore distributed as soon as possible. In other cases, you may want to save it until that particular aspect of the Project controversy becomes a hot topic or until that issue is discovered by the news media or a prominent politician.

As members of your group become more familiar with the issues, they can make, and take advantage of, opportunities to broaden their education efforts.

Educating the General Public

Your group wants to spread its message, keep your issues alive, broaden your support, demonstrate community backing at hearings and in elections, and raise money. Educating the public about the dangers of the Project makes all of these things easier.

The Media: The general public does not exist except as it is made up of individuals, families, and various groups. Even television advertisements reach only a part of the general public: those who watch a particular channel at a certain time. A thirty-second television advertisement may reach hundreds of thousands or even millions of people, but it costs a fortune, and its slick, impersonal nature may limit its effectiveness.

In your public education efforts, start close and move outwards. A big bang of a press conference announcing your group's existence and outlining its opposition to the Project will attract initial media attention. Choosing an unusual site — the proposed Project location, a local school yard, or an illegal trash dump, for example — may gain you added press coverage and help the public remember you. In all cases, be sure to obtain permission (if needed) to use the site, and by all means provide the news media with a clear map if it is not a usual location for press conferences (such as city council chambers or the federal building).

Usually, a particular reporter from each newspaper will be assigned to cover certain topics, or beats, like local politics, environment, school district, and other issues. (This is less true with the broadcast media, but you will still see certain broadcast reporters more frequently than others.) Pay attention to which reporter covers the beat that includes Entity and the Project.

One or two of your group's more articulate and well-informed members should introduce themselves to the reporter(s), provide phone numbers for contacts, and offer additional information whenever it is needed. No one in your group should make frequent and irritating phone calls to a reporter, but occasional tips or reminders of important upcoming events are usually appreciated. In return, the reporter may act as a tipster or quasi-inside source of information for your group.

Entity and other Project backers will also be bending the ear of this particular reporter, both probing for information and giving hints (intended or not) of future strategy. The reporter may telephone a contact in your group and ask for a reaction to a plan, or a lawsuit, or a consultant whom your group has not even heard of yet. If your group establishes a reputation as a source of good stories and accurate facts, the reporter may find it beneficial to establish a give-and-take relationship that results in your receiving as well as giving information. If, on the other hand, you make the mistake of crying wolf too often, he or she is likely to drop you and seek alternative sources of information.

During all your press conferences and media events, understand and take advantage of the needs of the news media. They want good visuals for the nightly news and eye-catching photos for the next edition of the local newspaper. (That's why politicians are forever posing in army tanks or astride police motorcycles.) Radio stations appreciate background noise, both chirping birds and rattling jackhammers, to give their reports a you-are-there quality.

Members of the media also appreciate your spokesperson speaking in a clear, sincere tone of voice and being well-informed without sounding like an electrical engineer or a lifelong government bureaucrat. Sometimes it is a good idea to have two people on hand to represent your group: a fact person to read the initial statement and answer technical questions and a more emotional person to express the concerns and fears of those most threatened by the Project.

If you get fifteen seconds on a local radio station or a minute on the local nightly TV news, you have been successful. Tailor your comments accordingly by including hard-hitting ten-second snippets (called *sound bites* in the business) that can be easily excerpted and broadcast.

Your press conference or media event may result in a newspaper article. Make sure the reporter gets a full information packet that includes your best fact sheets as well as names and phone numbers of group members to contact for further information.

From the point of view of the news media, an article or a story will be more widely circulated, the paper will sell more copies, and a broadcast news will reach more listeners if someone makes an inflammatory remark. So when a reporter calls you for more information, one of the things he or she may try to do is provoke you. Have some answers ready. Decide beforehand what is the worst thing you are willing to say publicly about Entity or other Project backers, and then do not exceed that when pressured by a reporter. Help out the reporter if you sense decency or sympathy. If there are matters that you would love to see Project backers asked, let the reporter know about them. He or she may be thrilled to be the first to ask prominent Project backers and then print or broadcast their unrehearsed replies.

Reporters are always looking for scoops, or exclusive stories. After your group's research takes off, you may have information enough for numerous exposés. In some cases you may wish to announce these yourself at official press conferences so that you can present your data and answer questions fully. However, the revelations may be taken less seriously and considered to be less credible if your group makes them, because, after all, you do overtly oppose the Project. In some cases, it may be preferable for you to leak certain information, confidentially or even anonymously, to the local press or other media. Let them pursue their own leads, check their own sources, and ultimately take the credit.

Understand, though, that something can be timely, newsworthy, and well-documented and yet never be printed or broadcast. This is because the news media are still parts of the business establishment of a city or region. Some news items will be judged too sensitive or delicate and will be ignored until a rival publication, sometimes in another city, breaks the story. Learn about the local leanings and rivalries among various players in the local news media and use them as best you can.

Be prepared for what the initial article on your group's opposition to the Project will be like. It will typically include a brief history of the Project, then mention the name and emergence of your group. A spokesperson for your group will be paraphrased and quoted a little, but the quotes will probably not be the ones that your group (or its spokesperson) would have chosen. The article will quote Project backers who have official-sounding titles (like Mayor or Director) and impressive credentials (university degrees, memberships in international science or business associations, or knighthoods). These are precisely the people whom Entity has had lined up for months or years, ready at this stage to make condescending but still usually fairly gracious comments about Project opponents.

Entity's tactics and strategies will be examined in more detail in a later chapter. At this point it is important to know that the newspaper article is not going to read like your newsletter and to understand that this is not the personal fault of the reporter who wrote the story. Reading through an introductory journalism textbook will make you much more prepared to deal with the media and their reporting conventions.

Your group may be able to run public service announcements (known as PSAs) on local radio stations. These messages must usually be very short (fifteen or thirty seconds is common), and their content must be neutral and a matter of public interest. So, while you cannot air a stop-the-project message, you can announce the location, date, and time of an important hearing. PSAs can publicize an important event and bring the name of your group repeatedly before the public.

Face-To-Face Contacts: Usually, the general public comes in small packages. Neighborhood groups, church organizations, social clubs, local chapters of national groups, environment and ecology-oriented groups, even baby showers and Tupperware parties, can provide opportunities for you to spread the word.

Often, groups are on the lookout for monthly or weekly programs. In these cases, the good news is that you are invited; the bad news is that they want to be entertained. But even if all you accomplish is familiarizing them vaguely with the Project and your group's name, it is well worth the time. You will almost always be allowed, even encouraged, to pass out literature, and you may be able to circulate mailing list or volunteer sign-up sheets as well.

Some groups will be cool to you, others generally supportive, and perhaps a few will support you wholeheartedly. Many organizations have a rather delicate public persona to maintain and may not be willing to risk their reputations by supporting you publicly, at least at first. They may offer informal aid instead in the form of shared technical information or political insights and perhaps loaned mailing lists.

These mailing lists can provide you with names of people who are already more active and concerned than average. They are excellent resources for expanding your range of contacts. When your group is larger and has a hefty mailing list of its own, you can offer to trade mailing lists with groups whose members you are eager to reach.

Do not be discouraged if a group whose members seem very sympathetic is hesitant to go public with its support. It is better to have their members' wholehearted, covert support than the group's lukewarm, public support. Wait until they are ready to give an enthusiastic public endorsement of your position. Such support comes slowly at first. A later flurry of public announcements of anti-Project sentiment will renew public interest in your cause, and correctly give the impression of a rapidly but solidly emerging base of support.

If your group is in a position to do so, hold a press conference a day or two before a hearing or other important event. Remind people of the hearing, state your main objections to the Project in simple language, and, perhaps announce that five more groups now support your position. If at all possible, ask representatives of each new supporting group to attend and make brief statements.

In your attempts to gain support, use all the connections that you can develop. Personal contact and word-of-mouth are always excellent ways to set up presentations and distribute information. You can also send cover letters and brochures to local groups offering a free talk or presentation. If that is not possible, send enough literature for distribution to the group's members at their next meeting.

By following the above suggestions, you will soon be inundated with requests for speakers, slide shows, and/or literature. Never turn down an invitation, and when new issues emerge, ask to go back to give an updated version. Members of community groups are often very active in other community events as well. These active and influencial people are excellent avenues for you to contact the mythical general public. You have the advantage of being real people. Entity's television advertisements and slick brochures will lack the personal touch and sincere urgency of your group's presentations.

Confrontations: In general, it is not wise to force yourself into situations where you are neither welcome nor invited. However, there are some exceptions. Various groups, government advisory boards, and even the news media (both print and broadcast) may set up public forums to discuss the Project. Entity may even stage some in order to give the impression that it wants to hear both sides and encourage discussion.

These forums may damage your cause more than any of Entity's public pronouncements or slick advertisements can, because your group may not be invited. That's right, your group may not be invited, even if you are generally recognized as the lead Project opponent. Instead, a few carefully selected experts or supposedly neutral observers may be asked to provide 'another perspective' on the Project. These events usually planned well in advance by Entity or its agents. If these set-up forums are allowed to proceed, Entity can re-frame the overall debate within a context favorable to the Project while discrediting your group by ignoring it.

In these situations, it is worthwhile to get your spokesperson on the forum agendas. Make the requests and ask for responses in writing. If firm but polite requests to organizers do not result in an invitation to your group to participate, then plan other avenues of response.

Your options are many. Hold a press conference in front of the forum site and claim that forum organizers are afraid to hear legitimate opposing views. Set up a picket line of demonstrators around the entrance to pass out your flyers. Attend the forum itself (if your members can slip in), and either pass out literature or punctuate the forum with well-planned questions. Another alternative is to host your own forum, simultaneously or afterwards, to demonstrate what a truly open forum looks like. If, as is likely, Entity refuses to send a representative, you can publicize that fact as well.

All in all, you are likely to gain at least as much publicity from these options as you will by attending Entity's forum. The general public has been duped numerous times, but it is getting more adept at smelling the rat. If there is a dead rat rotting in the vicinity of the Project, blow the odor around a little and let the news media help you. The only way to lose out is to sit by passively at fake debates or, of course, to fail to have your facts and arguments straight. Don't let either of these things happen.

Educating Public Officials and Other Community Leaders

After you get your information together and generate a modest but effective set of brochures and fact sheets, begin to set up appointments with Important People. The first wave of contacts you make should involve both those whom you believe may be sympathetic to your views and those who are powerful, though less likely to be sympathetic.

Your list should include elected officials, appointed heads of departments and agencies, prominent citizens appointed to government commissions, and prominent businesspeople. Specifically, start with city council members, local members of Congress, neighborhood association leaders, and Chamber of Commerce officers. Until you familiarize yourself with the intricate political connections swirling around any large proposed Project, it may be very difficult to detect potential allies, so don't write anybody off.

If you have done an outstanding job of public education and attracted much support or a few powerful backers, community big shots may actually contact your group and ask you to come in for a visit. That is quite rare, however, so be prepared to make repeated calls to set up appointments and to accept dates many weeks or even months in advance. Send a written acceptance and confirmation of your appointment, along with a modest sample of your literature (two or three pages at the most).

Sometimes, especially with the most powerful people, you will have to settle for talking with an aide or assistant. This usually means that the person is neither threatened by nor particularly interested in your group. That is all right in the beginning — take whatever opportunities you can get and make the most of them.

Arrive a little early for the appointment, even though the person with whom you are meeting will almost certainly be late. It is always advisable to send two persons from your group, both to act as witnesses and observers and to help each other out if difficult questions or situations arise.

As for the meeting itself, ask how much time is alloted for your appointment, and stick to it. Avoid going on and on until you literally are asked to leave. Bring literature with you: a copy of whatever you sent with your letter confirming the appointment and a selection of information on a wide range of topics. The person you meet with will probably not have read the literature you sent or at most will have glanced over it in the minutes just before your appointment. Assume the person has read nothing, and begin by politely introducing yourselves, mentioning the name of the group that you are representing, and outlining your opposition to the Project. The entire introductory segment of your interview should last no more than a few minutes. The entire meeting will rarely last more than fifteen minutes, so make the most of it.

Do not attempt to shame the person for not being familiar with your literature, and never become offended at what may be an abysmal ignorance of the issues involved. Be courteous and respectful when your short meeting is interrupted by phone calls and bustling secretaries.

Meetings with public officials and other prominent persons will be much more productive if you understand what they want and what you want. They want you to leave happy and impressed, and they will try to achieve this as cheaply as possible. You want their support in concrete actions rather than vague assurances.

Do some research and some thinking about each person you meet with in order to make appropriate requests. If the person is an elected official, you may ask for public support and a vote in favor of a particular item of legislation or an ordinance. You can consider asking the official to introduce a bill or a proposal which you favor. Or, you may ask him or her to look into the actions of a regulatory agency whose enforcement actions have been lackadaisical.

If the person is active in a business or professional organization like the Chamber of Commerce, National Association of Manufacturers, or a realtor trade association, you might ask that the organization in question consider passing a resolution opposing, or recommending caution in pursuing, the Project. Many people will balk at this, but you can then offer them a fall-back position and ask that your group be allowed time at the association's next meeting to explain your position on the Project.

Ideally, you will inject some doubt into the organization's support for the Project. It may be inspired enough to do a little investigating on its own. The best outcome would be for their study to confirm that the Project is dubious. The worst outcome would be that one more sloppy, slavish study is offered in support of the Project. That's not so bad; such studies are notoriously easy to critique, and you can hold a press conference to point out its shortcomings.

As a result of some meetings, you may get help in acquiring copies of certain documents that hitherto you have not had access to. Many important reports are withheld from your group and its attorneys (in part, because you will read and critique them) but are widely distributed among Project allies to bolster support. Don't appear desperate to get copies, but casually mention your need for them. This is a long shot, but it doesn't hurt to ask. You may strike gold.

The people you interview want to know how seriously they should take you, so they will almost always ask how large your group is. Either be honest or be vague when answering this question, but never exaggerate your numbers. If your group is not a formal one with membership dues and so forth, you may be able to answer honestly that you do not know and give a minimum estimate. Or, you can answer indirectly by saying that there were 650 people at a recent public hearing. Never offer the information that seven people do all of the work. (This is true of most groups, even the ones that seem incredibly professional and well-organized.)

During the meeting, one of you should take notes about the person's stated position, the questions he or she asks, and other people he or she suggests you contact. Some people like to feel powerful by rattling off names of other big shots with whom they are on a first name basis. Don't hesitate to call their bluff — ask them to contact their friends and get back to you with any information they obtain.

As the meeting ends, repeat your names and the name of your group, express your thank again for the interview, and encourage the person to feel free to contact you at any time for additional information.

After hearing from you, the official or businessperson may well call other big shots, report on your meeting, and ask them what they think. Many people will keep an eye on your group in order to determine whether or not you pose a serious threat or are just another bunch of crackpots. You must always appear respectful, organized, serious, and well-informed, but do be discreet about your group's strategies. Within a day or two of the meeting, send a note of thanks, including any information or literature you promised to obtain and pass along.

After an appropriate waiting period, call to see if they need more information, have questions for you, have learned any new information, have changed their views, and so on. This is probably a good time to attempt to schedule another interview.

The best possible outcome of your group's dialogue with a respected, powerful public figure is that he or she will want to latch on to your issue, embrace your position, become your leader, and ride to glory (public office, re-election, fame, whatever.) This is not a common situation, but it is by no means unheard of. A person, or even a group, may perceive an advantage in appearing to be identified with the common people, the abused masses, or the hard-working middle class and seek to use your group as a short cut to that end.

If such a situation occurs, be happy but beware. Happy because this means that opposition to Entity and/or the Project is becoming widespread and acceptable. Cautious, because if you have already reached this milestone, the last thing you need is to be perceived as serving the narrow interests of a particular individual or interest group (other than your own).

Hold serious discussions with group members about taking advantage of this support without selling out or losing your soul. You probably will need to discuss and reassess your goals. If your group does become hopelessly split between factions, it is better to separate under a truce flag than to fight it out in public. Nothing sours public support faster than the spectacle of formerly dedicated community activists clawing each other's eyes out in public.

How to Make a Presentation

A good presentation is a key to gaining broad-based, solid, public support for your opposition to the Project. It is an opportunity for you to demonstrate that you know your facts and can present them in a clear, effective manner. But this is not the only goal of a presentation. Your audience has heard, or will hear, Entity's version of facts in support of the Project. Your listeners will measure your credibility so that they can decide whether to trust your group or Entity. Always keep in mind that, while the content of your talk is very important, so too is your manner.

Who should give the presentation? Probably at least two members of your group. One person should be a fact person with a grasp of many technical details but able to see to the big picture as well. Another person should emphasize, in content or manner or both, the human side of the issue. For example, a woman might present a Project summary with technical data suggesting various hazards, or risks and then be followed by a man giving examples of how specific families or neighborhoods might be affected.

You should never allow a presentation to be made by someone who cannot summarize and be brief, rambles on and on without answering a question, talks above the level of his or her audience, or cannot explain issues well in everyday, ordinary language. No matter how right your cause is, how impressive your facts, you will fail if you repeatedly mismatch the speakers with the context.

For similar reasons, it is not advisable to have an attorney play a leading role in your presentations. First, attorneys can get so carried away with section twos, FONSIs, acronyms, and legal minutiae that their words will be lost on your audience. Second, attorneys cannot help but set the issues in primarily legal terms, which is rarely where good strategy lies. It may be helpful to have an attorney appear briefly to make a few points, explain a particular procedure, or answer a few legal questions. But keep it brief.

Those who represent your group should dress reasonably neatly. When in doubt, dress up a bit, but be yourselves. Other members of your group should stand at the doors, or at a table in the back of the room, with the usual pile of fact sheets, newsletters, sign-up sheets, petitions, and, if you have them, bumper stickers, T-shirts, and buttons.

How long should your presentation last? The answer is easy: exactly as long as was suggested, not a moment longer. If the host group says you have only five or ten minutes, stop after five and see if there are questions. (If there are none, work in another brief point or two.) If you are given forty-five minutes to an hour, stop after about forty minutes and ask for questions.

In most cases, twenty or thirty minutes will be the maximum time allowed. Never exceed the allotted time unless you are specifically asked to stay longer. If spontaneous questions and discussions have arisen and threaten to cut into the rest of the host group's program, volunteer to retire to the lobby (or the kitchen, or the anteroom) to chat with anyone interested in pursuing matters further. If some of your group members aren't able to follow time guidelines, don't send them to speaking engagements. No matter how bright they are, they will cost you support.

Avoid outright denunciations of Entity or other Project supporters (there are probably some present) and resist long litanies of boring facts and lists of numbers. Instead, slant your talk towards the interests of your audience. For example, if your audience consists of day care teachers, address issues concerning the health and safety of children. If you are talking to bankers, emphasize economic risks and uncertainties. If your listeners are farmers, talk about ground water contamination or soil erosion. Your group probably has enough information about the Project to fill many hours of presentations, so carefully select what will be most interesting and pertinant to any given group.

Use Sight As Well As Sound: Visual aids can be extremely helpful, but use them judiciously. One map after another for seventeen maps will seem like seventeen million. Chart after chart after chart brings on sensory overload in an audience, then numbness. Even stunning slides get old after a short while if they are not varied and accompanied by clear but interesting points.

You probably will use a map, or a few maps, to indicate the general location of the proposed Project and a closer view of the Project itself. Make sure that the maps include familiar landmarks, major intersections, street or highway names, and as little extra detail as possible. Take a little time to orient your audience verbally so they can follow the rest of your presentation.

These recommendations may seem obvious, but I have seen countless presentations in which, unknown to the speaker, the audience spent the entire talk whispering to each other trying to figure out the map.

A few of your most impressive statistics can be illustrated well by using simple graphs. Experiment with bar graphs or pie graphs, but don't get too fancy. Do not translate all of your data into charts and then flip chart after chart as you rattle off numbers. Your audience will miss or forget the major points in a jumble of information.

Before-and-after graphs are often impressive — imagine a simple bar graph of before and after traffic estimates, for example. Simple comparisons of Project options are often amenable to being charted. You could show a pile of coins representing current property taxes and contrast that to a pile representing property taxes under a proposed Project option. Sometimes, a simple list is effective. If some sort of chemical facility or power plant is proposed, just make a list of all the chemicals or other pollutants that Entity acknowledges will be emitted into the air, ground, or water from the facility.

Slides, enlarged photographs or sketches can also be very useful. Select them carefully, each for a specific purpose. Prepare a specific (and short) set of comments for each illustration. If your group is blessed with a photographer, encourage him or her to take pictures that illustrate your presentation. Many times, newspaper articles, pages of government documents, or textbook illustrations can be made into excellent slides. Have your group resolve to offer to help defray the costs of film and developing so that your photographer doesn't go bankrupt furnishing you with illustrations. And always document and acknowledge the exact source of any illustration.

Finally, organize your visual aids. Alternate between stark maps, and actual pictures of the Project site. Show the graphs illustrating financial risks, then show a picture of Entity personnel in the board room or driving expensive cars. Follow a list of chemicals to be emitted with pictures of billowing smokestacks or waste water pipes or orange foamy streams.

The Presentation Itself: Your presentation should do four things, probably in this order. First, establish rapport. Second, give a general picture. Third, describe the threat to the community. Fourth, tell your audience what it can do to help.

Establish rapport with brief introductions of the presentors, telling a little bit about how each of you became involved.

> *Hello, my name is ___. I'm a teacher at Jackson Elementary and I've been with NIMBY group ever since last March when I heard about plans to build a fertilizer plant upstream from the reservoir.*

> *Hi, I'm ___, and I'm an accountant. I first found out about the Project when a neighbor asked me to look over Entity's financial statements. I became very concerned about the numbers I saw and have been active with NIMBY group ever since.*

These introductions establish several things for the audience. They indicate that you are productive members of the community, interested in its general welfare. And, they suggest that, despite claims by Entity to the contrary, you do not go around looking for trouble. You are not disinterested parties by any means, nor are you seeking to benefit at someone else's expense. You are just doing what anyone in your audience would do when faced with similar circumstances.

(Individuals from Entity and other Project backers, on the other hand, are apt to be going around with poorly concealed dollar signs dancing in front of their eyes. Your audience, as the saying goes, didn't wash down with the last rain and will be able to evaluate the difference.)

Next, give your listeners the big picture. Show them a basic map, tell them the main idea behind the Project and a bit of its history. Summarize your group's main reasons for opposing the Project. Explain that you lack the time to go into all of the details, and remind the listeners that they can pick up more detailed fact sheets afterwards, subscribe to your newsletter, or, best of all, join your group as an active member.

Now, select a few of your strongest points, as tailored to this particular audience. Give enough background and detail so that your listeners knows that you are not speaking lightly. Make a claim, then back it up with facts. Make a second claim, back it up, and so on.

Finally, close your formal presentation by telling the audience what they can do to help. Don't let these potential allies walk away shaking their heads and saying *gosh, that's too bad.* Make specific suggestions for action to them. Ask them to sign petitions, write letters to important people (have a list of names, addresses, and sample letters available), sign up to volunteer, take extra literature for their neighbors, co-workers, or church groups, help you set up another presentation, help you do research, or give money.

Rehearse your presentation before your own group. If your cohorts are confused or bored, a group of outsiders surely will be. Take suggestions for improvement and try again. After a few adjustments and some practice under pressure, you will have built your presentation into a formidable public education tool.

Spreading Your Message

Informal speaking engagements before local groups will probably be the backbone of your public education efforts, but presentation opportunity should be missed. Pursue opportunities to set up a booth or table at as many public gatherings and public gathering places as you can. Festivals, shopping malls, athletic events, church bazaars, contests, county fairs, parades, and many other events provide opportunities to pass out literature, get petition signatures, and recruit volunteers.

As always, check with the sponsoring groups to make sure that you are welcome, and follow any rules that they have established to coordinate the events. It is a good idea to check with your lawyer as well. Shopping malls, for example, are a great place to distribute large numbers of fact sheets quickly to the general public. There is an ongoing controversy about the legality of doing so, however. In 1989 a Milwaukee lawyer was sued by a mall owner for passing out copies of the Bill of Rights. Court cases on the matter continue. Your lawyer should be able to advise you on local laws and conditions that apply to your case.

Any actions you take should be part of an overall strategy. Getting arrested for distributing your literature at the local grocery store parking lot may be one way to attract attention to your cause, but it may also backfire and drain your group's resources in a lengthy court battle that does not further your goals. If your goal is to spread information, you can do that without being arrested. If your flyers do not carry an organization's name or phone number, they are more difficult to trace. Usually you'll be warned before an arrest is made: Just leave and reappear at another parking lot across town. Whatever you choose, make sure that your actions match your goal, and that you have taken into consideration the various possible outcomes and consequences.

Some final reminders to ensure success in your public education efforts:

- Keep track of all of your correspondence, and send thank-you notes when appropriate to keep your name fresh in people's minds.
- Follow up on all expressions of interest in your cause.
- Once you have people's attention and interest, always tell them something specific that they can do to help.
- Keep copies of everything — fact sheets, letters, requests for appointments, legal notices, reports, whatever.
- And finally, try to stay organized and on top of things so that you don't miss opportunities.

If your group is able to follow the recommendations in this chapter, in a very few months Entity and Project backers won't know what hit them. However, public education by itself is usually not enough to stop a Project even if you have overwhelming support. You probably will have to carry your fight into the regulatory agencies and the courts. How to do this is the subject of the next chapter.

Anne Hagedorn, "Shopping Malls Become Free-Speech Battlegrounds," *Wall Street Journal*, Jun. 17, 1992; Daniel B. Moskowitz, "Ruling Redefines Malls' Right to Bar Activists," *Washington Post*, Washington Business Section, Nov. 11, 1991.

Chapter 8

HEARINGS AND COURT APPEARANCES

While your public education efforts continue, your group will find itself involved in a growing number of increasingly formal hearings and court appearances. Some will require the presence of an attorney and a few active members to handle the media and record the proceedings. At others, you will want, literally, to flood the place with supporters. Before describing each kind of hearing, we will review six goals for these events.

Six Goals for Legal Procedings

First, you want to gain a favorable ruling by the body in question. Hope springs eternal... You want the person(s) in charge to be convinced that the Project is a terrible idea, vote against it, or make such a recommendation to his or her superiors. Though your chances of achieving this at the beginning are nearly zero, proceed as though it were a plausible goal. You never know...you might be the first.

A more realistic goal is to delay or postpone the decision to proceed. Most likely Entity will try to push through a decision as quickly as possible (they call it 'cutting red tape' or 'streamlining the process'), because it is well aware that the longer the process takes, the more people will learn about the Project and the more upset everyone will become.

A third goal is to get something on the record. This means making a formal statement (in writing, under oath, or on tape) which then becomes part of the official, legal history of the Project. Both sides do this, and your attorney will advise you what needs to be put in the record. (If he or she does not, be sure to ask.)

In many cases, if a fact or issue was not raised at an early point in the controversy, it may not legally be considered later. In order to avoid having your hands tied at a later hearing or in a lawsuit, make sure that you have at least mentioned any issue that has any likelihood of coming up later.

Knowing this, and knowing also that on-going publicity works against them, Entity and Project backers, through their attorneys, will do everything they can to restrict the scope of any hearings and court appearances. For the most part, the definition of the scope of the hearing will be fought out by the eager-beaver legal eagles on both sides, but your group should be aware of the issues and offer what resistance you can.

A fourth and closely related goal is that of simply preserving your options by not skipping any of the possible steps. This is quite similar to the workplace grievance process. In many cases you may not be able to take an employer to court unless you have first exhausted (with unsatisfactory results) the company or agency grievance procedures. So, even if you are fairly certain that you will get nowhere by doing so, you must give it a try.

Regulatory law works much the same way. You must go through all steps of the official process in order to have the right to go to court in the end. So, even if the various hearings and other regulatory procedures are stacked against you, go through each one in order to preserve your other options.

Continuing public education is a fifth goal. Your group's members, outside supporters, members of the news media, government personnel and even Entity itself may learn something they did not know. Never give up on any of them. Bring updated handouts and sample newsletters.

A sixth goal may be to expand your outreach and membership. Like any public event, a hearing is an opportunity to recruit new supporters and fire up your old ones. Entity's employees and many Project backers will be getting fat paychecks to help them fight the blues when people boo them. Those of you opposing the Project will need another currency of support. Don't miss this opportunity to share both information with and appreciation of your supporters.

Keeping these goals in mind, the rest of this chapter covers four kinds of public events: public hearings, regulatory hearings, court appearances, and fake hearings. For each one we offer some brief background information, give some idea of how a typical event proceeds, and then suggest appropriate strategy and tactics for each.

The Public Hearing

A public hearing, in the sense of the term used here, is one in which members of the public are free both to observe and participate without having to meet any requirements at all (save perhaps providing some form of identification, and even this is rare.) A public hearing is held by an agency (the EPA or the Board of Health, for example) or other governmental body (a City Council), usually in a large public place like a high school auditorium, county courthouse, or council chambers. A scoping hearing, which defines what an environmental impact statement (EIS) must include, is an example of a public hearing, as is the EIS hearing itself.

The official purpose of such hearings is to gather information — sometimes they are specifically called *fact-finding* hearings. That means that you are there not as experts but as regular humans and that any statements you make will be taken, not as sworn expert testimony, but simply as what you think (known legally as *hearsay* evidence.) In reality, both Entity and the government (if they are separate) want to gauge public opinion and find out what you know, how well-organized you are, and how angry you are.

In some cases, holding a public hearing is completely discretionary. A City Council, for example, might honor a request for a public hearing even though it is under no legal obligation to do so. Such opportunities should not be overlooked.

Certain public hearings must be held whether or not anyone comes. Many others must be held if there is the slightest sign of interest — as little as one telephone call or letter can trigger a hearing. Still others must be formally requested, for example by a letter to an elected official and/or the government agency involved or by an official request from an attorney.

Make sure that those requests are made. Regularly read the public notice section of local newspapers, read the fine print and legal references in any official Project reports you have access to, and consult with your attorney about hearings that will be held only if they are specifically requested. If you fail to make the appropriate requests or miss a deadline, you run the risk of forfeiting your right to certain other hearings, legal proceedings, and perhaps even later court action.

An attorney is helpful but certainly not necessary for a public hearing, as long as you keep track of the legal implications of the particular proceeding. In fact, unless it is a very special case, most lawyers consider it a waste of time for them to attend a lengthy public hearing. There are relatively few rules and almost anything goes. This forum is for the masses and, as such, is rarely the place for legal niceties.

Too often, if no one says anything or makes a special request, public hearings are held during regular working hours, that is between nine and five on a weekday. Obviously, many people work during those hours and cannot attend. Always make it a point to request that some or all public hearings be held at times when more working people can attend.

Weekend opportunities are rare, but you may be able to schedule a hearing for one to nine P.M. on a weekday or for two consecutive evenings (if you think there will be enough public testimony). Sometimes one citizen's request will do the trick — few Entities want to run the risk of being accused of purposely scheduling a public hearing during the day when working people affected by the Project are unable to attend.

Usually elected officials react similarly. Many politicians who will not openly oppose the Project may be glad to help you out by giving a speech about the rights of hard-working Americans to attend public hearings without missing work. If just one or two local elected officials requests evening hours for the hearing, there's a good chance the request will be granted. Entity needs local support and there is nothing like helping a local official appear powerful in the eyes of his or her constituencies.

A Typical Public Hearing: The public hearing usually takes place in a large public place like a high school auditorium or large courtroom. As people are on their way into the room, they will be given the opportunity to sign up to speak. This usually involves filling out a card or signing a list. Though many Project opponents may prefer to remain anonymous, signing up to speak does little harm, because sign-up sheets are used, for the most part, as gauges of how many people wish to speak and as supplemental mailing lists for notices of future legal matters regarding the Project. And, if Entity really wants to know who you are, it scarcely has to wait around for you to sign up at a public hearing.

Unless Entity is extremely careless (this happens on rare occasions, usually to your favor), its representatives will make an effort to send out notices of hearings, copies of reports (the ones, like EIS's, that must by law be distributed), and other legal notices. This practice protects Entity from claims that it violated procedural law in pursuing appropriate authorization for the Project. As has already been mentioned, in many cases it is easier to prove procedural violations than substantive ones, and most attorneys will be eager to cover Entity's backside on this issue.

Inside the auditorium or hall, there will be a space set aside for the presiding officials. Usually they are three in number, white, male, ashen in complexion, and bureaucratic in attire. It will not be difficult to pick them out. (If a school board or city council is conducting the hearing, of course, its members will preside.) A small cadre of helpers will be scattered around the room to set up microphones, encourage you to sign in, and so on. If the public hearing is part of a formal EIS process (and in some other cases as well), the entire proceeding will be tape-recorded or videotaped.

A few minutes after the official starting time of the hearing, the presiding official begins by introducing himself and his colleagues and describing the general purpose of the hearing. He — and it's usually he — then states the rules governing the proceedings. This usually means that he explains how to sign up to speak, tells how long each speaker may talk, makes suggestions for handling an overflow crowd, and lets everyone know how and where to submit written testimony. In addition, he announces when to expect any results (in the form of a document, report, or decision) from this hearing.

Then the public hearing formally begins.

Usually Entity gets the first shot. Representatives of Entity present their case. Often this presentation is introduced by an officer or director of Entity. However, if the Project is unpopular or the opposition particularly vocal, a lower-ranking individual makes the opening remarks. The more successful your group is, the less frequently you will see someone from Entity's top management. CEO's and other big shots generally will not stand for being heckled, booed, or ridiculed, so they send proxies.

This fact is more than an interesting quirk about the perquisites of high positions. It is also a source of insight for your group. First, you can gauge your success by keeping track of who gets sent out to represent Entity in public forums (this is considered to be managerial combat duty). Second, it provides an opportunity for Entity to tailor each presentation to the expected audience. It also provides management with what, in the Iran-Contra era, became widely known as 'deniability.' If it sends an engineer, he or she can be as fuzzy about economics as a financial officer can be vague about technical aspects. An environmental officer might be unfamiliar with social impacts, while an attorney may be unwilling to discuss waste water discharges. The public relations person will know a little about everything and a lot about nothing (and be terrified that he or she will say something wrong and get into trouble with higher-ups.)

Entity's presentation will be a work of art, of sorts. Probably millions of dollars and several careers will hinge on the success of the Project, so Entity will spare no expense in preparing an effective presentation. Entity will be allotted more time for its presentation than your group will receive (probably no less than twenty minutes and no more than an hour, depending on the size and complexity of the Project, the number of people who have signed up to speak, and the temperament of the presiding officer.)

Expect charts, photographs, slides, artists' conceptions of the finished facility, scale models, and even video presentations to be part of Entity's pitch. It may also bring testimonials from supporters in other communities, praising similar Projects there.

(If it goes this far, be sure to get names and locations. Follow up on the rosy stories, for you are sure to find another side. Casting doubt on Entity's testimonials will be an excellent public education tool for you.)

Entity may also bring along a selection of industry booklets about the issue in question. Expect the usual range of titles: *Airplane Noise Stimulates Brain Cell Growth...The Unpublicized Dangers of Cholesterol Deficiency...Even Your Bicycle is Radioactive*, etc. Be sure to collect samples of all the literature passed out, and have your group's research division do a point-by-point analysis and critique. Make this into a brief pamphlet, give it a catchy title (humor always helps), and distribute it at the next hearing or other public event. It might even be worth a news conference if you are especially proud of it.

Take careful notes during Entity's presentation. In this hearing, new information or new versions of already available information may be offered. You will need to check it out. If anyone in your group has access to a home video camera, spend a few bucks on a couple of tape cassettes, set up your camera, and just tape the whole thing. Make absolutely sure that the sound track picks up every word uttered by Entity's representatives. You may catch them in some statements that will be extremely useful to your group at a later date. For the record's sake, state clearly on tape the date, place, and time of the hearing.

Something else may come out in the course of your opposition to the Project, often at a public hearing. Be prepared to hear outrageous misstatements, amazing distortions, and bald-faced lies. You may hear that Entity already has a permit that it does not have; that community Z in Idaho welcomed Entity's other Project with open arms; that Project will not emit malonium; that traffic levels will actually decrease; that safety equipment is 99.9 percent effective; that the City Council has already approved the Project; that no one's water wells will be contaminated; and on and on *ad infinitum*.

Since these individuals are not under oath, there is nothing forcing them to be truthful or objective and a lot of pressure on them to do or say anything that will promote the Project. Numerous escape routes are available to them, even when they are exposed. If you catch them in the act, they can say that they were misinformed, that they were given the wrong report, or that there is a difference of opinion on that subject.

Experts can, and have, testified, even under oath, to an amazing variety of falsehoods. There is no advantage in naively accepting everything that Entity representatives or backers say, especially at a public forum. There are ways to take advantage of statements of questionable veracity, so be alert and document everything.

After Entity's representatives make their presentation, the public comment period begins. There is a convention, usually adhered to, of inviting elected officials or other prominent community leaders to speak first. Typically, these individuals take the opportunity to support the Project strongly or, if they sense considerable opposition, to state that they want to make sure there is a full discussion of all aspects of the Project before it is approved.

Several standard hedges are possible here. Often the official vows not to make a decision about supporting the project until the JKL consultant's study comes out. Almost invariably, the study favors the Project, providing the official an opportunity to wave the report around at future public hearings. The official can also say that he or she wants to hear from constituents at the public hearing before taking a stand.

Rarely, a powerful public official will unequivocally oppose the Project. When this occurs, flood that official with letters of appreciation, supporting documents, fact sheets, and invitations to attend your group's meetings.

If the Project is already controversial, elected officials often will decline to speak at or fail to attend the hearing, sending an anonymous aide to represent them. This is either a sign of uncertainty or vacillation on their part (which is a good sign for you) or a sign of cowardice (also a good sign). In any case, it should be taken as a signal to step up your education efforts and lobbying.

Finally, after public officials have spoken, the hearing opens to the masses. The presiding officer reiterates the rules, explains time limits on individual speeches, and usually asks that there be no applause after each speaker in order to expedite the hearings. The names of those who asked to speak are then called.

Before starting their spiels, speakers must identity themselves for the record. Theoretically, the names are called in sign-up order or randomly, but practice often rearranges a sequence supposedly ordained by theory. As we'll see, Entity will seek to have its supporters (often absentee landlords with special incentives to support the Project) speak first. Your group should seek to have its strongest and best-informed representatives speak early.

Usually those who speak during the public comment period are overwhelmingly against the Project. Who would bother to come to the hearing if they thought that the Project was a great idea? Some in the audience will be undecided but concerned, eagerly listening to all speakers. Provide as much information as you can to everybody who attends, and then just let them go.

Attending a public hearing is often a very moving experience. Pregnant women speak of their hopes for the as-yet unborn. Parents express their dreams for their children. Gardeners bring in vegetables and express fears about toxins or polluted water supplies. Deeply religious folks express their faith in the Almighty and ask for guidance in making a decision that is good for all God's children. Patriots recite the Star-Spangled Banner and the Bill of Rights, and with a glance at elected representatives, refer to the Boston Tea Party. Solid, middle-class Americans who have never been rabble-rousers in their whole lives affirm that Mom-and-apple-pie families will not stand for having an inappropriate Project rammed down their throats. Usually meek and soft-spoken citizens verbally attack experts and elected officials alike, demanding answers. Folk singers sing tunes. Teachers ask officials to live up to their image in civics classes. In one poignant and courageous move, I saw one woman who lived in a trailer way out on a dirt road in the country dump a filthy baggie of crumbly brown coal on a table and demand that critical issues be addressed.

And here's the really amazing part: the three presiding officials sit in silent, blank-faced attention through each speech, hardly blinking, rarely, if ever, conferring or making notes. Then, no matter how passionate, or boring, or angry, or technical, or funny, or tearful the speech, the presiding official says, in what may pass for sincerity in some circles, "Thank-you for your comment." And the next name is called.

At the end of the hearing, the presiding official again thanks everyone — well, those who are left — for their comments, reiterates how and when any additional written testimony may be submitted, and explains what to expect next. Usually it takes months — a minimum of three or four if you are on a fast track or up to eighteen or even twenty-four otherwise before a report on the hearings will come out. In the case of federal EIS hearings, the report is supposed to reflect the nature of the oral and written comments and indicate a probable, tentative, or final decision by the appropriate agency on the Project in question. Less formal or voluntary public hearings, such as those held by city councils, may be ends in themselves, not culminating in any reports, decisions, or concrete actions.

Public Hearing Strategies: To maximize the benefits of participating in a public hearing, your group should focus on a few major issues.

The members of the media, presuming that they are in attendance, rarely stay more than twenty minutes. The period immediately preceding the hearing and the first half hour of the hearing are therefore critical for your group. If you are going to make contacts with the media — and you are, aren't you? — this is the time to do it.

This is not pandering to the media. It is realism. A minute or three of coverage on the local nightly news reaches thousands of people whom would otherwise go uninformed. Even if your group did have thousands of dollars to spend preparing a commercial for local television stations, you could not match the impact of a single decent news story.

Two of your best-informed and most articulate members should meet with media representatives just before the hearing opens. A brief press conference can be very effective. Make a brief statement, pass out fact sheets and related material (your press packet), and answer a few questions. The news media like local flavor, colorful stories, and raw emotion. Find a supporter willing to be used in this way, someone who lives right next to or in the middle of the proposed Project area. Let the media interview him or her and elicit candid and unrehearsed reactions.

Do not hesitate to use visual aids. Charts and graphs — if clear and understandable — can be very effective. Simply holding up a jar of contaminated water, a dead branch from a bulldozed tree, or an insulting or threatening letter sent by an insensitive Entity representative can liven up a television spot immensely.

This is why both you (and Entity) will want to present your best speakers at the very beginning of the public comment period, before the cameras disappear. Often, through mysterious means, Entity's backers are called to speak first at the hearing. (That way, they don't have to wait around, and they, instead of Project opponents, get a few precious seconds on the local nightly news.) Work to have a representative of your group included among the first few speakers. One way to do this is to have a person sign up numerous times, using slightly different versions of the name (for example, Barbara Bush...B. Bush...Mrs. G. Herbert Bush...Mrs. George Bush...G. H. Bush, and so on). The worst that can happen is that the sign-in cards are thrown out or that the person's name is, in fact, called several times. On the positive side, B. Bush may be called very early in the hearing, and her mailing address may receive four copies of the EIS — always useful for a group on a low budget.

Demonstrate public support by bringing a crowd to important hearings. Sometimes a roomful of angry voters can have a miraculous effect on a previously indecisive elected official. And, toot your own horn. Don't depend on the local paper to describe the hearing, write it up for your next newsletter — your way.

> ...*Over Eight Hundred Fired-up Local Residents Packed Tuesday's Public Hearings to Express Their Strong Opposition to...*

Continue recruiting by circulating sign-up sheets and newsletters, and be sure to sign up on other people's sign-up sheets. The more you know about what other groups are doing, the better off you are.

Though public education is a very large part of the significance of the public hearing for your cause, there are other important aspects. Use this public opportunity to put on the record, both orally and in writing, issues that have not yet been discussed.

In fact, in many cases, you should mention everything but the kitchen sink, because you have nothing to lose. Bring up any issue or concern that has any remote chance of being real: radiation leaks, smog emissions from traffic jams, termite invasions, toxic spills, erosion-caused flooding, or other harmful consequences.

There is a good reason for this tactic. In some cases, if a particular issue is not mentioned at an early stage (often, at public hearings), then it cannot be introduced later when it could affect the outcome of the entire process. This measure protects the integrity of the process and is designed to prevent Project opponents from saving a couple of really devastating issues until the eve of the decision date, then dumping them, so to speak, on the public.

One unfortunate consequence of this well-meaning proviso is that, since Project opponents start out ignorant, they may not have had the opportunity to study all aspects of the Project before the first public hearings take place. Hence, through no fault of their own, they are at a distinct disadvantage and should cover their backsides by mentioning a wide range of possibly relevant issues.

Before the public hearing, make a list of every single issue that might conceivably be important. Get ideas from other EIS's, newsletters, neighbors, newspapers, or any source. Then, at the public hearing, get one or two dependable people to sign up to speak last or near the end of the hearing. This person is your clean-up person. During the hearing, cross off each issue that is mentioned. By the end of the hearing, your list will be reduced to those issues which no one has brought up and your clean-up person can simply read them into the record. That does it.

Despite the odds, do your best throughout the whole hearing to convince agency personnel that the Project is a mistake. Chances are excellent that the whole process is wired in favor of the Project, but minds can sometimes be changed. The powers-that-be occasionally acknowledge that they have not thought of everything. Even if they continue to favor the Project, they may suggest modifications that acknowledge in essence the validity of your concerns.

Finally, don't hang up your chaps after an uproariously successful public hearing that brought you media fame, front-page articles, scores of new volunteers, and a movie-star mascot. This is just the beginning. While you sit and gloat, Entity will be preparing a counter-offensive — perhaps aimed at splitting your ranks, buying your acquiescence, or ordering another impressive consultant study. Nothing is irreversible.

Regulatory Hearings

Regulatory hearings are much more focused than the public hearings discussed above. The purpose of a regulatory hearing is to evaluate a specific item like a permit application or a request to alter a single provision of a permit. All testimony is sworn, whether it is from experts or from persons in positions to have privileged, firsthand knowledge about something.

An attorney is necessary in order to set up the hearing and participate in it. Testimony and cross-examination of witnesses is carried out according to the rules of administrative law (law written by an administrative agency). The hearing may go on for days, weeks, or even months, and the testimony is detailed, tedious, and often repetitive. Most or all of the action in the hearing will be directed by someone usually called a hearing examiner, normally between the hours of nine and five.

To explain what the hearing examiner does, we must digress briefly to explain the structure of a generic regulatory agency. An elected political figure (like a president, governor, or mayor) appoints an individual as director, or a commission as governing board, of a regulatory agency. This director or commission has the final say (outside the courts) as to the decision of the regulatory agency on a particular matter (for example, whether or not to give Entity a permit.)

Beneath this director or commission, a hierarchy of bureaucrats fans out, starting with a few deputies and assistant directors and finally ending twenty or thirty grades lower with the most menial clerks. Near the upper-middle of this structure are the people who actually preside over the hearings. They collect evidence, listen to testimony and arguments, sometimes have their own investigations carried out, and, in the end, render their decisions. These decisions are the bases for the recommendations which are then forwarded upwards to the director or governing board. The people responsible for these recommendations are the hearing examiners. In most cases, they have some expertise in the subject area that the agency regulates. Testimony can therefore be of a highly technical nature.

The two main participants, or parties, in a regulatory hearing are usually Entity, seeking a permit (or whatever it's called in that agency), and you, opposing the granting of that permit. The hearing examiner presides. Often, however, there are other participants: companies, organizations, or individuals who have sought and been granted the position of *intervenors*.

Intervenors may stand in support of Entity's permit request or in opposition to it. Or intervenors may have some other interest in the project of the Project. A citizens' group, for example, might intervene not to oppose the granting of the permit but seek to attach specific conditions to it. On the other side, the local Chamber of Commerce might intervene in order to encourage measures that would affect the Project's tax status in the community.

Sometimes the regulatory agency itself has intervenor status. As with the other intervenors, this team's attorney can present expert testimony, examine witnesses, and make whatever legal requests and maneuvers that applicable administrative law allows. If Entity has the resources to hire high-powered attorneys and experts, the regulatory agency's team (usually composed of relatively younger, less experienced persons receiving the public sector's lower salaries) are lightweights in comparison.

When all parties — Entity, you, and any intervenors — finish their presentations, the hearing examiner closes the hearing. A decision — really, a recommendation to his or her superiors in the agency — by the hearing examiner comes weeks or months later.

Hearing examiners usually render the safest, most conventional decision that is reasonably consistent with the expert testimony offered. They are unwilling to discount the testimony of any of Entity's well-paid experts unless the expert really shoots himself or herself in the foot. On the other hand, hearing examiners are familiar with the evidence presented and will be concerned that any recommendations be more or less compatible with it.

I emphasize this point because once you go above the hearing examiners' level, the whole game changes. The recommendation of the hearing examiner is sent up the bureaucratic pyramid until it reaches the director or the commission. The decision of the hearing examiner may be accepted and announced unchanged, it may be modified, or it may be completely ignored or reversed. The final decision, the declaration that will stand as the official ruling of the regulatory agency, is made by a political appointee.

A typical day at a regulatory hearing begins with Entity's lawyers and their expert witnesses for the day, your lawyer and your witnesses, and, perhaps, a lawyer or two from the agency filing into a hearings room. There probably will be a few secretaries and paralegals around, sometimes a reporter, and perhaps a few other observers. A court reporter, responsible for the official transcript of the proceeding, is also present.

If the hearing is routine or not widely publicized, there may be fewer than ten people in the room. If, however, the case is very controversial or involves setting a precedent because there is something special or novel about it (from a legal or regulatory standpoint), then dozens or, on rare occasions, even hundreds of people may be attracted to it like rubberneckers to a spectacular car wreck.

Lawyers and experts alike nearly always speak in very slow, even, monotones, as does the hearing examiner. The testimony is usually highly technical and may be repeated over and over, as Entity's attorney, the agency's staff lawyer, your own attorney, and then all three again ask the witness very similar but slightly different questions. Entity's attorney will try to demonstrate an airtight case, your attorney will try to poke holes in it, and the agency's legal representative may be trying to stay out of trouble, get a promotion, ingratiate himself with industry representatives, or uncover some facts — one never knows. Attorneys representing other intervenors are also given opportunities to participate, and the hearing examiner may question attorneys or witnesses.

The hours during which the hearing is actually held may amount to six or fewer per day. Morning hours of 9:30-11:30 and afternoon hours of 1:00-4:00 are not uncommon. Hearing examiners are like ship's captains: among them there is great variation in ability and temperament, but their word is law within the confines of their authority. Accordingly, recesses and behavioral expectations during the hearings vary according to whims of the hearing examiners.

(It is usually deathly quiet, save for the slow, methodical, monotonous voice speaking at the moment. I have often wondered how human beings could train themselves to speak so slowly, and why anyone would do so. It may be that the measured pace enhances one's ability to speak with the utmost care. But I don't buy that explanation. These experts and attorneys make $30-300 per hour for their performances, and I am tempted to believe that whole professions — consultants and attorneys, anyway — train their members to speak in slow motion in order to enhance their earnings. If attorneys and consultants got paid by the word instead of by the hour, hearings would undergo a drastic change in pace.)

The hearing examiners are usually in their early middle age. Youngsters need some experience before becoming examiners, so those just out of law school or graduate school do not yet qualify. Older, successful hearing examiners may be promoted to more senior bureaucratic positions within the agency or a sister agency, or, more likely, they will move into much higher-paying jobs in the private sector. Any Entity with controversial Projects ahead would love to have on board an experienced former hearing examiner as an advisor. (This movement of personnel between the private sector and government bodies is fairly common. This *revolving door* has been limited but by no means eliminated by ethics-in-government laws.)

In comparison to a public hearing — which usually has a slow, dry start, a crescendo of concern and outrage, an emotional catharsis, and then a gentle petering out until there is no one left to speak — a regulatory hearing is more like buying cloth by the yard, with the length of each day's swatch determined by the hearing examiner's never-revealed private appointment schedule.

Sometimes, during breaks, one side or the other will frantically try to line up a particular expert to testify on a point that has just come up. Or, attorneys will spend their time preparing (that is, coaching) one of their experts for what they expect will be rough (that is, hostile) cross-examination. During such drills, the expert will repeatedly rehearse the answers to expected questions.

In such a rehearsal, the expert is subjected to a barrage of difficult, confusing, and tricky questions to prepare him or her for the expected cross-examination by your attorney. If one of Entity's experts has become confused and given garbled and possibly damaging testimony in the morning, the crew (the attorneys and the witness) is likely to return after lunch like a team, down by one touchdown, bursting back onto the field with renewed dedication after half-time. The expert gets back on the stand, mumbles that he or she has had an opportunity to review his or her notes, and then gives an excruciatingly careful modification of previous testimony.

Unlike most public hearings, regulatory hearings lack strict time limitations. The hearing, as Alice in Wonderland would say, just continues until it reaches the end, and then stops. The process may last many weeks. Each day, the hearing picks up exactly where it left off the previous day, sometimes seemingly in the middle of a sentence. An engineer might be on the stand for days upon days, testifying about slopes, coefficients of expansion, and asphalt. Only when all experts from both sides have been questioned and re-questioned by the hearing examiner and by the attorneys for all parties and the regulatory agency is the hearing concluded. There follows a period of some weeks or months during which time the hearing examiner reviews all of the data and testimony before issuing a decision.

Regulatory Hearing Strategies: Your strategy for a regulatory hearing will be conditioned by financial considerations. If you are paying for all services, even a few days of hearings can be an awesome expense. Attorneys' and experts' professional fees run from thirty or forty dollars per hour (and that is dirt cheap) to ten times that much for real hotshots. In addition, you will probably have to cover travel and lodging expenses for your experts.

For various reasons, you probably should obtain copies of the testimony, especially that of opposing witnesses. Such copies (official *transcripts*, or parts thereof) are obtained from the court reporter services, starting at ten or fifteen bucks per page. To make matters even bleaker, the margins (top, bottom, right, and left) are expansive, oceanic in fact, and the testimony itself is typed at double- or triple-space. A fifteen-dollar page of expert testimony from a court reporter firm looks like a wedding invitation in the center of a full-sized piece of typing paper.

In short, the costs of extensive regulatory hearings are prohibitive for most groups unless you find a way to reduce these costs significantly. The first way to do this is to hire a sympathetic attorney who does some *pro bono* ("for the public's good") work and makes your group part of the *bono*. You still have to cover various filing fees, copying costs, and other unavoidable expenses, but you may be able to eliminate some of the attorney's costs.

There are benefits for an attorney who represents your group without expecting monetary payment. The individual can gain experience in regulatory law or whatever other areas of law your group is operating within. He or she may also make contacts with many committed individuals, perhaps even gaining fame if your group makes any headway against the Project. If there is anything especially curious, from a legal point of view, about your case, you may be able to attract high-caliber legal talent. If there is a chance that an important precedent — a standard for future conduct or legal decision — may be set during the handling of your case, an aggressive, ambitious attorney may be interested.

Do not overlook the possibility that a national organization or coalition will take an interest in or even support your case. Contact these groups with a brief cover letter explaining the general nature of your issue. Explain clearly why you think that it raises questions of national importance that fall within the purview of the group whose support you are seeking. Enclose a concise and precise summary of the legal issues involved. Avoid sending a desperate plea that does no more than wail *Oh, my God they want to put a toxic waste dump next to the school. What shall we do?* Your chances of receiving any aid are much better if you leave the impression that you are well-organized and have a clear focus.

Many national groups are already overextended and understaffed, so keep in mind that your chances of enlisting their active support are not great. However, there is nothing to lose by trying. Just getting on their mailing list and receiving their regular publications will help by providing additional sources of information. In addition, you may receive financial aid, legal support, and/or advice on locating appropriate expert witnesses as well.

Also try to round up some expert witnesses who will testify for principle rather than just for profit. The nearest large university is a good place to look for such people, but frankly, getting them to testify against Entity will be very difficult. Many of these experts will talk to you, help you obtain and analyze helpful studies and reports, discuss strategy with your attorney, and even attend your meetings and make helpful comments. But publicly testifying to what they have already told you privately is a different matter.

I have seen experts testify in public, under oath, to things directly opposite to data they discussed in private with members of a community group. I have seen experts suddenly cease all contacts with group members and even go so far as to pretend not to recognize them at public events. Such behavior is frustrating, but also understandable.

Take, for example, a generic engineer. Presumably this person is an engineer because he or she likes to do engineering. Whom can you work for as an engineer? A university, a private company, an engineering or consultant firm, or a government agency. Engineers who knowingly consort with or aid the enemy (i.e., groups like yours) have a difficult time obtaining or keeping most jobs. Forced to choose between testifying for your group and keeping a job, few will opt to give up job security and a steady income. And, like you, they have families, kids in college, debts, mortgages, and other financial responsibilities.

Even without your own paid expert witnesses, however, your group can get some mileage out of a regulatory hearing. There are probably numerous soft spots, weak points, and inconsistencies in Entity's case. Persistent cross-examination of its experts can expose many questionable aspects of testimony offered on Entity's behalf. Even if you fail to convince the hearing examiner that the Project is seriously flawed, you may succeed in eliciting sworn testimony that will be useful to you in other proceedings.

During the course of the hearings, your group should hold a few well-timed press conferences. One should be at the beginning of the hearings to explain your group's position regarding their purpose. If there is especially important testimony given during the hearing, a second press conference should highlight it. Finally, at the conclusion of the hearings, you should hold a third press conference to summarize what of significance was brought out during the hearings and to reiterate your group's position and hopes for a decision on issues involved.

Since the hearing in general and most of the testimony in particular is likely to be detailed, technical, and tedious, it is of the utmost importance that your press conferences not mirror these characteristics. If you hold a garbled and boring press conference even once, the news media will probably boycott you the next time, and with good reason. It is up to your group to explain why it is so shocking that Entity will have to dig twenty holes instead of ten holes or that the regulatory agency is going to allow the Project to skip provision *4b*. And if you cannot get the main point across in twenty-five words or less, do not expect to see anything about it on the nightly news.

Usually, there is no point in calling out the troops to attend regulatory hearings like those we have been discussing. It is probably sufficient if you can get one or two people to attend most of the hearings, keeping general notes on what is said, gleaning any new or shocking information that comes out, and lending moral support to your attorney, who will attend full time. Your regular newsletter should include updates on what happens at the hearings, but again, be sure to make the reports understandable to a general audience with some familiarity with the Project.

Court Appearances

Your group can end up in court in numerous ways, but the two most likely to get you there are to pursue an original civil suit or to appeal a regulatory agency decision.

If your group chooses to file a lawsuit against Entity or against the Project itself, the procedures to be followed will be defined by the case itself and the relevant state or federal laws. These cases have their own rhythms and peculiarities and cannot be discussed directly in this handbook. Instead, we'll focus here on what may happen in the judicial appeal of a regulatory decision; that is, when you take an agency to court and accuse it of not doing its job.

I mentioned earlier that you can only take take this step if your group has exhausted a particular agency's appeal procedures. This means that you must have proceeded through the labyrinth of re-hearings, appeals, and whatever other means of recourse are available within the agency. When you have exhausted all of these, you may then, and only then, take your complaints outside of the agency.

During the regulatory hearings, your group opposed Entity or the Project. In a court appeal of a regulatory decision, however, your group is actually opposing a government agency. The agency will be represented by its own legal counsel and almost certainly by legal counsel from the government itself (an attorney general or city attorney, for example.)

Put it bluntly. A regulatory agency, with an impressive staff of experts to call upon and years of experience in similar cases, spends days, weeks, or months evaluating the testimony of other recognized experts in the field and comes to a decision. The regulatory agency, defended by government attorneys, is tried by a government judge. A vociferous citizens group claims that the agency's recommendations are all wrong and should be reversed. Now what do you think the chances are that the citizens group's wishes will be granted?

Your attorney presents the case before a judge or in a courtroom. The participants are the same people as those at the regulatory hearing, except that there will probably be more lawyers and fewer experts.

There are two major differences between a regulatory hearing and a court appeal, one trivial and one exceedingly important. The trivial one is this: courtroom settings are much more elegant and stately. Expect to see ancient oak-paneled walls, banisters polished by the body grease of millions of nervous attendees, and so on.

The second difference is that the judge may know absolutely nothing about the substance of your case. The judge probably has broad experience in the law, but usually no expertise in a particular area within the purview of a certain regulatory agency. That is OK, because he is probably being asked to rule on the regulatory agency's behavior or procedures rather than on matters of substance.

A day in court can be every bit as tedious as a day at the regulatory hearings, but usually it is not. Lawyers can spend hours arguing back and forth, and this part has a little drama to it, even if the points are trivial or so obscure as to be invisible to the ordinary onlooker. The real tedium arises when attorneys spend hours in extended whispered conferences with the judge. This is like watching a chess match without being able to see the board. Someone will come by later and tell you who won or at least what happened. If you want an explanation, you have to pester your attorney and/or the one or two people in your group who were in on it.

The arguments here are likely to be about procedural matters. In order to argue for the significance of a certain procedural step or a particular technical requirement, details about the Project must often be introduced, even if they only provide general background information for the proceeding.

Something interesting happens here. The judge does not know much of anything about, say, the requirements or hazards of a semiconductor plant. Neither does either lawyer. The experts are either at home or stored at the back of the courtroom, but the attorneys hope they won't have to call the experts, which would involve much time and expense to both sides.

So, the lawyers, having recently memorized a few impressive sounding phrases about the Project in question, are both pretending to know a great deal about it. Each knows the other is faking, but neither knows how much the other really does know. Each lawyer makes the strongest case possible without pushing to the point where the other attorney will confidently question him, or even worse, correct him.

Meanwhile, the judge, who knows less about the Project than either lawyer, is doing his best to conceal his or her ignorance and confusion and wondering how on earth to rule in this case. Better judges make fewer efforts to hide their ignorance. They will often direct focused questions to the attorneys. A judge's request for clarification provides an opening for the attorneys to frame the issue, each according to his or her own perspective.

At some point early in the proceedings, the judge has to decide whether or not to accept the facts as presented to the regulatory agency. If so — and this is what usually happens — the judge will rule not on the facts themselves, but on whether or not they were appropriately handled and processed by the agency.

If the judge does not accept the testimony from the regulatory agency proceedings, that same evidence will be considered only if it is gathered all over again — *de novo* — in the courtroom. If the judge decides that a *de novo* proceeding is necessary, you are in for a very long and expensive trial. If your group really believes this is the way to handle Entity and the Project, go for it. But be aware that large amounts of your time will be devoted towards massive and on-going efforts to raise money and uncover damaging evidence.

If the trial is not *de novo,* it will probably be short. The judge listens to attorneys for both sides for a while, then dismisses them while deliberating. Moments, hours, days, weeks, or even months later (depending on the complexity and importance of the issue and the temperament of the judge), you receive a ruling on the issue at hand.

If the trial is *de novo*, it will go on for a very long time (or until your group runs out of money) and take on the character of a regulatory hearing with dumber questions asked.

In general, courts accept regulatory agency decisions unless there is overwhelming evidence of incompetence, neglect, or massive procedural violations. Procedural matters are more likely than substantive ones to provide your group with a persuasive argument.

As Alan B. Morrison reminds us, challenging a regulatory agency in court can be an exertion with dim prospects:

> You can almost always get into court and have it review your claim that an agency acted improperly.
>
> The court will review your claim and the agency's decision with care, but you have a decidedly uphill road to convince a court that the agency was wrong on the facts or in resolving policy choices. However, in exceptional cases, the courts will set aside an agency's decisions on the merits.
>
> The courts will insist that agencies dot their procedural i's and cross their procedural t's, but only those i's and t's that are required by law and not those that the judiciary thinks would be a good idea.

Court Strategy: Your group's strategy at a court hearing or trial should be similar to strategy at a regulatory hearing. Try to convince the presiding official to make a favorable decision, put critical information or statements on the record, and go through another step of the process to preserve your options and/or win delays.

Hold at least one press conference to explain what action you would like the court to take. If there are fireworks during the trial, explain their significance for the fight against the Project. And, when a decision has been made, explain it clearly to the public, express your approval or disagreement with it, and outline your next step.

As in regulatory hearings, the issues in a court case can seem exceedingly trivial and tedious to the rest of the world if they do not understand why they are significant. It is up to your group to explain this in a clear and timely fashion.

If, as is likely, your group is not satisfied with a court's ruling on your appeal of a regulatory agency decision, you can still continue the appeals process. Your attorney knows when and how to do this. Keep in mind that, in many cases, the further away from the original jurisdiction (the regulatory agency) you get, the better your chances of a fair hearing (local politics can exert tremendous pressures on a judge.) That's the good news. The bad news is that often, the further along you go in the appeals process, the more limited the scope of the subject.

Assume that Project has been granted the desired permit and that your group is appealing the regulatory agency's decision. In general, as you move along through the appeals process, fewer matters of substance and more matters of procedure are involved. Rulings in your favor will include reversals or invalidations of the decisions of lower bodies (lower courts or regulatory agencies). A refusal to consider the case or an affirmation of a lower court's finding usually means a setback for your group. An example of a middle course of action on the part of a court would be to send the decision back to the lower court or to the regulatory agency for reconsideration under slightly different conditions. (These slightly different conditions might include a requirement to consider evidence or arguments that were rejected during the original hearing).

Fake Hearings

Much of the controversy about the Project is likely to revolve around the issue of hearings. Project opponents will claim that Entity is trying to avoid hearings because it does not want the public to find out about the Project. Entity will reply that it held hearings and nobody came. Or, even more damaging, that it held hearings and no one was upset until these outside agitators came around spreading misinformation, getting everyone riled up.

At issue here is the flexible nature of the word *hearing*, often flexed by Entity to the max. Recall from Chapter Three that Entity will seek to line up support for the Project by quietly holding meetings to tell its side of the story. First, it probably will seek out prominent businesspeople and other community leaders, invite them to comfortable gatherings, and regale them with refreshments and displays of facts about what a great idea the Project is.

After a few community leaders have been lined up through these exclusive, invitation-only events, Entity representatives may try to reach a slightly broader range of people from the community. The goal here is to insure that the community's first glimpse of the Project is through Entity's eyes, and a very positive view it will be. During these so-called hearings, Entity will present the Project in glowing terms and take whatever steps are necessary to prevent Project opponents from even finding out about the hearings. The hope is that those who are exposed to Entity's version first will be vaccinated against the misinformation that Project opponents are sure to distribute.

Often after going to great lengths to avoid public hearings, Entity will now claim that it voluntarily held numerous hearings, even extra hearings not required by law. Never let claims of this nature slip by unanswered. They can be very damaging if the news media begin broadcasting them unanswered.

Instead, call Entity's bluff immediately. Find out who has made the claim, exactly what kind of hearings were supposedly held, when, where, and according to what statute. Usually when caught in this way, the Entity representative will stumble and stutter and retreat. Smoother ones will remain glib and confident, but exceedingly vague. Do not let them get away with this, for it is the kind of misinformation that can do your group great harm in the long run if you do not refute it at the outset.

Here a Hearing, There a Hearing...

What do all these hearings have to do with each other or with anything else? Sometimes a lot, sometimes almost nothing. We will try to sort it out briefly here.

Any public body can hold a public hearing. Sometimes, they are set up just to allow upset citizens to let off steam. In these cases, public officials will do little more than furrow their brows and look concerned, hoping that after the hearing, people will just go home and forget about the issue. A public hearing may also precede a vote, in which case the behavior of the public officials may be somewhat influenced by testimony offered at the hearing. However, the hearing still doesn't have any clear legal status: it is not part of a longer, procedurally defined process.

Some public hearings do have an important legal status, however, as is the case with scoping hearings and subsequent EIS hearings. Testimony presented at an EIS hearing must (supposedly) be considered in subsequent EIS documents. If a demonstrably relevant concern is mentioned in hearings but ignored in the final EIS, then the process may be procedurally flawed. Such a procedural error can lead to successful appeals in court. (In contrast, a public hearing that is an end in itself has no such tie-in to later legal action.) This is a good reason to put some organized effort into EIS hearings, sending documents to the headquarters well before deadlines, and using certified or registered mail.

At the end of the long EIS process, a final EIS and decision document are released. The recommendations are usually in favor of the Project, sometimes with minor modifications which are claimed to be safeguards. Once in a blue moon the final EIS actually recommends abandoning a Project, but this outcome is so rare that it should never be counted on, no matter how strong your arguments and evidence are.

The EIS process provides much information, many opportunities for public education, a very, very slim chance of having the Project halted, and the usual opportunities for appeals. It is more open and more understandable than most of the other administrative processes that accompany Entity's quest to get the Project on line. The only danger of pursuing the EIS process is that Project opponents expect victory and are dismayed when (surprise!) the final EIS gives the green light.

In most cases, public hearings have no connection to regulatory hearings. Regulatory agencies are much less inclined than are city councils or EIS bureaucrats to tolerate the circus-like atmosphere that public hearings (and democracy) entail. The scope of regulatory hearings is narrow and technical: *shall we issue this permit to allow discharge by so-and-so to a particular waterway?* Outside of the specific agenda, it is not the place to air wider issues.

Regulatory hearings are for specialists, lawyers, experts, and perhaps a few others who happen to be participants in or witnesses to certain actions. Regulatory hearings start in the agency and echo back and forth within it for a while until a decision is made. Sometimes, however, if the granting of a particular permit is especially controversial, a hearing examiner at a regulatory agency may, at his or her discretion, allow a miniature public hearing of sorts to take place before the real regulatory hearing begins. When this happens, the time allotted and the rules followed are those announced by the examiner. In such cases, rare as they are, the irate public is allowed to offer testimony and generally let off steam as highly paid lawyers and experts stand by. The testimony offered here, being unsworn, has no technical place at the hearing, but members of the public who have been allowed to speak out in this fashion may leave slightly mollified. The official, legally relevant regulatory hearing then takes place.

If your group is not satisfied with the regulatory agency's decision, you can sue the agency for not carrying out its duties. When that happens, the situation changes from you versus Entity on the regulatory agency's turf arguing over a permit to you versus the regulatory agency in court arguing over whether the agency has done its job correctly.

Just as your group may sue the regulatory agency whose decision you dispute, you many also sue the agency that carried out the EIS process. Almost any agency can do an EIS. Who does the EIS depends on which agency has jurisdiction over the proposed Project. And, just as Entity may hire a private consulting firm to draw up its permit application, a large federal agency may draw on the work of consultants to research and/or write up an EIS. No matter who participates in creating the final EIS, it is finally and officially the product of the agency that issues it.

On the surface it may seem that a few lone gladiators are sent out to do battle with Entity in the regulatory agencies and the courts. This is far from the truth. Even if an attorney and a few advisors or experts are the only ones physically present during most of a hearing, there is a massive, if hardly visible, group effort backing them up.

Good technical research and political intelligence will provide your gladiators with better information than money could buy. Sustained public education efforts will insure that fundraising has been successful enough to cover legal costs and will also enable you to turn out a good crowd when the situation requires it. When a decision is reached, it is likely to be framed in highly technical language. Your group will be able to translate it into ordinary language, explain its significance to the outside world, and suggest further courses of action.

We have now covered the major arenas — public debates, regulatory agencies, and courts — where the struggle against the Project takes place.

The realities of activism in the nineties demand that we now address the possibility that while performing in those arenas, your group becomes the object of intimidation attempts.

Alan B. Morrison, "Federal Regulation: Close Reins on the Bureaucracy," *The Nation*, Sep. 29, 1984, pp. 290-293. (Good analysis of federal laws, legalese terms, a general broad picture of the obstacles that citizens' groups encounter when trying to use the courts to their advantage. Special but brief treatment of the issues of standing, judicial discretion, and preclusion. Very readable and highly recommended. Morrison directs the Public Citizen Litigation Group, which he founded with Ralph Nader.)

Chapter 9

INTIMIDATION

No handbook for NIMBY activists would be complete without an overview of intimidation. Intimidation can take a number of forms, including smear campaigns and the circulation of misinformation and rumor about you or your group. It can occur at any phase of a NIMBY campaign, even when you and Entity are engaging in negotiations to settle the controversy once and for all.

Just as NIMBY tactics have evolved, so have the methods used by Entities and Project supporters. Are instances of intimidation increasing? Perhaps, but this may be a reflection of increased publicity and awareness. You may wage a NIMBY campaign for years without anyone in your group ever experiencing intimidation. On the other hand, it may begin early and intensify as the controversy heats up. No one knows how frequently NIMBY-related intimidation occurs. But if it happens to you, it doesn't matter what the exact statistics are. You need to be prepared. Understanding intimidation and knowing what you can do about it puts members of your group in a better position in case it happens to you.

As you read this discussion of intimidation, keep three things in mind. You may never experience intimidation. If you do, there are ways to respond that minimize its effects. There are also defenses you can use to discourage would-be intimidators from targeting your group.

Intimidation can be a tempting option for Project backers because the stakes are often enormous. Even a modest Project can involve over a million dollars. Many Projects cost hundreds of millions of dollars, some over a billion. In addition to all the money potentially involved, political careers, corporate careers, prestige, reputations, and egos may be on the line.

There are a lot of people out there with an eye on the Project. A consultant firm charging half a percent as a commission would earn $1,125,000 on a Project with a $225 million price tag. A construction firm awarded the contract to build it would earn 10, 20, or 30 times this amount, or more. Even a company hired to build a fence around it or provide toilet paper for its employees could amass a substantial profit. If the Project were stopped, these potential profits would disappear. To some Project supporters, intimidation may appear to be a cost-effective way of neutralizing opposition to a Project.

Intimidation attempts, unpleasant as they are, are a clear sign that your group is effective. Somebody among the Project's supporters is worried that NIMBY forces are making headway and threatening the success of the Project. This is good news.

The bad news is that sometimes intimidation works. People do get scared, and as a result they tone down their activism or abandon it entirely. The rest of this chapter is devoted to helping your group resist the effects that intimidation and the fear of intimidation can have.

What Is Intimidation?

Intimidation is any attempt to make you afraid to continue your activism by hurting you or your family in some way. It often takes the form of a hint or a threat, but can be much more direct, like a lawsuit or a bomb. The most common areas targeted by intimidation are your physical safety, your financial security, and your reputation.

Intimidation can come from Entity personnel or agents, people associated with government agencies, law enforcement personnel, Project supporters, or persons employed by any of the above. Intimidation may be overt or subtle, random or organized, direct or indirect, physical or legal. It may be aimed at anyone in your group, those collaborating with it or those associated with its members, including family and friends.

Intimidation comes in many forms. A few of them are listed here so that you can appreciate their variety. Simply reading about them before you have a more personal encounter may help you to respond in an appropriate and timely manner if the need arises.

People may bug your phones at home or at work, follow you around, or take pictures. Your home, yard, office, or vehicle may be vandalized or your files and records may be ransacked or stolen. Arsonists may target your home, car, or business, perhaps to cover up previous illegal searches or maybe only to destroy your records and scare you. A vehicle can have its brake lines disconnected or its fuel adulterated.

One long-used tactic is to embarrass you by serving you with legal papers in a public place or workplace. You may be blackmailed for real or manufactured reasons. Repeated and embarrassing drug searches can be scheduled at your home or place of work.

Some forms of intimidation focus directly on your ability to make a living. Your business may be boycotted or suddenly suffer a rash of lawsuits. You may find yourself blacklisted and your career moves blocked. Your current job may be threatened or eliminated in an unexpected organizational restructuring. More openly, your entire group, or some of its members, may be sued for slander or libel against Entity or Project personnel or for other alleged abuses of their rights.

Finally, you may be assaulted, or have strange inexplicable accidents. Threats, over the phone or through the mail, including death threats, are not uncommon.

Don't Count on the Cops

It would be comforting to think that the government, or some part of it, would vigorously seek to protect its citizens against illegal forms of intimidation, using the long arm of the law to locate and prosecute those responsible for the violations. Unfortunately, things do not always work out that way. To be realistic, you need to consider other factors.

If the Entity proposing the Project you oppose is part of the government, you are directly confronting government policy. But, even if your problem Entity is a private corporation, the proposed Project may be openly or tacitly supported by government. You may find that some powerful elected officials or a few government agencies share your opposition to particularly controversial Projects. But, most of the time, the activities of your NIMBY group may be at odds with government policy or goals.

What this means is that your group cannot count on the full and enthusiastic cooperation of law enforcement authorities. These various agencies — local police, state police, Drug Enforcement Agency, FBI, CIA, etc. — often feud among themselves, so you will not always find a coordinated, united front. In addition, they may be less than enthusiastic about investigating a report of intimidation from your group.

A reluctance to pursue your case takes two common forms. The first is a half-hearted, tardy, or sloppy investigation, hampering all further efforts to convict an intimidator or even to identify him or her. Or, law enforcement may simply refusal to acknowledge that the intimidation incident has anything to do with your NIMBY activism. This refusal essentially converts the intimidation incident to an instance of random violence or vandalism, thereby de-politicizing it.

While you should not interfere with an investigation carried out by a legitimate law enforcement agency or other government body, you might benefit from doing a little of your own investigating. At the very least, be as observant as you can and keep records of what you notice. Linking an intimidation incident to NIMBY activism may be possible only if you have well-documented evidence that a hasty *pro forma* investigation will miss. If your group has been assiduous in cultivating the interest and support of elected officials, their influence can be downright miraculous when it comes to putting life into a sluggish investigation.

Don't pester authorities with wild stories and paranoid fears that are not supported by evidence. Your best chance at gaining their cooperation is to treat them with respect while understanding their limitations.

Hope for the Best and Prepare for the Worst

Where intimidation is concerned, you don't have to expect it, but you certainly should be ready for it. Most activists experience little or no intimidation of a serious kind. But even if the possibility is remote, you should prepare to deal with it. Preparation by itself can often deter others from attempting intimidation. Just by assuming that something will happen, you are forearmed.

Assume that Project supporters sooner or later will launch a public relations blitz against your position, your group, or some of its members. Much of it will be pretty distorted if not downright untruthful. Assume that Entity will take legal actions (such as SLAPPs, discussed below) intended to silence your group or some of its members. And, assume that, at some point, other forms of intimidation will occur. Smear tactics are more or less part of the NIMBY landscape, and it is doubtful that you can do anything that completely eliminates them. But if you are ready, understand your rights, and know how to respond, you can minimize their incidence and effects.

Defenses

Take some time to analyze the weaknesses of your own group. Then, work on defenses which counter them. In the rest of this chapter, we'll discuss some of the defenses against and responses to intimidation which you can use as the basis for your group's plan of action. Plan occasional rehearsals for handling it. This strengthens your group and increases its resistance.

For example, during a meeting you can hold a practice session for delivering appropriate responses. What if so-and-so gets a telephone death threat? What if so-and-so's boss hints that he cool his NIMBY activism? And so on. Such rehearsals insure that you have thought out defenses and responses to each kind of intimidation. They enable everyone in the group to know that clear responses are available and ready to go. And they allow group members to understand that, by being prepared, they can weaken potential intimidation and lower its frequency. Because intimidation works best against groups or individuals that are vulnerable in some way, not knowing your rights, remaining unprepared, and feeling vulnerable makes you vulnerable.

Who is vulnerable? Physically or socially isolated individuals or groups are vulnerable. If no one knows who you are or what you are doing, who cares what happens to you? A group member who is in financial trouble or in a politically sensitive job is vulnerable. An organization that depends, or appears to depend, on one or two people for information, strategy, or money is vulnerable.

Neither your group nor any of its members should be left vulnerable because of isolation. Eliminate isolation through connections, communications, and visibility. Let people know where you are and visit or contact those members who are physically isolated or live alone. Phone those who live far away often. Where possible, always have a partner or a witness with you; don't go around alone, especially if you are carrying important documents or going to a meeting or a hearing.

Take pictures or video tapes of members of your group, Entity's representatives, other Project supporters, and members of the general public at hearings and other public events. They establish who was there, are available for current or later use in your newsletter, newspapers, and other literature, and are good to have on file. Your group should be visible in the community, maintaining contacts with churches and other community organizations, giving presentations, and generally keeping in touch and making your presence known. You should also get on the mailing list of national organizations whose goals overlap with yours, sending them regular but brief updates on your activities.

Threats to a group's or its members' financial security are quite effective and dangerous, especially if they come as a surprise. It's important to anticipate, acknowledge, understand, and mitigate such threats. If a group member has a politically sensitive job, he or she should be extra careful at work, especially when dealing with controversial or delicate matters. Trusted witnesses should be present during potentially troublesome transactions. Copies of records, documents, and papers should be kept or filed at a second location. Much of this is standard operating procedure in bureaucracies, where the phrase *cover your backside* was invented.

Where a person's financial security or career may be threatened, provide a safety net of support. This involves anything from contacting public services already available in the community to assuring the vulnerable person that there is a spare bedroom or couch available in a group member's house, should need for it arise.

SLAPP and SLAPP-back: One special form of financial threat deserves special attention: the *SLAPP.*

SLAPP, a term coined in 1988, refers to a Strategic Lawsuit Against Public Participation. According to Stephanie Simon, writing in the *Wall Street Journal*:

> Corporations and developers have filed hundreds of civil suits against individuals or community groups in the past decade, [Ralph] Nader said. Usually, the plaintiffs allege libel, defamation, or interference with business in an effort to stop protesters from voicing criticism.
>
> Targets of SLAPP suits are varied: individuals who complain about development projects in letters to the editor, activists who lobby against industrial polluters, neighborhood groups that fight to uphold zoning restrictions.

SLAPPs are often dropped or eventually dismissed, but that is little comfort to those being sued, because fighting them is an extremely expensive, time-consuming process. For this reason, many feel that SLAPPs have been effective means of discouraging critics from speaking out and pursuing their activist agendas.

In the last few years, activists have begun filing countersuits, called SLAPP-Back suits, alleging libel, abridgment of first amendment rights, malicious prosecution, and related abuses. Both general and punitive damages have been sought. One St. Louis activist was awarded $86 million in damages in a successful 1991 suit.

Though some SLAPP-Back suits have been successful, the legal process is expensive and time-consuming. Several states have enacted laws that provide specific protection for the First-Amendment rights of persons testifying or speaking out as part of a public debate. Such state laws make SLAPPs easier to fight but cannot eliminate all possibility of such intimidation.

The Citizen's Clearinghouse for Hazardous Waste (CCHW) offers a fact sheet on SLAPPs (called the *SLAPP Back Fact Pack*) and monitors related court cases and legislation.

If your group is SLAPPed, SLAPP back. There is a growing body of experience and precedents around the country to aid you in your counterattack. But, as is the case with all intimidation, don't let a SLAPP response distract you from your group's original goals.

Decentralize: Your defenses against intimidation are greatly enhanced by taking precautions to prevent one or two individuals in the group from becoming targets. Concentrating information, responsibilities, or influence makes you vulnerable; dispersing them protects you.

Share information with the entire core group of your NIMBY organization, keeping each other informed of new developments and even rumors. Share responsibilities within your group as far as practical, rotating jobs when possible. This acquaints various members with information that they previously received only secondhand or in summary form. Active members of your group should frequently document in writing what they are doing. This makes information widely available for newsletter summaries and historical reviews of the NIMBY campaign and becomes part of your permanent records. Keep duplicate copies of important records in more than one location. Consider giving complete copies of sensitive documents to a lawyer or to someone who is widely trusted but is not an active member of your NIMBY group.

Just as you should never allow one or two people to be, or appear to be, the brains of your operation, don't allow your group to become dependent on one or only a few sources of money. Not only will the decision-making process be skewed if you do so, but disproportionately influential individuals could also be tempting targets for intimidation.

When members of the group sort themselves into areas of expertise, some degree of specialization is inevitable and desirable, since it matches individuals' talents to areas where they can make the greatest contribution. But, rather than focusing on such specialization, the group should downplay it to avoid setting certain people up as targets.

Simple Precautions: Finally, while pursuing the structural defenses described above, do not neglect to follow the usual security measures that are appropriate for your community. Follow safe habits and stay alert. Do not become obsessive about security. This will tear the group apart, causing members to lose effectiveness in the NIMBY campaign — exactly the result that intimidators want. But, do be reasonably careful.

In addition to the other measures mentioned in this chapter, be sure that you follow standard security practices regarding your home, office, workplace, and vehicles. Having a phone is a relatively inexpensive and effective precaution. A 'caller i.d.' feature, if available, can be very useful. Don't spend a lot of time alone and out of touch with group members or friends. Let people know where you are. Keep up the maintenance on your home and car so you can better avoid things like flat tires when you are all alone on a dark country road.

Avoid Martyrdom: When the stress and high stakes of a NIMBY campaign collide with the fear and adrenalin of an intimidation incident, some unfortunate side effects can result. A targeted individual may acquire an inflated sense of his or her own importance, taking off on an ego trip that forms the basis of a martyr complex. Living out this martyrdom can become a career in itself, even a self-fulfilling prophecy. A targeted individual needs support and compassion, not adulation. Help all members of the group retain a sense of realism and a focus on collective goals. If fears generated by an intimidation attempt have failed to derail your group, don't let a budding martyr succeed.

If you are reasonably careful, know your rights, and do not present an enticingly easy target, your chances of being subject to intimidation are much reduced. If potential intimidators know that their efforts probably won't scare you from acting on your beliefs, they have less incentive to try. If they do, keep up the defenses mentioned here, and move on to your responses.

Responding To Intimidation

If anyone in your group, or the group collectively, is the recipient on intimidation attempts, take it seriously and react immediately. Your reaction must be twofold: continue, or even intensify, your NIMBY activities and respond to any attempts using the following suggestions.

Don't let intimidation achieve its purpose. Don't respond in kind, retaliate with threats, or reciprocate vandalism. There are much more powerful and effective means of responding at your disposal. Develop a contingency plan for your group that covers the actions described below.

The plan should outline specifically who does what so that action can be carried out as promptly and efficiently as possible.

Call the active members of your group and inform them of the situation. Offer physical and emotional support to the person or persons involved. This might include anything from staying with the person to providing safety-net services and support until the situation stabilizes.

Contact all relevant authorities, including the police, other law enforcement agencies and, if appropriate, the district attorney. If possible, press charges against any suspects. Ask for copies of any police or incident reports and stay informed about the progress of any and all investigations. Publicly demand an investigation if authorities appear reluctant to pursue on their own initiative. Sloppy investigations and refusals to investigate are bad signs, and may indicate that authorities are linked in some way to the incident(s). Make a public issue of this.

Call your group's lawyer to notify him or her of any attempts and to get legal advice. Make a list of the names of several lawyers familiar with your group who specialize in civil liberties, First-Amendment rights, criminal investigations, whistle-blowing, SLAPPs, and other related activities. Don't wait until something happens and then get out the phone book to seek legal help. Be prepared.

Document everything. Whether the authorities launch an investigation or nor, gather all the evidence you can, interview people, photograph (if appropriate) anything at the scene that could be relevant, and get names of witnesses and their statements. Write everything down, label all photos or videotapes, make sure you have duplicate copies, and keep them in a safe place.

This documentation should include any unusual behavior or events prior to, during, and after an intimidation incident. Witnesses who are not members of your group are very important here. If no outsiders are present during the incident, bring some in as soon as possible to witness the aftermath and any remaining evidence.

Within twenty-four hours, or less if you can manage it, contact the media and issue a statement about the intimidation attempt. (Have an attorney review the statement beforehand.) The statement should include a brief description of the incident, followed by (1) a declaration of your group's intent to pursue all legal means to see that the intimidator is identified and prosecuted to the full extent of the law and (2) an affirmation of your continued, uninterrupted opposition to the Project.

Inform the media that further press conferences, statements, or more lively actions may follow and that you will keep them informed.

Using a list you prepared during your planning for intimidation, communicate with similar groups in the town and country, local and regional civil rights and civil liberties organizations, and state or national groups that work on similar or related issues. You may also want to include local, state and national elected representatives, and, perhaps, officials from Entity as well.

Hold an open discussion of the event within your group. If you have a newsletter, write a brief account. If investigations stall, if you feel that authorities have not handled the incident appropriately, or if you simply want to reemphasize your commitment to activism, you can plan a demonstration of some sort. A public spectacle draws attention to your group and its dedication to working against the Project as well as to any legal or Constitutional issues that may be involved.

Design press events well to take advantage of the power of symbolism. Picketing an office building where government authorities are dawdling over an investigation may be appropriate. Or hold a candlelight vigil (always visually impressive) while giving a public reading of the Constitution or the Bill of Rights.

Finally, avoid becoming obsessed with the intimidation incident itself or paranoid about everyone and everything. Treat such events seriously, respond forcefully, and take a public stance. Just don't take away from the on-going efforts required to stop the Project.

Never underestimate the ugly potential of intimidation. Most acts of intimidation stop short of violence. But not all of them do. I personally knew one activist who was beaten under extremely suspicious circumstances. Another received death threats because of her opposition to a particular Project. A third activist was brutally murdered at a critical point in a NIMBY campaign. None of these cases was ever solved. (In the case of the homicide, there was not even any specific evidence linking the woman's death to her activism. On the other hand, the investigation was carried out in an inarguably sloppy manner, especially in its early days immediately following her death.) Bad things can happen, even if not very often.

Intimidation is very much a mind game. The intimidator has already won if you spend excessive time worrying about or anticipating threats. Don't give intimidators such an easy victory. Just having thought about the material in this chapter makes you better prepared to handle any intimidation attempts that might be thrown in your way.

Now move on. The next chapters cover three of the toughest issues that you probably will have to face in the course of your NIMBY campaign.

Stephanie Simon, "Nader Suits Up To Strike Back Against 'SLAPPs,'" *Wall Street Journal*, Jul. 9, 1991; Paul Duggan, "Bowie Woman Finds Activism May Carry $8 Million Price Tag: Some Say Contractor's Suit Against Development Foe Is Intimidation," *Washington Post*, Jun. 24, 1991; Citizens Clearinghouse for Hazardous Waste (CCHW), "Operation SLAPP-Back," Everyone's Backyard, 1991 Annual Report; Robert D. Richards, "Suing to Squelch: A New Way to Keep Activists Quiet," *Washington Post*, Aug. 6, 1992.

Chapter 10

JOBS VS. ENVIRONMENT

If your NIMBY movement has been successful in gaining favorable governmental decisions, helpful delays, and increased public support, congratulations. But don't think that things will begin to get easier. On the contrary, they will become more difficult and more complex.

Of the three tough issues covered briefly in this and the next two chapters, the first two, *Jobs versus Environment* and *Alternatives,* come on very soon. The third, *Negotiations*, often takes longer to develop. But you must be ready for them all.

The Job Issue in a Nutshell

At some time during the course of almost every NIMBY battle, you will be hit with the *Jobs-versus-Environment* argument. Project supporters will claim that the jobs which the Project will provide outweigh any minor adverse environmental effects that it might have. In practice, the Jobs-versus-Environment argument comes in several forms, but its general outline is usually the same. Because of the recurring similarities, you can train yourselves to recognize any of its incarnations and formulate counter-arguments at a glance.

The most common forms are the class version, the race version, and the organized labor version. I do not endorse these arguments or the language they use. They are stated here in roughly the same way as you will probably hear them.

The Class Version: This version holds that jobs for working class folks are more important than having hiking trails for the rich or insuring that affluent homeowners have good views from their living room windows. Listeners are reminded that most of society's dirty work is done by the working class so that white collar workers can drive their expensive cars over smooth roads and have properly flushing toilets. Those who would deprive the working class of good jobs are described as selfish, ungrateful, spoiled, and lazy.

The Race Version: Here, white folks are contrasted to blacks, Hispanics, Asians, Native Americans, or whatever minority group is most evident in the community or region. White folks, the argument goes, can afford to think about whether or not a facility is pretty, smells good, or puts out two parts per million of some invisible chemical. But, minorities have to think about jobs to support their families and don't have the luxury of considering aesthetics first. This version pulls the same guilt strings as the class form of the argument and, in addition, plays on the racist fears of some whites that if society doesn't provide a minimum number of jobs, the minority groups in question will continue to weigh down the welfare rolls (and later the voter rolls) with a multitude of non-white offspring.

The Organized Labor Version: is used when construction, operation, or any other aspect of a Project is likely to involve union labor. The argument is couched in terms not of jobs in general, but good, union jobs filled by highly qualified workers — the cream of the labor force. In the proposed Project we finally have a chance, goes the argument, for hard-working Americans to earn a decent level of pay for good solid work. But instead of supporting such an opportunity, the anti-Project forces are trying to ruin it while while turning a blind eye toward or even supporting other projects that use non-union, sweat-shop, minimum-wage unqualified scab labor.

In the three classic forms of the Jobs versus Environment argument described above, the argument is spoken by a member of the group (worker, member of a minority group, union member) or someone like a family member who is closely associated with it. The argument is addressed to both the ruling elite (the ones who finally make the decision, a group usually dominated by affluent white males) and to those opposing the Project (often an uneasy mix of working class and/or minority activists joined by religious or environmental groups.)

Many Project supporters (here calling themselves the pro-jobs faction) sincerely believe that Jobs versus Environment is a fair statement of the issue. They will defend their view with conviction, emotion, and eloquence, no holds barred. At any public forums, you can expect to find construction workers in their hard hats sneering at non-productive tree-huggers; black pastors questioning the ethics of spoiled backpackers who have never done a day's work in their lives and don't have orphaned AIDS babies to support; and union men (and maids) railing against the shoddy workmanship and slave wages of scab labor.

The shrillness of these debates often unleashes a flood of long-suppressed mutual stereotypes, shouted against a backdrop of questionable generalizations. If the quality of the debate falls to alternating between the vicious and the vacuous, the whole community becomes vulnerable to Entity's manipulation. Such a situation helps Entity by splitting people who should be allies, using guilt to score public relations points, and diverting debate from the real issues.

A liberal member of a legislature, commission, council, etc., may have been elected by a coalition of minorities, organized labor, and environmentalists. This member is often a white male with no labor background who therefore may be desperate to prove himself to minority and/or union groups. The NIMBY activist needs to be realistic about the pressures that can be exerted within the political system. Few people in the position of this legislator can stand up against the combined effects of minority and union support or survive being labeled an anti-jobs candidate, whether the label is fair or not.

If your NIMBY issue has been successfully packaged as Jobs versus Environment, your cause has, by extension, been labeled anti-jobs and perhaps anti-growth as well. If you allow Project supporters to frame the debate, you will find yourselves in a deep hole labeled anti-jobs, anti-growth, selfish, short-sighted, and insensitive to the needs of minorities and working people. This is not the way to gain community support.

To assist you in disarming the jobs versus environment taunt, we'll turn first to jobs, then to the environment. Finally, we will face the more fundamental issue that encompasses each and transcends both.

Jobs: A Job Is Not A Job Is Not A Job

In people's minds, stable employment is the key to everything from financial security and health insurance to self-worth and personal fulfillment. When people are tuned into jobs, talk jobs to them.

If the Entity purportedly providing these jobs is an established one, look into its past claims and ask questions of Entity representatives at public forums. What have other communities been promised in the way of jobs and how did things turn out? Specific facts about how well previous projects fared in providing jobs often provide a much-needed dose of reality to a community on the verge of being swept away by exaggerated visions of imminent prosperity.

Also check the track records of similar facilities operated by other entities. Were the jobs they provided the unmixed blessing that the communities anticipated? Did Entity close up shop and move south of the border to Mexico the day after the peso was devalued? Such questions, among others, can provide insights into possible futures of the Project you yourself are facing.

Explore the difference between the jobs associated with two separate phases of the Project: the construction phase and the operational phase. Jobs associated with the construction phase (often one to three years or more) are usually more numerous, higher paying, and less permanent.

For the several-year period of construction, your community may need to provide housing, transportation, roads, infrastructure expansions (sewer lines, water and electricity hookups, etc.), schooling for children, health and hospital facilities, and increased police, fire, and emergency services for the expanded work force and their families. Costs for inspecting and monitoring new facilities may increase.

If the work force resides within your city or county, you may benefit from increased property and/or sales tax revenues that can be used to cover some of the costs associated with these improvements and expansions. If a substantial proportion of the construction phase work force resides in another community, however, your own local government may find itself bearing many of the costs but gaining few of the benefits from the temporary construction jobs that the Project brings.

During the construction phase of power plant construction, to take one case, a small number of professional and skilled-labor jobs will be supplemented by a much larger number of semi-skilled and unskilled-labor positions. All of those employed will require housing and other infrastructure-related services while construction is underway. Specialized businesses (such as small grocery stores, bars, restaurants, and related entertainment facilities) will provide spin-off jobs and increased local tax revenues. Often, they will also require expanded services such as police protection and traffic control measures.

During the operational (post-construction) phase, the work force shrinks. Your community may have to continue to pay off the principal and interest on the ten-, twenty-, or thirty-year bonds that financed improvements (the expansion of the school system, for example) that are no longer needed. This is the 'bust' part of this boom-bust cycle, in which short-term financial benefits to a community were insufficient to pay off long-term costs. This is when permanent residents of a community find that higher taxes, increased fees, rising rates, and reduced services (from road maintenance to libraries) are the price for the short-term boom. Evaluate all construction phase employment figures with long-term effects of a boom-bust cycle in mind.

Long-term effects, like the development of some forms of cancer, take decades to show up. Many long-term effects only become apparent after years, long enough for construction to have been completed and regular operations to have settled in. By that time, the thrill of having provided a hundred new jobs will have faded somewhat, and the community can begin to evaluate whether the revenues and other benefits to the community outweigh the added costs, inconveniences, and environmental damage.

In the case of the power plant, some of the construction-phase employees (especially professional, technical, and managerial ones) may stay on during regular operation of the facility, but their number is likely to be reduced from the construction-phase peak. The rest of the construction crew may be laid off.

Projected operational-phase jobs should be carefully scrutinized. How many will go to local residents, how many to executives, managers, or technicians transferred from Entity's other facilities or hired away from similar facilities elsewhere? How many will be entry-level jobs available to those currently unemployed or entering the job market for the first time? Does Entity have a policy regarding hiring a certain percentage of local residents and providing training if necessary? Will it offer employment opportunities to minorities, women, the disabled, or other often-discriminated against job seekers?

Will the jobs provided be seasonal or cyclical? Will the number of unemployed swell or shrink every spring or winter? Is the industry subject to frequent or unpredictable business cycles that may disrupt the local economy? Is it dependent on government research grants or the vagaries of military funding policies? Can it realistically provide more or less stable employment for a period of five years, ten, or twenty?

Will the facility, if successful, put any locals out of work? Will the old grocery store, the old hotel, the old Dairy Queen, or the local print shop go out of business or have to shut down? Has Entity offered any guarantees that it will patronize already-existing local businesses? Will it buy its staples, toilets, or light bulbs, locally or have them shipped in from distant sources? Will it advertise in local newspapers, have its public relations brochures printed at local print shops, and encourage its employees to live nearby?

Are there other businesses or industries that would not feel comfortable in your community because of the Project? If you hope that your town will become a tourist mecca, sportsperson's paradise, or retirement haven, think twice about welcoming with open arms a hazardous waste dump or dog food factory. Does the proposed Project have the potential for a catastrophic accident like a nuclear meltdown or the massive contamination of your community's water supply?

In efforts to convince people that the short-term, possibly illusive benefits of a relatively small number of new jobs outweighs the many certain or probable future costs, sometimes some fairly outrageous arguments are offered. In one case I know of, a major defense contractor was seeking to locate a large production facility in a medium-sized city. Environmentalists pointed to the substantial water use requirements and inevitable increase in water treatment capacity requirements for the city. The pro-jobs factions countered that the facility was a relatively clean industry. Union officials noted with approval that the facility was a union shop and insisted that this would have the effect of raising the overall wage rate and increasing local unions' influence.

Fiscal conservatives doubted that the economic benefits to the community would ever make up for the substantial tax breaks and extra-low water and electricity utility rates that the Project had been offered, but enthusiastic 'pro-growthers' chided them for being timid and backwards. Peaceniks who opposed military production facilities on principle wondered whether such a plant should be encouraged at all. Their pleas were all but drowned out by energy activists who were convinced that once the facility was built, its managers could be convinced to retrofit its production facilities from military hardware to solar collectors and other politically correct products.

The facility was approved and built. The city soon began an extensive and expensive expansion of its water treatment facilities, due in part to this facility's substantial requirements. Neither wage levels nor local unions' political clout increased appreciably. While services were reduced or cut, local taxes and fees for services went up, and utility rates increased dramatically as residents had to pay for the mushrooming indebtedness of their city. The plant eventually began laying off workers when the federal military budget was trimmed.

Needless to add, it never produced a single solar collector.

The people who want to put the Project in your back yard are influenced by national and international events and conditions. Their selection of your community was the last decision in a long chain of analysis and calculation. If Canada tightens its environmental regulations governing the steel-making process, steel makers may find it advantageous to cross into the U.S. Don't forget that their reason for doing so is to make cheaper steel by using dirtier processes, not to provide jobs. Or, political instability overseas may lead a chemical company or waste disposal outfit to shift some operations back to the United States. If they choose your community, it is because they think they can still profit if they charge less for burning your waste than you would have to pay to haul it off. This price differential is partly the result of fewer and fewer countries accepting foreign waste.

What makes your community look good to an industry one year can be a liability the next, depending on the global situation. And many of the factors that affect the success of a Project are beyond your control or due to things you have no way of finding out about. Providing jobs for your community is not one of Entity's goals. It is simply a side-effect. Taking jobs our of your community (or dumping waste into it) is not one of Entity's problems: it is also a side-effect.

Entity may come to your community, thrive, and bring prosperity for decades. Or it may come in, start up, incur local debts, hire a bunch of locals, mishandle a lot of potentially dangerous materials, and then go bankrupt. No one really knows which way fortune will turn. However, a private Entity will probably know its break-even point: how long the Project must last or how much it must produce before its costs are recovered. Entity will probably tell the local community that it plans to be there forever, even if it knows it can still come out ahead if it folds after a frantic three years. Private Entities have their plans figured down to the last penny — there is no reason for communities to be pacified and silenced by vague dreams of jobs, jobs, jobs and the eternal boom they herald.

If you stop and think a moment, it is clear that we do not want jobs at any price. Drug abuse provides a multitude of high-paying jobs for smugglers, arms dealers, distributors, street dealers, and the lawyers that defend them. It also increases the demand for law enforcement officers, bank tellers, prison guards, social workers, arms manufacturers, emergency room technicians, and a variety of counselors and therapists. The news media and book publishers exploit the hysteria generated by drug abuse statistics and gory gang shoot-outs. Even the medical supply industry benefits from increased sales of hypodermic needles and other drug-related paraphernalia.

Despite the enormous number of jobs created by drug abuse, few would conclude that the drug industry should be encouraged because it provides so many opportunities for gainful employment. People make judgments about the desirability of an enterprise or an industry on the basis of factors other than the number of jobs created. Any Project that Entity wants to bring to your community should be evaluated in terms of the same broad range of considerations and values.

So, when your community wants to talk jobs, talk jobs. But talk about realistic job prospects, not wild pie-in-the-sky scenarios that not even Entity's out-of-state investors believe. Try to anticipate and evaluate:

- The entire long-term impact of the Project and its jobs on your local community. The jobs promised are rarely as numerous, as good, or as stable as the promises implied.
- The indirect costs, from short-term infrastructure improvements to long-term debt incurred. These are often dramatically underestimated.
- The uncertainties caused by unpredictable political and economic conditions. These are minimized by Project supporters who also ridicule the risks of accidents, social dislocation, or environmental problems.

No two Projects are quite alike, so each NIMBY controversy has to produce its own particular set of arguments on the Jobs-versus-Environment issue. But no Project is so unique that it justifies members of your community going around in a starry-eyed daze, ignorant of a Project's probable consequences.

Some of these consequences are so-called environmental ones, and it is to the environment that we now turn.

Environment: You Don't Know What You've Got Till It's Gone

In their haste to categorize you, brand you or label you in a way useful to them, Project supporters will try to identify you with buzzword issues — spotted owls, the ozone hole, wilderness hiking, for example — and then label you environmental extremists. Don't rise to take the bait.

Instead, carefully, patiently, and without apology explain what you are concerned about. You will find that it is a good deal less global than the greenhouse effect. You will also find that, if you look closely, it has a dollar sign attached to it. If you simply remember to explain specifically what you are defending and to attach a dollar sign to it, the environmental extremist label just won't stick.

If you are a homeowner, one of the things you are defending is the value of your property. Despite anything Entity may claim about the absence of unpleasant side effects, the fact remains that many Projects (landfills, waste dumps, power plants, airports, weapons testing ranges, etc.) will devalue adjacent and nearby property, because no one really wants to live near one. A house is worth thousands of dollars more because it has a view of the mountains. Clear-cut the mountain, or build a paper mill there and your property values will go down. If you are a renter, remember that whoever owns your building will not appreciate lowered property values, either.

You are probably also defending yourself and your family (and your community as well) against the potentially adverse health effects of the Project. Your fears may range from asthma and annoying respiratory complaints to nervous system injury and cancer from airborne mutagens or carcinogens. Avoiding costly and debilitating health problems also makes economic sense.

Or, you may oppose the Project because you are defending against the possible degradation of your immediate environment. Anything from eroded hillsides, to the stench of car exhaust and lead from vehicle emissions, to the razing of natural park areas where kids can play or the polluting of creeks or watercourses in your neighborhoods can threaten your standard of living. Often, 'quality of life' has an economic value for both an individual homeowner and the wider community.

Think of trees in the fall, sunlight glancing off the brilliant reds and yellows, the hillsides alive with fall colors. Many places benefit economically from this yearly riot of color as tourists flock to see the autumn leaves. All the motels, lodges, restaurants, gas stations and souvenir shops that serve these sightseers bring dollars into the local economy and support jobs.

Some years, for whatever reasons, the leaves don't participate in the fall ritual. They simply turn brown, curl up, and fall to the ground. Many local businesses see red during these brown years, when the tourists go elsewhere. It becomes obvious that, unlikely as it may sound, even leaves turning color have an economic value for a community or region.

This value is one that, theoretically, a community could possess in perpetuity, with no more investment than is represented by *not* cutting the trees down and *not* fouling the air or water so much that the trees die. The obviousness of the value is not compromised by the fact that an exact economic price cannot be placed on it. Nevertheless, no approximation or even acknowledgment of such economic values enters into most discussions about economics and the environment.

Our lack of attention to recognizing and maintaining specific environmental sources of value that were always there has taught us a hard lesson: the economic value of a healthy environment is often most evident when it is nearly gone. Let's use an example to sketch out the environment in economic terms.

The Water Example

From the whole environment, consider just water. Unlike air, which we're hardly conscious of using unless ours is polluted, and unlike raw land, which city dwellers may hardly even see for days on end — water is pretty much an obvious daily necessity. From your first brush of the teeth in the morning to the last flush of the toilet at night, you use it all day long.

We started out on this continent with a seemingly infinite supply of pure water, all for free. Imagine a city growing up, as many of our great ones did (by no mere coincidence), on the banks of a river. We'll look at three phases in the history of this city, emphasizing the economic value of water, an important part of the environment.

Phase 1: The water was seemingly infinite and pure. It had an infinite economic value — it ran turbines or mills, irrigated crops, provided process water for industry and fishing and recreational value for tourists. The cost of keeping this source of infinite value was zero or negligible: we only had to refrain from threatening its quality or supply.

This would have been a matter of taking two fairly simple precautions which in fact we didn't take: don't deplete the supply by taking more water out than was put back in — a simple principle we have been applying to our checking accounts for years — and don't dump anything into the river, lake, or aquifer that would lower its quality.

Cheap and easy as this option would have been, it was not practiced with any consistency by those of us who lived and worked along rivers. By the mid-twentieth century, we were at Phase 2.

Phase 2: Water supply was not as dependable as it once had been, but it was still used for free (or nearly so), and as quickly as possible, by citizens and industry.

Decades of industrial activity in the city and upstream, residential development, and the intense use of agricultural chemicals, all punctuated by periodic acid rains, lowered the quality of the river a few notches below pristine.

This change may have gone unnoticed by all but a few. Industries found the river water less than ideal, so they spent resources to cleanse it further (using resources that decreased their profits, and, in turn, jobs and tax revenues). Some local residents noted that the local water no longer had a taste they could brag about. More often they filtered it before drinking it themselves, accepting the extra costs, lower quality of life, and lower property values.

Sport fishermen or restaurant suppliers noticed decreasing numbers and size of prized fish and perhaps an increase in the numbers of less desirable species. As word spread among water recreationists that the water wasn't what it used to be, a few marinas shut down, taking the nearby bait shops and convenience stores with them.

The supply of water was also affected. Because of overuse or increased demand, the river could no longer be depended on always to provide abundant water at critical times. To make up for this, the city and industry had either to tap alternative and more expensive sources of water (and pay extra costs) or curtail water use (and lose income).

In economic terms, the original nearly infinite value of the river had declined. An abundant supply was no longer certain, water quality was down, the fishing industry was in decline, recreational use dropped off, and some industries had to do some purification before using the water in their industrial processes.

But it wasn't economic collapse. Factories could still provide jobs and the guy who once rented boats and sold minnows could operate a forklift. The woman who owned and ran the corner store could do inventory. No big deal, so far. Continuing business as usual lead directly to Phase 3, but that was not the only option.

A modest investment could still have recovered the losses that the economic value of the river experienced. Especially dirty sites could have been cleaned up, and the withdrawal of water could have been monitored and regulated. Laws prohibiting dumping of waste or impure effluent anywhere in the watershed could have been strictly enforced.

After a few years of reestablishing the abundant supply of pure water — putting back the value of the river lost by carelessness and neglect — the full economic value could again have been realized: all the tourism, sport fishing, great tasting drinking water, ample supplies for industry, and no necessity for extensive water treatment for residents or business.

But if steps were not taken during Phase Two to reclaim the economic value of the river, the city ended up in Phase Three. See if this sounds familiar.

Phase 3: Effluent continues to be dumped upstream and in town. The water quality quietly continues its decline. A couple of species of algae or water plants now dominate the river ecosystem. The fish population is reduced to a few hardy and not very appetizing species.

Fishing, tourism, and recreation are by now nearly nonexistent in the river town, which has lost revenues, lost taxes, lost jobs, and lost its quality of life. Water skiing exhibitions are a thing of the past.

Meanwhile, industry and related services provide local jobs. New suburbs, more lawns, new industry, and an expanding service sector — all signs of success and progress — put additional demands on the city's water supply.

The river now flows with the health-threatening organisms (like *E. coli*) that have always been a danger when human or animal wastes are not kept separate from the water supply. These traditional contaminants are joined by benzene, pesticide runoff, PCB's and other, more modern toxins.

The old water treatment plant has been revamped several times to expand and add new processes that remove undesirable components from an ever-growing waste stream. But, eventually, the old plant can no longer be jerry-rigged to handle the increased volumes of highly polluted water. A new, larger, state-of-the-art water treatment plant is necessary to provide the clean water that once just flowed down the river.

During the planning phase of the new plant, the city learns the true extent of pollution. Heavy metals abound in the river sediment. The river ecosystem is reduced to a handful of species from hundreds or thousands. Area ground water is not only depleted by excessive pumping but also contaminated from seepage of carelessly disposed-of industrial by-products.

Financing the new plant to remove the pollutants in the water from industry practices, government neglect, and personal carelessness raises rates dramatically. Water that was once free for the pumping, or nearly free, now costs a bundle.

Property and municipal sales taxes increase, and user fees are instituted. On top of all that, the bonds sold to finance the new treatment plant won't be paid off for thirty years.

In order to meet the payments on the bonds in a timely manner and retain a good bond rating so it can borrow more money for other projects, the city must collect progressively higher revenues from a large and growing number of water consumers.

But, local industries respond to higher water rates and stricter water quality standards by cutting back on production and employees, then by shutting down and moving away. Their contributions to the tax base shrink, associated industries decline, and the service industry which fed, clothed, and entertained the now laid-off workers finds its customers gone or broke.

Because jobs are lost as industry cuts back, shuts down, or moves out, yesterday's wages no longer infuse the local economy. The city finds that it no longer has the large and growing number of water consumers it once touted from whom to collect water fees and other revenues. In fact, the number of rate payers is shrinking.

The city still owes the same amount of money to pay off its new water treatment plant, money that must be extracted from a shrinking rate base. Even the rocket scientists understand that water rates and other municipal charges are going to rise even more.

The city is in a mess, and everybody knows it. Those who could do so profitably (like the industries and major retailers) have already escaped to set up shop in the next about-to-boom borough across the county line or across an international border. Those who remain are pointing fingers at each other trying to assign blame for what still seems a surprise to some even though it has been developing for decades.

A heavily indebted city, its economy sagging, its recreational facilities downgraded, its schools under-funded, is no boon for property values. A real estate crash brings a loss in property values for individuals and families and a loss in tax revenues for the city.

Here we have a once grand and thriving city in the bust phase of the cycle. Its resource base — the water that once fueled its economy, from tourism to agriculture to industry — is now a liability, costing millions in cleanup costs to get back to zero.

Land, air, soil, trees, or any other natural resource — all parts of the environment — can be similarly evaluated from a strictly economic point of view. In each case, economic losses are evident.

Lost Economic Value: The question arises: what happened to all of this lost value? If the river once was of essentially infinite economic value and now is worthless or even a liability, where did the value go?

Consider an agribusiness that depletes the ground water supply beyond the point where it could ever recover its former abundance.

Crops had been grown and marketed without considering the price of water. Assuming that labor costs were kept as low as possible while crop prices were the highest the market would bear, some of the value lost by the river was pocketed by the agribusiness in the form of higher profits.

Agriculture uses the vast majority of the water supplied in the U.S. — seventy to eighty-five percent or more depending on exactly how you define and measure it. Residential users pay more than a hundred times more per gallon. (For a dollar, city residents in the Southwest get a few hundred to a thousand gallons of water. For the same dollar, farmers get 40,000 to over 100,000 gallons).

This price differential means, among other things, that residential users are not only subsidizing dirt-cheap water rates for agribusiness, but they are also paying a disproportionate share of the clean-up costs made necessary by pesticide and herbicide contamination of surface and ground water.

Industry tends to pay water rates that are much higher than those paid by agribusiness but usually somewhat lower than residential rates. Though industry uses only five to ten percent of the water supplied in the U.S., its relatively low consumption stands in great contrast to its huge potential to devastate water quality. Dumping even a small amount of toxic waste can pollute a vast underground aquifer or a long piece of river, often irreversibly.

Inappropriate disposal of toxic substances might save the industry what it would have cost to dispose of the materials safely — in many cases, a substantial amount. Again assuming the lowest possible labor costs and the highest possible produce prices, the industry increases its profits by the amount it saved by dumping the wastes in a ravine somewhere. Substantial as these increased profits are likely to be, the amount is certainly far less than the amount of value lost by the river in its transformation from infinite source of pure water to toxic cesspool.

So the economic value lost by the river has gone into past profits for some and present and future costs for the community or region as a whole. Some of the costs were not charged to anyone, but passed to the public (in the form of decreased quality and supply) and to future generations (in the form of deferred cleanup costs). There's still no such thing as a free lunch. The fate of our economy is entwined with the fate of our rivers. The future of our industrial infrastructure is tied to that of the natural infrastructure.

Undermining The Natural Infrastructure

We are accustomed to hearing the bureaucrat's or banker's definition of infrastructure — electric distribution lines, water and waste-water drains and pipes, roads, telephone lines, parking lots — all the 'hook-ups for humans' in their contemporary industrialized manifestation.

Contrast this nuts-and-bolts infrastructure with another kind of infrastructure, the natural infrastructure. It differs little from what is generally termed the environment, but by calling it the natural infrastructure I hope to emphasize the continuity and inseparability of the two terms.

The natural infrastructure includes earth, air, fire, and water; the day and the night; the land below and the firmament above; the rivers that flow down to the sea; all the creeping things that creep upon the earth; all the swarming things that swim in the sea; all the flying things that flit through the air, all the herbs bearing seed. The natural infrastructure also includes human beings, affecting them and being influenced by them in turn.

In your own town, the natural infrastructure includes the air in your neighborhood and the soil in your garden. Look at the past history of your yard and whatever has blown in from the lead smelter or refinery or power plant. Is it healthy to eat your own carrots and tomatoes? If not, is your community likely to sustain any industry that depends on agriculture or thriving natural areas?

Your natural infrastructure also includes your water supply. Many high-tech industries and laboratories depend on a steady supply of pure water for their processes. If they have to put excessive efforts into cleaning dirty water or pay rates that are too high, such enterprises will go elsewhere.

Your natural infrastructure probably includes some acid rain, too, probably generated elsewhere. Acid rain costs you money when it damages buildings, roads, bridges, parking lots. It is also very harmful to the finishes of new cars. (Some car manufacturers have altered their production and transportation practices so that their new cars aren't pitted by acid rain by the time they reach dealerships.) Acid rain is also bad for many crops, peanuts among them. Communities whose natural infrastructure is consistently pelted with acid rain (or dust) can expect to miss out on jobs in industries harmed by the effects of acid rain.

Job-producing enterprises have thus also been producing costs for which no one has been held accountable. Careless disregard for our natural infrastructure has left costs that take the form of used-up or destroyed resources (trees, oil, coal, diamonds, clean water, fish, pretty scenery). Related costs take the form of ruined health of workers (black-lung disease and asbestosis are but two examples); health costs for their families and communities are also common (children with congenital defects and community-wide health effects of living near a toxic waste dump are but two more.)

The costs of resource destruction and adverse health effects continue to accumulate whether or not anyone is made accountable. Everyone suffers higher prices from the destruction or waste of resources which could have been used more carefully or even sustained permanently by better management. The costs of environmentally caused health problems are partly borne by the families involved and partly shared by the whole society as higher insurance costs, more expensive health care, and a less healthy (and probably less productive) population.

For perhaps two centuries, many of these costs have been pushed into the future so that those not yet born would have to pay the long-overdue bill, compounded by neglect, for ravaged resources and carelessly handled wastes. Some of the costs have been shunted to certain sectors of the population which have borne more than their share: members of poor and/or minority communities who have long suffered the costs of having waste dumps nearby, for example. But all of us are now paying for the frequently self-serving excesses of the past. Many now wonder, along with Wilderness Society President George T. Frampton, Jr.: *Why must the public bear the cost of private gain from the destruction of common resources?*

The accumulation of unacknowledged costs is catching up with us and shaping our day-to-day economic realities. The creation of wealth (not to mention the pursuit of happiness) is possible only in the context of a viable natural infrastructure. Or, as a report by the Council on Environmental Quality puts it, a healthy environment makes wealth possible. Once the natural infrastructure is no longer viable, the possibility of generating wealth is gone with it. Once we fill our empty spaces with waste dumps, cut down all of our trees, pollute our lakes and rivers, and fill our air with noxious fumes, what kinds of jobs do we expect our children to have?

Which brings us full circle to a recognition that there is an economic value to having a healthy natural infrastructure. Destroy that, and no amount of roads, telephone lines, and power plants can provide for a healthy economy.

Conversely, an ailing natural infrastructure hinders the creation of wealth. Economic costs of pollution include lost productivity and increased health care costs for workers and others in the affected community. As many communities already realize, the costs of environmental cleanup are staggering. As the agricultural capacity and water quality in an area decline, food, water and other needed resources must be imported from areas not yet despoiled. Eventually, the costs will outweigh the benefits, and the last job-producing endeavors will move out if they can, shut down if they must.

Jobs *versus* Environment makes no sense once you realize that a healthy environment is necessary for a healthy economy. Whether you are looking at a great river or a tropical forest, the degradation of the environment is inevitably followed by the loss of jobs. Sometimes, the process takes generations; at other times, it begins in only a few months or years. But it follows inevitably. Jobs and the environment are inextricably linked. Choosing between them is like choosing between eating and breathing. We need both.

Jobs AND Environment

The Jobs-versus-Environment argument, then, is never the real issue. It comes up frequently, not because it is the real question but because it is so powerful a slogan that even the merest mention of it plays hard upon the public imagination. It is a false issue, a red herring, a convenient distraction to make the discussion of the real issue(s) impossible. In the Jobs-versus-Environment debate, and increasingly in other controversies as well (like housing costs and availability, for example), environmentalists and environmental considerations are made scapegoats for whatever ails the economy.

Consider the example of the Endangered Species Act (ESA), which has been blamed for loss of jobs, higher housing costs, failed industries, and most of the economic ills that have befallen the U.S. in the last couple of decades. The facts show that only a fraction of one percent of projects have been stopped because of ESA considerations. But that has not stopped critics from crying *Spotted Owl!* whenever they wanted to stir up fears and emotions.

Other environmental policies have also been blamed for job loss, even when the loss of employment is clearly related to other factors. During the corporate takeovers of the 1980s, for example, many corporations went deeply into debt to buy other corporations. In order to pay off their loans, many had to cut back operations, sell off parts of their businesses, and lay off employees in order to make debt payments. In spite of the obvious causes of unemployment, many of these same mega-corporations have sought to blame vague environmental laws or over-regulation for the job losses which were caused by their own corporate irresponsibility.

Another often overlooked factor in job loss is the role of government subsidies. Some industries or businesses get direct or indirect financial benefits from the government through tax policies (e.g., special provisions or loopholes) and assistance with infrastructural support (roads and dams, for example). A shift in tax law or an abrupt reduction in government subsidies can shake up an industry which is losing it governmental buffers against market forces. The resulting unemployment is often blamed, not on tax loopholes or government subsidies, but on the twin scapegoats of the age: over-regulation and environmentalism.

Such scapegoating often leaves the underlying causes of unemployment untouched, puts the blame in the wrong places, and discourages positive discussion of what can be done.

The Real Issue

The real issue is how to have jobs (and, more generally, provide for our material needs) without destroying the environment on which we ultimately depend for satisfying these needs. The real challenge is to to sustain and protect the natural infrastructure while still building and using whatever kind of nuts-and-bolts infrastructure we require.

The question posed by this issue is huge. It encompasses everything from technical questions about agricultural capacity and appropriate technology to the philosophical questions about the nature of humanity and the universe posed by utopias for thousands of years. Fortunately, it is also beyond the scope of this book.

I can set aside this question without guilt because it is one that each community must decide for itself. Gone are the days when people could go around seriously assuring each other that the future lies in plastics or mutual funds or fractals or biotechnology. Each individual community can and must decide its own future, or it will risk becoming a waste dump for the bright ideas that no one else wanted in their own back yard.

We have to play catch-up. In order to regain a position in which a healthy natural infrastructure can support wealth-creating activities — jobs — we must both clean up or repair that which we have damaged, starting with air, water, and land, and work to create wealth in such a way that the natural infrastructure will be maintained in a healthy state.

The task is endless, but so are the possibilities. Passive communities can stop holding their collective breath, waiting for some bigshot company to dangle a few jobs and millions in incentives. Active communities choose their futures, inviting certain industries or companies or starting their own. All jobs are not created equal. Communities that set their own speed limits and regulate the sale of alcohol should not hesitate to take an active, aggressive role in shaping local employment as well.

Together, people can mold a future that is safe and sustainable by choosing jobs that make them healthy and proud.

Would you rather be famous for your employee-friendly and environmentally benign factories or for having one of the top ten most dangerous toxic waste sites? For your whitewater rafting and good fishing or for the river that once was so polluted that it caught fire?

Rich white suburbs are not the only places that can decide their own fates and then make it happen. The Institute for Local Self-Reliance (2425 18th St. NW, Washington D.C. 20009-2096) offers a multitude of well-researched ideas for communities that want to do just that.

Even Entity is likely to acknowledge that we have all been irresponsible. Entity is likely to say, "This project is *our* way of addressing the problems we have inherited from the past. Can you do any better?"

This question of alternatives comes up much sooner than you might expect in the course of your own NIMBY campaign. Before you have presented even half of your arguments against the Project, people will ask you what you can offer instead. Your ability to give a credible answer to this challenge is at least as important as your long list of criticisms of the Project.

John M. Berry, "The Owl's Golden Egg: Environmentalism Could Boost Lumber Profits and Prices," *Washington Post*, Aug. 4, 1991; William L. Dwyer, "The Owl and the Law," *Washington Post*, Jun. 25, 1991; George T. Frampton, Jr., "You Have a Dirty-Smokestack Attitude" (Letter to the Editor), *Wall Street Journal*, Feb. 4, 1992; David Hatcher, "Mill Dies; Town Comes to Life," *High Country News*, April

5, 1993, p. 13; Mark O. Hatfield, "Can't See the Forests for the Endangered Species," *Washington Post*, Jun. 12, 1992; Leo Heagerty, "Its No Use Blaming the Owls" (Letter to the Editor), *Wall Street Journal*, Feb. 4, 1992; Edgar R. Jones, "It's No Use Blaming the Owls" (Letter to the Editor), *Wall Street Journal*, Feb. 4, 1992; Ken Kenworthy, "Wildlife Protection Stops Few Projects, Study Asserts," *Washington Post*, Feb. 11, 1992; Jessica Mathews, "The New Dogma of Environmentalism: It is the kind, not the amount, of economic growth that makes the difference," *Washington Post*, Jan. 3, 1991; Mathews, "Green, Inc," *Washington Post*, Mar. 15, 1991; Mathews, It's Not Jobs vs. Endangered Species," *Washington Post*, Jan. 26, 1992; Mathews, One Man's Land Is Another's Pollution," *Washington Post*, Jan. 23, 1992; Mathews, "It's Not Jobs vs. the Earth," *Washington Post*, Jan. 23, 1992; Mathews, Achievements at Rio," *Washington Post*, Jun. 14, 1992; Stephen M. Meyer, "Environmentalism Doesn't Steal Jobs" (Op Ed), *New York Times*, Mar. 26, 1992; Dwight Nickerson, "Jobs Exported to Japan Along with Our Logs" (Letter to the Editor), *Wall Street Journal*, Feb. 4, 1992; Mark Rey, "It's No Use Blaming the Owls" (Letter to the Editor), *Wall Street Journal*, Feb. 4, 1992; John C. Sawhill, "Saving Endangered Species Doesn't Endanger Economy," *Wall Street Journal* (Counterpoint), Feb. 20, 1992.

Chapter 11

ALTERNATIVES

You will learn a lot more about alternatives as a NIMBY activist than you ever expected to. Ironically, it will often be Project supporters or Entity employees who push you in this direction. Their dual strategy of concealing information and belittling their opponents ultimately works against itself and, fortunately for Project opponents, points you toward the best counter-strategy. This is how it happens.

We Are All Parts of the Problem

Entity works to dull people's concern and discourage them from pursuing other options by concealing not only the unpleasant aspects of the Project itself but also any knowledge of alternatives to it. But even as Entity is trying to conceal things from the public, a second part of its strategy comes into play: accusing opponents of being ignorant, uninformed, and irresponsible.

The only good response to accusations of ignorance is to make sure they are not true. As you learn more about the Project itself and the alternatives that Entity would rather ignore, you are frustrating Entity's efforts at concealment and contradicting their accusations of ignorance and irresponsibility. A typical scenario might work out this way.

Entity will try to embarrass you by implicating you personally as part of the problem or by challenging you to come up with a better idea. Don't you use electricity, buy industrial products, generate garbage, and feel safer knowing that convicted felons are behind bars? Put boldly, do you really want to live in a world without power plants, factories, waste dumps and prisons? Of course you don't, claim the Project supporters, so therefore you NIMBYs should bear your part of the social burden by tolerating such a facility in your community.

That's the argument in a nutshell, and though it's a little simplistic, there is a basic soundness to it. NIMBY activists are challenged, in both a personal and a global sense, to go one better than others in the society around them.

Let's look at the personal side first. Perhaps it's not entirely fair to expect NIMBY activists to exceed the standards expected of others in a community, but it's not a bad idea. And, if you don't, fair or not, your credibility will be damaged.

For example, if the Project is a waste dump, landfill, or incinerator, you will be asked to account for your own generation and disposal of wastes. Do you throw out materials that could be recycled? Do you use more paper or packaging than is necessary? How do you get rid of used motor oil, dead batteries, old cleaning supplies, leftover garden chemicals, and other hazardous household materials? Ask yourself the same questions about your workplace — how does it measure up?

In order to answer these questions and then clean up your act, you have to educate yourself. Part of this self-education consists of little more than looking around with new eyes. Focus, perhaps for the first time, on your own trash, marveling at how much packaging material you throw out and reading the scary labels on many common household products.

A second part of your education involves going to the library to learn about alternative products and recycling opportunities and reaching out to the wider community to find out about efforts already underway locally and regionally to reduce the quantity and the toxicity of garbage.

Once members of your NIMBY group have learned to be better examples, you can spread the word to others in your community. With every fact sheet about how terrible the proposed Project is, hand out a second one about what people can do to reduce the community's waste problem. You'll make a much better impression if you have something positive to offer.

Your Back Yard Is The World

While you are gathering information, do a little snooping, a little research, and a lot of talking; change some of your own personal practices, encourage others to do likewise, and learn about community-wide aspects of the problem. You have already begun to tackle the more global aspects of alternatives.

On the negative side, you learn how much garbage even a small business or a home can generate without improving comfort or productivity. You have seen bureaucrats and managers react fearfully to outside suggestions and even friends and co-workers stubbornly resist small changes. You now know how incredibly difficult it can be to obtain the most basic information from a government office or agency.

What once may have seemed to be a simple matter of garbage has now taken on added dimensions as you grapple with waste creation, alternate materials, re-use options, biodegradability, recycling, multiple layers of government jurisdiction and inertia, collection and transportation issues, and the simple fact that most people would rather not think about garbage unless they have to.

On the other hand, you have probably found a great deal of sincere concern and made contact with many groups and individuals who are already working on different aspects of solutions. You begin to visualize what it would take for your community drastically to reduce and simplify its waste stream. And, if it will work for your home, workplace, and community, it will probably work for others as well.

By the time you become involved in trying to encourage broad-ranging responses to what started out as a local problem (the Project), laws, regulations, interest groups, finances, and other social complications are likely to loom as just as large as, if not larger than, the more immediately evident technical problems.

Some of your ideas can be put into practice by a slight change of habit at home or a conscious shift in buying patterns. (Do you really need the lotion in a glass jar, shrink-wrapped in plastic, inside of a cardboard box in a plastic casing?) Others may require the cooperation of local businesses or the changing of local ordinances. Still others may involve national policy or legislation. Your NIMBY group will not be able to bring about such huge changes by itself. But you can point the way and head out in the general direction.

When you sketch out alternative solutions to the problem that the Project is supposed to solve, you will have gone a long way toward achieving the credibility your group needs in order to be effective. And if you are simultaneously doing what you can in your own home and community, you're already part of the solution.

A waste dump is just one among dozens of kinds of unwanted Projects. A power plant is another kind. If your NIMBY group is fighting against a power plant, you will have to evaluate, improve, and defend your personal electricity usage while you are addressing the needs of your community or region as a whole.

Pursuing alternatives to the construction of large power plants need not involve loss of productivity and comfort. Reducing the need for electricity, using it more efficiently, and meeting needs in different ways each can be pursued in countless alternative ways. All have been hot research topics since the mid-seventies, and the technical advances made since then are impressive. The only limits on applying such techniques have been the lack of public enthusiasm and the indirect government endorsement of business as usual. A NIMBY controversy often provides just the incentive needed.

Put your own NIMBY struggle in the context of national energy use, and be able to discuss the big picture. This enables your allies to see you as part of the solution instead of part of the problem, and it makes it more difficult for Project supporters to dismiss you as uninformed, selfish crackpots.

Entity, of course, will shift its arguments as is convenient. No matter what kind of Project it is, Entity will adhere to this three-part charade. After implying that there are no alternatives, then criticizing Project opponents for not presenting any, Entity shifts to a third approach, claiming that there may be alternatives but "time is running out and it's too late to pursue them now." Or, if people still harbor hope for them, Entity will label them exotic and consign them to the circular file next to hula hoops, perpetual motion machines, no-exercise weight-reduction plans, and cold fusion.

All of these tactics represent an effort to avoid a full discussion of alternatives. There are literally hundreds of books, magazines, newsletters and organizations whose focus is to provide ideas and suggestions for alternative approaches. Many people have a healthy interest in these issues already, but there is no motivation quite as inspiring as the thought of a Project in your own back yard.

Waste dumps and power plants are examples of Projects that may be opposed for economic, aesthetic, and environmental reasons. Other Projects you may oppose involve potential negative effects stemming from social or cultural concerns rather than environmental ones. Prisons, low-income housing projects, highway interchanges, and shelters for the homeless are examples of this slightly different form of unwanted Project. Again, fairly or not, if you want to retain your credibility in the debate, members of your group will have to demonstrate personal purity and offer plausible alternatives.

Take prisons — correctional facilities — for the example here. Project supporters will taunt you by asking if you want rapists and murderers walking the streets. When you answer in the negative, they will pounce: Aha! — then you must be in favor of prisons but just too selfish or hypocritical to accept having one in your own back yard.

Your community probably produces its share of criminals, white collar or otherwise. Don't you send them away to be locked up in prisons elsewhere? So why should your own area be immune to doing its share in providing for correctional facilities? If you find yourselves hemming and hawing when you are asked this question — and you will be asked — Project supporters will utter a well-deserved *Gotcha!*

Prisons are the waste dumps of our social system. Not long ago, we didn't want to know where our garbage went after the big smelly truck took it away. We weren't interested in hearing about the yellow gook that oozed out of the ground over in the chemical company's vacant lot. Now as landfill costs escalate and we are finding toxic materials all around us, we are paying dearly for past neglect of this issue.

What we once lumped together as garbage we now realize includes a wide range of materials: some easily re-used, others more difficult to recycle, some so difficult that we would prefer to isolate them and maybe stop making them altogether. Many analysts now suggest a cradle-to-grave awareness of our industrial processes and waste stream. Careful consideration of a given product would begin with its raw materials, follow their processing, transport, and use, and conclude with an understanding of possible disposal options.

One would hope that a society that lavishes such close attention to soft drink cans could exhibit similar thoroughness and concern for people who find themselves on the wrong side of the law. *Get 'em off the streets and lock 'em up* is just as short-sighted and temporary a solution to crime as the all-purpose county dump of yesterday was to waste.

Does this mean that members of your NIMBY group have to become experts on the criminal justice system in this country? For the most part, yes, it does mean that. Unless there is some screamingly obvious reason why a prison should not be located in your community, you will need to be able to discuss alternative options just as you would with a proposed waste dump or power plant.

You might begin by asking who goes to prison and who does not? What convictions are met with prison terms? What are the bulk of prison inmates locked up for? Is this the best option? Should some perhaps be in hospitals, drug treatment facilities, community service or job training programs, or half-way houses? There is usually a much wider range of options available than those Project supporters have considered. Sometimes a comparative look at the approaches of other states or even other countries can provide fresh insights.

All the while you have to face the conflicting views of everyone from those who think prisons should be like medieval dungeons to those who believe they should be run like celebrity fat farms. You will hear from people who would, without question, lock up all drug addicts, or all doctors who perform abortions, or all corporate CEOs, or all trial lawyers.

It won't be a pretty picture. But when your group has learned about the range of issues facing the criminal justice system today, you will already be part of the way toward offering alternatives. When you start asking questions and making suggestions, you have already gone beyond your role as anti-something activists into the realm where, suddenly, things become very complex and simple judgments very difficult. The meaning of the term *alternative* begins to encompass not only a different way of handling waste, using electricity, or labeling people, but a different approach to making decisions as well.

The new dimension present in this more profound kind of alternative is that those affected by a decision now participate in making it. This shrinks Entity from 'Major Player' to 'Villager' and then burdens each 'Villager,' big and small alike, with greater responsibility.

New Ways Of Thinking

Summarizing this brief exploration of the idea of alternatives, your first task is to accept that you bear some of the responsibility for creating the need that the Project supposedly addresses and then to demonstrate that you are doing everything you can to reduce your personal contribution to the problem.

The second task is to offer solutions that would make the Project, as planned, unnecessary. These suggestions may involve ways to cut the problem at its source (reduce garbage generation, reduce crime) or to find alternative ways of handling it (recycling, drug education and treatment centers). They probably will include both community efforts and state and national initiatives.

Members of your group have probably been too busy to notice how much they have changed during the whole process. You probably know as much about alternatives to the Project you are fighting as you do about the proposed facility itself. Public forums now feature a more highly educated public, exchanging ideas that were notably absent from early meetings and hearings.

Project opponents, newly awakened and inspired members of the community, unasked third parties, uninvited consultants, and even Project supporters eventually begin coming up with all kinds of quirky new ideas and angles no one had even considered. Many of these ideas, had they been taken seriously years before, would have made it possible to alter the Project drastically, perhaps even to make it unnecessary.

However, by now, too many careers, egos, studies, and funds have been committed for Project backers to consider abandoning the Project. Often at this point all parties realize that they should have faced the difficult issues and worked them out together years before.

Entity often realizes that it has needlessly antagonized and polarized the community. Recently inspired NIMBY activists realize that they should have paid more attention to the fine print of local politics. Such hindsight only highlights the soundness of the best possible alternative, the alternative that should have been chosen at the beginning: participatory democracy.

We Are All Parts of the Solution

The participatory democracy alternative requires that everyone be involved as soon as a possible problem appears on the horizon — not years later when a few private and public big shots have already sewn up the whole package and await public endorsement or acquiescence. Therefore, your first response when a Project supporter confronts you with the *What would you do?* taunt should be to insist that the local community be involved at the outset.

Various reviews of NIMBY activity in the last fifteen years or so suggest that Entities still do not consider this approach to be a viable option. One recent study of NIMBY controversies concluded that, in general, the sponsoring institutions (what we have called the Entities) have typically withheld important information until critical decisions were made and made no attempts to communicate seriously with locals until serious opposition arose.

One would hope that something short of NIMBY-gridlock would inspire Entities and other planners to abandon their continual efforts to impose fully-hatched Projects on un-consulted locals. If Entities and potential Entities hear this enough times — that they should involve the broader public in devising solutions at the earliest moment — it may eventually be possible for now-warring groups to work in a genuine partnership. Until those better times, however, NIMBY activists are condemned to a more adversarial setting.

Even within the now-traditional confrontational context of NIMBY activists versus Project backers, there is room for negotiation or conciliation. If a NIMBY movement demonstrates over time that it can gain and retain strong community support, amass relevant information, raise funds, and succeed in regulatory agency and courtroom contexts, it may find itself puzzling over an unexpected knock on the door: Entity's legal representative will appear, hat in hand, friendly as ever — and say (probably to your lawyer) — *Can't we work this out somehow?*

This moment may be years in the making. It is simultaneously the most gratifying and the most dangerous moment in your NIMBY campaign thus far. Entity wants to negotiate. This offers the possibility of conciliation, compromise, finding a middle way, a heretofore unappreciated option that meets most or many of the needs of both or all parties.

It also opens the possibility that you can throw away in an instant the fruits of several years of struggle.

The next Chapter explores some of the pitfalls and possibilities of negotiating with Entity.

Charles Piller, *The Fail-Safe Society: Community Defiance and the End of American Technological Optimism*, Harper Collins, 1991. (This analysis of NIMBY activism under another name includes three useful case studies and a good though brief discussion of tradeoffs and conditions.)

Chapter 12

NEGOTIATING WITH ENTITY

Entity has approached you to talk it over. I'd like to encourage you to rejoice, give each other high fives, and break out the champagne. I'd like to, that is, but I can't, because you have entered the most treacherous waters thus far in your NIMBY campaign.

It is certainly an accomplishment to have induced Entity to offer to negotiate, and since this is a victory of sorts, your group deserves congratulations. However, a few hard facts about the Entity team should cool your euphoria a little.

- They have done this before.
- They chose the timing for this break.
- They know why they're doing this, while you do not.

In these negotiations, you will be eaten alive if you aren't sharp.

Negotiations, Entity-Style

To maintain your perspective, remember what you have learned so far in your NIMBY campaign. Every action by Entity is a potential source of information waiting to be interpreted. When Entity hired a new law firm or changed the Project design plans, you saw that as a signal, a tactic reflecting a larger strategy. The same thing was true when Entity managers changed their PR team or withdrew a permit application.

The offer to negotiate is no different. It may reflect a change in tactics or even in overall strategy but not necessarily a change in goals. It doesn't mean that you have won.

Always ask *why?* It is important to figure out why Entity strategists have suddenly suggested negotiations. There are many possible reasons.

Entity may be trying to get specific information from you. It may suspect that your group knows about certain things that could harm its cause considerably. Without asking you directly or waiting to find out the hard way, it may be using the guise of negotiations to probe your representatives. Often, a NIMBY group has a great deal of information but is not aware how important some of it may be. Entity may know that you have a certain fact but not know if you realize how useful it could be.

In order to avoid making Entity's job easier, do not give out any information — facts, tactics, or even opinions — in a negotiating session. In the early phases of the negotiations, instruct your representatives to listen, not talk. They can bring back Entity's pitch to your whole NIMBY group, where you can decide on a response under less pressure. At a later time, you may decide to trade information for something from Entity — information, documents, or some other clear gain. Remember that information can be very valuable, and do not give it out except as part of an explicit tit-for-tat.

In other cases, Entity negotiators may be involved in a more general fishing expedition — an attempt to find out more about who your most influential members are, the ways in which your group is most vulnerable, or the tactical surprises you may be preparing. Your own representatives must resist all impulses to brag about your contacts, drop hints about upcoming events, or give out any information, however trivial it may seem at the time. A full report of each negotiating session should be brought back to the wider NIMBY group and discussed before an official response is prepared.

Sometimes, Entity's offer to negotiate is an attempt to mislead your group, or to plant some false or misleading information. If you take the bait, Entity may succeed in distracting you or diverting your group away from some very effective actions. An Entity representative may casually suggest, for example, that *X* has hurt them a great deal but *Y* doesn't bother them at all. (This probably means that the reverse is true.) Listen to their claims, but do not share your views with them or confirm or deny their suppositions.

In general, Entity will neither tell you the real reason it initiated negotiations nor reveal which of your actions are really hurting them. It may be especially eager to conceal the fact that some particular NIMBY tactic has it very worried, because it knows that such a revelation would provide priceless information to you. Your group should be equally wary of unintentionally giving Entity similarly useful information.

Even if Entity's first overture seems casual or even off-hand, there is nothing accidental about it. Its timing probably has been thoroughly calculated. Entity representatives may engage you in negotiations at any time in order to stall you. It may be tempting to shift your focus suddenly away from hearings and regulatory agencies and toward talks. In fact, if the negotiations are not quickly resolved or ended, it may prove nearly irresistible to do so. Unproductive discussion and speculation about ongoing negotiations can take up countless hours of *your* precious time. This may be the precise reason that Entity approached you.

Though offers to negotiate early in a NIMBY campaign are rare, they are not unheard of. Early contact may be a sign that your group is on to something good (i.e., threatening to Entity) and Entity wants to head you off at the pass, derailing your efforts before you realize how effective they are. Early offers to negotiate may indicate that Entity is trying to offer you some meaningless concessions before you realize how good your chances are or before you learn more devastating information about Entity operations. Entity may know, for example, that it is about to be indicted for massive violations of environmental regulations at another facility. Entity knows that news of such a development will weaken its credibility and local bargaining position considerably. So, before the news hits the fan, Entity's team wants to cut some kind of a deal with Project opponents.

Whatever the precise motives, offers for early talks are usually a sign that you are doing something very right. Carry on, full speed ahead, while attending Entity-initiated talks and doing little but listening carefully and asking a few questions.

More often than not, Entity will make its first offer to negotiate when you are well into your NIMBY campaign and on the eve of some important event. This event might be the opening of a hearing, the beginning of a trial, or a filing deadline of some kind. Entity then uses the deadline as a lever to pressure your representatives to lose their cool, slip up, reveal information, feel pressured to exceed the role of listener that they agreed to play, or, perhaps, even make arrangements under pressure that they are not authorized by your NIMBY group to make.

If yours is like most NIMBY groups, you are always short on funds and always have too much to do. Negotiations, new to you, difficult, and time-consuming, will be a big deal for your group. Therefore, Entity can try to stretch your resources and your nerves to the breaking point by engaging you in long, drawn-out, frustrating negotiations. Meanwhile, your group may end up dropping some other actions that had Entity very nervous indeed.

Entity managers never put all of their eggs in the same basket, but they'd love for you to do so. And if they can arrange to hold the basket for you, all the better. Dropping everything to engage in fruitless negotiations does exactly that.

Negotiating with any Entity team is a tough assignment. Send members who are cool-headed and firm. If there is a trusted, experienced negotiator among you, send that person along as part of your team. Whomever you send, however, make sure that neither your NIMBY group nor its representatives ever makes any decision under pressure. Much of the pressure you feel will have been created or intensified by clever psychological warfare on the part of Entity. And most of the deadlines and other absolutes which Entity uses to flex its muscles are much more flexible than Entity reps let on.

As your NIMBY group surely recognizes by this stage in the game, Entity is powerful and adept at using its power. But it, too, has limitations and specific needs. If you can begin to understand these limitations and needs, the negotiations process will make a lot more sense to you.

For example, if Entity is a company whose primary source of revenues is building waste incinerators, it will not make any money unless it can build an incinerator, period. That fact sets certain limits on its negotiations. Entity might agree to building a small incinerator, or a faraway one. It might offer to build a softball field or contribute to the volunteer fireman's squad. But it's not going to agree to set up a giant recycling center to replace the proposed incinerator. A government agency in charge of waste disposal, on the other hand, might agree to exactly that.

Do some background research and listen carefully; you may be able to see the situation from Entity's perspective. If you can do this, both Entity's next move and your best counter-move become obvious, and you are on your way to becoming a formidable negotiator.

Preparation for Negotiations

Entity's initial offer to negotiate may catch your group off-guard — that's to be expected. But there is no excuse for being unprepared for the rest of the negotiations.

First, draw up a list of your group's priorities and goals, much as you did when the group first formed. What is most important to achieve? Which goals are non-negotiable? What are you willing to give up in exchange for real concessions? Consider several different scenarios and alternatives, and talk over how your group should react. Take steps to make sure you won't feel quite so raw when unexpected situations develop during the actual negotiations. Develop a list of alternatives and supplementary demands, so that you are not just passively reacting to Entity's deft moves.

Once you have clarified and reaffirmed your own goals, keep reminding yourselves of them. Focus on getting what you want in the negotiations. Do not be distracted by efforts to change your opponents' values or opinions. Attacking Entity's values will not help your cause, whereas convincing them of the reasonableness of your goals may. Also avoid childish attempts to get revenge or make Project supporters look stupid or foolish. Such attempts will not help you achieve your goals and may poison the negotiating atmosphere.

It may seem odd to be told to remember your goals. How could you forget them, after months or years of fighting for them? Unfortunately, it happens all too often.

Shifting attention, even temporarily, from fighting against a Project to negotiating with Entity can rattle the mind. This is partly because the significance of negotiation is easily misperceived by NIMBY activists. Negotiation, to paraphrase Winston Churchill, is not the end of your struggle. It is not even the beginning of the end, but it may be the end of the beginning.

Negotiation is just another part of the NIMBY process, a continuation of what you have been doing all along in public hearings, regulatory agencies, and courts. If you take this to heart, you may be able to avoid the sudden mental paralysis that often seizes NIMBY activists when they sit down at the negotiating table.

Entity representatives bring to the table all the same devious tricks they have employed since the beginning of the campaign. They also bring knowledge of and experience in a wide range of more personal tactics specifically designed to confuse and intimidate you without your knowing it. In order for these tactics to succeed, however, NIMBY activists need to forget where they stand, how much they have accomplished, what they want, and how much of it they have achieved.

Little things can make big differences. Consider how important the physical setting of your negotiations can be. Have you ever gone to a restaurant and been given a table next to the rest rooms? Do you remember the constant stream of people going back and forth? The crack of light and clicking of the lock as the door opened and closed?

Now, do you remember what you had to eat? Probably not. It's as easy as that to lose your sense of goals during a negotiating session.

Take an active role in setting up the procedures. Never agree to meet in Entity's offices or in their law firm's plush conference room. You will be ill-at-ease and easier to bluff. It is a psychological disadvantage to meet on your opponent's territory, so demand your own place and time. Invite Entity's representatives to come sit out on the neighbor's porch or in your living room. When they are out of their element, you have the advantage. Their glib explanations and slick sales pitches will sound like what they are.

Settle for a neutral site only as a last resort, and before you agree to it, do not hesitate to inspect the place ahead of time. If Entity representatives really want to negotiate, they won't let demands such as these stop them.

Expect Entity's representatives to make last-minute requests for changes in time and place. This is a standard tactic to shake you up. Don't let it. If you start to act desperate or even worse, grateful, Entity will know that you are putty in their hands. Play hard to get. After all, Entity requested the talks, and it wasn't so they could do you a favor (though they will pretend that it was.)

Do not hesitate to assert yourselves during the actual negotiations. If a session is going nowhere or going badly, or if you feel pressured or confused, simply break it off. You do not have to give a reason. Similarly, if a series of negotiations sessions seems to be stagnated, let the Entity representatives know that you will continue meeting with them only when they have something new to offer. It is as simple as that. Again, you need not (and should not) answer their questions about your reasons for such an action — just do it.

Before negotiations, prepare questions, positions, strategies, and tactics. Then role-play a negotiating session, with members of your group playing both Entity representatives and your own. This is the single most useful thing you can do to prepare for the actual negotiations. It may sound silly to some of you who haven't played a dramatic role since *Cinderella* in fourth grade, but it works.

Choose your own negotiating team, probably two or three people. Never let Entity have any influence over your choice of negotiators. Entity representatives may try to initiate talks on their own with one or two members of your group. Or, they may let your group know which members they would like to see on your negotiating team. Either action is a blatant effort to disrupt your group's leadership structure. It does not matter whether your group has a well-defined, hierarchical structure or a much looser one in which five people talk things over until they come to an agreement. If you allow Entity to choose who they will talk to, the natural decision-making structure of your group will be distorted as the chosen ones take on the special role of being Entity's favorites.

This tactic is an effort to divide and conquer, to sow seeds of discord, and to dictate your agenda by means of controlling certain individuals. Entity's negotiators may exploit differences that already exist among members of your group or exploit the differences they create by treating your members differently. Do not allow any special relationships to develop between Entity representatives and your own. One safeguard against this situation is to send a different negotiating team to each session, without letting Entity know who to expect. This approach also enables your group to hear a wider range of opinions on Entity's negotiating positions.

Never send fewer people on your team than Entity sends on theirs. Entity may unexpectedly bring along an extra person, just to distress you. You can have a group member waiting outside, or you can even refuse to participate if the new unauthorized person attends. If you send a team of two, they should have differing personalities and approaches. This will increase the depth of your negotiations, and enable you to play the Good Guy/Bad Guy negotiating ritual described below.

It is difficult to generalize about how to negotiate, because negotiations can take on so many nuances. However, unless your negotiating team is an experienced one, do not give them the authority to reveal any information or make any deals without consulting your NIMBY group. This limits Entity's ability to exert pressure on inexperienced group members who might easily give away the store without even knowing it. Having to consult your group also gives your negotiators time to think over proposed deals that seem less desirable in the light of day.

Finally, as part of your preparation for negotiations, read up on the subject. There are numerous books and many articles written about negotiating, a few of which you will find in the bibliography. None that I know of are written specifically for the NIMBY activist, but any of them would be helpful for an inexperienced negotiator and well worth the time spent.

At the Negotiating Session

The Good Guy/Bad Guy technique: A standard negotiating ploy which you are very likely to encounter is the Good Guy/Bad Guy gambit. This is also used in interrogation sessions and goes by many other names, such as *Hot 'n' Cold* and *Mutt 'n' Jeff.* Many organizations keep this technique in mind when they choose their two top officers. Think back to high school. If yours was anything like mine, it had a principal who was a quiet, mild-mannered man that many of us thought was 'cool' (the Good Guy). On the other hand, most of us were at least a little scared of the vice principal (the Bad Guy), a large, no-nonsense man with a booming voice who just happened to be the football coach as well.

Entity might use the Good Guy/Bad Guy technique something like the following:

Bad Guy first reminds you how powerful Entity is and how insignificant your NIMBY group is. Entity governs over millions of people or earns millions of dollars a year. Entity has built dozens of facilities similar to Project and has never encountered any opposition or missed a single deadline. Entity spends more on legal counsel in a year than you will earn in your lifetime without batting a single eyelash.

By this time your own group's representatives are beginning to feel intimidated. With only a dozen really active members, $76 in your bank account, and no background in NIMBY matters, your opposition to the Project begins to seem a little pathetic. That's how you are supposed to feel after Bad Guy's performance.

Now it is Good Guy's turn. It is usually a he, but more and more frequently it will be a woman or a member of an ethnic minority, someone calculated to stimulate your sympathy glands. Good Guy comes across as kinder and gentler, willing to see your point of view, sympathetic. He or she will not deny that Entity is very powerful but will insist that it is more or less benign. Project supporters are reasonable, sensitive people who think that something can be worked out. Good Guy will usually suggest that even NIMBY activists know that the Project is really not such a bad thing. He/she will continue to say that, although it would be unrealistic to try to stop the Project, a few concessions might be worked out.

Just when your NIMBY reps are beginning to think that they should grab anything they can get, Bad Guy takes over again. Bad Guy belittles Good Guy's implied offer and insists that The Board of Directors or whoever is really in charge of Entity would never accept concessions. He goes on to say that the negotiators represent the soft-hearted faction at Entity, and implies that if you don't deal now, the rest of Entity would just as soon burn you at the stake. Then he asserts that NIMBY folks could even be sued and be financially liable for Entity's losses due to delays. To bolster his position, Bad Guy rattles off references to successful Projects and defeated Project opponents. By this time, the inexperienced NIMBY negotiator identifies strongly with Good Guy and is having a hard time remembering any of the warnings offered before negotiations began.

Good Guy steps in as the White Knight and tries to see how little can be offered in exchange for NIMBY activists' complete acquiescence. If your representatives find themselves in this position, they are victims of an effective Good Guy/Bad Guy performance. Before they give anything away or make any deals whatsoever, they should retire from the negotiations and clear their heads.

Guarding against the potentially devastating effects of the Good Guy/Bad Guy technique is not difficult if you are familiar with the technique. Instead of allowing yourselves to be sucked into the drama, sit back and admire it. As you let Entity's reps play out their roles, you will learn something of their strategy. If you are feeling confident and want to return the favor, act out your own version of Good Guy/Bad Guy for Entity's benefit. (This can be risky, however: be sure you know what you are doing.)

Other Techniques: There are lots of other ploys Entity may use, and lots of things you can do to weaken Entity's more practiced negotiators. A few will be presented here, but remember that such a brief summary cannot turn you into legendary negotiators overnight.

Entity's negotiators will have a well-worked-out game plan and a specific pitch to use on you. Interrupting their performance can throw them off balance. So, ask questions, say you don't understand, ask them to explain or to rephrase things. This approach can not only disrupt their game plan, but it may also lead them to slip up and reveal things that they intended to conceal. You may also be able to detect inconsistencies or weak spots as you listen to them reiterating what they have already said.

Ask for proof of their statements. When Bad Guy says that the Board would never accept this or that concession, ask how he or she knows this. If one of Entity's representatives asserts that it would be illegal for Entity to agree to a certain provision, ask for documentation of that claim. Whenever possible, insist that Entity's claims be backed up by specific, written evidence. You may even be able to use the negotiations to acquire documents that have previously been withheld. And if you do receive written documents (especially legal opinions) as part of the negotiation process, be sure to have them evaluated by your own experts and lawyers. A legal opinion is just that — an opinion, one among many.

Whether or not the session is being tape-recorded, take notes, even about things that seem unimportant. This enables you to recreate and analyze the tactics and strategies that are being applied. But do not make public statements about the status or goals of the negotiations unless such public statements are a clear part of your own strategy.

Always keep in mind the very real possibility that Entity representatives are secretly tape-recording all negotiating sessions. With current technology, this is easy enough to do and you cannot prevent it without going to a great deal of trouble and expense. Consider two possible tactics regarding taping. One is to enter the room and immediately ask in a loud, clear, voice, "Are you taping this session?" If they are not, fine. If they are, they will record their own true or false answer to your question. This may be useful later if you ever gain access to the tape. They may also unconsciously touch, pat, or look at the location of the bug. Either way, you will get a heads-up reaction from them.

Alternately, your group can cover itself by requesting that the sessions be taped openly. This usually involves each side using a recorder to tape the other's recorder taping the session. But at least you are protected. Consult your lawyer about the taping issue before you decide on a course of action.

Entity reps may attempt to shake you up or anger you by making personal attacks or insinuating remarks during negotiations. Do not lose your cool, and do not respond in kind: personal attacks have no place in your strategy. Never lose sight of your NIMBY group's goals and priorities that you have formulated during calm, measured discussions outside of the tense and disorienting negotiating context.

Entity's negotiators will try to use language that puts their views in the best possible light. Accepting their language is an early and dangerous step toward letting them frame the argument and set the scene. So when they refer to a *materials handling facility,* gently insist on calling it a *waste dump.* If they persist in saying *surface mining,* counter with *strip-min-*

ing. Do not let their use of fancy, confusing, or euphemistic terms soften your positions or tactics.

Throughout the negotiations, Entity representatives will bring up new topics, subjects, or ideas that you did not expect to hear and are unprepared for. They do this for two reasons: to gauge your reaction and, in so doing, sharpen their future tactics, and, second, to try to surprise your negotiators into making hasty judgments or decisions.

Let Entity bring up such new topics, but refuse to discuss or react to them until a future session. This gives you a chance to consider them while you are not under pressure — exactly what Entity is trying to avoid.

On the other hand, do not hesitate to bring up new, unanticipated topics for consideration by Entity's negotiators. You do this for the same reasons they do, and your team may be more successful at it because Entity probably does not expect your negotiators to display such ingenuity or sophistication.

For example, you might ask Entity reps, out of the blue, if they would be willing to consider two facilities, each one-half the size of the proposed Project, instead of one large one. Or, you might suggest that they voluntarily reveal Entity's complete tax returns for the five previous years. By airing unexpected ideas in this way, you are creating opportunities to evaluate their unrehearsed reactions and to put little seeds of concern into their heads about what you may be up to.

As you float such trial balloons, take care not to reveal your broader strategies indirectly or imply that you would agree to a particular concession. Use introductory phrases like *what if... let's suppose that... what would you think of...* in order to make certain that the suggestions are only exploratory. Prepare some of these ideas ahead of time so you can toss them on to the negotiating table at the appropriate moment.

Experienced Entity negotiators have a million ways to make you feel pressured. They may suggest that you are losing public support, that they are about to convert one of your prominent supporters, that the Board of Directors is losing its patience with your group, that an upcoming election might benefit Project backers, that important deadlines are coming up, *ad infinitum*. As with other statements by Entity, ask for evidence, written if possible. Also remember that most deadlines are much, much more flexible than Entity would have you believe. With all its influence, Entity is an old hand at bending rules and regulations. Finally, make sure your NIMBY group is well aware of any real deadlines and prepared to deal with them appropriately.

The superior negotiating position is one in which you know and understand their real deadlines, but they do not know yours.

Cooptation and Tricks

If the negotiations get off the ground at all, Entity representatives will probably make you an offer.

Whenever a NIMBY group makes a deal with Entity and settles for anything short of complete victory, the question of co-optation is raised. In a typical settlement, for example, Entity will compensate the NIMBY group for its legal costs, offer some advisory or coordinating role for NIMBY activists, and modify the planned Project in some way, all in exchange for the group's agreement to end its opposition to the Project.

For some, this progression will reflect wisdom, prudence, and the spirit of true compromise. Others may feel that you have been co-opted, or bought off, in exchange for money, a role on some meaningless committee, and a few insignificant alterations in the Project.

The specter of co-optation is not new. It has led to some rather nasty fights among NIMBY activists who thought they were on the same team. Sometimes when Entity offers a settlement, a NIMBY group splits into two factions, one wanting to accept the settlement and the other wanting to go on fighting. An internal power struggle may occur until one side signs an agreement with Entity while the other splits off to continue opposing the Project. Sometimes the two factions even end up facing each other in court over which has the legal right to use the original group's name.

During this whole spectacle, the public often becomes disgusted and confused over who stands for what. Both groups suffer a reduction in credibility, neither can raise the funds it needs, and both lose public support. This is the kind of self-destruction that makes Project backers jump with joy, because it usually means the end of effective opposition to the Project.

Evaluating when success has been attained is particularly difficult after years of NIMBY fights have frayed nerves, changed lives, and altered the political terrain. It is a good idea to familiarize yourselves with some cautionary tales about other NIMBY negotiated settlements so that you can avoid some of the pitfalls often associated with them.

Keeping in mind problems of co-optation, here is a brief discussion of some of the main kinds of offers you can expect.

Entity May Offer You Something Irrelevant: For example, in exchange for withdrawing all opposition to the Project, it will offer to build the community a softball field, a health clinic, a new public library, or some other innocuous public facility. It might be very nice to get such a facility, but that has no relation to the reasons for your opposition to the Project in the first place. The main result of your accepting such offers may be that you will end up feeling somehow indebted to Entity. This weakens your bargaining position considerably.

Entity May Offer You Something Inconsequential: Inconsequential offers include such things as the opportunity to choose one representative on a fifteen-member board, the setting up of yet another task force to study your concerns, or a ten-percent down-sizing of the proposed Project. Again, such offers, in themselves, present no significant improvements to the current situation and may result only in a less favorable bargaining position for Project opponents.

Entity May Offer Something Unreal: That is, Entity representatives will offer to give up something that they don't have, couldn't get, or didn't want anyway. They may offer to give up all rights to a piece of land that they have already (unknown to you) sold to someone else or determined is of no value to them. Or, they may promise not to do something that they already know regulators will absolutely prevent them from doing.

The infinite variations on this tactic of offering a phantom concession are limited only by Entity's cleverness, which is substantial. Examine every offer as thoroughly as you possibly can, and do not rely on Entity's own evidence as proof of anything. Trading everything for nothing is an excruciating way to end a promising NIMBY campaign.

Tricks: Similarly, the number of tricks Entity negotiators can play on you is limited only by your alertness. If you are contemplating signing a document or memorandum of agreement or understanding, be sure you understand every semicolon. Obscure or confusing wording, legalistic jargon, fine print, footnotes, and even other documents or laws merely referred to in the agreement can be the Trojan horse of your downfall. Everything you ever heard about the 'fine print' is true: you cannot be too careful.

Even after you have researched every possible pitfall and understood and approved a final draft of an agreement, you are not out of danger. Entity negotiators can whisk away the draft copy to be typed up, during which process one or two tiny details of punctuation will be changed to your great detriment. Even if you do not suspect that this has happened, insist on time to examine the final copy as carefully as you did the draft.

This next point may seem obvious, but make sure that the people you are dealing with have the authority to make good on their promises. If you do not take this precaution, you may end up giving away concessions to people who lack the authority to uphold their side of the bargain. Also make sure that the agreement will be binding even if there are personnel or management changes. The president of a company or the head of a commission that you made an agreement with may be gone within hours of the final signing. Or, the company may be acquired by a corporation that is not legally bound to honor prior agreements. You will need competent legal advice to design an airtight document to withstand such tricks.

This is but a brief sampling of the tricks that may be tried on you. New ones are being devised all the time. People spend whole lifetimes dreaming them up. Watch your step.

The Real Offer

Entity may do one other thing. It may make you a real offer. That is, its representatives might offer to give you something you really want in exchange for your giving them something they really want. If your group is in a position to determine that the offer is real, practical, and the best deal you can get, you may want to accept the offer. (All the *if's* here are arguable, so evaluate the offer carefully.)

However, keep this in mind: Entity will offer to give up something only if it is afraid of losing the whole thing. And if Entity is afraid that it may lose the whole thing, your group is in an excellent position — perhaps even close to winning. And if you are winning, why negotiate for something less?

Often during the course of an acutely confrontational NIMBY campaign, well-meaning outsiders, ranging from old friends to professional mediators, will suggest that NIMBY activists and Entity skip the confrontation part and jump right into sincere, productive negotiations. If this approach seems to work for your group, by all means pursue it. Usually, however, such attempts at conciliation are premature because neither side is ready. Why is this?

At the beginning of a NIMBY controversy, NIMBY activists are still focused on the narrow issue of opposing the Project. They do not yet see themselves as part of the situation that the Project is supposed to address, and they are not inclined to devise regional or global alternatives because they have a fire to put out, here and now. Entity, meanwhile, is not interested in serious talks because it has already hot-wired the political process and is not yet convinced that NIMBY activists will ever earn the right to be negotiated with.

The very fact that they are waging a NIMBY campaign changes the context in which it occurs. After a while, new conditions exist. Everyone (Entity, NIMBY activists, the larger community) becomes more familiar with the myriad details of the Project itself, why is was proposed, and how it may alter the community. Both sides are learning something about the other's point of view, needs, and concerns.

NIMBY activists realize that they must do much more than just fight against something. They must see the larger picture and be willing to offer and perhaps help implement alternatives. This is true in both a community and an individual context.

Entity realizes that it cannot just brush off the concerns of community members. Meanwhile, everybody wishes that everybody had been consulted earlier. Entity realizes that it should have talked to people outside of its narrow ring of experts and community leaders. NIMBY activists realize that they themselves have to do more than go to work and watch TV to maintain a healthy (in all senses of the word) community. This is participatory democracy in its best sense, and this, ultimately, should benefit all.

In the critical, early stages of a NIMBY controversy, these conditions are rarely satisfied, and Entity has a whopping advantage. That is where this book comes in. It should improve your chances of reaching the point where you can choose if and how negotiations are to occur.

You have now completed this brief guided tour of a NIMBY campaign. Now browse through Part II. In it, you will find a collection of short examples, anecdotes, and stories, all selected to provide you with hints and insights useful during your own NIMBY campaign.

Geoffrey Aronson, "Antinuclear Sellout: The Co-opting of CASE," *The Nation*, Dec. 4, 1989, pp. 678-683.

EPILOGUE

What if everyone became a NIMBY activist?

It would attract even more attention to both NIMBY activists and the Projects they oppose while at the same time intensifying two trends that are already underway. On the one hand, it would increase the pressure for completion of NIMBY Projects. On the other, it would reduce or eliminate the need for such Projects.

In the first trend, we see Entities changing the ways in which Project siting is accomplished by making greater use of the 'carrot-and-stick' approach. More and larger incentives are offered to communities to induce them to accept Projects. Sometimes, outright grants of large sums of money are promised if the community even says *maybe*. In an impoverished community, such offers are almost irresistible. (The government's attempt to handle its growing radioactive waste storage problem provides examples of this technique.) This is the 'carrot.'

The 'stick' is the use of increased government pressure or power to force acceptance of unwanted Projects. The little stick approach, already in widespread use, is to exempt Projects from laws obviously intended to apply to them. (Projects have already been exempted from the Endangered Species Act and the National Environmental Protection Act by means of riders attached to unrelated bills in Congress.) Such exemptions give Project opponents much less to work with in the legal arena and put Projects on the regulatory fast track.

The big stick approach is not yet common but may become so if NIMBY gridlock threatens. The government may pass state-of-emergency laws, stripping citizens of many of their civil rights and drastically streamlining the red tape that safeguards due process. Under emergency conditions, the usual regulatory maze and legal maneuvers that go with it are largely irrelevant. If the need for landfill space or toxic waste dumps becomes acute, for example, the executive branch might simply declare a state of emergency based on the threat to public health and send out security forces to stand by while a dump is constructed.

The second trend which NIMBY gridlock would intensify is a more hopeful one. This is the reduction of NIMBY-causing problems at their sources instead of attempts to hide them until they become unmanageable. Businesses and industries would seek out ways of manufacturing, transporting, handling, or wrapping their products which do not produce the unwanted byproducts that are by now clogging our collective social and environmental arteries. Governments would establish incentives that encourage rather than discourage responsible practices.

Government could set the pace by reforming itself and becoming a good example of how to carry on rather than the bad example it has so often been. A government that frequently exempts itself from its own laws and only sloppily enforces regulations elsewhere inspires little confidence, much less cooperation or enthusiasm, among those it asks to make sacrifices for the public good. Experts who tell others how to live will never replace the power of a good example.

But the most important aspect of any effort to reduce problems at their source is the involvement, and usually the leadership, of ordinary citizens. People who work for government and private business can work for change from within. Everyone can vote for people and policies that favor tackling problems at their points of origin rather than hiding their consequences in underground dumps and barbed-wire prisons. Voting with dollars by spending your cash at businesses that encourage responsible alternatives to current practices is as effective as voting at the ballot box. We all can help reduce problems at the source by setting examples in our personal lives, modifying our own lifestyles where appropriate.

If everyone became a NIMBY activist, they would have first-hand, irrefutable, up-to-date knowledge of how their government really works. Well-informed citizens are much more difficult to fool than those who are only as close to their government as thirty-second sound bytes can bring them.

Tear the NIMBY cover off this book. What remains is a guide to how your government works, not in theory but in practice. The application of this knowledge is by no means limited to NIMBY matters. Knowledge of how to work in an electoral campaign can also be used to evict a bad legislator or to put in a good one. Referendums can be used not only to eliminate bad ideas or Projects but to initiate better ones. The same skills that you use to lobby against an unwanted Project can also be used to lobby for positive community changes. Instead of waiting for an Entity to dash in with a gift-wrapped package deal, you can design and work for your own ideas of what a community center, a recycling program, a housing project, or a school system should look like.

The skills and insights which this short book — or a long NIMBY campaign — provides can help level the playing field on which ordinary citizens, long at a disadvantage, contend with corporations, government agencies, joint ventures, and other incarnations of power long accustomed to dictating to an ill-prepared citizenry.

During the course of a NIMBY campaign, your understanding of government will be profoundly changed and deepened. Just as dramatic will be the transformation of your view about how each citizen, yourselves included, can be a part of a larger change. As you refine your ability to evaluate and influence the views of others, your self-confidence will grow as your opinion of the value of experts wanes.

What about the author, a self-styled expert who once worked in a NIMBY campaign and is now trying to cash in on the naïvete of NIMBY activists by selling them a how-to book? Why take her advice?

Fair enough. Experts, myself included, should be advisors, not decisionmakers. This book will be helpful in any NIMBY campaign, but it is those affected who should make the decisions.

In the history of the progress of this nation, somebody had to pick the cotton. Somebody had to build the railroads, work in the factories, fields, and slaughterhouses. Somebody had to provide child labor, mine uranium with bare hands, be cannon fodder for war, stand around in army uniforms testing chemical weapons, work endless hours at low pay in fast food joints. Now, more somebodies have to endure the health hazards, dislocation, and inconvenience of Projects like toxic waste dumps and smelly factories. Without some serious changes in the way decisions about such facilities are made, the same anonymous somebodies will be called on again to sacrifice so that others may prosper.

NIMBY activism is not an obstruction but a stimulus to finding lasting solutions instead of temporary and often devastating technofixes. In NIMBY activism, people take an active role in shaping their futures and in running their government instead of letting it run them. That may well be the most lasting and worthwhile result if everyone became a NIMBY activist.

Before you return to the daily grind, remember that the real issue behind all NIMBY controversies is the desire to have a world where no one has to be a NIMBY activist. Your back yard is as good a place to start as anywhere.

Part II

A Browser's Dictionary of Tips and Tricks

ACCIDENTS WILL HAPPEN

Imagine how sorry Richard Nixon's secretary must have felt when she realized that she had inadvertently erased 18 minutes of a critical presidential tape! That's how an Entity feels when some irreversible accident comes along and alters the legal lay of the land. Accidents will happen. You can bet on it. Sometimes you can even anticipate and predict them. (One man who became something of an expert at stalking corporate polluters has reported that in one case, plant employees frequently knew ahead of time when periodic 'accidental' spills were going to occur.) In fact, one way of preventing some 'accidents' may be to predict them a little too accurately in a public forum, preferably the local newspaper. Then, Entity may feel forced to deny that they would have ever dreamed such a thing.

Is there a particular document, of which only a single copy exists, that contains information damaging to Entity's case for the Project? Do not be surprised if it is inexplicably lost. And do not be surprised if it is a government agency that loses it. If at all possible, before they know that you know how important the document is, get one or more copies made in the presence of reliable witnesses.

Is there a particular natural or geological feature at the Project site — a cave, a cliff, a sinkhole, a little stream or spring — the presence of which is especially inconvenient for Entity's design plan? Is there an archaeological site that may warrant extensive (and time-consuming) excavation, or worse yet, status as a historic landmark? Is there a structure (an old school house, a church altar, a factory chimney) that local history buffs might be interested in preserving? Is there habitat supporting a colony of an endangered species in or near the Project area?

If the answer to any of the above questions is yes, or even perhaps, then expect a bulldozer. A piece of construction equipment just being 'stored' on site, will inexplicably fill in a sinkhole or cave in a precipice while being parked. Or, 'careless workers' will plow right through a known (to others) archaeological site. The old factory kiln will be crushed and leveled by a road crew who thought it was just a pile of gravel. Niches of rare habitat will be trampled by 'local hoodlums' seeking a place to kill an illicit six-pack.

Be ready for the destruction of critical evidence and for the sworn testimony that will be lined up to vindicate Entity of any wrongdoing or malfeasance. Once the evidence is gone, it's gone — unless, of course, you have documented it as part of your baseline study (see Chapter 5). Expect the worst of Entity and expect the rest of the legal system to look the other way, or at best, to shrug its collective shoulders. Be prepared with well-documented evidence that pre-dates Entity's destruction of data.

See *THE FISH AUTOPSY; GOING THE EXTRA MILE; GOVERNMENT REGULATORS WILL PROTECT YOU; MUDDYING THE WATERS; NORMAL ACCIDENTS; REST IN PEACE; SET IN (SOFT) CONCRETE; SMILE, YOU'RE ON CANDID CAMERA ... OR ARE YOU?*

Gabriel Escobar, "Bid to Save 2 NW Sites Bulldozed," *Washington Post*, Aug. 4, 1991; J. Madeleine Nash, "The Fox: He Stalks the Wild Polluter," *Business and Society Review*, no. 11, Autumn, 1974, pp. 11-13.

ACCOUNTANTS' TRICKS

If viewed with a careful, critical eye, Project-related annual reports or other financial documents can reveal exceptionally good information.

However, clever accounting techniques can be used to conceal many financial transactions from the layperson, so you may need some outside help with your analysis. It may be worthwhile to consult an accountant to help you understand Project-related documents. Take care to find one who has not benefited from an ongoing relationship with Entity or prominent Project backers. If you are on friendly terms with any accountants, by all means ask one for help. Or, go through some basic accounting textbooks and flip through some of the many accounting journals that a business library will carry. (Also familiarize yourself with the roles performed by the *internal* auditor and by the auditing firm that performs regular *external* audits of a corporation.)

Some financial analysts (Thornton L. O'Glove and David W. Tice, to name but two) specialize in detecting hidden messages or information in annual reports. Unfortunately, their newsletters, directed at big investors, cost thousands of dollars per year. These may be available in specialized business libraries or through sympathetic investment analysts or professors who teach courses in tax law, accounting, and the like.

No one knows accountants' tricks better than accountants themselves. And nothing inspires internal reform like the threat of outsiders coming in to clean house. The possibility of federal legislation requiring accountants to report evidence of fraud to regulators has led accountants' firms and organizations to develop their own sets of guidelines as to the appropriate roles of both internal and external auditors and to set expectations that outside audits by accounting firms should meet. (Representative Ron Wyden [D-Oregon] keeps tabs on this and related issues.) Such guidelines may result in somewhat less misleading financial reports.

It is not easy to gain insights from documents designed to obfuscate, but Project backers will not expect you to have enough sophistication even to try. The potential rewards, in the form of information, are enormous.

See *ENVIRONMENTAL AUDITS; MOUNTAINS OF MATERIAL; NUMBERS GAMES; WHISTLEBLOWING IN THE WIND; YOU BUY THE BEER, I'LL BUY THE BUBBLES.*

Anon., "Coopers and Lybrand Agrees to Tighten Audit Practices" (Associated Press), *Washington Post*, Dec. 13, 1990; Lee Berton, "Accountants Issue Guidelines to Prevent Manager Fraud; Legislator Assails Them," *Wall Street Journal*, Mar. 13, 1991; Alison Leigh Cowan, "Wall Street: The Gumshoe of Annual Reports," *New York Times*, Jun. 10, 1990; Thornton L. O'Glove with Robert Sobel, *Quality of Earnings: The Investor's Guide to How Much Money A Company is Really Making*, (New York: The Free Press, 1987) .

AN ACRE OF PREVENTION

If you are not yet in the midst of a major NIMBY battle, consider ways of taking land out of circulation — tying it up so that it is next to impossible to develop the land in any way. The Nature Conservancy (NC) is probably the best-known organization that does this. The NC acquires pieces of land that it considers especially appropriate for preservation in their natural states and then takes steps to insure that development is prohibited or limited on those tracts.

With its limited resources and specific criteria, the NC is selective about which lands it seeks to preserve, and many great parcels of land will not meet its requirements. As a mainstream, privately funded organization, NC has received criticism from all sides. Some dislike the fact that as a result of its policies and practices, large acreages can be removed from the tax rolls in rural areas where the loss of revenue is a great blow to local governments. Others have accused the NC of selling out to corporate development interests in order to swing deals that preserve only a trivial amount of land. Despite its many detractors, the NC has provided an option for those seeking to prevent certain lands from falling victim to poorly thought out Projects.

There are other ways to attach conditions to, or *encumber*, the use of land. Probably none of them would withstand the full force of the federal government's efforts. (If a national emergency were declared over the need for hazardous waste facilities, for example, many regular procedures would be suspended). But any of them might offer some protection for lands threatened with an unwanted facility. Even if such measures ultimately fail, dealing with them will cost Entity time and resources and give you time to consider other strategies.

See *'TAKINGS' AND THE FIFTH AMENDMENT: PROPERTY RIGHTS; REST IN PEACE.*

Robert Cahn, *Footprints on the Planet: A Search for an Environmental Ethic* (New York: Universe Books, 1978) includes a chapter on the Nature Conservancy and other land trust options; David E. Morine, *Good Dirt: Confessions of A Conservationist* (Chester, CT: The Globe Pequot Press, 1990) describes the author's fifteen-year association with the Nature Conservancy.

ACT LOCALLY

If you are reluctant to depend on federal authorities to enforce existing regulations in a firm and timely manner, do not hesitate to turn to state attorneys general, local district attorneys, or city attorneys.

Mark Green notes in a very useful and encouraging article that state and local officials are increasingly stepping in to fill what he terms a "regulatory vacuum." In the areas of anti-trust law, environmental law (including workplace and health issues), and consumer protection, it is often these authorities who are at the forefront. Jessica Mathews chronicles another hopeful sign, the application of criminal statutes to issues once treated only through civil law.

See *HEADS I WIN/TAILS YOU LOSE: THE PRE-EMPTION ISSUE.*

Mark Green, "State A.G.s Move In: Filling the Deregulatory Vacuum," *The Nation*, Oct. 23, 1989, p. 441; Jessica Mathews, "Energy Policy: Where the Real Action Is," *Washington Post*, Nov. 8, 1991.

ALL THE ANGLES

In seeking vulnerable areas in Entity's plans for the Project, leave no stone unturned. Check out every angle you can think of, and then think some more and check some more. The Achilles's heel can turn up in some pretty unexpected places. Here are some examples to inspire you.

Cranwaste: According to the *Wall Street Journal*, one company was indicted for a potential violation of a 1987 amendment to the Clean Water Act. The company was allegedly dumping extremely acidic cranberry wastes into a Massachusetts water system, potentially harming the Nemasket River and nearby wetlands. It turns out that the cranwaste also kills bacteria and thereby impairs the normal functioning of sewer systems.

Handle With Care: A 1988 article, again in the *Wall Street Journal*, describes a proposed biological weapons experimental area in Utah which was supposedly made safe by multiply redundant systems to insure against accidental release of biological warfare agents. The viruses were to be carried to the facility by way of ... the U.S. mail.

Poaching With Oil: In the wake of a catastrophic oil spill, the U.S. Justice Department accused the oil company of violating the Migratory Bird Treaty Act of 1916 because oil owned and transported by the company (or a subsidiary) killed migratory birds without a permit. According to L. Gordon Crovitz, this meant that "accidentally spilling oil is akin to hunting out of season." It's a little more complicated than that, but this instance does demonstrate that creative interpretations of laws and regulations need not be confined to the corporate boardroom. The Justice Department also sought to hold the oil company accountable under the little-used Refuse Act.

Ice Nine: Snow-making technology for ski resorts has come a long way and uses some little-known methods. Bacteria — *Pseudomonas syringae*, also known as 'Snow Max' — are pumped out with cold air and water to make snow. The bacteria slow down water molecules, causing the water to freeze at warmer temperatures than usual. In case of problems, there are other bacteria which slow the freezing process. Is there any danger from spraying this kind of bacteria around the ski slopes? Who knows?

Assault With Battery: Increasingly, state and local jurisdictions are applying criminal statutes to actions usually considered as workplace safety issues. For example, Mark Green reports that corporate officials have been convicted of homicide (when a worker was killed by exposure to cyanide gas) and of assault with the deadly weapon, mercury.

See *STRANGE BEDFELLOWS DEPARTMENT.*

Anon., "Ocean Spray Faces Federal Charges of Water Pollution," *Wall Street Journal*, Jan. 29, 1988; James Coates, "Bacteria snow fertilizer stirs fears at Colorado ski resort" (Chicago Tribune Service), *Austin American Statesman*, Dec. 16, 1984; L. Gordon Crovitz, "Justice for the Birds: Exxon Forgot to Get a Hunting License," *Wall Street Journal*, Mar. 20, 1991; Mark Green, "State A.G.s Move In Filling the Deregulatory Vacuum," *The Nation*, Nov. 23, 1989; Con Psarras, "Just Think How the Postal Service Handles Packages Marked 'Fragile,'" *Wall Street Journal*, Apr. 5, 1988.

APPLICANT VS. OPERATOR: IS THIS THE PARTY TO WHOM I AM SPEAKING?

The *Entity* proposing a Project may not be the *Applicant* which seeks the necessary permits or the *Operator* which finally builds or runs the facility. At regulatory hearings, it is the Applicant (obviously) that seeks a permit for a Project, whether the Project is a toxic waste incinerator, a landfill, a new manufacturing plant, or whatever. The Applicant can be a parent company, an electric utility, a consortium, or a newly created company, among other things. Entity may intentionally avoid naming itself as the Applicant.

It is the Applicant whose history with similar Projects and reputation is evaluated at regulatory hearings. If the Applicant is a company newly created by Entity, there is no history and little reputation to review. Likewise, if Entity itself is new or if the Project under review is Entity's first foray into a new area, Entity may choose to name itself as Applicant, since there are no horror stories of past bungling or mismanagement to be uncovered. On the other hand, if Entity is an organization with a past, then it will create a new company or organization to name as Applicant so that there is no past to be evaluated.

After the Applicant has accumulated the necessary permits, Entity will award a contract to someone else — the Operator — who will actually build or run the facility. The Operator may have a history of sloppy management of other such Projects. But the Operator is not evaluated by the regulatory agency, so the Operator's history at managing similar Projects is not reviewed.

Operators often have no history. This is because a parent company will set up a freshly named, brand-new subsidiary each time it bids on a new contract. This insures that Project opponents seeking to learn about the Operator's record will find nothing. In order to get a clue about what to expect, citizens have to find the Operator's parent company and then investigate other subsidiaries of the parent company that might be operating similar Projects. Since subsidiaries of the same parent company may be no more alike than siblings with the same parents, such investigation may reveal little useful information. And even if information does surface, one subsidiary's poor record does not constitute proof that another will be as irresponsible.

The reliance on companies without a past is an interesting inversion of an earlier pattern where a company's long, proud history of high quality and community service was a tradition to be proud of. The implications for underlying values are disturbing, to say the least.

There is a further twist to the Applicant-versus-Operator phenomenon. During the permit-acquisition process, Entity (which may or may not be the Applicant) may be assuring Project opponents that it will guarantee that standards are met and accept full responsibility for all future Project operations. But during contract negotiations with the Operator, Entity will often turn around and insist that the Operator assume full responsibility for future problems. The Operator will use the same approach with subcontractors. In the end, if something goes wrong, Entity and all of its stand-ins will blame the fly-by-night outfit that finally did the dirty work.

Different terms may be used to designate the players in your NIMBY project. Applicant and Operator are just two examples of some of the labels that may be appropriate in a specific case.

If your NIMBY group suspects such shenanigans before they occur, you may be able to thwart some of Entity's clever maneuvers, request specific written and binding assurances, or at least cast some doubt on Entity's credibility by publicizing such slippery distribution of responsibility.

See *'BAD BOY' BILLS; DIFFERENT STROKES FOR DIFFERENT FOLKS.*

ARROWHEADS, ANYONE?

A sure-fire way to gain popularity and community support for a dubious Project is to publicize its archaeological, historical, or paleontological aspects. Entity can arrange to have archaeologists from a nearby college excavate a site. Public tours can be offered, the news media can be invited, some kind of permanent exhibit can be planned at the Project itself or at a nearby site.

As far as Entity is concerned, it doesn't really matter whether it's arrowheads, the farmhouse where a famous person lived, or dinosaur bones. Any Entity with available funds and PR know-how will take advantage of these and similar opportunities to demonstrate its community ties and civic commitments. In many cases, praise is due Entity for such efforts. Just guard against the tendency to allow good deeds to mask the overall deficiencies of the proposed Project.

See *MANAGEMENT'S VIEW; A SPOONFUL OF SUGAR; UNWANTED MATERIALS COMPANY.*

'BAD BOY' BILLS

Bad Boys, or *Bad Actors*, are Entities (often corporations) that have a history of violating environmental laws or of misrepresenting their past environmental records. *Bad Boy bills* are laws that forbid the granting of permits to these entities or prohibit government bodies from doing business with them.

Numerous organizations throughout the country are pushing for Bad Boy legislation at state and national levels. If passed, these Bad Boy bills will provide positive incentives for companies wanting to do business with the government to operate in an environmentally appropriate manner. (A Bad Boy bill affecting companies that manage waste disposal facilities was recently passed by the North Dakota legislature.)

See *APPLICANT VS. OPERATOR; ENVIRONMENTAL AUDITS; BEYOND YES AND NO; STANDARD OPERATING PROCEDURE.*

BADGER HOLES

You might hear anything at a regulatory hearing. To illustrate this, I've selected the most absurd example that I've ever run across. I was actually present at the hearing when this one came up, so I will not bother to cite further references.

At this hearing, an electric utility was seeking a permit from a state agency that regulated water quality. The water quality permit was one of many permits that the electric utility needed in order to gain final approval to strip mine an area for lignite (a young, dirty coal). A special team of lawyers and consultants working for the utility was in charge of getting the permit.

At issue was the possibility that mine seepage, runoff, and the extensive pumping associated with strip mining would degrade an important underlying water-bearing formation, a sand aquifer.

It was a well-known fact, conceded even by the electric utility, that extensive tunnel-mining had occurred throughout the general area for several decades in the early part of this century. At least six small companies had done large-scale mining, but records of the exact locations and extent of the underground tunnels were poor or nonexistent.

Local residents, many of whose families had owned land in this rural county for generations, knew a lot about the previous mining activities. Sinkholes — areas where the ground above abandoned mines had collapsed, leaving an irregular depression — were not uncommon, and in some of them, you could see into deep holes underneath. On one person's land, a stock pond had disappeared literally overnight, evidently draining into an old abandoned mine shaft.

Because the network of old mine shafts riddling the area was an obvious threat to the integrity of the mining process and the quality of the underlying aquifer, opponents of the strip mining project thought that evidence of sinkholes in the Project area would be enough to result in denial of the permit.

Several of us who attended the hearing were therefore astounded to hear the testimony of one of the consulting firm's experts. After testifying repeatedly that he had found no evidence of previous mining or underground mine shafts in the permit area, he was pressed about the nature of the mysterious holes that everyone knew were there. What could they be?

"Badger holes," the expert suggested. None of us were sure that we had heard right. When the attorney for Project opponents repeated and rephrased his question, the same answer came back: badger holes, badger holes.

It is difficult to argue against such an outrageous statement. I later delved into the literature on badgers and found that not a single sighting of a badger had ever been reported in that county.

More disturbing is the fact that the badger hole story apparently did nothing to discredit the testimony of this expert witness, one of the two who presented most of the utility's expert testimony.

It is often wise to concentrate your efforts on procedural matters rather than matters of substance. It's difficult to beat the 'experts.'

See *STUDIES AND MORE STUDIES; A WORD ABOUT EXPERTS.*

BAIT AND SWITCH

Sometimes the same action is legal if it is performed for one purpose but illegal if it is performed for another. It may be legal to cut trees and clear land for an agricultural purpose, such as plowing a field or planting a goat pasture, but illegal to clear land for industrial or residential development, for example.

Now, imagine that Entity owns or controls some land and knows that an endangered species currently living on the land will certainly no longer live there if the habitat is drastically altered, say by clearing. It is a simple matter for Entity to have the land cleared, ostensibly for agricultural purposes. That eliminates the endangered species problem by destroying the species' habitat. Entity can then wait for a spell, experience a change of heart, and obtain the necessary permits for the residential or industrial development of the site.

This kind of bait and switch tactic can take many forms. A crew may gain access to your property in order to conduct a safety inspection but once there do informal surveys and exploration. Other versions of this tactic are being invented and applied daily. Many of them are not illegal, falling into the category of loopholes that are very difficult to plug without tough rules about intent.

Probably the best your group can do to counter such techniques is to see them coming and to take steps that will blunt their effectiveness. Baseline studies, even informal ones, may help. Sometimes the bait-and-switch tactic can even be used against an Entity. Its legal counsel will be enraged to see your group successfully apply this technique in another direction.

See *ACCIDENTS WILL HAPPEN; REST IN PEACE.*

BE CONSISTENT

The criterion of success is success, not consistency. "If it works, do it," may as well be the motto of any Entity seeking to carry out its goals. If you always keep this in mind, you are less likely to be confused by seeming inconsistencies in Entity's behavior.

One week, Entity may praise a regulatory agency or government administration for being diligent, open, and thorough because it reopened a hearing to consider new evidence. The next week, the same Entity may denounce the same regulatory agency for stalling, excessive government red tape, and caving in to political pressure because it reopened a hearing to consider new evidence. This may at first seem inconsistent, but that is not the case at all.

Entity is not for or against reopening hearings. It is *for* outcomes that favor its goals and *against* those that detract from them. In the above case, Entity expected to benefit from the first reopenings and suffer from the second. It is bad public relations to announce "We're against the hearing because we think it'll hurt us," so other language is used. 'Thorough' is praised; 'caving in to pressure' is condemned. Lawyers who handle cases like these day after day giggle knowingly at such inconsistencies. You should also learn to take them in their true spirit — as opportunistic moves that may offer you some insights.

See *DIFFERENT STROKES FOR DIFFERENT FOLKS.*

BECOME A SHAREHOLDER

During the 1970s, the so-called public interest movement began experimenting with new and creative ways of trying to influence the policy and actions of corporations. Some of these tactics might be helpful in your group's struggle to defeat whatever Project that threatens you.

In his book, *Lobbying the Corporation*, David Vogel gives a brief history of the public interest movement's efforts, explains the most frequent tactics, and offers a bibliography that is invaluable aid for opposing certain kinds of Projects. The book is recommended on all three counts. Here I will limit myself to a brief summary so that your group can determine whether or not this sort of activism is appropriate in your case.

The public interest movement exploits the fact that, in most large, modern corporations, the owners of the corporation do not directly control it. While stockholders or shareholders literally own the corporation, it is the corporate management that controls its policies by making all of the decisions. Investors (the owners) may have little knowledge of what corporate management actually does. And, until the last two decades, as long as quarterly dividends were satisfactory, investors had as little curiosity as they had knowledge.

By concentrating on the hitherto mostly neglected powers of shareholders, public interest groups have attempted to influence corporate policy, obtain information not otherwise available, and broaden their public education efforts. In order to get a foot into this door, you must either become a shareholder yourself (by buying a few shares of stock) or gain the sympathetic ear of an institutional investor. (A teachers' retirement fund or a union pension fund is an example of an institutional investor.) Increasingly, the people who manage these funds must listen to the concerns of individual contributors about how their money is invested.

Shareholders have certain rights, including the right to introduce resolutions at annual meetings. These *shareholders' resolutions* may be blunt attempts to influence corporate policy, say, by directing management to close a particular factory, improve its occupational health and safety practices, modify its hiring practices to include more women and minorities, or stop making a particular product line. Vogel points out that such resolutions are rarely successful in their primary goals, seldom gaining more than a few percentage points of investor support if and when they come up for a vote. However, these efforts may succeed in other ways.

Substantial publicity may accompany a noisy shareholder fight over corporate policy. Especially if coordinated with more public shows of support, the introduction of a resolution may draw the attention of the whole financial community (including potential lenders and potential investors) along with members of the news media looking for a good story. Publicity itself may hurt the corporation: who knows what the repercussions will be when the public at large hears that PQR, Inc. is seeking to bulldoze a historic church in order to put in a toxic waste dump?

The publicity thus generated may have beneficial effects even if it does not immediately bring about a change in corporate policy. Investors may sell their stock in PQR, Inc., or decide against increasing their holdings. Increased public awareness of the issue may make your group's fundraising efforts more successful. And the corporate management itself may even be a little more sensitive to community issues in the future.

Shareholder resolutions can also call for the corporation to reveal certain information about its practices to investors or even to conduct and make available surveys or studies of certain aspects of its operations. Such resolutions are known as *disclosure resolutions*. If successful, these can provide information unavailable from other sources. A disclosure resolution might, for example, ask what proportion of employees at a new facility are to be hired locally and then trained for particular jobs. Or, it might request information on the disposal of dangerous chemicals that are byproducts of a manufacturing process.

One of the most substantial accomplishments of this public interest tactic has been to initiate and shape public debate on issues that were later addressed in federal legislation. However, as *Lobbying the Corporation* makes clear, shareholder resolutions require considerable time, effort, and resources and should therefore never be undertaken lightly. If, from this brief summary, any of these tactics appear to be a potential tool for your opposition to a particular Project, look into it further. With the help of an attorney and guides like Vogel's useful book, you should be able to decide if you want to make this tactic a part of your overall strategy.

You may learn a lot as a shareholder without even offering resolutions. Just by being a shareholder you will receive, prior to the annual meeting (usually held in the spring), any proxy statements regarding the meeting. These statements explain much of the routine business that will be conducted at the meeting. They may also disclose a great deal of less routine information about compensation and any special arrangements that the company or its representatives have made. Some of the information revealed in this manner may be useful to your group and/or embarrassing to Entity, so don't neglect seemingly dry-looking proxy statements as a source of information.

See ACCOUNTANTS' TRICKS; ENVIRONMENTAL AUDITS; THE HATFIELDS AND MCCOYS.

Frank Edward Allen, "Shareholder's Resolutions Mushroom Since Valdez," *Wall Street Journal*, Mar. 25, 1991; Earl C. Gottschalk, Jr., "Proxy Statements Offer Juicy Tip-offs at Some Firms," *Wall Street Journal*, Apr. 17, 1991; Thomas J. Neff, "Manager's Journal: Shareholder Muscle Cutting Into Corporate Fat," *Wall Street Journal*, Feb. 4, 1992; David Vogel, *Lobbying the Corporation: Citizen Challenges to Business Authority*, (NY: Basic Books, Inc., 1978); James A. White, "Shareholder-Rights Movement Sways A Number of Big Companies," Wall Street Journal, Apr. 4, 1991.

BEHIND THE BERMS

Part of your success in opposing the Project will depend on your powers of observation. Your cause will be helped immensely if you notice subtle things going on in your community, especially in areas in or near the proposed Project location.

Some human activities seem to be watched more carefully than others. People are sure to talk if they see a strange man with land surveying equipment at the end of the street or a group of men in three-piece suits pointing at houses. Important as these activities are, they are not more important than what is going on behind the berms.

A berm is a wall of dirt, gravel, or vegetation, often like a levee, that is erected in order to keep people from wondering about what is going on behind it. The berm may consist of dirt only, overgrown with weeds, flowers, shrubs and whatever other invasive species have colonized it. It may be little more than a three-to-four foot tall lip built to obstruct a clear view from passing cars. In other cases, berms may be twenty-foot high mounds that go on for miles. They may be planted with fast-growing trees that form a solid visual barrier. To give the illusion of dense forest, a barrier berm can be backed up by a hundred yards of vegetation left in place along roadways.

The extent and visible effects of human activity are gently concealed behind well-placed berms. Though, with a few exceptions, there is no law against ugliness, people are often shielded from the unsightly long before similar protection against the unhealthy is offered. So long as visual input is pleasant, or at least not unpleasant, people will tolerate a robust assault on their other senses, including their common sense.

Vast expanses of the countryside have been carelessly quarried for gravel, sand, and other minerals, leaving lunar-like landscapes and often bringing undesirable changes to water quality and supply. But as you drive through the center of such an area, the gravel truck ahead of you bouncing stones off your windshield, you will see no sign of the quarry itself, thanks to an extensive levee-like berm that parallels the road.

Thanks to berms, logging trucks, carrying raw logs whose tips brush the pavement, can pass by all day long as you drive through what the view from the road tells you is a forest wilderness. A rolling, winding tour through the countryside is unspoiled by unsightly strip-mined land and spoil piles because a strategically placed berm, its grassy expanse dotted with wildflowers, gently intrudes. Scrap metal graveyards and chemical waste dumping grounds, gigantic piles of coal, rusty barrels sprinkled here and there, and all manner of unspeakable things that gurgle in the night also rest unperturbed, concealed behind innocent-looking berms.

Take an interest in berms. Look to the side as you drive along berm-lined roads. Crane your neck, listen. Bring some binoculars, a camera. Berms are only the most physically obvious aspect of Entity's campaign to keep your group ignorant as long as possible. Don't help it out by looking at the berms instead of behind them.

See *MUDDYING THE WATERS; STEALTH GARBAGE; WHAT IS THAT FUNNY SMELL?*

BEWARE THE MASKED RIDER

NIMBY activists have become much more sophisticated during the last decade, especially in the use of the regulatory process. Today, Entities must work harder, hire more experts, pay for more studies, jump through more regulatory hoops, and spend more money on public relations and propaganda than before. But, as with warfare, stealth is playing an increasingly prominent role. Entities are escaping the power of regulations by using all kinds of clever ways to place themselves outside of regulatory oversight.

In some cases, a Project can simply be exempted from a particular law. Many surprised people, for example, were infuriated when they learned that a 1988 law exempted the proposed Mt. Graham observatory from the National Environmental Policy Act.

In other cases, jurisdiction over a particular Project can be transferred from one agency to another. The real reasons usually have to do with the expected ease with which permits are granted, while the official reasons range from convenience or expertise all the way up to national security.

Sometimes an exemption is even more complex. There may be a law, for example, that prohibits using acquired federal military lands for a certain purpose. Entity may propose a Project for that purpose on a piece of acquired federal military land. Aha! you think. Gotcha! But you are too late, for several years earlier, Entity had a local Congressal representative arrange for that one particular piece of acquired federal military land to be exempted from the general prohibition against the stated purpose.

How are such exemptions accomplished? Often by attaching *riders*, or unrelated amendments, to bills in Congress. Many times, the bill is a popular one expected to pass without much opposition, and the rider is attached at the last minute by a powerful member of Congress, often one from the district or state for which the Project is planned. Often the rider applies to only a tiny piece of land, or one particular Project, but that is enough to give relatively clear sailing.

Such tactics are as effective as a stab in the back, and are similarly difficult to prepare for or counter. Try to keep track of any pending legislation that might affect your Project, and be ready to launch a blitzkrieg campaign if you catch the rider before a vote. And do not fail to bring it up during the next reelection campaign.

See *BUT THAT'S AGAINST THE LAW; GOVERNMENT REGULATORS WILL PROTECT YOU; THAT'S NOT OUR DEPARTMENT DEPARTMENT; THE LAW OF THE LAND.*

BEYOND YES AND NO

Despite the high cost of elections, referendums, and ballot initiatives, there are some clever and effective ways of using the ballot box without asking citizens to vote a simple *YES* or *NO* on the Project. One excellent example comes from South Dakota.

Construction on a megafill — a huge landfill — was about to begin. Project opponents put an initiative on the state ballot "requiring that all megafills be approved by the State Legislature." State voters approved the proposal. The initiative shifted the responsibility for the decision from the regulatory agencies to elected officials, who were more likely to be receptive to citizens' concerns.

This meant, of course, that if the legislature took no action, the megafill could not go forward. In order for a megafill to be built, state legislators would have to vote specifically in favor of it. Any legislator considering such a vote would then have to stand up to heavy lobbying by citizens who opposed South Dakota's becoming the trash can of America.

NIMBY activists should also note that it is much easier to pass an initiative that merely requires the state legislature's approval than one which, for example, prohibits all megafills.

There are also several proposals in the U.S. Congress to expand states' rights to refuse to accept out-of-state waste. Such bills are often referred to as *Right To Say No* bills.

See *'BAD BOY' Bills.*

Anon., "Just Whose Backyard Is It?" *New York Times*, Dec. 2, 1990.

BID RIGGING

Bid rigging occurs when an Entity which seems to be seeking bids openly on a contract is in reality working to pre-determine the outcome by heavily favoring a certain bidder. Although this practice is common in the private sector, among corporations in many if not all industries, you are more likely to run into it among government entities, because it shows up more where the bidding process is likely to be more public. Government entities are usually expected to award contracts to the lowest bidder that can do the job. There may be some conditions attached to this — the 'specs' (specifications) may call for a U.S.-owned company or a company that uses union labor, for example. Within those guidelines the contract is supposed to be awarded to the lowest bidder. (The idea is that the government is simultaneously rewarding efficiency and spending taxpayer dollars wisely.)

If the government agency involved (or factions within it) wants to control the external environment a little by steering the contract in a certain direction, it must do so surreptitiously and without raising suspicion. It does this by including in the fine print of the bid specs — the detailed specifications of what is needed — some technical or practical detail that it knows can only be satisfied by one bidder, the favorite.

An example will clarify this. Suppose that, for political reasons, Entity wants to buy all of its computer paper from company QWE. The business climate is very competitive, however, and several companies will probably bid lower than QWE. Entity must find a way of awarding the contract to QWE without making it seem that the bidding was rigged in any way.

The procedure is fairly simple. First, Entity finds something unique about QWE — say, it is the only company that will deliver paper supplies on Saturday mornings. Second, Entity works up a story about how the success of its whole operation depends on being able to receive emergency paper deliveries at odd hours. Third, the bid specs are written to contain vague requirements (like 'flexible deliveries') that Entity personnel will later reveal can only be satisfied by Saturday deliveries. When bids are opened, it turns out that the lowest acceptable bid is from QWE, the only company that can deliver on Saturday mornings.

Though the principle is simple, pre-determining a bid award without raising suspicions (or inspiring lawsuits) is an art and a science. In the above example, Entity runs the risk of another company saying, "Hey, we'll deliver Saturday mornings" and disrupting its bid-rigging attempt. The tailored specs are usually much more subtle and sophisticated than the example given here. To see how it's done in real life, read through some court records of cases where one company has alleged that another has been involved in bid irregularities.

Needless to say, exposing bid irregularities in Project-related contracts will not inspire confidence in Entity or the Project.

See *THE INSTITUTIONAL ENVIRONMENT*.

BLACK AND WHITE AND READ ALL OVER

There is an overwhelming amount of printed material available on NIMBY-related subjects. Your group needs to find the most useful stuff first and to avoid wasting time on books that just are not what you need.

Though I have tried to provide some useful tips throughout this book and in the bibliography, you are still on your own for much of the reading that lies ahead. A valuable shortcut in your search for the right book is the book review.

Most book reviews include a brief summary of a book's contents along with some clues about its biases and the reliability of its perspective. A quick scan of a book review can save you hours of slogging through a library's stacks and reading over hundreds of pages of perhaps not very relevant information.

A librarian can help you locate book reviews of current and non-current books, by consulting indexes and using other search techniques. To make sure that you are not overlooking a real jewel of a book because one critic didn't like it, consult at least two book reviews. Just this amount of research alone will save you time and frustration in the long run.

BOYCOTTS

One of the many tactics that your group may consider is the boycott.

A boycott is an organized refusal to purchase goods or services from a source that is doing something considered undesirable. After the 1989 Exxon Valdez oil spill in Alaska, for example, many people boycotted Exxon gasoline in order to express their disapproval of the way Exxon handled the spill. Like many boycotts, this one was controversial because the issue was complex. Some opposed the Exxon boycott because the records of other oil companies, they felt, were no better than Exxon's.

The purpose of a boycott may be to call public attention to an issue, reduce revenues of businesses that are undesirable in some way, or ultimately, to pressure a company to change its practices.

Most of the boycotts we hear about in the news are nationwide or even world-wide boycotts. These are often coordinated by large organizations with lots of resources at their disposal. Some have been effective at forcing changes in policy. If you want to learn more about how extensive and complicated the boycott scene is, check out Todd Putnam's Seattle-based *National Boycott News* or Dana Milbank's article about it.

Your group is more likely to be interested in a more modest local boycott, perhaps of businesses that actively support the Project. A boycott won't be effective unless people know about it, so make an effort to publicize the purpose and goals of your action. Put it in your newsletter, mention it in public appearances, advertise it on T-shirts, and perhaps even picket and pass out literature at carefully chosen sites. A well-planned boycott can perform a public education function in addition to encouraging a business to reconsider its views.

As with all other tactics and strategies, the pluses and minuses of a boycott should be carefully considered before you go ahead with it. Evaluate your group's priorities and resources, get legal advice, and if you decide to launch a boycott, do it right.

See *GETTING THEIR ATTENTION.*

Lynn Duke, "Proliferating Boycotts Turn Buying Power Into Political Clout," *Washington Post*, Apr. 14, 1991; Dana Milbank, "Being a Consumer Isn't Easy if You Boycott Everything," *Wall Street Journal*, Apr. 24, 1991; Todd Putnam, *National Boycott News*.

THE BUCK IS PASSED

Whether we turn to toxic waste dumps, abandoned strip mines, massively contaminated military bases across the nation, or the abuse and near-destruction of the Everglades (and southern Florida's water system), the story is the same. After companies have gone bankrupt, disappeared, or otherwise ceased to exist in financially viable form, it is the government (if anyone) that steps in to clean up the mess. And the costs of fixing up the problems fall to the taxpayers, ratepayers, and other ordinary citizens.

For example, a *Wall Street Journal* article reports that water and sewer rates in Boston increased by thirty-nine percent between 1990 and 1992 as rate payers were asked to pay for cleaning up Boston harbor. In general, according to the same article, "[the] costs of clean water are making it a scarcely affordable luxury for the poor in some U.S. cities."

In the case of private companies, profits have long been channeled into executive salaries, stockholder dividends, or new fast-buck enterprises. With government Entities, (like the military, acknowledged by some to be the largest single source of inappropriately-disposed-of hazardous wastes), the story differs slightly. They go from community to community looking for new sites to move the problem to, promising that this time they'll do it right.

Examples of fulfilled promises are so rare and cases of botched or mismanaged Projects so plentiful, that even the most enthusiastic backers of new, improved Projects (*It's not like the old days!* they'll croon) will be hard put to come up with any genuine instances of proper behavior. Mining an industry's (or an agency's) sordid history will not undo its mistakes, but it can help those in the present to better prepare for the future.

See *GOVERNMENT REGULATORS WILL PROTECT YOU*; *PROMISES TO KEEP.*

Anon., "Report Calls Military Nation's Worst Polluter" (Associated Press), *New York Times*, Mar. 17, 1991; Bill Richards and Andy Pasztor, "Special Invoice: Why Pollution Costs of Defense Contractors Get Paid By Taxpayers," *Wall Street Journal*, Aug. 31, 1992; Keith Schneider, "Toxic Cleanup Stalls Transfer of Military Sites," *New York Times*, Jun. 30, 1991; David Stipp, "Poor Pay a Big Price To Drink Clean Water," *Wall Street Journal*, Jan. 15, 1992.

BURNING TOXIC WASTE

If you're confronted with a plan to burn (they call it incinerate) toxic or medical wastes, expect the pro-Project propaganda to repeat the usual claims. Project supporters will declare that incineration of such wastes is well understood and poses no risks (or, they might say, "no significant risks") to human health. There are serious problems with this claim.

A toxic waste incinerator (like other combustion systems, from your car engine to a coal-fired power plant) is sensitive to variations in procedure. Sometimes unsatisfactory results are impossible to ignore, as when a supposedly inert pile of incinerator ash exploded. (The incinerator had been operating at a lower temperature than that necessary to destroy — i.e., turn into gaseous form — the dangerous chemicals.) At other times, operational errors become totally invisible, as when a container of dioxin (one of the most toxic materials known) was accidentally burned with other wastes and vented into the atmosphere.

Many existing toxic waste incinerator operators have less-than-reassuring records of taking care of the hands-on details that are necessary to bring actual operations anywhere near the level of safety claimed by proponents. Past violations have included failures to test samples of chemicals before mixing them together for incineration and loading the incinerators improperly, thereby increasing the dangers of a catastrophic accident and the likelihood of hazardous atmospheric emissions and solid wastes (ash).

Incineration of toxic and medical wastes — the latter is still not adequately regulated by the federal government — can, under very carefully controlled conditions, reduce the toxicity of materials being handled. However, in actual operations, these carefully controlled conditions are very difficult to maintain. Air emissions and solid wastes may actually be much more dangerous than claimed.

The difference between what can be achieved and what will usually occur during regular operations is critical in considering the probable effects of many Projects. Entity representatives will continually claim that the regulations require this and that; be sure that your questions and arguments bring them back to a discussion of historical performance and realistic operating conditions.

See *BUT THAT'S AGAINST THE LAW; GOVERNMENT REGULATORS WILL PROTECT YOU; MEDWASTE AS A TROJAN HORSE; TURNING THE HEAT UP; WHAT IS THAT FUNNY SMELL?*

Jeff Bailey, "Concerns Mount Over Operating Methods Of Plants That Incinerate Toxic Waste," *Wall Street Journal*, Mar. 20, 1992.

BUT THAT'S AGAINST THE LAW

Sometimes people think that just because there is a law against something, they are protected. I have seen Entity representatives successfully soothe and silence a roomful of angry NIMBY activists simply by reciting laws and regulation numbers, as if the words themselves provided insurance against all possible problems. Some laws spell out in no uncertain terms protection for endangered species; others still seem to state unequivocally what can and cannot be done to a public park; others give local governments jurisdiction or veto power over Projects proposed by outsiders. Numerous other legal and regulatory obstacles can appear to stand between a planned Project and its completion.

Unfortunately, the mere presence of a law does not work any better with personnel matters or pollution than it does with muggings or vandalism. In order to explain this and add an unpleasant dose of reality, I will give a short review of a few things that they don't tell you in a civics textbook.

In theory, a law has a life cycle something like this. An elected Congress (the *legislative* branch), passes a law, which is then sent to the appropriate regulatory agency (part of the *executive* branch), whose top people are appointed by the president. The regulatory agency translates the law (e.g., reduce particulate emissions by ten percent) into rules and regulations (e.g., at a type *A* facility, particulate emissions slall not exceed *x* tons per hour for more than three hours out of every twenty-four.)

Regulations are very specific and may involve specifying certain alternatives (for example, equipment *p*, *q*, or *r* must be used) or setting minimum or maximum levels. After the regulations have been written and approved, the regulatory agency coordinates the system of monitoring, licensing, and enforcement. If the enforcement becomes difficult or nasty, the Department of Justice, the part of the executive branch which is charged with enforcing the law, may be brought in to help. If the enforcement action involves lawsuits, criminal penalties, or the like, the case may be taken to court (the *judicial* branch of government.)

This process is especially vulnerable to political or bureaucratic manipulations at two junctures: first, in the transition from law to regulation, where subjectivity and obstructionism come to play, and second, in the enforcement of the regulation, where the practical differences between regulation and application can become more than apparent.

There are many different ways in which a law can effectively be rewritten while it is being transformed into regulation. The process can be fast, or it can be so slow that it never completed. (There are numerous examples of the latter situation. Drugs have gone unevaluated, emissions standards for hundreds of chemicals have remained unwritten, and dozens of species have gone extinct while waiting to be listed as endangered.) The regulations can be very strict in interpreting the law or very loose. And by shifting emphasis, the regulations can actually change the sense of the law.

Perhaps the best example of the ability of the executive branch to subvert Congressional intent through the regulation-writing process is President Bush's Council on Competitiveness, set up in 1989 supposedly to resolve interagency disagreements about regulations.

Under the Reagan Administrtion, the Office of Management and Budget was authorized to evaluate the cost-effectiveness of proposed regulations before regulatory agencies wrote their final versions. Reagan's executive order opened the door for economic considerations to influence the translation of Congressional legislation into actual regulations. But it was President Bush's Council on Competitiveness, chaired by Vice President Dan Quayle, that became the crucible where critical segments of regulatory law were actually worked out.

The Council on Competitiveness has made a significant impact on the way regulations are written and implemented. According to Bob Woodward and David Broder:

- The Council has quietly and imperceptibly interceded in many regulatory controversies, often (and intentionally) without leaving so much as a "fingerprint" record of its activities.
- Vice President Quayle claimed to possess a *carte blanche* from President Bush to intervene in the regulation-writing process ... whenever he thought it necessary.
- The latitude given the Council on Competitiveness allowed the Bush Administration to circumvent the historically and legally sanctioned right of interested parties to make public comment and on-the-record arguments about proposed regulations.
- The Council on Competitiveness became one of those "informal, back channels outside public or congressional purview" which keep policy decisions in the hands of insiders and, to many critics, violate the principle of open government.

A prominent critic, Michael Weisskopf, gives numerous examples of how the Council on Competitiveness gave big breaks to many industries, usually by allowing them to avoid troublesome and costly regulations that were the specific intent of Congress. In one case, the Council re-inserted wording "easing expensive pollution control requirements for electric utilities," after Congress had explicitly rejected such wording three times.

In general, the Council on Competitiveness acted 1) specifically to override the clear intent of Congressional legislation, 2) to give breaks to industries to exempt them from laws intended to protect the public's health and safety, and 3) to bring about a dramatic reduction of citizens' input into the writing of regulatory law. It would be difficult to find a better example of the vulnerability of Congressional legislation to regulatory tampering. Many of the issues raised by the Council will eventually be argued in court. But until the judicial system works its way through a long, slow appeals process, the work of the Council will stand.

Desire to control and direct the process that shapes legislation and translates it into regulation is by no means a characteristic peculiar to Republican administrations. In his first months in office, President Clinton took steps to disband the Council on Competitiveness and to replace the Congressionally-mandated Council on Environmental Quality with a White House Office on Environmental Policy. Ostensibly intended to highlight and coordinate environmental policy, these moves may also make it easier for a new administration to dilute environmental law and use selective enforcement of regulations for partisan political ends.

As far as enforcement is concerned, a regulatory agency can be lax in enforcement of a certain set of regulations because its personnel are not enthusiastic about them to begin with. Or, the failure to enforce can be the result of lack of funding. If Congress fails to appropriate sufficient funds to an agency, enforcement is not possible. Sometimes this situation is purposeful, enabling Congress to tell one constituency that a tough law was enacted and tell a second constituency that there is no way for the law's provisions to be enforced. For a brief but scathing description of some of the consequences of understaffed and underfunded regulatory agencies, see the comments of Bruce Stutz's on EPA and Superfund.

In sum, discretion is the name of the game. Especially when the legislature and the executive are controlled by different political parties, it is not difficult to see that the enforcement branch of the government (the executive) might not be especially eager to carry out the laws passed by the legislative branch (the Congress).

Given the broad discretion with which regulations are actually applied and the limited funding for extensive enforcement activities, it is not surprising that many regulations are hardly enforced at all or that most monitoring and sometimes even testing is done by those being monitored and tested. Many regulatory activities are minimally carried out, while most of the effort goes into those few areas that have been singled out by political pressure as critical.

Congress has reacted to lackadaisical enforcement and loosely written regulations by writing more specific and detailed legislation. This requires similarly detailed regulations which require much time and effort to promulgate.

Years of waiting, reams of paper, expensive days in court, and concerted political pressure lie between a law as written and a law enforced. Keeping this in mind will help you view your task much more realistically.

See *DAMAGE CONTROL AND FOIA; GOVERNMENT REGULATORS WILL PROTECT YOU.*

Ann Devroy, "Clinton Announces Plan to Replace Environmental Council," *Washington Post*, Feb. 9, 1993; Timothy Nash, "Clinton Establishes White House office on Environment," *Wall Street Journal*, Feb. 9, 1993; Robert Pear, "U.S. Laws Delayed By Complex Rules and Partisanship; Many Deadlines Missed, *New York Times*, Apr. 28, 1991; Michael Weisskopf, "Rule-Making Alters Reach of Clean Air Act," *Washington Post*, Sep. 21, 1991 and "Quayle Council Official Had Role in Acid Rain Rule Action; Hubbard Also Owns Stock in Electric Utility," *Washington Post*, Dec. 6, 1991; Bob Woodward and David S. Broder, "Quayle's Quest: Curb Rules, Leave 'No Fingerprints': Council on Competitiveness Is Back Channel for Business," *Washington Post*, Jan. 9, 1992; Bruce Stutz, "Environment: Cleaning Up," *The Atlantic*, Oct. 1990, pp. 46-50.

CLEAN-UP JOBS DEPARTMENT

The next time someone complains to you that it's just too costly to meet stringent standards and clean up the environment, tell them about the industry that such cleanup has generated. As Bruce Stutz observes: "In an age marked by an overabundance of waste, regulation, and litigation, here is an industry that thrives on all three."

Stutz notes that the pollution-abatement-and-control industry, known as PAC, is growing at 20 to 30 percent a year and in one year (1988) took in almost $100 billion and created almost 3 million new jobs. Timothy E. Wirth, former senator from Colorado, recently estimated that the 70,000 businesses in the domestic environmental services industry have generated $270 billion in sales, $22 billion in corporate profits, $76 billion in federal, state, and local revenues, and some 3.5 million jobs. Jobs in demand range from specialized real estate appraisers to laboratory technicians to hydrogeologists.

Some believe that the twelve-nation European Community (EC) will provide unparalleled opportunities for U.S. companies. As Patrick Oster has observed, the EC has been passing environmental legislation at a frantic pace. American companies, with twenty years or so of experience in responding to similar domestic legislation, are particularly "well positioned to take advantage of the opportunity" created by these recent EC initiatives. These opportunities are nothing to sneeze at. Oster notes that Western Europe's expenditures for environmental services are expected to reach $171 billion by the year 2000.

PAC industry growth is the economic silver lining to the environmental cloud that some have seen only as a threat to the economy. Point this often-ignored fact out when someone challenges you with the *jobs versus environment* argument.

John Burgess, "Seeking Pollution solutions: Environmental Services Industry Foresees Boom Times Ahead," *Washington Post*, Jun. 14, 1990; Barnaby J. Feder, "Wringing Profits from Clean Air," *New York Times*, Jun. 18, 1989; Rose Gutfeld, "Pure Plays: For Each Dollar Spent on Clean Air Someone Stands To Make a Buck; Alternative Fuels May Grow into Major New Industry as Polluters Change Ways," *Wall Street Journal*, Oct. 29, 1990; Scott McMurray, "Cleaning Up: Chemical Firms Find That It Pays to Reduce Pollution at Source; By Altering Processes to Yield Less Waste, They Make Production More Efficient," *Wall Street Journal*, Jun. 11, 1991; Patrick Oster, "EC Rushing To Clean Up Environment: U.S. Firms Benefiting From New 'Green' Laws, "*Washington Post*, Jun. 6, 1992; Bruce Stutz, "Environment: Cleaning Up," *The Atlantic*, Oct. 1990, pp. 46-50; Timothy E. Wirth, "Easy Being Green — Lighten Up, Loggers — Environmentalism Actually Creates Jobs," *Washington Post*, Oct. 4, 1992.

COMMON SENSE NEED NOT APPLY

Remember all those things in the 'common sense' category that your mother always wished you had and you finally got? Well, forget them. The sooner you get rid of your load of common sense, the faster you will begin to understand how laws, regulations, courts, and bureaucracies really work.

Consider the idea of 'prime farmland.' Some regulations limit development on prime farmland or provide for special measures seemingly intended to protect it as one of our country's precious resources. A closer look at the regulations, however, will reveal that this protection is actually quite limited.

What is prime farmland? One would think that the term refers perhaps to soil types that are exceptionally good as farmland, to land that farmers generally agree is very fertile, or to something of that nature. But in many cases, lands like those just described are not considered legally to be prime farmland at all and so receive no protection from prime farmland clauses.

How can this be? Prime farmland is defined by use, not physical characteristics. That is, land will meet the legal definition of prime farmland only if it has been used to grow certain specified crops for, say, five of the last ten years. If it does not meet this criterion, then no matter how fertile the soil, it gets no protection. Similarly clever definitions are sprinkled throughout regulatory law, rendering much of it almost worthless.

Take the treatment of hazardous waste as another example. Common sense might dictate a process along these lines: medical people or scientists would identify and inventory the sorts of materials which are hazardous to life. Then a technical person would write up rules that would apply to the handling of such materials. Right? Wrong.

From the beginning, some materials and wastes from certain sources have been defined as non-hazardous, no matter what they contain. Such wastes are specifically exempted from the category of hazardous waste as far as the law is concerned.

In cases involving these substances, even if you can find compound *Q* in a pile of waste and find in reference books that compound *Q* is, in fact, highly toxic, you may also find that, in relevant legislation, the regulations applying to hazardous waste do not apply to compound *Q*.

Occasionally, the courts uphold a common-sense interpretation, as when the Supreme Court recently rejected claims by the mining industry that mining waste should not be considered subject to hazardous waste regulations. But exemptions, exceptions, loopholes, and other special considerations are likely to apply in ways that a normal human being would never expect. Assume the worst, and if somehow common sense does apply, be pleasantly surprised.

See *NUMBERS GAMES; THE RATINGS GAME; A ROSE IS A ROSE IS A ... TULIP!; TESTING, TESTING ....*

Anon., "Mining Not Exempt From Waste Rules: High Court Rejects Industry's Appeal," *Washington Post*, Jun. 26, 1990.

THE CREDIBILITY GAP

A stubborn public often finds it impossible to believe that Entity's representatives — lawyers, experts, prominent citizens, university folks, community leaders, businesspeople — would lie, cheat, or steal. Their credibility as the overwhelmingly white, male mainstream — the so-called backbone of this country — is very difficult to shake, even in the face of overwhelming evidence.

On the other hand, the reverse is true of your group. No matter how well-informed you are, how well you document your arguments, how neatly you dress, how respectful your silence is when you know you are being lied to in public — many people have lingering doubts that you could really be right when so much of the establishment is aligned against you.

While it takes a near-avalanche of evidence to shake people's confidence in Entity, often a mere snowball — sometimes just an ice crystal — is enough to undermine severely the credibility that your group has built up. And Entity knows how to throw snowballs while making it look like they came from somewhere else. Expect to deal frequently with nasty rumors of 'unknown' origin. The rumors may run the gamut, but usually they focus on the reputed personal habits of prominent group members — those who Entity thinks are the leaders or the brains of the operation. Some of the more interesting snowballs are the following.

Outside Agitator Theories: You will hear that your group is run by one or two outside professionals who came into town just to stir up trouble, presumably just for the fun of it. (Anyone who attends regulatory hearings just for the fun of it needs to have his or her head examined). Some versions of this rumor also claim that your group is receiving large amounts of money from some mysterious source (anything from the Communist Party to the Moonies.)

In some cases, Entity may actually believe that these rumors are true. This reflects two things about how Entity backers think. First, they cannot believe that any plain old citizens could be critical enough, on their own, to doubt the glittering promises and benefits the Project offers. And second, they cannot believe that people will do so much work (the research, the organizing, the newsletter preparation, the coordinating, the fundraising and on and on) without getting paid for it. Since lawyers, accountants, consultants, and other experts seem to agree with the highest bidder, people like NIMBY activists who 'call it as they see it' for free seem incongruous (and more than a bit suspicious) to them.

When damaging claims are made publicly, take the opportunity to refute them publicly, if indirectly. At a news conference, you can introduce a few (keep it to a very few) group members and briefly mention that they were born and raised in the county, have lived there ten years, or have sent three generations of McGillicutties to local schools.

Some members of your group probably *are* relative newcomers, having chosen your area for its schools, natural beauty, convenient location, jobs, or other perceived advantages. Rather than apologizing (as if these people were second-class citizens) make a positive statement out of the situation. These newcomers are people who were, and continue to be, aware of the advantages that your community provides. This fact speaks well for your community and provides you with yet another palpable reason for wanting to preserve its character by preventing Entity and the Project from threatening it. The fact that these newcomers are willing to put forth the effort to help defend and protect your community speaks well for them. Far from being outside professional agitators, they are new community members with a stake in its future, the very kind of people whom anyone would be pleased to call neighbors.

The Toenail-Picking Perverts: Other rumors are less likely to get started at public forums and may be more difficult to combat. You may be astounded to hear, perhaps from a sympathetic or shocked neighbor, that Entity employees are going around saying that members of your group pick their toes at public meetings, do not wash regularly, or live in pigpens. Through the grapevine, you may also hear that Project opponents prefer exotic, immoral, perverted sexual practices, that their kids are juvenile delinquents, or that they are involved with illegal drugs or Satanic cults.

Often the suggestion is made that there is some connection between the alleged illegal activities, the strange hours that group members keep, and the fact that they always seem to have enough money to support their efforts against the Project.

Never mind that some people work nights or have jobs that require frequent out-of-town travel or that 10:30 PM may be the only time that working people opposed to the Project can get together and plan. Never mind that group members can produce legitimate doctors' prescriptions for every last dab of antibiotic cream. Never mind that opponents have modest funds for newsletter costs and attorneys because they scrimp and save. Once started, these toenail-picking rumors are surprisingly difficult to stop. However, as with other dirty-trick type tactics, you are not powerless to respond.

Your best response is your example. Continue to carry yourselves well, dress presentably in public, be respectful of public officials even if they are lying, and most important of all, keep your facts straight and present them clearly and often. Resist the impulse to respond publicly to ridiculous rumors. Calling a press conference to claim that you don't pick your toes in public, that you are not sexual perverts, that little Jimmy is not a car thief, or that you don't get your funds from a crack ring is like Richard Nixon's public plea that "I am not a crook." It only calls attention to the allegations while distracting attention from the real issues.

You should also resist the temptation to make similar attacks on Entity or Project personnel, even if they are true. Pointing out that the Project Director took kickbacks or that Entity's chief attorney is an alcoholic will only erode your credibility and make you look desperate. Your group already carries a disproportionately heavy burden of proof. Don't make your job more difficult by allowing irrelevant pseudo-issues to intervene. Of course, if you do have solid evidence of kickbacks or other illegal activities, share it with the local newspapers and district attorney's office; cooperate but don't try to do their jobs for them.

Looney Tunes: One of the most unfortunate tactics that you may find yourself facing is the effort to portray key members of your group as mentally unbalanced. Again, don't be too shocked to hear claims that a member of your group supposedly has a interesting psychiatric history ... is mentally troubled ... never really got over Viet Nam ... burned out his/her brain in the sixties ... is paranoid or strangely unpredictable.

This is an old, old, tactic, one which has been used, with varying success, against women, minorities, religious sects, immigrants, labor activists, peaceniks, and almost anyone else who has ever dared to challenge an established set of beliefs. Today, for example, it is frequently used against those who question the medical establishment and those who blow the whistle on fraud and government waste.

Again, there is no sure-fire antidote to the Looney-Tunes attack, but acting crazy sure isn't it. Here, more than anywhere else, your actions speak loudly. While it may be good to reexamine and reevaluate your beliefs and actions periodically, don't let the 'nutso' claims divert you from following your heartfelt and well-thought-out beliefs. After all, those who knew that the earth was flat once derided their opponents as the equivalent of perverts, nuts, and quacks. You are in good company.

A Final Word on Credibility: Why are Entity or other Project backers resorting to name-calling and dirty tricks? There are two reasons. First, because your campaign has been effective and they are worried. Second, because they are reluctant to talk about the issues that your group has been raising. Why? Probably because your criticisms are unanswerable.

Rather than comparing facts, head to head, it's easier to direct people's attention elsewhere by claiming that you are nuts, sick, drugged, or otherwise incapacitated. While it is not fun to have your good name slandered by nameless whisperings, you may be encouraged if you take it as a sign that Entity is feeling desperate. This is good news for you.

See WHISTLE BLOWING IN THE WIND.

DAMAGE CONTROL AND FOIA

The purpose of the Freedom of Information Act (FOIA, discussed in Chapter 5) is to make it easier for citizens to find out what the federal government is doing. One result of FOIA's success has been the evolution of new sets of informal procedures designed to circumvent, or at least dull, the force of the law. Once in a while we get a glimpse from the inside of how this is accomplished.

In June 1993, *Harper's Magazine* printed excerpts from an internal NASA document outlining how to deal with anticipated FOIA requests. Four of the strategies noted were:

- Throw out as many of your notes as you can. Rewrite the ones you keep so as to "minimize any adverse impact should they be publicly disclosed."
- Throw out drafts of documents.
- Use yellow stick-ons to comment on documents. That way, if the documents must be disclosed, you can release the stick-ons separately from the documents so it is difficult if not impossible to make sense of either the documents or the stick-ons.
- Don't refer to other documents, because this might make the first document easier to understand and lead readers to other useful information.

We can be sure that NASA is not the only federal agency or government body to have taken steps to blunt the effect of FOIA. The strategies outlined in the NASA document remind us of two lessons that a NIMBY activist must always keep in mind. First, the mere existence of a law does not insure that it will be enforced or that it will work. Second, Entities, regulatory agencies, and other players in a NIMBY controversy keep evolving, adapting, and developing new methods of protecting themselves and achieving their goals.

See *BUT THAT'S AGAINST THE LAW; GOVERNMENT REGULATORS WILL PROTECT YOU.*

Anon., "[Instructions] Lost in Space," "Readings," *Harper's Magazine*, Jun., 1992, pp. 25-6.

DELAYS

Everyone knows that delay is part of your strategy. (Conversely, rushing things through is a part of Entity's strategy.) No matter how serious or substantial your concerns, Entity will claim that you are just using delaying tactics, and you will claim that they are critical issues. However, Entity has at least two weapons to use against your delaying tactics: asking you to put up a bond and claiming that your legal actions are 'frivolous.'

The use of a bond can be amazingly intimidating. It works this way. Chances are that Entity (and/or other powerful groups) has already invested substantial sums of money in the Project. It has a timetable for progress on the Project that justifies its financial investment. Entity may claim that your actions cause delays in getting the Project underway and that these delays, in turn, cost it money. Accountants and lawyers get together and determine that each day of delay costs, say, $10,000. Then, they calculate that the delay from a particular appeal or other action may last 45 working days, thereby costing Entity $450,000 overall.

Armed with these calculations, (and depending on the specific legal provisions and procedural protocol that apply), Entity may ask that your group put up a bond for $450,000 to be given to Entity in the event that the proceedings are decided in Entity's favor. Often, just the threat of a bond is enough to scare people off. It goes without saying that very few groups can afford to set aside that kind of money in order to take a chance on winning an appeal. (And even for those that can, it is not clear that this is a wise use of half a million bucks).

The suggestion that you be required to put up a bond is an attempt to intimidate and is often very effective. Often the request is a bluff and is denied by the presiding official. However, your group should be aware that Entity may convince a hearing examiner or judge that a bond is appropriate, thereby effectively forcing your group to withdraw from a hearing.

Entity may also claim that a particular suit is frivolous — insubstantial, trivial, or without merit, advanced not on its merits but only as a delaying tactic. Lawyers from both sides will get a chance to argue about this before a judge, who will decide whether the suit has any merit.

Though the determination of frivolity is often thoroughly subjective, it is not good for your group to get a reputation for introducing frivolous suits. Requiring a bond and successful claims that your pleadings are frivolous are two ways that Entity can cut short your legitimate attempts to delay a Project or to examine its merits.

DIFFERENT STROKES FOR DIFFERENT FOLKS

Entities make a regular practice of telling different versions of a story in different forums. In this way, everybody hears what they want to hear, and the real story may never be told at all. Following are two examples of the use of this technique, both drawn from my experiences with regulatory agency proceedings.

The Clay Layer: At one hearing on a water quality permit, a major issue boiled down to the thickness and degree of continuity of an underground clay layer. (This may seem trivial, but the success of many operations hinges on matters as seemingly inconsequential as this). Project opponents claimed that the sometimes thin (eight to twelve feet) and sometimes discontinuous clay layer was not substantial enough to protect the major aquifer (water-bearing layer) beneath from the extensive strip-mining operations proposed for the Project. Entity claimed that the clay layer was essentially continuous and usually thicker than twenty feet and that it would amply protect the underlying aquifer against contamination.

It turned out, however, that Entity was making a substantially different argument at another hearing. In the second hearing (before another regulatory agency), Entity was trying to convince the agency that someone else's proposed Project was not viable because it would degrade an aquifer. This Project involved strip mining in an area characterized by the same geological formations as Entity's own Project. Here, the clay layer was seventy-two feet thick and apparently continuous. However, in these second hearings, Entity's representatives came across like born-again environmentalists, fearful that a clay layer merely seventy-two feet in thickness would provide insufficient protection for the aquifer in question.

Entity's representatives will make whatever arguments they deem necessary in order to further their ends. In this case, the integrity of an aquifer was not really the issue for them. Their concern was getting their own permits granted and seeing a competitor's denied. Arguments about the clay layer were simply means to different ends.

Reference to such apparent hypocrisy on the part of an Entity is not a germane argument at regulatory hearings, because it is not directly relevant to the merits of a permit application. However, the exposure of such hypocrisy is a very effective public education tool.

How Dusty Is It? A strip mine, especially in the arid West, can be a very dusty place. Various dust-suppression techniques are applied to the mine itself, as well as to stockpiles of ores and topsoil, haul roads, and any transport facilities and transfer points. Though there are some 'high tech' methods to reduce dust, spraying water still plays a large role (*if* there's water — another critical factor in the arid West). The use of surfactants mixed in with sprayed water is also a widespread practice in the industry. (A surfactant, short for surface-active agent, is any one of several chemicals that are used with water to aid in dust suppression.)

In this case, Entity was attempting to get two separate permits for a mine-mouth power plant and associated mine. One permit was from the state Water Commission and the other from the state Air Control Board.

The Water Commission was concerned that surfactants from extensive spraying could contaminate surface water from runoff and underground aquifers from percolation into underlying strata. So, Entity's representatives assured the Water Commission that they had no plans to use surfactants. (Note that they did not promise *not* to use surfactants; instead they repeated firmly that they had *no plans* to use them.)

The Air Control Board, on the other hand, wanted assurances that dust suppression efforts would be successful. So, Entity representatives told this agency that, of course they would be using surfactants to achieve maximum effectiveness of their dust-suppression efforts.

And so it goes. Pointing out the discrepancy did not prove to be an effective tactic at either hearing; both permits were granted. Nevertheless, public education efforts exposed this opportunism and provided yet another example of Entity duplicity.

See *BE CONSISTENT; HAVE IT BOTH WAYS; THAT'S NOT OUR DEPARMENT DEPARTMENT; WORDS AND MORE WORDS.*

THE ELVIS PRESLEY MEMORIAL TOXIC WASTE DUMP

The act of naming holds a special power. Once someting has been named, the name and the thing together assume an aura that is more than the sum of its parts. Because Entity will stop at nothing to enlist a few more supporters for the Project, expect it to try to tap into the power of naming as well.

This represents but one more attempt to get you to lose track of what the issue really is. The issue is the Project itself, not whether or not it is named after a civil rights leader, a saint, a local volunteer firefighter who died saving a child's life, a martyred labor leader, the president of the PTA, or a school crossing guard.

When you expose this cheap tactic for what it is, Entity will pout that it only wanted to honor so-and-so for his or her contributions to the community and so on and so forth. You can always suggest to Entity that so-and-so might well have wanted to see the issues discussed instead of wasting time on the side issue of naming.

See *ARROWHEADS, ANYONE?; A SPOONFUL OF SUGAR; IF IT QUACKS LIKE A DUCK; MANAGEMENT'S VIEW; UNWANTED MATERIALS COMPANY.*

ENVIRONMENTAL AUDITS

Environmental audits — "systematic examinations of environmental performance," in the words of David Thomas — are increasingly common, especially in the U.S. and Europe.

The spread of environmental auditing is not difficult to explain. First, anti-pollution legislation is becoming more rigorous. Second, the cost of dumping, rather than recycling, waste is rapidly increasing. Third, insurance companies and shareholders are more nervous about the huge liabilities caused by environmental disasters. Fourth, a company's pollution record is an important component of its public image, not least among environmental groups.

In addition, U.S. Securities and Exchange Commission (SEC, the body that requires 10K reports) now expects companies to disclose any potential liabilities connected with environmental cleanup under the federal Superfund law. Current annual reports and 10K filings now contain more information than in the past about a company's environmental practices. This does not mean that they will tell all, but it is a start.

Data on environmental documents filed with state and federal agencies are now being collected and organized by several electronic data companies which offer their services at a price to interested persons. Some of the main companies in this area are: Ensite (Denver); Environmental Audits (Lyonville, Pennsylvania); the Environmental Risk Information Center (Alexandria, Virginia); the Petroleum Information Corporation (Littleton, Colorado); Toxicheck (Birmingham, Michigan); Vista Environmental Information (San Diego); and Environmental Data Resources (Southport, Connecticut).

The idea of an environmental audit and the requirement of environmental assessment are still new, and the criteria for evaluating them are still evolving. Federal law and court cases will surely play their parts in shaping future environmental evaluation standards.

The potential to be overwhelmed by this mass of information is a danger. The sometimes prohibitively high cost of using environmental data services is another deterrent. But if other efforts have failed, your group might consider this approach to information gathering.

See *APPLICANT VS. OPERATOR: IS THIS THE PARTY TO WHOM I AM SPEAKING?; 'BAD BOY' BILLS.*

Diana B. Henriques, "Wall Street: Tracking Environmental Risk," *New York Times,* Apr. 29, 1991; David Thomas, "Hemmed in on all sides (Electricity supply industry)," Industry and the Environment special section, *The (London) Financial Times*, Mar. 13, 1991; Thomas, "Fruits from a worthy labour," *The (London) Financial Times*, Mar. 27, 1991.

ENVIRONMENTAL RACISM

Environmental racism is the practice of siting undesirable facilities in or near neighborhoods where non-whites live. The facilities may range from landfills to radioactive waste storage facilities, from sewage treatment plants to toxic waste incinerators. Studies by the General Accounting Office and by Dr. Benjamin Chavis, Jr., for the United Church of Christ's Commission for Racial Justice, have concluded that African-Americans, Hispanics, and Native Americans are much more likely than whites to live close to an undesirable and very likely hazardous facility.

Here are a few examples cited in the 1987 Chavis study:

- The largest hazardous-waste landfill in the nation holds waste from forty-five states as well as several foreign countries. It is located in Emelle, Alabama, in Sumter County, which is almost eighty percent black.
- The South Side of Chicago, which is predominantly African-American and Latino, contains the greatest concentrations of hazardous waste sites in the United States.
- Six of the Houston's eight municipal incinerators and all its landfills are situated in areas which are predominantly African-American.

Some have argued that undesirable facilities are located in *poor* communities, white or non-white, and that *class* is a more important factor than race in such siting decisions. Social scientists can argue the exact causes, but it seems clear that relative powerlessness, be it due to race or class, is an important factor in siting decisions.

Would you look in Donald Trump's neighborhood for a place to store hazardous waste? How about some acreage near George Bush's Kennebunkport retreat? Of course not. Why? High land values are part of the explanation. A related reason is that affluent whites, with political connections, easier access to information, and resources (from social networks to cash) to fight against such facilities, present a hornet's nest of problems and low probabilities of success to people seeking such sites. As Sidney Plotkin notes:

> Well before the Union Carbide Disaster in Bhopal and the Chernobyl nuclear meltdown in the Soviet Union finally exploded the myth of a benign industrial science, Ameri-

> cans were reluctant to make room for the dangerous and undesirable functions of industrial capitalism. In the more exclusive neighborhoods and communities, such issues rarely arose: it was simply unthinkable to locate factories next to suburban split-levels. So corporations and government builders followed the paths of least resistance to rural backwaters and urban industrial districts, where people did not have the power to pull in the welcome mat. (Plotkin, *Keep Out*, p. 2)

Affluent whites are the original NIMBYs. They are also usually the stealth NIMBYs, because they have rarely even had to raise their voices. Now that other groups are making their voices heard as NIMBY activists, government and corporate planners have begun to claim that the NIMBY syndrome is selfish, backwards, and even unpatriotic.

NIMBY activism has raised issues of citizen participation as local groups have organized to participate in a system long dominated by a few players accustomed to making decisions about the fate of others. 'Environment' has come to mean not just wilderness hiking trails for affluent whites, but safe neighborhoods and work environments for people of color. NIMBY activism may succeed where affirmative action and Supreme Court rulings have failed in bringing all Americans — white or not, affluent or not — into the mainstream of participatory democracy.

Sometimes, though, even being white and influential is not enough to protect people against an undesirable Project. Many residents of Georgetown, a pricey neighborhood in Washington, DC, were disappointed when preliminary approval was granted to a Project they strongly opposed. The Project in question was not a toxic waste dump but a comparably benign cogeneration power plant. As of this writing, several appeals are still possible. Nevertheless, the increasing NIMBY activism on the part of people who never used to worry about such issues may be a good sign, whether it reflects desperation on the part of Project backers or increased awareness and concern on the part of formerly apathetic and privileged classes.

Despite occasional cases like the Georgetown example, environmental racism is still blatant, especially on the international scene. Industrialized countries have long treated their Third-World or less-developed trading partners as dump sites. (For an example that is frightening and very close to home, see Edward Cody's, "Expanding Waste Line Along Mexico's Border.")

There is even the possibility that such practices will become more overt and openly advocated. Following are a few excerpts from a December 1991 memorandum written by Lawrence Summers, the World Bank's vice president for development economics and chief economist, as reported by Michael Weisskopf. (For the record, let it be said that Mr. Summers has indicated that he feels that his memo has been misunderstood.).

- *Just between you and me, shouldn't the World Bank be encouraging more migration of dirty industries to the [less developed countries]?*
- *...under-populated countries in Africa are vastly under-polluted...*
- *I think the economic logic behind dumping a load of toxic waste in the lowest*

wage country is impeccable and we should face up to it.

Unfortunately, increased NIMBY activism in the U.S. has contributed to the use of other countries as dumping grounds for our waste.

The issue of environmental racism is taking center stage in the nineties. Dr. Benjamin Chavis, Jr., who coined the term, is now the Executive Director of the NAACP (National Association for the Advancement of Colored People). Under Chavis' leadership, the NAACP and others are filing lawsuits claiming racial bias in the siting of hazardous facilities.

The Clinton administration has initiated measures that may make it easier to address the issue directly. These include using the 1964 Civil Rights Act to fight environmental racism and drafting new EPA guidelines to consider the cumulative effect of multiple pollution sources in new ways. Carol Browner, the head of the EPA, has acknowledged that "low income and minority communities have been asked to bear a disproportionate burden of this country's industrial lifestyle." The new buzz words are 'environmental equity' and 'environmental justice.' It will take time to determine whether these reflect a policy with substance or propaganda in blackface.

See *SOUTH OF THE BORDER; STEALTH GARBAGE; UNWANTED MATERIALS COMPANY.*

Edward Cody, "Expanding Waste Line Along Mexico's Border," *Washington Post*, Feb. 17, 1992; D'Vera Cohn, "University Power Plant Has Georgetown Steaming: Neighbors Split over Cogeneration Plan," *Washington Post*, Sep. 29, 1991; Cohn, "Power Plant at GU [Georgetown University] Gets DC Approval: 56-Megawatt Generating Unit Would Sell electricity to Pepco," *Washington Post*, Feb. 15, 1992; Melissa Healy, "Administration Joins Fight for 'Environmental Justice,'" *Los Angeles Times*, Dec. 7, 1993; Elizabeth Martinez, "When People of Color Are An Endangered Species," *Z Magazine*, Apr. 1991, pp. 61-65; Sidney Plotkin, *Keep Out: The Struggle for Land Use Control* (Berkeley: University of California Press, 1987); Keith Schneider, "Minorities Join to Fight Toxic Waste," *New York Times*, Oct. 25, 1991; Julia Flynn Siler, "'Environmental Racism': It Could be a Messy Fight," *Business Week*, May 20, 1991; Michael Weisskopf, "World Bank Official's Irony Backfires," *Washington Post*, Feb. 10, 1992.

EX PARTE ANIMALS

It is usually illegal for a judge, a hearing examiner, or anyone else who is supposed to be fair and impartial to have secret, unofficial discussions with any party in a particular dispute. This kind of prohibited communication is called *ex parte* communication.

The exact definition of *ex parte* communication will differ, depending on the jurisdiction the case is in and the set of administrative procedures which apply. But in general, both parties (you and Entity), or your representatives, have a right to be present when either one is talking to a judge, a hearing examiner, or any other government official who is supposed to be evaluating the merits of a case.

In spite of this, *ex parte* communication is quite common. It may occur at a meeting in a club, in a bathroom, during a phone call, or indirectly through an intermediary. Often it is a very easy and natural thing. Powerful people who work with each other regularly are often friends. They socialize together, see each other at dinner parties, go dove hunting or riverboat gambling together, and have ample opportunities to chat about business.

Ex parte communication can accomplish a variety of ends, sometimes for both parties. One side may be looking for a tipoff as to which way a decision is likely to go or when it will be made official. This can obviously provide unfair advantage in future strategy. Or, one person may mention some unflattering and little known information (perhaps false) about the other party in hopes of influencing the proceedings against that party. In the most insidious scenario, one party may get together with the judge and hammer out a compromise of sorts that leaves both winners and both looking good in the eyes of the public.

Ex parte communication is usually difficult to detect and almost impossible to prove. But knowing it exists will help you to anticipate some of its possible effects. If you have well-founded suspicions that *ex parte* communication has occurred, keep in mind that hearings and court cases may present opportunities to question those whom you suspect while they are under oath.

THE FINE PRINT

The fine print is all it's cracked up to be, and more. Here are some particulars to watch for.

Captain May I? The word *may* gives permission to do something but does not require that it be done. *Shall*, on the other hand, is an order to do something and carries much greater legal weight. Some of the most heated arguments over laws and regulations involve the distinction between *may* and *shall.*

A law may state that a regulatory agency "shall establish and enforce" standards. That's an order. If the law only says that the agency "may" establish standards, forget it. Similarly, if it is stated that a company subject to regulations "shall take such and such measures," you are being given something you can use in court.

Often, a given piece of legislation or code of regulations will be sprinkled with *shalls* and *mays.* The *mays* are almost meaningless; the *shalls* you can work with. Do not overlook this critical difference when you are quickly glancing over the fine print or when you are seeking to influence legislation under consideration or pending regulations.

Develop a Plan: Sometimes laws or regulations direct an agency or company to develop a plan, for example, to control excess runoff, reduce the volume of hazardous waste, or increase the level of public input into its decision-making process. Often the plan is developed, shown off before the news media and public groups, and heralded as "a great step forward in controlling (or reducing or increasing) ..." whatever the goal was. But watch for the old 'develop a plan' trick. In some regulations, the process stops right there. There is no requirement that the plan be applied, followed, or enforced — just developed. Entity can derive great public relations from such development, while your group hits a dead end if you try to sue for enforcement.

See *INSTANT CLEANUP; HAVE IT BOTH WAYS; TESTING, TESTING...; WORDS AND MORE WORDS.*

THE FISH AUTOPSY

Many illegal emissions or discharges go relatively unnoticed, at least at the time of the event. Not so with discharges that kill fish. Fish go belly up, begin to smell, and wash up on river banks or collect in little eddies. Dead fish are difficult to ignore. In fact, if it weren't for dead fish, we might never learn about many toxic discharges.

Accidents that result in dead fish can occur during the planning, preparation, construction, or operating phase of a Project. Dead fish attract the attention of the news media, law enforcement agencies, and, often, appropriate regulatory agencies.

If it seems pretty clear from the outset that Entity is involved in the event, Entity personnel step in, take responsibility for ten dead perch, and start up the damage control wing of the public relations squadron.

If Entity appears to be accepting at least minimal responsibility for the incident and seems to be proceeding in a respectable manner, other would-be participants usually back off and let Entity handle it. This is one of the times when Entity personnel are very efficient.

Very quickly, they gather up all the dead fish they can find, have their tissues 'tested,' and announce that the cause of death of the fish was something fairly innocuous-sounding. Two favorite causes of death are suffocation from silt in the gills and a little excess ammonia or chlorine in the water. Entity then closes its investigation into the matter.

In the aftermath, the fish disappear, the tissue samples disappear, and no copies or descriptions of the autopsies or laboratory analyses are available. The outside world never finds out exactly what the fish tissue was tested for or if the water at the time of the accident contained toxic levels of numerous other suspect chemicals and, if so, what caused the apparent discharge in the first place. Regulatory agency personnel are usually missing in action during critical periods, only to reappear later to sample clean (or cleaner) water.

Being familiar with this typical routine before a fish kill occurs may enable your group to stir up the waters a little bit. As soon as you hear of the kill, try to get to the site (before it is completely cordoned off to 'protect the public') and get as many fish samples and water samples as possible. Do this in the presence of witnesses if you can, and document exactly when and where each sample was taken.

Then, as soon as possible, before the samples degrade or decay completely, get them analyzed by reputable analysts. The analysis will be easier, and perhaps cheaper, too, if you have done previous research and can tell the analyst what to test for.

Many important characteristics of the water at the time of the accident will have changed by the time testing is done. Obviously the temperature, an important variable, will change. The pH (acidity) of the water will almost certainly change as well. If any very short-lived radionuclides were present in the water at the time of sampling, they will continue their radioactive decay. An analyst may be able to detect their residues, or 'descendants,' even after a period of time has elapsed.

The presence of some compounds in both the fish and the water, however, will be essentially unaltered even after the passage of hours or days. Your alternative samples may provide you with useful information of exactly the sort that Entity may be trying to keep from you.

The lesson of the fish is that you should never trust any tests or information provided by Entity, and always, where possible, seek alternative sources of information.

See *TESTING, TESTING ...; YOU'RE ON CANDID CAMERA ... OR ARE YOU?*

A FOOT IN THE DOOR

One of the most effective and persuasive techniques Entity can employ to gain approval of a large Project is to use a very gradual, piecemeal, incremental approach. This technique is recognized and discussed by C. Northcote Parkinson in his humorous but deadly serious book, *Parkinson's Law*, but it acquired its most memorable label — the *foot-in-the-door technique* — years later in a psychology article by Jonathan L. Freedman and Scott C. Fraser.

The principle is that once even a tiny part of a much more extensive Project is agreed to, it is more difficult to oppose the next little piece, or the next, or the whole thing. The most common versions of the foot-in-the-door technique follow one of two paths. The first is to start small and then add on or expand; the second is to begin operations for the stated purpose and then seek to change over to a less acceptable one.

For example, Entity might first request permission to construct a maintenance building, a storage area, a pilot project, or some other fairly small, innocuous-sounding facility. If approval is granted, the facility is built quickly and with great care. After perhaps gaining some public support for this undertaking, Entity will seek to enlarge it or build a giant production factory next to it. Or, Entity may get permission to build one kind of facility (say, a small garbage incinerator) then quietly begin to carry out plans to expand or modify it for burning toxic wastes as well.

If your group has agreed to Entity's original request, you are disadvantaged in two ways. Not only have you deviated from a consistent strong, 'Just-Say-No' stance, but you may also find that your legal recourse is now limited. It is often much more difficult to intervene successfully in the regulatory process to oppose an expansion or modification than it is to oppose the original Project, however small the expansion or modification may be.

Once Entity has built anything at all, it is much more difficult to oppose. The explanation offered for the expansion or change often involves factors beyond Entity's control, increasing sympathy for its plight. Common excuses include things like: the economy changed, and Entity must now change or go bankrupt; the regulations were altered, and now financial viability depends on changing operations; or the parent company was the victim of a corporate takeover and new management wants to restructure operations.

Entity may have planned out its whole sob story ahead of time, knowing how susceptible many people are to pleas of hard times. It is best to avoid getting yourselves into such a position in the first place. Foreknowledge of the tactic should alert you in this regard. If you don't catch Entity until there is already a foot in your door, explain and expose the whole strategy to the public in the hope that you can alert everyone to Entity's overall strategy.

See *YOU BUY THE BEER, I'LL BUY THE BUBBLES; PROMISES TO KEEP.*

Jonathan L. Freedman and Scott C. Fraser, "Compliance Without Pressure: the Foot-in-the-Door Technique," *Journal of Personality and Social Psychology* 4 (1966), 195-202; C. Northcote Parkinson, *Parkinson's Law* (Boston: Houghton Mifflin, 1957).

FULL-COST PRICING

Full-cost pricing is an idea that could potentially reduce the need for costly clean-ups and waste dumps while making those who use a product or service pay for its real costs. It would also make companies and consumers aware of the real costs of any particular product. It is a concrete and realistic alternative to business-as-usual, and can be recommended by NIMBY activists challenged to come up with constructive suggestions. And, to top it all off, it has been strongly endorsed by Dow Chemical Company Chairman, Frank Popoff!

Full-cost pricing means what it sounds like it means: the *price* of a product would reflect its actual cost, including the environmental costs of producing, transporting, using, and safely disposing of it.

Take diapers, for example. The price of disposable diapers would include the costs of obtaining and processing petrochemicals and the resulting pollution it causes, the energy cost of making the diapers, and the landfill and recycling costs of disposing of them, among other things. The price of cloth diapers would include the real cost of growing the cotton (including pesticide manufacture, use, and cleanup, and the actual costs — not the subsidized costs — of the water used for irrigation), plus the costs of manufacture and transport. Laundering services would also charge the full cost of cleaning up the diapers. Their prices would reflect the costs of the detergents, chemicals, and water used in washing and rinsing as well as the clean-up costs associated with later water treatment.

Consumers could then choose between diaper options in full knowledge of what the real environmental costs were. Producers of disposable and cloth diapers would know the real costs of each product and would not be using higher prices for one product to subsidize 'losers' — products that would never succeed in the marketplace if full-cost pricing were applied.

In practice, full-cost pricing would run into many difficulties, though not insurmountable ones. As we learn more about actual costs and as new methods are developed, the relative prices of different items in a full-cost pricing system would fluctuate. But at least market price would bear some resemblance to actual product (or service) costs.

Container deposits are a step in the direction of full-cost pricing. Say the cost of disposing of a jar, or manufacturing a new one, is ten cents. Ten cents is then added to the price of the beverage but returned to the consumer if the container is recycled, thereby saving disposal or manufacturing costs, reducing environmental damage, and giving the consumer an incentive to recycle.

If full-cost pricing became widespread and reasonably accurate in reflecting actual costs, then lower-priced products would also be more environmentally benign ones. That's a real marketplace.

See *RECYCLING AND APPLE PIE.*

Martha M. Hamilton, "Making a Product's Cost Reflect Pollution's Cost," *Washington Post*, Nov. 29, 1992 and "Firms Saving Money by Preventing Pollution," Washington Post, Jun. 17, 1992; John Holusha, "Learning to Wrap Products in Less — or Nothing at All," *New York Times*, Jan. 19, 1992; Jessica Mathews, "Ecology in the Marketplace: Profits and Environmentalism are Not Opposed Objectives," *Washington Post*, Nov. 9, 1992; Marlise Simons, "Europeans Begin to Calculate the Price of Pollution," *New York Times*, Nov. 9, 1990.

GETTING THEIR ATTENTION

Sometimes, despite your best efforts to increase public awareness (or gain corporate or government attention) through press conferences and similar mainstream tactics, the issue just doesn't catch on. You may be tempted to try something to make your concerns a little more difficult to ignore.

A number of attention-getting tactics have been used widely by the civil rights and labor movements earlier in this century. Their potential applicability is much broader. So, too, is their legal ambiguity. Henry David Thoreau may be one of your heroes, but many of these tactics may not be firmly established on the side of mere civil disobedience. In all cases, be sure that you have consulted an attorney and understand the legal ramifications and implications of your choices beforehand.

Most of these campaigns involve a three-part attack. First, get 'their' attention (whoever 'they' may be); second, demonstrate that you have broad public support; and third, make your demands. Your efforts may be wasted if you accomplish the first two without providing the third: a clear yet brief statement of what you would like to see happen.

Some activists have held *shop-ins* to get the attention of a grocery store or other large merchandising chain. In this tactic, numerous shoppers have gone to the store, filled their carts with merchandise (sometimes including ice cream), and then 'forgotten' them in the aisles of the store. A related tactic has been called *cross-filing*. Here shoppers have picked up merchandise from one part of the store and 'inadvertently' put it back somewhere else.

The regular operations of a governmental office or private business have been disrupted through the use of a tactic called a *phone-in*. At prearranged times or on prearranged days, large numbers of people have called in to the selected agencies, businesses, or offices. Callers asked routine questions or expressed interest in certain questions or topics previously agreed upon. When a banking institution was the focus of the campaign, the group designated a day as *money-changing day* and asked people to show their opposition to the Project by going to the bank and asking for change for large bills — and then going to the next teller and changing their coins back to bills.

When these and similar tactics were accompanied by explanatory literature (leafletting at the entrance is very effective), the institutions involved, the larger public, and the news media were made aware of the concerns.

Sometimes, if employees of Entity or the Project backers support your group's position, they themselves can take on-the-job actions to demonstrate their support. People cannot just throw their jobs away, however, so their actions must be well-planned and carefully considered. In some cases a work slowdown ('Italian strike') or a 'work to rule' period (where each and every rule is followed completely, absolutely, and literally) can send a powerful message up the line to management.

Do exercise caution lest the wrong people be affected or alienated by your efforts. Neither management nor shareholders stock groceries, answer phones, or handle day-to-day transactions, so be courteous to and considerate of the persons with whom you deal directly. Not only are they not the enemy, they are potential allies. Make sure that these people are not left with the feeling that your dissatisfaction is with them personally.

Some of these attention-getting tactics may flirt with the line separating the legal from the illegal; a few may actually cross over and risk costing your group far more than it could possibly gain. It is up to your group to decide if and when such tactics as those described above are appropriate and to take measures to prevent such actions from backfiring or exposing innocent people to legal, physical, or professional jeopardy. The last thing you want to do is to leave the public with the sense that you are willing to embrace any unseemly means to achieve your ends. Entity will use the opportunity to paint you with that brush, and if it is successful, your larger goal may well be lost.

See BOYCOTTS; ISSUE OF THE WEEK.

David Vogel, *Lobbying the Corporation: Citizen Challenges to Business Authority* (New York: Basic Books, Inc., 1978).

GHOST PERMITS

Entity may be astute enough to set up a situation that will simultaneously allow it an easy escape route while wasting the time and resources of Project opponents. Such an orchestrated scenario might look something like the following.

Let's imagine a case where regulations state that if *a, b,* and *c* are true, Entity will need a Type 1 discharge permit. Entity hires a team of lawyers and consultants and begins the long process of getting the permit. Project opponents scrape together some resources and put up a fight against it. This process might go on for years.

In the meantime, two things happen to Project opponents. First, they put a lot of effort into the process, probably diverting resources from other promising areas. Second, they start to think that they may actually be able to convince the regulatory agency overseeing the process that the permit should be denied.

Now, step back a moment. With the large number of federal, state, and local laws and regulations, tempered by a constantly changing (one might say, deteriorating) regulatory climate and further modified by court cases and appeals being decided daily, it is not always clear exactly which permits are required for a given Project. Entity is very well aware of this, but Project opponents who understand the regulatory ropes less well have become more and more focused on fighting against this particular Type 1 permit.

Suddenly, when Project opponents think that things are going very well indeed, Entity pulls the rabbit out of the hat. Its lawyers march into the regulatory hearing and announce that a Type 1 permit is not necessary for the Project because it will not involve requirement *b* mentioned above. Then they will pack up their briefcases and suggest that the hearing be closed.

Such tactics may surprise the regulatory agency as well as Project opponents. The whole scene has shifted to an argument over whether or not the Project involves *b* and therefore needs the Type 1 permits. Project opponents will be flabbergasted and totally unprepared to argue about provision *b*. Meanwhile, Entity's team has been planning this strategy for some time, so they are ready with piles of documents and very persuasive arguments.

Some further observations are in order. Entity may have been planning this switch all along or it may have come up with the idea mid-stream because Project opponents were doing better than anticipated in the hearings. It may even have changed a detail of the Project in order to exempt it from the Type 1 permit.

However Entity came to use this tactic, it is a powerful one and difficult to anticipate. It is a good reminder to Project opponents not to put all of their eggs in the same one or two baskets. A hearing that seems to be going too well can be a trap.

See *SAY NOW WHEN YOU START CONSTRUCTION; TRIGGERS; WE'D LIKE TO BUT.....*

GOING THE EXTRA MILE

No idea is so bad that it cannot be modified by an even worse idea. When Entity wants to develop a Project or fix up one that has gotten tripped up in its own complications, it will stop at nothing. If you express concern about an adverse effect of the Project, Entity experts will immediately explain how they will mitigate it. The problem is that their 'solutions' are often no more than the successful masking of a symptom or, all too frequently, the cause of further problems. Here are some examples of the kind of technological 'solutions' that have been proposed.

Toad Mating Zone: In Texas, the once widespread Houston toad is now an endangered species limited to a few rural counties between Houston and Austin. One of the reasons for the decline of the toad is that its habitat is being destroyed. Its mating and reproductive habits require what biologists call 'intermittent streams' — streams that are dry most of the year but flowing during spring rains and other periods of heavy rainfall. (Texas has a lot of streams like that.)

A public utility company, intent on strip mining hundreds of acres of Houston toad habitat, promised to reconstruct special intermittent streams for toad-breeding on land reclaimed from its mining operations. The responsible regulatory agencies bought the story, and so the range of the Houston toad has been further reduced while the range of human strip mining has expanded.

Meanwhile, the population of Houston toads continues to decline, primarily because of the habitat destruction that reconstructing these intermittent streams was supposed to avert.

Pumping Iron: "Scientists trying to battle the 'greenhouse effect' have seriously proposed dumping hundreds of thousands of tons of iron into the ocean to create giant blooms of marine algae that could soak up much of the excess carbon dioxide believed to be responsible for global warming." So begins an article by William Booth about an idea endorsed by the National Research Council, an arm of the National Academies of Sciences and Engineering. Apparently the iron stimulates the growth of algae and phytoplankton, which absorb CO_2, one of the greenhouse gases, while carrying out photosynthesis. Enthusiasm for the project was high.

One marine scientist was quoted as saying, "You give me half a tanker full of iron, I'll give you another ice age." That gets to the core of the matter.

All That Glitters: In the gold mining industry, attempts are made to keep birds away from cyanide-flavored ponds by covering the ponds with nets, firing noisy cannons, and playing electronic bird distress calls.

Fanning the Fumes: Mexico City, notorious for air pollution that brings tears to the eyes and chokes the breath, is considering a plan to use giant fans to blow the bad air out of the city when air pollution reaches dangerous levels. A hundred fans, each 150 feet in diameter, would be arranged around the city to blow the hot, dirty city air up through the layer of cool air that often forms above the Valley of Mexico. The Mexican National Autonomous University Engineering Institute will study the fan idea. (One recent idea rejected by authorities was to cut notches in nearby mountain ranges to increase air flow in the valley.)

Unfortunately, as these examples suggest, Project supporters rarely even consider removing the cause of the problem as a possibility. It's up to your NIMBY group to convince people ahead of time to address the core issues instead of hoping for engineering magic when things go wrong.

William Booth, "Ironing Out 'Greenhouse Effects': Dumping in Oceans Proposed to Spur Algae," *Washington Post*, May 20, 1990; Edward Cody, "Mexico City Eyes Wind Machines: Proposal Aims to Halt Rise in Air Pollution," *Washington Post*, Feb. 22, 1992; Robert Reinhold, "Unusual Accord Opens the Way for a Gold Mine," *New York Times*, Nov. 25, 1990.

GOVERNMENT REGULATORS WILL PROTECT YOU

Today, the U.S. government in general, and the military branches in particular, are regarded as the perpetrators of the worst toxic cleanup mess in the nation: the problem of radioactive wastes. For a half century, the government has handled its nuclear-weapons-related projects without much interference, so presumably we can get a glimpse of the real government at work.

Public participation (except for paying for it) was next to nil. The usual bureaucratic paper-shuffling among relevant agencies was kept to an absolute minimum while the military and national security organizations did it 'their way.' Civil liberties — *Sergeant, have your men dump these barrels where the sun don't shine* — were no big deal, and the occupational safety of the 'grunts' was hardly considered. The mantra of national security was an effective shield against public disclosure of what was going on, even during Congressional inquiries. Even when national security was not at issue, Congress was often no help at all, as when it exempted the Department of Energy from OSHA (Occupational Safety and Health Administration) regulations.

The outcome should be a lesson about what happens in the absence of outside interference or public scrutiny of any kind. During the 1980s, for example, the Department of Energy maintained a steady policy of resisting any attempts by the EPA or state environmental agencies to force nuclear weapons plants to abide by existing environmental laws. According to Keith Schneider, this stonewalling allowed government contractors, perhaps with the knowledge of government officials, to violate all sorts of health and safety standards. Contractors reportedly stored chemical and radioactive wastes without obtaining the proper permits, failed to act when these wastes began to leak, and illegally disposed of hazardous wastes, some of which were toxic.

Unless you rid yourselves of the notion that the government acts primarily and consistently to protect the public against external risks (be they microscopic emissions or incoming Scuds), you will be vulnerable to Entity's most shallow and transparent arguments in favor of a Project. The mere presence of a mega-sized government bureaucracy and millions of lines of regulatory law does not insure that any serious regulation is achieved. If you are ever tempted to believe the oft-repeated stereotype of government regulators who over-regulate facilities in the name of protecting the public or the environment, just remind yourself of the government's handling of its own nuclear weapons production facilities.

The regulatory community's handling of non-nuclear issues is not much better. The delay of a particular regulation even for a few weeks or months can save an industry or a company millions of dollars. The pace of writing new regulations from legislation already on the books during the 1980s slowed to a pace that makes the glaciers seem speedy. According to a recent report (1991) by the Inspector General of the Department of the Interior, thirty-four species became extinct before they were even listed as threatened or endangered under the Endangered Species Act.

Largely due to EPA's sluggishness in writing regulations, many major industries have escaped regulation of one or more critical areas of operations. For example, according to critic Michael Weisskopf, liquid waste discharges from "hazardous waste treatment facilities, industrial laundries, hospitals, commercial solvent recyclers, transportations equipment cleaners, used-oil reclamation operations and conditioners of chemical and fuel drums" are all currently *not* subject to federal regulations.

For the purpose of fighting your NIMBY battle against an unwanted Project, it does not matter whether government regulators are lazy, incompetent, overworked, or in cahoots with those they are supposed to be regulating. What matters is that history demonstrates repeatedly that you cannot count on a combination of Entity's or industry's voluntary compliance or governmental monitoring and regulation to protect your health, rights, or environment. Once that misconception is cleared away, you can begin planning your own strategies.

See *BADGER HOLES; BUT THAT'S AGAINST THE LAW!; COMMON SENSE NEED NOT APPLY; THE FINE PRINT; NORMAL ACCIDENTS; GHOST PERMITS; SAY NOW WHEN YOU START CONSTRUCTION; HEADS I WIN/TAILS YOU LOSE; INSTANT CLEANUP; NUMBERS GAMES; STANDARD OPERATING PROCEDURE; THAT'S NOT OUR DEPARTMENT DEPARTMENT.*

Keith Schneider, "U.S. Takes Blame in Atom Plant Abuses," *New York Times*, Mar. 27, 1992; Matthew L. Wald, "Nuclear Fingerprints All Over, but Try to Find the Hands," *New York Times*, Jun. 7, 1992; Michael Weisskopf, "Default on Industrial Effluent: With EPA Water-Pollution Controls Lacking, Duty Falls to States," *Washington Post*, Dec. 30, 1992.

THE HATFIELDS AND MCCOYS

You would not want to get all of your information about the Hatfields from the McCoys, or vice versa, but what a place to start. Industry usually closes ranks when faced with outside threats (consumer groups, environmentalists, neighborhood activists, unions, etc.), knowing that a united front is stronger when facing an enemy. So, usually, the members of an industry, or even closely related industries, refrain from sniping at each other in public.

Not so always. If the stakes are high or if the pie is shrinking, we are sometimes presented with a spectacle of the big guys duking it out in full view. This means a public exposure by each of the perceived flaws in the other's plans. This information, sworn to by the best experts in the business, will then be available to anyone opposing either or both.

Two brief examples will provide a glimpse of how such conflicts might arise. Imagine that two electric power companies are vying for permission to build a power plant. A power company must receive permission from state and/or federal authorities before building a power plant — not only on environmental grounds, but also on grounds of the public need. Two competing companies (either can be public or private sector entities) may each claim the right to construct and manage the proposed plant. In their regulatory tussle to prove whose plan would be cheaper, more efficient, more environmentally sound, and in general, preferable, a great deal of damaging information about both proposals emerges. If the proposals involve more than one fuel, those of you seeking information will get a free bonus.

As I write, such a heavyweight bout is actually in progress between two consortiums, each of which wants to build the facility to produce tritium (a radioactive gas) for the U.S. nuclear weapons program. These two consortiums are led, respectively, by major players in the nuclear industry and include some of the largest engineering, design, and construction firms in the world. With a $5.6 billion price tag, the incentive to win the contract is considerable. Project opponents have already recognized that a comparable opportunity to gather information may not soon be repeated.

See *BECOME A SHAREHOLDER; DAMAGE CONTROL AND FOIA.*

Thomas W. Lippman, "DOE Reactor Splits Nuclear Industry; Two Syndicates in All-or-Nothing Contest for $5.6 Billion Contract," *Washington Post*, Apr. 3, 1991.

HAVE IT BOTH WAYS

The public relations staff of an Entity trying to succeed in a Project has a very difficult job, often because it must overcome, mask, or minimize the effects of the work done by Entity's other subdivisions. Here is one of the many tactics used in an attempt to maintain a positive public persona in that context.

Entity's governing board, or another visible committee of some kind, will have a study done about something that sounds wholesome and positive, such as how to contribute more to the well-being of the local community. The report will come out and include a number of rather strong and perhaps costly recommendations about what Entity could do to further its civic responsibilities. After some discussion Entity's board or committee will accept the report. The PR department (perhaps now named Public Information to downplay its purely propaganda function) will generate news releases, video clips, and a host of similar vehicles for getting the word out. Often local news media run these packages unedited.

Months later someone may notice that Entity has taken no steps toward implementing any of the recommendations in the Blue Ribbon Report. Persistent questioning will eventually reveal the explanation: Entity has accepted the report, but that does not mean that it agrees with the findings or even considers it appropriate to follow the recommendations. As a matter of fact, it may disagree and have no intention of following the recommendations. But it has been basking in the warmth of good PR for many months.

Don't let Entity get away with something as cheap as developing a plan. Press Entity representatives to find out if the plan is also the policy. Ask about the specific steps Entity will complete within the next year, for example. And if Entity does not follow through, jump on every opportunity to let Entity embarrass itself with its own forgotten words.

See *DIFFERENT STROKES FOR DIFFERENT FOLKS; THE FINE PRINT; GHOST PERMITS; MANAGEMENT'S VIEW; UNWANTED MATERIALS COMPANY.*

HEADS I WIN/TAILS YOU LOSE: THE PRE-EMPTION ISSUE

Pre-emption can wipe out years of efforts on your group's part, so it's worthwhile to familiarize yourselves with the problem at the outset.

Greatly simplified, the following is what pre-emption is all about. Sometimes both a state and the federal government have regulations concerning the same issue, say, air emissions from a factory. If these laws are conflicting, then, because of Article VI of the U.S. Constitution, the federal law applies and the state law does not. State law has been pre-empted.

Often in the past, federal laws have been stricter, and states have therefore been required to meet the higher federal standards. But what if the states have stricter standards? May states enforce their own more stringent standards, or do the federal standards, even though they are less strict, automatically pre-empt the state standards?

In reality the issue is even more complex, because often it is not absolutely clear which standards are stricter. To illustrate, imagine the following situation regarding compound *ABC*. Suppose that federal standards state that hourly average emissions may not exceed ten ppm (parts per million) more than four times in a thirty-day period. And suppose state standards specify that maximum emissions may not exceed five ppm more than once each 24-hour period. Federal standards allow four hours per month of unlimited emissions, while state standards allow unlimited emissions once daily but require emission levels under five ppm for the rest of the day.

Unless you know a great deal about compound *ABC*, about its health effects at different concentrations, and about how the factory is likely to operate, it is extremely difficult to evaluate the strictness of provisions such as these. On top of this, the factory operator may prefer the federal standards in some areas and the state standards in others (as may you.)

More and more frequently, states are passing and attempting to enforce standards different from and often stricter than federal rules. The legal status of these stricter, state regulations depends upon the federal and state agencies which are involved, the administrative procedures which apply, and the determinations that have been made in recent court cases. Right now, pre-emption fights are very tricky, costly, and time-consuming. Perhaps eventually the air will be cleared somewhat by Supreme Court decisions and/or an act of Congress to clarify the matter. Until then, try to steer clear of lengthy pre-emption cases that you may very well lose.

See *ACT LOCALLY; BUT THAT'S AGAINST THE LAW; THE LAW OF THE LAND.*

Michael Weisskopf, "*EPA* Upholds State on Tougher Environmental Laws," *Washington Post*, Jun. 2, 1990.

HORSE TRADING AND POLITICAL CORRECTNESS

There are a number of national organizations, coalitions, and umbrella groups that work towards achieving clusters of related goals. Some are primarily concerned with the environment, others with consumer issues, human rights, working conditions, children's rights, nutrition, and a host of other matters. The achievements of these groups have made all of our lives safer, cleaner, and more fulfilling.

In the course of your NIMBY battle, it may make sense for your group to seek support — financial or otherwise — from one or more of these well-established groups. You may seek, gain, and benefit from the assistance of such groups. But while utilizing the advantages that association with such groups may bring, keep two things in mind. First, there are inter-group strains and conflicts that you may be unaware of which may end up hurting your efforts. Second, though your NIMBY problem is a central issue in your life, it may look like a bargaining chip to outsiders. We'll take up each in turn.

Within each activist field — the environment, for example — there is a range of groups from the radical (Earth First!) to the mainstream (Sierra Club). There are also many nuances of method (monkeywrenching versus litigation versus legislative lobbying, for example) and goals (new policies, getting good people elected or appointed, stopping Projects, or changing the relations of power).

Though these groups may in many ways be headed in similar directions and benefit from many of each other's successes, they also compete for media attention, supporters, funding, and legitimacy. Allying your group with one of them may cause you to be identified with it, thereby limiting the assistance that you might receive from another. Or, the organization may be more interested in receiving membership dues and your group's endorsement than in participating materially in your particular NIMBY controversy.

In the matter of bargaining chips, remember that a national group has a big agenda and broad goals. It must to some extent choose controversies that it considers to be both important and winnable. In the process of selecting and prioritizing its goals, some issues inevitably fall by the wayside or get compromised away. In return for concessions from industry in one area or for favorable language in a legislative package, for example, support for particular issues like your own NIMBY problem might be dropped, or worse, specifically excluded. Having your core issue manipulated in this way is not only frustrating, but it can do significant legal and public relations damage to your cause.

If you are working as part of a wider coalition and you object to seeing your main concern swept under the rug or traded for another supposed benefit, you can expect to be criticized (attacked is often a more appropriate word). It is fairly standard to be called selfish and divisive, to be castigated for not being team players, or to be accused of not thinking about the big picture.

This is the same opening salvo used in attacks on any NIMBY movement, so you should already be somewhat adept at handling it. It is disconcerting to be thus criticized by people or groups who you thought were your friends or allies. Unhappily, it is often disputes between the most similar groups that become the most bitter.

IF IT QUACKS LIKE A DUCK...

When the Audubon Society bought a large tract of South Carolina oceanfront property, many people expected that the environmentally sensitive area would be preserved. Instead, the area is slated to become a golf course, with the Audubon Society benefiting financially. Has the Audubon Society changed its tune? Not exactly. The National Audubon Society still frowns on golf course development because of the massive use of pesticides and fertilizer in maintenance. The 'Audubon Society' is a New York group that apparently marches to a different drummer. Confused? You're supposed to be.

With this example in mind, let's see if you can guess what these groups are about. *The Fur Farm Animal Welfare Coalition?* It's a public relations group for the fur industry. *The Abundant Wildlife Society?* It's a pro-hunting property rights group in Wyoming. *The Center for the Defense of Free Enterprise?* It spends its time fighting against the Endangered Species Act. *The National Wetlands Coalition*, with its logo of a duck flying out of some cattails? It's a lobby group for oil companies and other land developers. *The Environmental Transportation Association?* It represents waste disposal companies and railroads. *People for the West?* This is an outgrowth of the Western States Public Lands Coalition, which has financial backing from Chevron, Homestake Mining Co., and Energy Fuels Co. (a producer of uranium.) What about a company called *Safety-Kleen*? It provides services to generators of hazardous waste. And the *Environmental Conservation Organization?* It's a Chicago-based property-rights group founded by the Land Improvement Contractors of America.

As NIMBY controversies become more and more a matter of public relations and control of information, the appearance of vaguely but suggestively named groups, sometimes linked to industry or other specific constituencies, has become more common. Their names may sound wholesome, positive, and vague. Their activities range from lobbying in the national and state capitals to distributing brochures in problem areas in attempts to sway public opinion. Many times, their members sincerely believe in what their groups are trying to accomplish.

Often these groups claim, or strongly suggest, that they are grass-roots groups, or sort-of-spontaneous alliances among local citizens or small businesses which have banded together in an effort to protect their individual interests. One such group is described by Cindy Skrzycki as a 'small business' group founded by some phone company 'relatives' to lobby against bills that would limit the activities of such companies.

Though these groups may be partly or wholly funded by large trade organizations or industry lobbying associations, their legal structures often insure that they are not subject to disclosure laws which would make it easier to find out who really funds them. A Ralph Nader-backed, non-profit group headed by John Richard has done some of your research already and has published a directory of *Essential Information* that provides background information on these and other groups.

Organizations like these are legal, powerful, persuasive, and proliferating. If a vague-sounding group starts hanging around your backyard, find out about its history and backers, and make sure that others know what to expect. The group may even try to form a local chapter to disguise itself as another home-grown, grass-roots group. If it does, you can even try to attend their meetings! Don't be the last to know what their tactics will be.

See *MANAGEMENT'S VIEW; RECYCLING AND APPLE PIE; UNWANTED MATERIALS COMPANY.*

Kirstin Downey Grimsley, "The Birders and the Birdies — Audubon's Name Use in S. Carolina Golf Course Deal Angers Environmentalists," *Washington Post*, Sep. 29, 1993; John Lancaster, "Western Industries Fuel Grass-Roots Drive for 'Wise Use' of Resources," *Washington Post*, May 16, 1991; Cindy Skrzycki, "Companies Adopt Grass-Roots Lobbying Tactics to Push Programs," *Washington Post*, Feb. 3, 1992.

INCENSE, PEPPERMINT

In an advanced technological society such as ours that has a competitive market niche for anti-woodpecker paint to prolong the useful lifetimes of wooden utility poles, it should come as no surprise that there is a whole sub-industry devoted to masking unpleasant sights and smells.

Ever wonder where that intense cherry smell in the office bathroom comes from? Do you know anybody who uses cherry perfume or cologne?

The same people who can answer those questions can also tell us a lot about our industries. One smell expert, Richard Duffee (who founded Odor Science and Engineering, Inc., of Hartford, Connecticut), once made "a blend of industrial deodorants strong enough to overcome the stench of a five-foot pile of rotting carcasses," according to Robert Tomsho. What you can see coming out of smokestacks and what you can smell as you drive by can be — or may already have been — modified. The color of stack gases can be altered; the smells that fill the air can be masked or improved; there is even technology available to add opposite kinds of sounds to cancel out unpleasant noise and reduce associated discomfort.

The absence of unpleasant smells or unsightly plumes billowing from smokestacks does not indicate that the air quality is good. Chemical masking, and the fact that many dangerous materials are odorless and invisible, must be considered. Likewise, unpleasant smells and visibly ugly plumes do not necessarily indicate the presence of a health hazard. (In certain light, for example, water vapor looks downright demonic.)

To evaluate potential health hazards, you need access to reliable sampling data, technical research, and the advice of a technically competent person whom you trust. If you make health claims after only pointing at a smokestack and sniffing the air, you run the risk of looking (and being) the fool.

See *WHAT IS THAT FUNNY SMELL?*

Robert Tomsho, "This Nose for Hire," *Wall Street Journal*, Jun. 11, 1992.

INSTANT CLEANUP

Between 1987 and 1989, the American aluminum industry drastically reduced the amount of toxic pollutants that it emitted into the environment.

Did it do this by cutting back operations? By shutting down older, dirtier plants? By changing its manufacturing processes? By installing improved pollution-control technology? No, no, no, and no. It did this by successfully lobbying the EPA over a period of years to remove aluminum oxide from its list of toxic pollutants.

A similar process is now underway regarding dioxin, considered by some to be among the most potent carcinogens in our environment. Spearheaded by a well-known doctor from the U.S. Centers for Disease Control in Atlanta, the campaign first surfaced when he made statements suggesting that dioxin, which is used heavily in the paper industry, was hardly dangerous at all. The study on which he based his pronouncement had reviewed and reinterpreted a couple of older studies which had originally been provided by interested people in the industry. New research suggesting that dioxin was highly dangerous was ignored. In spite of the scientifically questionable 'new interpretation' of dioxin, press coverage has been sympathetic to industry goals.

It's not uncommon for such significant policy changes to occur after similar, pro-industry reinterpretations of old results. As for dioxin, the EPA may be on its way to weakening the restrictions on the chemical's presence in the environment. If such changes are made, many lawsuits and insurance claims will no longer have a chance of being collected.

Be on the alert for similarly creative methods used by both the public and private sectors to improve an industry's public image. There is always a story behind the story.

See *THE FINE PRINT; GOVERNMENT REGULATORS WILL PROTECT YOU.*

Jeff Bailey, "Dueling Studies: How Two Industries Created a Fresh Spin On the Dioxin Debate; Paper and Chlorine Groups Revisited Old Data, Came to Some New Conclusions," *Wall Street Journal*, Feb. 2, 1992; Laura Sessions Stepp, "In Search of Ethics; Alcoa Pursues a Corporate Conscience Through Emphasis on 'Core Values'," *Washington Post*, Mar. 31, 1991.

THE INSTITUTIONAL ENVIRONMENT

In order to understand, perhaps even to predict, an Entity's response to certain situations or events, the external context must be considered as well as the internal one. Consider Entity's total environment. When sociologists speak of an organization's environment, they are not referring to air, land, or water. They are referring to the social, political, and economic context within which the organization functions, including the regulations and permit requirements that govern Entity's operations.

The institutional environment includes, for example: the suppliers from whom Entity acquires raw materials, supplies, fuel, and whatever else it needs to function; the transportation network that brings in these supplies; the systems that distribute any products, be they books, bombs, or electricity; employee organizations, other bureaucracies, insurance regulations and companies; even the local community, its news media, and other private and public organizations.

An Entity's environment also includes competitors, both foreign and domestic. In the case of a product like electricity or phone service, the competition may include federal, state, or local government agencies, public utilities, or other quasi-government entities. Alternatives to the product or service that Entity offers are also part of the relevant environment. If Entity handles waste materials, for example, the shipping industry, the recycling industry, the incinerator industry, and the firms that offer special landfill arrangements may all compete for the same business. Similarly, if Entity is in the energy business, alternative energy sources or fuels, and even conservation techniques are competitors in Entity's environment.

Generally, Entity has more control over its internal operations that it has over this external environment. It is clear that changes in the environment can affect the organization. More often overlooked is the fact that the reverse is also true. An organization often seeks to reduce the uncertainty it must face by controlling its environment as much as possible. If control of the environment is difficult or impossible, then an organization will seek to buffer itself by reducing uncertainty from this quarter.

If price fluctuation poses risks for an organization, for example, it may seek to enter into long-term contracts to minimize this problem in the environment. Other arrangements or understandings may be made between or among organizations. Three-cornered arrangements — organization *A* buys from organization *B*, which buys from organization *C*, which in turn does business with organization *A* — are not uncommon. These may be very effective but difficult to trace. Megacorporation *A* may buy large quantities of steel for construction from company *B*, which gets its coal from a mine owned by *C*, which controls the insurance company that offers *A* a very favorable insurance contract.

An organization's environment also includes actual or potential foes or rivals. Such forces can be dealt with by co-optation (bringing token outsiders in some way into Entity's decision making process and thereby neutralizing their criticisms) or by using special arrangements that take the edge off Entity's perceived negative presence. It has been claimed, for example, that during the 1930s the Tennessee Valley Authority essentially bought off possible opponents by favoring the white and wealthy farmers over the relatively powerless poor and minority farmers within its jurisdiction.

Another fairly common way of controlling potentially antagonistic elements is to award large contracts to potential foes. As we saw in the discussion of "Bid Rigging," this is fairly easy to accomplish, even when contract awards are made through a public process. Unless someone tips you off about exactly what to look for, it is extremely difficult to spot such items and next to impossible to prove that they reflect a deceptive intent.

Regulatory agencies are a ubiquitous part of the environment for most organizations, and it is obviously desirable to be able to predict, if not control, the actions of such agencies. Three aspects of the Entity-regulatory agency relationship are particularly important to understand.

First, most contacts between Entity and the agency are tedious and bureaucratic, and only a very few incidents generate any kind of disagreement or controversy. In all likelihood, a long-term relationship and pattern of behavior has already been established.

Second, there will almost certainly be a revolving door between the two organizations, with many Entity personnel having been trained and 'aged' at one of the regulatory agencies that monitor it. People who were once co-workers and friends may be uncomfortable when they find themselves structurally opposing one another. More importantly, they may suspect that at some future time they will again be on the same side. Expect kid gloves.

Third, the relationship between industry and agency may not be quite as adversarial as it might appear. Do not take too seriously the common business and industry complaint that the regulatory agencies are sources of unnecessary red tape and little else. This makes it sound like they harass business on behalf of government for the benefit of the people. The opposite may actually be the case. There is reason to believe that in many industries, regulatory agencies effectively help to eliminate small and independent business and to pave the way for the domination of the particular industry by a few big players. This means among other things that you may find some surprising allies among smaller firms who also feel abused by the big guys.

See *BID RIGGING; THE HATFIELDS AND MCCOYS; LOOKING FOR HELP IN ALL THE RIGHT PLACES; STRANGE BEDFELLOWS DEPARTMENT; KEEP OUT.*

Charles B. Perrow, *Organizational Analysis: A Sociological View* (Monterey, CA: Brooks/Cole Publishing Company, 1970).

ISSUE OF THE WEEK

In the beginning, your public education campaign will be conducted through major public announcements, hearings, and other external events. After this intensity cools, both the news media and the public will be ready to move on to other issues unless you work carefully.

Even if the issues are very important, no one wants to hear the same old lines day after day. In order to keep your issue alive in the public's mind and to continue deepening the public's understanding of it, your group may need to actually plan your own public education campaign.

Develop a series of themes, each covering another aspect of the proposed Project. You might include air quality, property values, water discharges, employment, worker safety, taxes, Entity's history regarding similar Projects, and so on. Then highlight — in talks, press conferences, mail campaigns, or whatever public education formats you have found effective — one issue per week or per month, depending on the rhythm of events. In this way, you can cover numerous aspects of the Project without boring your audience. It will receive new information periodically, and the Project issue will not fade away.

See *GETTING THEIR ATTENTION.*

THE JURY

If your group ends up in court at a jury trial, you might benefit from knowing about a movement afoot concerning the power of juries. It could work for or against you, depending on the situation, but forewarned is forearmed.

As described by the Wall Street Journal,

> [J]uries in criminal cases possess an absolute but unadvertised power to ignore the dictates of the law. As a practical matter, a jury can know a defendant is guilty but simply refuse to convict him....Jury-power activists have a good deal of inspirational early American history on their side. They point out that in pre-Revolutionary days, colonists who served on juries made a practice of refusing to convict defendants for breaking British laws they deemed unfair.

An organization called the Fully Informed Jury Association (FIJA) seeks to insure that "juries be told the truth about how much power they have." FIJA National Headquarters, are located at P.O. Box 59, Helmville, MT 59843 (800-835-5879).

See *THE LAW OF THE LAND.*

Stephen J. Adler, "Courtroom Putsch? Jurors Should Reject Laws They Don't Like, Activist Group Argues; It Says Juries Have the Power And Need to Be Told of It; Establishment is Horrified. Adherents are a Diverse Lot," *Wall Street Journal*, Jan. 1, 1991.

KEEP OUT!

NIMBY controversies are part of a larger context that involves the meaning of private property and property rights. The underlying questions have been at issue since even before this country gained its independence over two centuries ago.

In his excellent book, *Keep Out: The Struggle For Land Use Control*, Sidney Plotkin explores the ways in which two frequently opposing interests often overlap. The *exclusionary* interest arises when an individual or a group claims the right not only to do what they please with their own property but to exclude other people or uses. A neighborhood exercises an exclusionary interest when it excludes certain groups from living there or prohibits certain uses of land within the neighborhood (massage parlors, for example). The right to use and to exclude have always been subject to some limitations, usually to prevent the obstruction of an adjacent property owner's exercise of his or her rights.

The *expansionary* interest is represented by a government or an agent (such as a corporation) designated by a government. The expansion (of government rights over private property rights, in effect) is usually justified on grounds that it serves the general public good (interpreted variously in different eras by the powers that be.)

The exercise of condemnation powers (the use of eminent domain) — for railroads, reservoirs, military facilities, highways, and later for urban renewal, power plants, hazardous waste dumps, etc. — is the most obvious example of expansionary interests. Increasingly, these interests may also include limits on the use of private property, even rigorous limits. Prohibition against building on property in a wetlands area or against siting a chemical facility in an aquifer recharge zone are examples of the extension of an expansionary interest from land condemnation to strict regulation of land use.

There are few purists in the controversy between exclusionary and expansionary interests. Persons with exclusionary NIMBY sentiments about their own neighborhoods may be pleased to learn that expansionary interests have succeeded in acquiring land for a needed power plant in other neighborhoods, for example. This lack of purism and consistency can also be seen on a larger scale. An energy corporation may favor a federal law to allow it to condemn land for an oil pipeline but shrink from this expansionary view when the same government limits the company's use of its own property by imposing strict environmental standards.

On a more local level, zoning is also a two-edged sword. It can serve exclusionary interests by excluding toxic waste dumps from a residential area. However, it can also be used to establish a commercial zone along a street in the same neighborhood, thereby permitting forms of development not desired by neighborhood residents.

Potential conflicts between exclusionary and expansionary interests exist among individual property owners, neighborhoods, municipalities, states, and even the federal government. The resolution of struggles among these multiple jurisdictions over already-complex issues of property rights and the public good often takes place in the courts. In the absence of a clear, overall federal land use policy, delays resulting from such litigation often work to the advantage of NIMBY activists.

NIMBY conflicts are not essentially between the individual and society but between different interests that are sometimes allies and sometimes opponents, depending on the particular issue involved. An entire planning profession arose as an attempt to work out the inevitable and time-consuming clashes among these varying interests. Some would argue that planners have become yet another interest group, one that has continued a tendency to plan *for* instead of *with* many members of a community.

If NIMBY issues are ultimately resolved at the national level, there is the risk that legitimate concerns of states, municipalities, and neighborhoods will not be carefully addressed. On the other hand, if all exclusion-versus-expansion issues were resolved at the local level, we might never get a highway built.

See *THE INSTITUTIONAL ENVIRONMENT; THE HATFIELDS AND MCCOYS; 'TAKINGS' AND THE FIFTH AMENDMENT.*

Sidney Plotkin, *Keep Out: The Struggle for Land Use Control* (Berkeley: University of California Press, 1987).

THE LAW OF THE LAND

Your group may find itself in the position of being able to influence legislation. The legislation may be at the federal, state, or local level. If Entity itself has proposed the legislation — and this is not uncommon — then the proposed law, even if it seems innocuous, will probably either give Entity more power or let it off the hook in some way (for instance, by transferring the regulation of Entity's activities to a more sympathetic agency).

Pending legislation might also be proposed by other interest groups, including ones like yours. These may limit Entity's power, tighten regulations, broaden regulatory powers, or in some other way expand or contract the reach of someone's arm. In any case, your group can and should lobby for or against the legislation, and you should probably testify at public hearings as well. But before you throw yourselves wholeheartedly into this effort, be sure that your efforts are appropriate.

First, get a copy of the actual draft of the law, resolution, or ordinance. Never accept offers of summaries or main points in lieu of the real thing. Then, go over it with a fine-toothed comb with your attorney and with someone with technical expertise. Identify the weaknesses, limits, and loopholes in it, and publicize them widely in an effort to attract and demonstrate public support.

Some laws are written in a certain way specifically to insure that they will be difficult if not impossible to enforce. Others are allowed to become law because no one (except a few naive citizens, perhaps) expects that they will ever be enforced. Think about this next time you hear some plaintive whining about over-regulation.

Long-time bureaucracy-watcher Amitai Etzioni puts it this way:

> [A] good part of the laws passed are not meant to be implemented, at least not systematically and effectively. Passing laws is part of the make-believe or theater of politics, in which politicians try to placate two (or more) opposing camps. They give one faction the law (saying, in effect, 'you see, I took care of it') while the other faction more or less retains the freedom to pursue activities which violate the law.

Etzioni then offers some guidelines for determining if a piece of legislation is intended to be effective or just cosmetic. These criteria will help in evaluating potential legislation before or after passage.

- Check the size of the fines; unless fines are large and consistently applied, they may be considered just one more small percentage of Entity's regular operating costs.
- Find out how widely the results of an enforcement action can be generalized. In legal parlance, anticipate the issue of a class action.
- Determine whether or not, and under what conditions, actual human beings (corporate directors, bureaucrats, elected officials, company owners, technical experts, etc.) can be held liable for any problems associated with the project. (Problems might range from things like sudden chemical explosions and meltdowns, to long-term health problems for neighbors or employees, to reduced property values downwind of the Project.) Entity will run a tighter Project ship if there are people who will be subject to substantial fines or even prison terms if things go wrong.
- Find out who may take action in the event of a suspected infraction. This is the issue lawyers call *standing*, or *standing to sue*. A law with enforcement teeth in it will not restrict standing to one-armed blind dwarves living in caves under the Project. Rather, it will extend standing to a wide range of interested and potentially affected citizens.

See *BEWARE THE MASKED RIDER; BUT THAT'S AGAINST THE LAW; GOVERNMENT REGULATORS WILL PROTECT YOU ; HEADS I WIN/TAILS YOU LOSE.*

Amitai Etzioni, "There Oughta Be a Law — Or Should There Be?", *Business and Society Review*, Winter, 1973-74, no. 8, pp. 10-11.

LOOKING FOR HELP IN ALL THE RIGHT PLACES

It is usually not productive to spend a lot of your group's time trying to change the minds of persons or organizations who think that the Project is a fantastic idea. Whether you are trying to enlist the support of legislators or neighbors, don't waste time and resources antagonizing those least likely to share your views. Instead, start with the easy ones.

This means not only your natural allies, but those who may initially be disinterested but who will experience no negative repercussions if they support you. Seek out those who, at first, don't care at all about your issues and will neither benefit from the completion of the Project nor suffer if it is halted. If you get to them early, they may support you solidly and steadfastly because their support for your cause does not harm them, economically or politically. For example, if you are trying to get legislative support for a bill to regulate the toxic waste dump industry, don't start looking for it among legislators who get half of their campaign contributions from that industry. Look instead among those whose campaigns are not dependent on waste-company contributions and whose constituencies support them already for their stands on other issues. Sometimes you can amass a lot of support from legislators who are less vulnerable to repercussions from annoyed and regulated industries.

LOOSE WIRES AND EXTRA WIRES

Always be on the lookout for loose wires, especially if an effort is made casually to discard the circumstance as without significance. Surprisingly often, monitoring equipment or pollution abatement equipment is simply disconnected. If there are no records of violations of regulations, then no action can be taken against the violator.

Coal scrubbers, for example, which remove some of the sulfur from the fuel at coal-fired power plants, reduce the power generated by five percent. Five percent of, say, a thousand megawatts is fifty megawatts, a lot of electricity not to sell. Think about it — others surely do.

When monitoring equipment is disconnected, the reason usually given is that it needed to be calibrated. When the component itself is disconnected, the usual reasons are maintenance or repair. At many facilities, the down time for the combination of calibration, routine maintenance, and repair insures that the facility is almost never operating under the conditions described in proposals, permit applications, or licenses. Keep your eyes open for evidence of these tactics both on site and in regulatory agencies.

Extra wires can be as interesting and insightful as loose wires. Often a special arrangement is made to bypass annoying pollution control or safety equipment. In other cases, special wiring can provide favorable conditions for a particularly powerful customer. It may take a highly trained technician or engineer to spot such anomalies. But there are tricks in every trade, and by knowing a little bit about what to look for, you may stumble upon one or two of the many disturbing practices that are too common in business and government today.

See *GOVERNMENT REGULATORS WILL PROTECT YOU.*

Jonathan P. Hicks, "Will Coal, the Plentiful Old Standby, Pick Up Speed?" *New York Times*, Aug. 26, 1990.

THE MALIGNED LETTER

A letter is sent out on the stationery of some widely respected, influential group. The letter praises the proposed Project and urges readers to carefully consider the following fine reasons for supporting Entity's plans. The usual reasons are then listed, and the letter closes graciously. Large numbers of people receive the letter.

This is a standard trick, one that can usually be used effectively only once (typically just before an election or another Big Decision). The organization's name and stationery has been used without the group's permission. When the official leadership figures out what has happened, it issues a letter and/or holds a news conference to clarify the organization's position regarding the Project. (Probably, it has or can take no position, at least officially).

But despite retractions, the damage has already been done. The impact made by the first letter will often exceed the impact of subsequent letters, especially if they contain complicated explanations and apologies. Sometimes, the retraction is not even issued until after the Big Decision has already been made.

Usually, in cases such as this, the influential group is genuinely upset, if not downright angry, about what has happened. In some cases, however, a group allows itself to be used in this way and issues a retraction later to officially clear itself of any wrongdoing. Keep in mind the possibility of this happening. It could even happen to your own group.

See *ACCIDENTS WILL HAPPEN.*

MANAGEMENT'S VIEW

Don't just rely on my biased views about how Entity personnel think. Go directly to the source, or, at any rate, to a source. There is no better way to get a succinct look at how Entity will respond to your group's opposition than to look at a recent management textbook. Go to a large public library, a university library, or a business school and pick out a few textbooks that are used to train managers to handle challenges like the one your group presents.

Until you can do this for yourself, consider the following summary of one typical public relations handbook for management.

What most of us normal, everyday people consider to be issues — things like regulations prescribing certain standards, consumer groups monitoring business performance, employees wanting a safe workplace, or stockholders asking for reform (or even disclosure) — are termed 'challenges' by management. Often, a challenge is translated as a 'pain-in-the-behind.' The typical management response is to hand the challenge at hand over to the public relations specialist. The point is this: a real issue to you is a PR problem to them. Never forget this, because, as insulting as it is, it can work in your favor.

A crisis occurs when one of the issues — a challenge — reaches a point where it can no longer be ignored. The immediate cause of such a crisis can be anything from a natural disaster to a lawsuit. When a crisis occurs, according to the management handbook, the first line of defense is to "contain the damaging effects of the crisis on the company's reputation." This is accomplished by, among other things, prohibiting employees from talking to the news media, and keeping the news media "away from victims, survivors, and relatives." We see once again how threatening the spread of information is to Entity.

Handling a group like yours falls under the category "Dissident Group Activity" — anyone who disagrees with Entity's world view and goals will automatically be considered to be a dissident. A range of tactics may be useful, among them avoiding or outmaneuvering the group and isolating the group by exposing is as a collection of social deviants. (There is no definition or elaboration of what a 'social deviant' actually is.)

The typical management handbook also discusses a number of ways to foster what it terms good community relations. Most are familiar, but it is worthwhile to remind ourselves how baldly they are stated. Donations and other corporate contributions "help to build community good will, improve the corporate image, and strengthen a company's political power." Sponsoring "little league teams, bowling teams, tennis tournaments, horse/dog shows, essay and crafts contests, presentations of annual trophies and cups, marching bands," concerts, and other exhibits builds a corporate image associated with humanistic and civic values.

In a related tactic, managers are urged to set up, foster, and control various groups in the community. Then, the group can perform various charitable and good-will activities such as sponsoring summer scholarships, putting on summer or winter bashes for local kids, or erecting statues or monuments to local notables.

Managers know that the idea of a new facility of some kind — a Project — is likely to cause problems. According to the management handbook, many of these problems are the result of some abstract "fear of change" among the community. Without saying it directly, this phrase suggests that there is something a little old-fashioned and a little irrational about reluctance to support Entity's new planned Project. Management's analysis goes further. These fears are more than irrational. They are exaggerated and unrealistic because they are rooted in ignorance, incomplete information, and rumor. The standard claim that Project opponents are uninformed or misinformed is thus trotted out again.

Expect Entity mouthpieces to haul out this familiar litany over and over again: its opponents are old-fashioned, irrational, and ill-informed. Proving that you are none-of-the-above will level the playing field a little and maybe give you a chance to address the real issues, but management will do all it can to prevent this.

In times of special stress, as when a new facility is planned, management is counseled to hold meetings with community groups and to work on recruiting a reliable and influential team of sympathetic local movers and shakers. This cadre is likely to include, among others: prominent members of the local business community, such as owners of large retail outlets or automobile dealerships, lawyers, realtors, bank presidents, or insurance brokers; media moguls, such as newspaper publishers or radio and television station owners; civil luminaries such as the heads of the PTA, the local service club, or the chamber of commerce; important officials, such as the fire or police chief, the town librarian, or the superintendant of schools; leaders of local political parties or civic groups; and anyone else who Entity believes has local influence.

This has just been a glimpse of what is inside a typical management handbook. Check a few out in the library yourself. Know what tactics to expect and try out a few on Entity itself.

See *THE CREDIBILITY GAP; UNWANTED MATERIALS COMPANY.*

Nathaniel N. Sperber and Otto Lerbinger, *Manager's Public Relations Handbook* (Reading, MA: Addison-Wesley Publishing Co., 1982), for example.

MEDWASTE AS A TROJAN HORSE

The idea of medical waste stops many people dead in their tracks. Fears of AIDS, germs from decayed body parts, and the possibility of contagious disease surround medwaste with a protective aura that can lead otherwise savvy activists to suspend their usual watchfulness. And because many people won't touch medwaste with a ten-foot pole, the need to dispose of the relatively small volumes of it has been used as a powerful seduction for constructing hazardous waste incinerators, often near heavily populated areas.

But the same kind of thoughtful analysis that has permited a drastic reduction of residential trash in many areas can work for medical wastes as well. The first step is to consult medical personnel who are committed to safely reducing the volume and danger of medwaste instead of those who stand to benefit financially or otherwise from the construction of incinerators.

The volume of medical waste can be substantially reduced by a variety of measures, only three of which are mentioned here.

- The amount of waste can be reduced at the source. Instead of being thrown together, different types and levels of medical waste can be kept separate from the beginning so that they can be treated separately later. This would reduce the volume of wastes that require special treatment.
- Many instruments can be re-used. Glass and metal are long-lasting and amenable to a wide range of sterilization techniques, some of which were in widespread use in the recent past.
- Alternate methods of de-activating disease-causing organisms can be used in place of incineration. These methods include photo-degradation, bio-degradation, and the use of safe chemicals, among other methods.

An industry that pursues its profits by incinerating will not hesitate to play on people's fears about the bogeyman of medwaste. NIMBY activists can point to other safe methods of managing necessary medical wastes while warning against the well-documented dangers of incineration.

See *FULL-COST PRICING; RECYCLING AND APPLE PIE.*

MOUNTAINS OF MATERIAL

Entity will be reluctant to release to the public any information except a few glossy public relations brochures. What it does release will probably come in as slow a trickle as is legally possible. However, through the application of various right-to-know laws and participation in various public hearings, your group will eventually gain access to more detailed, less glossy information.

As Entity realizes that it will have to release many studies, reports, and documents, it may try the *mountains of material* technique. The phrase was actually used by attorneys in a regulatory battle in Texas. One side released literally tons of papers, for the most part not organized so as to be understood by outsiders, in response to a list of specific and focused questions asked by the other side.

In this approach, Entity releases reams and reams of papers, reports, documents, computer printouts, copies of purchase orders, logs of monitoring equipment — mountains of material to be sure. Entity knows that non-specialists, and even sometimes specialists, will almost literally drown in such overwhelming amounts of unexplained and uninterpreted data.

As outsiders who have in the past probably complained that Entity was insufficiently forthcoming about producing information, you cannot easily now complain about too much information. Unless you are pursuing a highly structured *discovery* process, you probably have no legal recourse when the mountains of material appear.

Finding the information you originally sought will be like looking for a needle in a haystack, but having access to original documents can still prove useful to your group. If you sift through carefully and patiently enough, you just might gain some legally significant insights into Entity's mode of operations. As always, have your priorities clearly in mind before you dive into mountains of minutiae that will take months to digest.

Don't feel singled out if you become the victim of the *mountains of material* technique. It can be, and has been, used to befuddle corporate or government experts as well. Consider what happened in Texas when two large utilities were feuding in a regulatory environment that would probably permit only one of them to build a huge power plant complex.

Entity *Y* thought of itself as a blue chip utility and regarded its rival, Entity *X*, as a not-very-well-meaning and incompetent upstart. Entity *X* had done extensive studies, far exceeding the minimum necessary. This left it wide open to sniping by Entity *Y's* attorneys, who went over every page submitted by Entity *X* with a fine-toothed comb. For its part, Entity *Y* was infamous for not giving out information and followed that historic pattern in this feud as well. It offered as little information as possible, relying on its reputation and ruthless legal offense to carry the day.

A key issue revolved around which of the two Entities could provide the cheapest and most reliable electricity for the region. Financial data, energy use patterns, and detailed plans for construction and operation of the proposed power plants were argued down to the last penny, kilowatt-hour, and lump of coal. The language of the regulatory agency called for fiscal year data, so all the original testimony and reports followed this convention.

But Entity *X* felt that Entity *Y* had submitted its impressive conclusions without providing the supporting data upon which their conclusions were based. After much legal wrangling, the regulatory agency finally allowed Entity *X* to make supplemental information requests to Entity *Y* and directed the latter to comply.

Entity *Y* complied, all right, delivering literally tons of raw data, computer print-outs, and other hardly identifiable information to Entity *X*. The icing on the cake was that most of the useful data was tabulated by calendar year instead of fiscal year. It is virtually impossible to translate complex data from a calendar year framework to a fiscal year framework without knowing other things that Entity *Y* had no intention of explaining to Entity *X*.

Of course Entity *Y* claimed that that's all they had, and Entity *X* had little recourse because the data had in fact been delivered.

Even apparently successful informational requests can backfire if you forget that Entity is an old hand at having the last laugh. It is difficult to keep your sense of humor, however, when it happens to you.

MUDDYING THE WATERS

Look for tactics like these when evaluating a proposed Project or reviewing a Project history.

Remember the diesel oil spill in the Monongahela River near Pittsburgh in early 1988? After the spill was announced publicly, companies along the river called authorities to find out the spill's location. Eventually officials began to suspect that all kinds of other dangerous waste (containing chloroform, methylene chloride and trichloroethane — all used as industrial solvents) was being dumped where it would be masked by the original oil spill.

Many facilities routinely disconnect their monitoring equipment during times of heavy emissions, if not permanently, so proving the suspicion is another question. Likewise, if the facility in question has stacks or other large sources of air pollutants, it may release the really dirty air at night time when it is less likely to be noticed. With water-borne emissions, expect release during big storms or other catastrophic events.

See *LOOSE WIRES AND EXTRA WIRES*

Anon., "Firms Dumped Toxins During Spill, Experts Say," *Austin American Statesman*, Feb. 22, 1988; Wolfgang Saxon, "Monongahela Oil Spill threatens Water Supplies in Pittsburgh Area," *New York Times*, Jan 5, 1988.

A NICE GUY LIKE YOU

What's a nice guy like so-and-so doing working for Entity's Project? The most important thing about this question is that you should not be wasting your time thinking about it.

Entity probably has many nice guys working for it, and will certainly send as many of them as possible out to face the public and attempt to calm fears about the Project. This is a conscious tactic designed to disarm members of your group and the public, shifting attention toward this likable person and away from what you know are the hazards of the Project.

If you feel your resistance crumbling and find yourself wondering how such a humble and charming fellow could be on the wrong side of any issue — think of this. Your group is also full of nice, likable people, but is that fact inducing Entity's representatives to gush with sympathy and cancel or alter the proposed Project? Heck, no.

See *RED HERRINGS.*

NORMAL ACCIDENTS

In retrospect (that is, after an accident has occurred), it is often easy to look back at a situation and describe it as an accident waiting to happen. Too often we just leave it at that, perhaps hoping that someone else will figure out how we could have foreseen it.

Somebody has. Charles Perrow has reviewed a range of technologies — including petrochemical and nuclear facilities, dams, mines, weapons and space research, aircraft and airways, DNA research, and shipping — and come up with an insightful and persuasive analysis of the kinds of systems in which accidents are inevitable, or "normal" in his terminology. Here is a glimpse of his findings.

Normal accidents occur in systems that share a few key characteristics. (Nuclear power plants are great examples of such systems, so you may find it helpful to think of the Three Mile Island accident as you read these characteristics.) First, the system has many components (parts, procedures, and operators), all of which are arranged in a complex way. (That is, it's not one, long, linear process where *A* leads straight to *B* leads straight to *C*, one which can be stopped easily at any time.)

In such a system (with many components in a complex arrangement), it is obvious that many small failures — things such as faulty switches, burned-out light bulbs, minor operator errors — will occur. Such failures are not expected to be catastrophic because numerous back-up and emergency response systems — also complex — are in place.

A second characteristic of a system that will, according to Perrow, experience normal accidents is that two or more failures (of parts, procedures, or operator judgments) — failures that may be trivial in themselves — can interact in unexpected ways. For example, part *P* (a light bulb on a gauge) might fail at the same time that part *Q* (part of the back-up system) is off-line for maintenance. The failure of part *P* might leave operators unaware that a problem was developing. The inactive status of part *Q* might deactivate the emergency system that would have (probably) either alerted operators to the problem or shut down the now-dangerous system.

But the problem is just beginning. For one thing, the operators may not know that anything unusual is happening. There is so much going on, that in a system with literally billions of components, they may not know that part *Q* is not on-line. They have no way of knowing that the light bulb in a particular gauge should be blinking *danger*. The complex system, with all of its gauges, back-up systems, and interdependent processes (for example, pumps that automatically go on when temperature in a given area or temperature gauges reach a pre-established threshold), continues to function and react. Until other things go wrong, the operators will be unaware that there is a problem. And by the time they are aware of the problem, they will be unable to act appropriately because they have no way of knowing what else has happened.

At Three Mile Island, it took many months of sifting through computer data, numerous interviews, and much technical analysis before a reasonable scenario of what had happened could be constructed. This circumstance illustrates an inherent contradiction in high-risk systems because the very procedures that are necessary during normal operations are hopelessly inadequate during emergencies.

Here's why. During normal operations, a centralized control team must know exactly what each operator is doing so that one person does not do something that will interact with another component and endanger the whole system. Operator procedures must be fixed and exact. However, crises are much more likely when events for which there are no clear procedures occur. The lack of procedures, combined with operators' ignorance of the exact state of affairs, means that operators must take independent action based on their best guess as to what is happening.

Without suggesting that back-up systems and redundant safety features should be eliminated, Perrow notes that these measures add to the complexity of a system and decrease the likelihood of timely comprehension of the problem. An example will clarify this.

Suppose that, in order to insure the accuracy of control-panel information about a very important measurement, there are not one but two gauges measuring the amount of water in a tank. Now suppose that one shows that the tank is empty and the other that it is full. Is one gauge broken? Which one? Is the tank empty or full? Or is it half full, but both gauges are malfunctioning or disconnected?

Assume that a partly full tank could account for observed leakage and that an empty tank would explain overheating. What if other gauges suggest both leakage and overheating? Are both of these gauges accurate, or is one or both faulty, and if so, which one? And so on ...

Even in this oversimplified hypothetical case, the possibilities multiply rapidly when a possible doubt is introduced about each piece of information. In nuclear technologies, the catastrophic potential is immense while in other technologies accidents may be more frequent but more limited in catastrophic potential.

In *Normal Accidents*, Charles Perrow offers a framework for evaluating and reducing the risk of accidents in various industrial technologies. It's a great aid in taking a fresh, critical look at a proposed Project.

See *FISH AUTOPSY; GOVERNMENT REGULATORS WILL PROTECT YOU.*

Charles Perrow, *Normal Accidents: Living With High-Risk Technologies* (New York: Basic Books, Inc., 1984).

NUMBERS GAMES

Numbers and statistics have long been the domain of planners, bureaucrats, technicians, salesmen, scoundrels, and liars, among others. By carefully picking and choosing your numbers and how you use them, you can prove almost anything you want to prove. Entity already knows this, as the following examples illustrate.

The One-Percent Solution: "Removes 99% of pollutants!" In an effort to ease fears about pollution, Entity will often make comments like this about its air pollution control equipment. The ninety-nine percent is usually by volume, which means that ninety-nine percent of the total volume is removed. Sounds pretty good.

Well, maybe not. It may mean that the big stuff (over two microns in diameter) that your body's own defenses can handle quite well is removed. The remaining one percent consists of the tiny particles that reach your lungs with little interference and are extremely difficult (if not impossible) for your body's own defenses to handle. In addition, that ninety-nine percent rating is contingent on regular and careful maintenance — a rarity to say the least, especially when the operation of the control equipment itself requires a lot of expensive electricity.

(The above example is roughly accurate for the electrostatic precipitator, one of the two or three main ways of removing airborne pollutants resulting from combustion processes.)

Here is another creative use of numbers, this one involving the joys of averaging. The new version of the Clean Air Act allows an electric utility to combine the average emissions of all of its power plants together. This makes for good-looking numbers, but does not help those who may live downwind of the dirtiest plant.

What's Good For The Goose Is Good For The ... Gorilla: "The new law is stricter/ stronger/more effective than the old one because in the old law, only fifty percent of the polluters had to meet the standards. Now, under the new law, the standards apply to all polluters."

This kind of claim is usually made by a government agency to shore up its image as a tough regulator ('putting teeth in the regulations') or by an Entity advertising its supports of the new regulations. If anyone (like your group) has criticized or opposed a new set of regulations, then Entity will complain that troublemakers like you are just never satisfied and that you are habitual obstructionists. So, it is pretty important for your group to know the reality behind the claim.

The reality may well be that even though all polluters must meet current standards, the standards have been lowered. Some Entities can now pollute more than they did before. In addition, the original law may have only applied to large polluters, say the hundred largest companies that were responsible for ninety percent of the pollution volume. The new law may apply to thousands of other smaller companies which were responsible for only ten percent of the overall pollution. The end result is that the major polluters can pollute much more and the many small-scale polluters must take expensive measures to reduce their pollution. (This sort of ruling is usually particularly hard on small, local businesses.)

To check claims like this one, always figure the net effect: not how many companies are regulated but whether or not the amount of allowable pollution is increased or not. Sometimes it is better for half of all polluters to meet high standards than it is for all polluters to meet lower standards.

Leaners Only Count In Horseshoes Entity holds a press conference to announce the results of the Hooper Study, which shows that no more cancer deaths will occur among people exposed to chemical *X* than among those not exposed. Such a study might be about cancer or another disease, about chemical *X* or another environmental factor.

Any number of statistical tricks (not to mention outright fraud) can be employed to obtain these favorable results. One of the most common is to substitute death for disease. In example above (a made-up study but an illustration based on an actual case), the study focused on deaths and deemphasized tumor rates. Had tumors been counted instead of deaths exclusively, the reported cancer rates would have been much elevated in the exposed population.

Silk Purses And Sow's Ears Unpleasant facts can be repackaged in more palatable form, a skill Entity will be a master at. This is especially easy to do with numbers.

One of the unpleasant facts of life is increasing electricity and water rates. Watch carefully how such increases are expressed. Would you rather see your rates go up 12 percent each year or see them triple in less than a decade? Which sounds better? Actually, they're both the same. A flat $100 rate in year one, increasing at 12 percent annually amounts to $221 after 7 years and $310 after 10.

When an Entity is complaining about its own costs, it will take the *triple in ten years!* approach. When explaining your rate increases, it will say *twelve percent per year.* Always remember to make a few back-of-an-envelope calculations before breathing a sigh of relief.

Pollution by Dilution There are lots of laws and regulations that prescribe the quality standards which water discharged from a site must meet. These standards are often expressed in terms of how many parts per million (*ppm*) or parts per billion (*ppb*) of a particular element or compound may be released. A regulation might require, for example, that water discharged from a factory may not exceed eight ppm of lead.

One cheap and easy way to meet these standards is to let the faucet run. That eight ppm standard can be met by mixing factory byproducts with enough city water to attain a lead concentration under the threshold.

On the positive side, it can be said that this is perfectly legal and that streams or lakes in the nearby watershed will be fed by relatively clean water. On the other hand, consider that the factory may already be paying below-average costs for its city water. Residential water users may therefore be subsidizing the waste of water by a factory so that it can meet the statistical standards that are supposed to ensure environmental wellbeing. At a time when clean water resources are becoming more precious and water rates in general are rising, it is questionable whether pollution by dilution represents a responsible use of water resources.

See *GOVERNMENT REGULATORS WILL PROTECT YOU; LOOSE WIRES AND EXTRA WIRES.*

Matthew L. Wald, "A New Geography For the Coal Industry; The 1990 Clean Air Act will help some regions and producers while others suffer," *New York Times*, Nov. 25, 1990.

OTHER PEOPLE'S GARBAGE

Most communities are in the import-export business. They export garbage. All this garbage has to go somewhere, and increasingly it's small, poor, rural communities like McDowell County, West Virginia that do the importing. Proposed Projects in such places are forcing people to come to grips not only with what to do about their own trash, but also whether to accept imports for a price.

"Other People's Garbage," by Elizabeth Royte, is a case study of how one community wrestled with the issue and then, at least temporarily, rejected the option of playing host to a huge landfill. Royte's article is a thoughtful and fact-filled glimpse into a dilemma facing a large number of rural communities throughout the United States.

Elizabeth Royte, "Other People's Garbage — The New Politics of Trash: A Case Study," *Harper's Magazine*, Jun. 1992, pp. 54-60.

PROFESSIONALISM AND YOU

Entity knows that the people in the neighborhood right next to the proposed Project are probably never going to be convinced that it is a great idea. This is no problem for Entity, which can simply claim that those few dissenters are being greedy, selfish, unreasonable, and non-civic-minded.

On the other hand, Entity does have to be concerned when others, less directly affected, also begin to oppose the Project. If a local nurse speaks out to oppose the Project because of health-related concerns, Entity brings out its own doctor to testify that the nurse's health concerns are unfounded. If a chemistry professor from a local college brings up concerns about toxic chemicals, Entity will counter with statements from someone with advanced chemistry degrees from famous universities.

Many other professionals from the local community will hesitate to speak out, and those who do speak risk being subjected to attempts to discredit them. Such hesitation is instilled, and the subsequent discrediting enforced, by one's own peers under the banner of 'professionalism.'

The idea of the professional, and of professionalism, leads a double life in the English language. Many connotations are favorable. A profession is considered to be superior to a mere trade, a vocation. Professionals are expected to understand the pure, theoretical aspects of a field as well as the merely practical, applied aspects. The word professional is itself used as explicit praise, as in *she did a very professional job* or *it looked very professional*.

But the concept also has a dark side, suggesting insincerity, something done for money and not out of conviction. Someone may be pejoratively described as a *professional Don Juan* or a *professional agitator*. Still another dark side of professionalism is illustrated in phrases like, *a professional procrastinator* or *a professional leech*. These suggest that an activity, acceptable in small doses, pursued excessively, warrants 'professional' status.

Despite the tainted edge to some meanings of professionalism, many people cringe if someone suggests that their behavior is unprofessional. As a result, the possibility that someone may be accused of being unprofessional is a powerful negative sanction influencing that person's behavior.

A teacher may be accused of being unprofessional for showing too much interest in students. A nurse may be so accused if he or she joins an employee rights organization. An accountant is slapped with the unprofessional label if he or she goes outside of regular channels to call attention to fraud.

Professionals who speak out against the Project, even if they confine their comments to their own fields, risk being called unprofessional and even damaging their careers as a result.

Part of the meaning of professional is tied to a person's particular area of expertise. This means not biology in general but the egg-laying patterns of *Polygonia faunus*, not all of chemistry but factors affecting the boiling point of dimethylnitrosamine, not engineering as a whole but the creep strength of steel alloys.

With areas of expertise so narrowly defined, almost anyone whose studies do not exactly match the issue in question can be called unprofessional if he or she claims to draw on professional expertise in expressing an opinion. There is a Catch-22 aura around the whole situation. Any old biologist is not good enough to comment on the biological aspects of the Project; you need one whose area of expertise coincides with Project issues. So, too, for chemists, engineers, and other technical experts. Therefore, the only experts who can testify legitimately, without inviting criticism for lack of professionalism, are Entity's own hired hands (its experts and consultants). It is no surprise what their views will be.

At this point the dark side of professionalism returns not to haunt but to help your cause. The testimony of paid professional experts will be accepted by regulatory agencies and the courts, even though many rightly see the networks of experts as a racket of sorts. But regular people, members of the community whom you hope to convince, may distrust that same testimony simply because it is bought and paid for. What pleases the courts may irritate the citizenry.

This is one of those times when it becomes most clear that there are at least two battles going on simultaneously in the war against the Project. One battle is waged in the regulatory agencies and the courts, among lawyers and experts and bureaucrats. A second battle is waged at the grass roots for the hearts and minds of your neighbors, church group members, PTA's, bowling leagues, and garden clubs. If you can convince enough people to oppose the Project, you may still win the war against the Project while losing in the courts. A full-fledged grass-roots rebellion can make certain powerful people realize that the Project is politically untenable.

Be ready to counter suggestions that so-and-so is behaving unprofessionally by speaking out against the Project. Just as the taunt *chicken!* is usually a call to do something dangerous or stupid, the taunt *unprofessional* is a call to someone to shut up and return to the feed trough. Both taunts require courage to ignore. Both are easier to reject if they are seen clearly for what they are: cheap, desperate attempts to influence behavior by people who know that reason is on the other side.

See *A WORD ABOUT EXPERTS; STUDIES AND MORE STUDIES.*

PROMISES TO KEEP

Do not expect promises, pledges, or other assurances from Entity to be good predictors of future behavior. Entity's leadership and policies can and do change, often with the specific purpose of making it easier to wiggle out of past promises.

Entity will probably promise to do things like provide certain facilities, maintain certain standards, or perform regular monitoring of its performance. Sometimes the promised facilities are never set up. More often, they are partly or completely installed but then not maintained and allowed to fall into disrepair and disuse.

Getting it in writing will not necessarily help, either. After all, laws and regulations themselves are in writing, and it is difficult to achieve even partial compliance with them even when you have the assistance of armies of lawyers and experts.

Broken promises litter the files on events as famous as front-page headlines can make them, and they are just as common in less publicized controversies. Afterwards, the small pleasures and limited public relations benefits of saying *We told you so* are far outweighed by the damage done.

Rather than asking for verbal or written promises about standards and operating procedures, you might request instead that representatives of your group (or better yet, representatives of the public at large) be allowed to make regular and frequent inspections of records and facilities during construction to insure that no hanky-panky is in the works. Be sure to specify that you want informed observers (technicians, accountants, or lawyers for records and probably engineers for construction) to make the observations. Entity will turn this down faster than you can say toxic waste dump, but the refusal itself makes good public relations for you and allows some of Entity's true colors to show through.

See *THE BUCK IS PASSED; GHOST PERMITS; A FOOT IN THE DOOR; ACCIDENTS WILL HAPPEN; STANDARD OPERATING PROCEDURE.*

THE RATINGS GAME

Entities often seek to assure people that everything will be fine by referring to the standards that they will meet. They point to the laws governing their behavior and the regulations requiring them to achieve certain standards in order to convince you that compliance will be have to be complete and that enforcement will be virtually automatic.

But there is a third standard that Entity can use to soothe concerns when some large pieces of equipment (anything from a nuclear reactor to a super-security system in a prison) is part of the Project. This is the rating of the equipment.

Instead of inviting outsiders to review the past performance of similar equipment, to test the actual performance of the equipment, to monitor it at surprise intervals, or to measure the effects of it, Entity will cite a supposedly objective rating of the equipment. Often this rating is comparable only to other official ratings — that is, it does not bear much resemblance to actual performance and is not expected to.

But Entity will bet that most people don't know this. When asked about this or that potential problem, it will cite the impressive-sounding ratings of the equipment and avoid discussing the erroneous idea that ratings can somehow also describe the probable performance.

Whenever possible, ask for actual historical data — the records, not the ratings. These are likely to be a good deal less impressive than the ratings. Of course, they will be much more difficult to obtain.

See *NUMBERS GAMES; GOVERNMENT REGULATORS WILL PROTECT YOU.*

RECYCLING AND APPLE PIE

With all the media hype surrounding the recent rush to market 'green' products, the promise of recycling has taken on almost mythic proportions. As you evaluate a Project, you will increasingly run into claims that Entity is using recycled this or that or plans to recycle jumbo percent of its own such-and-such.

The increasing popularity of the term recycling (if not the idea) has already led to intense arguments over what real recycling is. A brief look at this civic-minded phenomenon may therefore be in order.

Recycling simply means re-using something that ordinarily or previously would have been thrown out. In this most basic sense, recycling does not specify what kind of use it got before the item was thrown out. Nor does it require a particular type of re-use afterwards. Sometimes, the way in which a particular material is recycled seems worse than not recycling at all. In other cases the term *recycling*, though technically and legally accurate, is misleading.

The *recycled* label can play the role of a roomy Trojan horse, offering an opportunity for all kinds of practices to slip in unexamined as part of a Project. In at least one case, for example, legal loopholes have enabled companies to dispose of their hazardous wastes without making public reports simply by declaring that they are recycling the chemicals. There's no reason for claims of recycling to escape examination while other aspects of the proposed Project are under close scrutiny.

One of the most familiar recycled goods is paper. In the paper business, there are several kinds of recycled paper. Some recycling involves post-consumption paper — paper (like office paper) that has actually been used at least once. Other recycled paper products contain no post-consumer-use paper, being made instead of various kinds of wood waste that was previously not used in paper-making. Some feel that labeling waste wood products as recycled is cheating, while others see both practices as positive steps. Evaluate it within your own framework, but do be aware of the controversy surrounding recycling.

Recycled non-aluminum food cans have some uses that might surprise you. Some of the recycled cans are sold to scrap metal companies which in turn sell them for use in making new steel cans. Many cans from places like California, however, are used in another way. Steel from the cans is shredded and used to make dissolved iron, which is then spread on huge open-pit copper mines. This allows enhanced recovery of the copper from poor ore and delays the expansion of the mines. The steel cans are literally recycled, but critics have expressed dismay that recycled materials are being used to increase the profits of such an environmentally devastating process as open-pit copper mining.

Used oil, like the stuff you drain out of your car, is quite toxic, containing all kinds of things that it didn't when you put it into your crankcase. The recycling of such oil often involves little more than collecting it and burning it as fuel — in the process releasing (into the air or as solid toxic waste) the materials that made it so toxic in the first place. (The EPA reported that in 1990 alone, 815 million gallons of used oil was burned as fuel.) Cement companies have even been paid to recycle toxic chemical wastes by burning them as fuel in their cement kilns.

And how about this recycling idea. Take waste ash (containing, among other things, lead, cadmium, dioxins, arsenic, and mercury) generated in the eastern U.S. where no one wants it in their back yards. Send it to Nicaragua where it can be used as a construction material for building roads through dense tropical forests in areas where torrential rains help spread the toxins through the ecosystem and where workers and those who use the road can be exposed. The Nicaraguan government gets paid for each shipment accepted, but almost all of the money goes to various handlers and businesspeople outside of Nicaragua. The United States disposes of toxic waste cheaply and can even call it recycling; intermediaries profit handsomely; and a developing country gets a load of toxic material that is a hazard to both human health and the integrity of the tropical forest ecosystem. (This proposal was actually considered seriously, but it had to be set aside temporarily following the outcry that arose when details of the operation were made public.)

What are some of the lessons to be learned from this quick overview of recycling? For starters, just because recycling is involved does not mean that the idea is necessarily a good one. Recycling has a wide range of meanings and applications, each of which needs to be evaluated on its own merits and with a particular context.

The success of recycling efforts — at least for the present — will depend on our collective ability to establish more or less stable markets for recycled materials. Once established, these markets have the potential to create a backlash and make the recycling business a market-driven one. For example, a municipality might find itself more or less forced to sign a long-term contract with a recycler guaranteeing certain amounts of trash — or pay an extra fee. This would encourage consumers to maintain a steady trash stream as opposed to minimizing their throwaways.

The recognition that recycling is part of a complex web of interrelationships among local, national, and international politics and labor, trade, and materials economics will enable you to evaluate the alternatives before you more dispassionately. But even without a global understanding of everything that recycling entails, you can at least examine your immediate options with a cradle-to-grave perspective — one that follows materials from the moment of their extraction until they and residual byproducts are safely at rest.

See *THE FINE PRINT; FULL-COST PRICING; MEDWASTE AS A TROJAN HORSE.*

Mitchell Cohen, "Green Tide/Toxic Imperialism: Exporting Pentagonorrhea," *Z Magazine*, Oct. 1990, pp. 78-79; Jock Ferguson, "Cement Companies Go Toxic," *The Nation*, Mar. 8, 1993; David S. Hilzenrath, "Oil Companies' Recycling Ads Called 'Flagrantly Misleading,'" *Washington Post*, Apr. 24, 1992; John Holusha, "Making Recycling Pay: In Solid Waste, It's The Breakdown That Counts," *New York Times*, Mar. 31, 1991; Jay Mathews, "How San Francisco's Discarded Cans Are Recycled to Aid Mining in Utah: Use in Copper Extraction Raises Complaints From Environmentalists," *Washington Post*, May 5, 1991.

RED HERRINGS

The term *red herring* originated in the late nineteenth century when it was used to describe the practice of throwing smelly smoked fish in the path of hounds during a hunt. The smell so confused the hounds that they were unable to follow the more subtle scent of their prey. Today the phrase is used to describe an argument or idea that so confounds the reasoning process that the thread of an argument is lost in the muddle.

The use of red herrings in public debate is widespread, often during controversies about regulatory policy. If it is not countered, the red herring can be very effective in anti-NIMBY campaigns.

A classic use of the red herring technique appeared in a *Wall Street Journal* piece by Jack Kemp, who argued that excessive environmental regulations have made it very difficult if not impossible for many working class and even middle-income families to buy their own homes. In particular, Kemp argued, regulations requiring various impact statements, the protection of endangered species, the regulation of drainage and runoff, and limits on construction in ecologically sensitive areas have increased construction costs so much that only the well-to-do can afford to purchase even modest homes.

This seemingly simple argument, if taken at face value, has three immediate consequences. First, it drives a wedge between two groups who should be natural allies: environmentalists and those who cannot afford to purchase a home. This wedge can make it more difficult for these groups to work together on issues that affect them both.

Second, Kemp's argument discounts the benefits of environmental regulations. Those benefits include: discouraging fast and shabby construction with associated unsafe use and disposal of potentially dangerous materials; reducing local and regional flooding (thereby protecting property values) and guarding against the degradation of the area water supply; and fostering long-term sustainable economic growth by protecting the natural infrastructure that makes such growth possible. (Wetlands, for example, contribute to the long-term viability of the natural infrastructure in such ways as preserving ground water quality and protecting fish and shellfish populations.)

The third consequence of blaming environmentalists for the nation's housing woes is that attention is diverted from the actual causes of the problem. Any serious inquiry into the so-called housing crisis would examine the full spectrum of potential causes, including changing income patterns in the U.S. during the last two decades, tax policy (including breaks and loopholes seldom available to any but the upper income brackets), and bank lending practices (like redlining), among others.

For those who toss out such aromatic red herrings, it is easier to hurl accusations on imaginary issues than to acknowledge underlying causes. The most harmful aspect of the use of red herrings in public debate is that it allows the accusers to frame the issues. Opponents are then left to try to re-state the issues in less misleading terms. As in a debate, the trophy often goes not to the one with all the evidence, but to the one who has most convincingly stated the problem.

See *WORDS AND MORE WORDS.*

Jack Kemp, "Free Housing From Environmental Snobs," *Wall Street Journal*, Jul. 8, 1991.

REGULATION-DRIVEN PROFITS

Given the large numbers of federal, state and local regulations, the regulatory environment is a major factor in company decisions. Details of regulatory law can have major effects on investment and operational decisions.

Many public utilities are heavily influenced by the most minute legal details. A public utility commission often sets a guaranteed rate of return on investment that a utility company may be allowed. The commission may also control certain aspects of the company's operations and finances, such as the costs which can and cannot be passed on to ratepayers.

Consider in this context the dilemma of a power company required to reduce the sulfur emissions from its coal-fired power plants. Two basic ways to reduce such emissions are 1) to burn low-sulfur coal, or 2) to install scrubbers, a common type of sulfur-removal equipment for power plants and similar facilities.

All other things being equal, low-sulfur coal is more expensive than the higher-sulfur variety, while scrubbers are costly to purchase, install, and operate. What do the regulations say? Some states will allow companies to pass on to ratepayers the cost of lower sulfur coal but not the cost of scrubber installation. High-sulfur coal it is, then. Scrubbers are not installed, and air pollution is greater than it needs to be.

Such seemingly minor provisions with major impacts are not uncommon in the regulation business. When you feel that you have a solid understanding of various related regulatory details, your group might consider it worthwhile to lobby to alter such legal details. If you do, always take care that you are not just being used as a front by a clever corporation that shares none of your goals and will double-cross you if it serves its interests.

See *THE INSTITUTIONAL ENVIRONMENT.*

REST IN PEACE

Cemeteries are very special places in the eyes of the law. The law — well, the letter of the law, at any rate — contains special provisions concerning the treatment of cemeteries and the disposition of human remains found therein. In general, access to the cemetery and the cemetery itself must be preserved, while remains can be moved or removed only for very compelling reasons and/or with consent of descendants. If there are any cemeteries within or near Project boundaries, you should begin looking into legal aspects of the case. Morbid as it may seem, cemeteries can become bizarre battlegrounds.

Check first to make sure that the cemetery meets legal definition of a cemetery. (Very old Native American burial grounds may not qualify as regular cemeteries, but they may be eligible for legal protection as Native American religious sites or as archaeological sites.) If the area is generally recognized as a cemetery, if the grave markings are legible, and if any relatives of those buried there can be located, you are 'in luck.'

Find out who owns and controls the use of the cemetery. Even if it is a quiet, rural cemetery where no one has been buried for decades, the rights and obligations of the various involved parties can be very complex. Consider that someone (or a company, or a government agency) owns the land on which the cemetery is located. That entity may or may not also control various rights to resources on the land.

For example, one entity may have the right to cut and sell lumber from trees in the cemetery. A second entity may have the right to use the surface water but only in accordance with certain permit provisions. (It may not have yet bothered to get the permit, in which case you may have a mini-permit fight on your hands in the future if you lose on the cemetery.) A third entity, subject to yet an another set of regulations, may retain the right to any subsurface minerals or oil that may be located there. In addition, the land may be leased on a ninety-nine-year lease to a certain church association or religious group, whose activities are limited by a particular charter or practice.

At first glance, it may seem that the presence of a tiny cemetery in the proposed project area may be a godsend (forgive the pun), sure to throw a monkeywrench into Entity's plans.

Dream on. Imagine this: quietly a team of Entity lawyers and assistants has done all of the legal research on the cemetery in question. Remember, this is not their first time. There are legal minds out there who specialize in turning cemeteries into non-cemeteries. While your group is still wondering if the cemetery will be affected by the Project, Entity agents (usually not mentioning Entity or Project) are out negotiating.

Before you know it, they will have bought surface rights, subsurface rights, water rights, and any other rights that may be available. They will have located surviving family members (with relatives in the cemetery), and induced them to sign papers granting permission for the disinterment of remains.

Never mind what these people — former holders of partial land rights or relatives of the deceased — were told. Entity (or more likely, its representatives) can say anything necessary to get those signatures. All that it puts in writing is in the contract. If not challenged, this verbal strategy can be extremely effective.

There are all kinds of ways to get someone to sign a contract that is contrary to that person's interest. A few common tactics are:

- The negotiator does not reveal who the real client is. A false name may be offered, sometimes along with a convoluted story. Or, the negotiator announces that the client wishes to remain anonymous.
- The agent says that everyone else (all the other surrounding landowners, or all the other relatives, for example) have already agreed. This general agreement (usually a fiction) is then used as evidence that the deal offered is reasonable and used to suggest that resistance at this late date will only hold up the whole thing.
- The negotiator does not want you to be able to get any independent, outside information about the deal he/she is proposing. Hence you are not told the names of any others who are being offered similar deals and you are not given a copy of the agreement until you have signed it (and maybe not even then unless you ask).
- The negotiator implies that the terms of any agreement will never be better and will worsen significantly if you do not settle very soon (now). Obviously, this is another attempt to pressure you into signing before you have a chance to look into the situation.

The overwhelming superiority of Entity in expertise, access to experts, lawyers, government records, and sheer intimidation power, along with its ability to sweeten deals with impressive and immediate financial rewards — all this makes effective countermeasures difficult. But there is much you can do, especially if you get active early.

Project backers will try to clear up most issues like this before the Project is even made public. But often, there are still loose ends to tidy up. Your groups needs to be able to scan the Project terrain, quickly pick up on possible trouble spots like a cemetery, and then act quickly to capitalize on them before it is too late.

A church organization can abandon a cemetery in a flash. Property rights and other claims are transferred, distant relatives sign unintelligible legal papers, and before you know it, bulldozers are leveling the area and the cemetery is gone. Disinterment is supposed to be done with care and respect, but if it is done during the night or with no witnesses, who can say it wasn't? Who can then dispute the claim that a particular box contains the remains of Uncle William?

All you can do is try to get to the interested parties before Entity's representatives confuse them with threats and promises. If you get there soon enough, and have some clear-cut legal issues and some firm parties/allies, an issue like a cemetery can tie up the Project for years.

See *ACCIDENTS WILL HAPPEN*.

THE RIGHT TO POLLUTE

Because of the way air pollution laws are written, a company has what is essentially a right to emit a certain specified amount of pollution. It may also have some leeway as to where it can use the right. It may, for example, be able to use up all of its pollution rights on one plant or spread them around among several. And under new laws if it does not use up all of its pollution rights, it can trade or sell them to another company. This has opened up a whole new area of laws and negotiations.

In practice, a company might build a new plant and install state-of-the-art pollution control equipment while leaving one of its old plants to spew extra-dirty air. Where a company chooses to do most of its polluting will depend on the cost, the likelihood of enforcement, the buying vs. selling price of pollution rights, and the local political climate, among other factors. Your group should make itself a major part of the local political climate, but keep in mind that the new market in pollution rights is a new and tricky factor.

See *THE INSTITUTIONAL ENVIRONMENT*.

Robert D. Hershey, Jr., "New Market is Seen for 'Pollution Rights'," *Wall Street Journal*, Jun. 14, 1989; Matthew L. Wald, "A New Geography For the Coal Industry; The 1990 Clean Air Act will help some regions and producers while others suffer," *New York Times*, Nov. 25, 1990.

A ROSE IS A ROSE IS A ... TULIP!

If things seem to be going pretty well for your group, you have figured out relevant laws and regulations, participated in hearings, succeeded in your public education efforts, and gained widespread support for your cause — things could change completely in an instant. For Entity, with its vast network of connections, its political clout and its army of lawyers, has a really impressive array of resources at its disposal. In addition, if Entity is a government body or is closely allied with one, access to the centers of power is awfully easy.

One thing it can do is change the rules mid-stream, as has happened with the *wetlands* designation. The 1989 definition of wetlands was extremely inconvenient to a wide variety of investors, developers, and even some government agencies. So, in 1991 a change that would drastically reduce the amount of acreage legally defined as wetland was proposed. Though the executive branch cannot rule by decree, it has great leverage in the regulatory realm and will probably succeed in its redefinition of wetlands, at least until the courts have a chance to set some precedents.

Cumbersome as it sometimes is to change a law, regulation, or definition, that option is often much easier and less costly than improving the Project to meet regulations or convincing the NIMBY opponents.

See *BEWARE THE MASKED RIDER; GHOST PERMITS.*

SAY NOW WHEN YOU START CONSTRUCTION

When you are dealing with regulatory law and a determined Entity, you will find that even the 'ifs, ands, and buts' have 'ifs, ands, and buts.' Be ready for Entity to propose all sorts of creative ways to get around regulations that you think are quite clear. Consider the following example, which hinges on the meaning of the word *construction*.

An electric utility company was planning to build a two-unit power plant in which some parts of the facility were to be common to both units. Construction on Unit One began in June 1975 while Unit Two was started in October 1976. These dates were widely reported both by the utility itself and in area newspapers.

At the time, EPA required a particular permit for facilities such as this for construction which began after June 1975. In keeping with this, no permit application was filed for Unit One, but in 1977, a permit application was filed for Unit Two.

In 1980 the utility discovered that Unit Two, without modifying its design, would have particulate emissions several times higher than would be allowed by the EPA permit.

A flurry of letters went back and forth between EPA and the utility until the utility made an argument that the EPA would accept. The argument went something like this: The date October 1976 was chosen to identify the beginning of the construction in order to satisfy the definition of construction used by a *state* air quality board. However, using the EPA's definition of construction, the utility determined that construction of Unit Two had in fact begun in June 1975, simultaneously with construction of Unit One.

The EPA bought it, the permit application for Unit Two was withdrawn, and another coal-fired generating unit was exempted from more stringent air quality regulations.

See *COMMON SENSE NEED NOT APPLY; YOU BUY THE BEER, I'LL BUY THE BUBBLES.*

SET IN (SOFT) CONCRETE

When you are reading through thousands of pages of highly technical drawings, engineering diagrams, and descriptions of multiple back-up systems, all clothed in scientific jargon and sprinkled with numbers and unfamiliar symbols, it is easy to find yourself being swept along and feeling reassured that everything will probably work all right. Here's an example to remind you that the on-site reality seldom matches the clean diagrams.

The Department of Energy (DOE)is trying to clean up thousands of sites used during half a century of production of nuclear bombs. Much of the time it doesn't know exactly what materials it is handling because decades of neglect, mishandling and mixing of wastes has occurred.

One major facility was using what are known as *solar evaporation ponds*, even though it knew that little evaporation occurred. Instead, the mix of cancer-causing solvents and heavy metals was seeping into the ground water beneath the site. To halt the seepage, management decided to mix concrete into the ponds. No pilot studies or other tests were performed to evaluate whether or not this step was a good idea or not. What happened was that the concrete did not set. Now the DOE has over ten acres of ponds of toxic, unhardened concrete and no assurance that the seepage has been stopped.

There are thousands of examples like this one. Keep this in mind before you let an engineer with colored maps and a pointer convince you that everything is under control.

See *GOVERNMENT REGULATORS WILL PROTECT YOU; BUT THAT'S AGAINST THE LAW!*

Matthew L. Wald, "The Adventures of The Toxic Avengers Have Barely Begun," *New York Times*, Sep. 15, 1991.

THE SIGNIFICANCE OF SIGNIFICANCE

Government and corporate spokespersons and official documents use many words — like the *significant* in *significant impact* — that seem to have clear, common-sense meanings. Do not assume that the legal sense of a seemingly familiar term (such as significant impact, alternative, best available technology, or mitigation) will match your common-sense understanding of it. Often the real, legal sense will surprise, amuse, or enrage you. Just make sure that your surprise, amusement, or anger comes early in your struggle and not after a critical hearing when it is too late.

See *WORDS AND MORE WORDS; COMMON SENSE NEED NOT APPLY.*

THE SILVER LINING

There is no lack of creativity in the effort that goes into justifying Projects. For example, some environmentalists and fishermen oppose the destruction of already existing but out-of-use offshore oil rigs because they provide a mini-environment for plant and animal species. This is a far cry from claiming that offshore oil drilling has an overall positive effect on the environment.

A dedicated PR team working for Entity will make it seem like there was hardly any place for poor little fish to hang out until Homo sapiens began building piers and oil drilling platforms. Or, ignoring the rapidly accumulating evidence that power lines pose a health risk to animals from cows to humans, they will print stunningly beautiful pictures of hawks perching on transmission line towers, as if the birds had been doomed to flap their wings eternally before we humans kindly set up special perches for them.

After the 1990 Clean Air Act passed, the Lumpa Coal Company, whose coal is among the cleaner grades, printed up T-shirts with the motto: "Lumpa Lite Coal: Burns Great, Less Polluting." (The name is obviously a pseudonym, but the T-shirt was real.)

The best defense is a good offense, and Entity will find ways of attacking opponents for their insensitivity to

Entity's supposedly good deeds. This is just one of many tactics designed to distract you from the central issue of the Project. It is not whether fish live near an oil rig or whether birds perch on transmission lines. The central issue is whether or not the Project will be a safe, appropriate, and desirable alteration to your community.

See *RED HERRINGS.*

James P. Sterba, "Save the Oil Rigs? Yes, some say, they are Habitat-Forming," *Wall Street Journal*, Apr. 29, 1988.

SMILE, YOU'RE ON CANDID CAMERA ... OR ARE YOU?

Video surveillance cameras are used in many high-risk operations to insure that there is a record of events in sensitive areas. Such cameras can detect and record both physical changes (cracks in containment building walls, for example) and human activity (like vacuuming out radioactive water).

These videotapes can also potentially record and preserve evidence of inadequate safety measures and inappropriate environmental procedures. At least potentially. In at least one case, bright security lights aimed at video cameras rendered the cameras totally ineffective.

The case in question may not be earthshaking in itself, but represents just one more example of how reasonable precautions and safeguards can supposedly be inadvertently circumvented. Never put all of your eggs in one basket — never rely on a single camera or document or testimony that Entity can render worthless by means of what appears to be an accident.

See *ACCIDENTS WILL HAPPEN; GOVERNMENT REGULATORS WILL PROTECT YOU.*

Thomas W. Lippman, "Uranium Pollution Probed at Oklahoma Plant," *Washington Post*, Apr. 29, 1991.

SOUTH OF THE BORDER

It's no surprise when an industry goes across a border (or an ocean) in order to take advantage of drastically lower wage scales or less strict environmental regulations. But until relatively recently, electric power plants tended to be in or near the region that they served.

However, with the rapid linking of electrical grids during the last decade, vast areas share access to essentially identical power supplies. When you turn on a light in Lackawanna, you are usually getting your electricity from a nearby power plant. If, however, that plant is down, you can still use electricity pumped into the grid from somewhere else, perhaps hundreds of miles away.

Connection to the grid can provide several advantages. First, it can provide back-up electricity in case of an outage. Second, it can offer utilities the opportunity to buy the cheapest electricity available at a given time. As demand goes up, more expensive power plants gear up and join the less expensive ones already generating. All things being equal, the most expensive plant will be the last to be used. (Line losses from sending electricity long distances and contracts for guaranteed electricity sales are two factors that would alter the simplistic model outlined here.)

The grid system also has some drawbacks. The complex system is susceptible to what Charles Perrow calls "normal accidents." The cheapest electricity may be coming from the oldest and therefore the dirtiest (least environmentally sensitive) power plant. By making traditional borders obsolete, the grid system permits the legal evasion of environmental laws or other regulatory oversight, an increasingly attractive and frequently pursued option.

With the surge in public opposition to many Projects, the socio-political climate can be as important a factor as the regulatory environment. Increasingly, operators have built their power plants away from the strength of public opposition and imported the power back in.

This practice has become a tradition in California, where relatively pristine communities are ringed, at politically safe distances, with the infrastructural support facilities necessary for their vigor and comfort. The phenomenon is also apparent internationally. Italy has been planning a very large power station to be built in the former Soviet Union. Likewise, a French consortium has proposed to build two nuclear power plants in Hungary for electricity to be exported to Germany and Italy.

It is no longer possible to ignore the fact that everywhere is some body's back yard. Unfortunately, some people's back yards are still deemed more equal than others.

See *ENVIRONMENTAL RACISM; NORMAL ACCIDENTS.*

Charles Perrow, *Normal Accidents: Living With High-Risk Technologies* (New York: Basic Books, Inc., 1984);
David Thomas, "Hemmed in on all sides (Electricity supply industry)," (Industry and the Environment special section), *The (London) Financial Times*, Mar. 13, 1991.

A SPOONFUL OF SUGAR

Often, in an effort to 'sweeten' a proposed Project, Entity will decorate it with unrelated tinsel in an attempt to distract attention from the Project's massive flaws and make the whole package seem more palatable. The sweetening can occur before the Project's approval, during the construction phase, or even after regular Project operations begin.

Entity will seek to maintain good public relations (which it calls 'being a good neighbor') as long as successful Project operations are at least partly dependent on public support. Even after the Project is operating, Entity will probably have occasion to come back to a public body (a city council, a regulatory agency, whatever) to make further requests. It may need permission to expand the facility or eliminate certain safeguards, or it may seek tolerance and forgiveness for promises it has already broken.

The sugar in these combinations is often wonderfully disjunctive. A waste disposal company that became successful by dumping unspeakable toxins just 'south of the border' will offer to have its facility be a model of recycling and promise to recycle eighty percent of the on-site generated trash. The backers of a mega-loop highway interchange that will pave/flatten/wipe out two minority neighborhoods and a park will promise to construct a modern playground as partial compensation for neighborhood dislocation. Or a gigantic physics experiment will house an innovative habitat reconstruction. (In Batavia, Illinois, almost all of the area within the ring of a massive particle accelerator was replanted with indigenous prairie species, some of which had grown there prior to European settlement.)

Sweeteners like these are not chosen lightly. When Project backers realize that some opposition may arise, they appoint a task force or hire a consulting firm to run interference for them. Who is likely to be most upset about a particular project? What 'perks' would that group find to be most irresistible?

For example, if an older, tightly knit ethnic neighborhood in decline is to be razed, Entity will promise job training for that particular group and promise to hire *x* number of workers from what had been the neighborhood. If the habitat of an endangered species is to be destroyed, Entity will help set up a nature preserve — elsewhere, of course. If historic preservationists are concerned about the destruction of century-old structures, Project backers will set up a special museum or contribute toward preserving some other similar structures, away from the Project area.

Many professionals and academics are especially susceptible to this sort of subtle bribery. Of course biologists and hydrologists want to be working, doing studies, strutting their stuff. Entity can probably fund a few of each for years on less money than it takes to launch a serious television advertising campaign. Archaeologists want to excavate — hire them to do surveys and studies, give them a place to sit around sorting pot sherds, and keep them happy. Economists like to analyze and count; hire them to do a study to estimate the effect of the Project on the local economy. Entity will help as much as possible, provide data that is conveniently available, and maybe even throw in some computers and office space.

Entity knows that professionals and academics so employed are less likely to turn in research strongly critical of the Project. Universities and private consulting firms are equally susceptible to the slight clouding of vision that often accompanies lucrative or long-term research grants or contracts. University researchers, consultants, private engineering firms...none of these are independent, scientific, objective researchers, no matter what they say or how often or emphatically they say it. They are interest groups whose business happens to be research and/or information.

Having said that, it should also be said that most researchers are honest, competent, and conscientious, that they love their work and want to do it accurately and meaningfully. Some or most may even personally oppose the Project. However, they also want to keep their jobs and their positions and to preserve the comfortable standard of living to which they are no doubt accustomed. Throwing them a bone in the form of a consulting contract or research facility may be more than enough to forestall any possibility that professionals or university faculty or administrators will officially oppose the Project.

See *A WORD ABOUT EXPERTS; THE ELVIS PRESLEY MEMORIAL TOXIC WASTE DUMP; MANAGEMENT'S VIEW; ARROWHEADS, ANYONE?*

Christine Mlot, "Restoring the Prairie," *Bioscience* vol. 40, no. 11, Dec 1990, pp. 804-809.

STANDARD OPERATING PROCEDURE

Entity's public responses to environmental accidents and Project crises paint a picture of the generic, standard operating procedures to be expected of Entity. Based on real events, here is a succinct summary.

While the Project is being planned or discussed, Entity will make many promises about the future measures it will taken and the capabilities it will attain. Some measures will be skipped entirely, never put in place at all. Others will be at least partly set up, then phased out after a few picture-taking sessions. Other measures will be set up but not maintained and allowed to fall into disuse or disrepair. Still others will be established halfheartedly, using inferior, less safe, cheaper materials or inadequately trained personnel.

Meanwhile, Entity will fight against other safeguards, saving money during such delays by continuing less safe, not-yet regulated practices. Monitoring equipment will not be set up at all, set up incorrectly, or set up in an appropriate manner and then not maintained properly. Records may be fabricated, as is convenient.

Then the accident, long predicted by Project opponents, will occur.

The immediate post-accident response will fall far short of what was promised. Extensive public relations work by Entity will downplay the weak response and present the public with a picture of heroic and selfless good deeds on the part of Entity personnel. In the aftermath, the amount of damage will be understated dramatically.

This, in a nutshell, is the cycle. In its general outline, it seems pretty constant and applies equally well to private and public sector Entities. On the public side, the military branches of the U.S. government provide numerous outstanding examples. Military treatment of toxic and hazardous waste is generally recognized as unsurpassed in its lack of respect for regulatory and procedural law.

Historically, Entities have an remarkably negative record for keeping promises, maintaining safeguards, or generally protecting the broadest public community interest. In view of this, the burden of proof, a heavy one indeed, should fall on Entity to demonstrate its seriousness and competence rather than on community groups to justify their concerns. Your group can insist on framing discussion in such a way that the public does not forget this.

See *GOVERNMENT REGULATORS WILL PROTECT YOU; ACIDENTS WILL HAPPEN; PROMISES TO KEEP.*

Charles B. McCoy, "Broken Promises: Alyeska Record Shows How Big Oil Neglected Alaskan Environment," *Wall Street Journal*, Jul. 6, 1989.

STEALTH GARBAGE

Especially during the last decade, NIMBY activists and other concerned citizens have used regulatory law to their advantage. Such groups have had some success in delaying, stopping, or modifying Projects that they felt were inappropriate. Their successes have not gone unnoticed.

Responses to these successes have gone in two directions. First, pressure has been brought, with some success, to change the regulatory laws. In some cases, the regulations have been changed to make requirements and standards less stringent. In addition to easing the standards themselves, changes have reduced opportunities for public participation. This has been done, for example, by limiting the scope and number of hearings or by making it more difficult to get standing to participate.

A second direction has been to avoid confrontation. Entities have sought to settle possibly controversial matters before they have reached the hearing stage and to avoid drawing attention to controversial Projects until most or all legal requirements have been met. The treatment of garbage provides an excellent example of this second direction.

Only a few years go, an unsightly, smelly mess known as the *poo-poo choo-choo* — a railroad shipment of sewage sludge — gained notoriety as it traveled around the country while bureaucrats tried to find a landfill that would accept it. The waste industry learned a valuable lesson from that train's embarrassing journey.

Today, some of the most unpleasant and dangerous waste materials are shipped in clean, shiny, sealed railroad cars that are unmarked or labeled only in code. Train shipments, which generally attract less attention and cause less air pollution or traffic congestion than truck shipments, are increasingly the method of choice for transport of potentially controversial cargo. Garbage shipped in this way has earned the nickname *stealth garbage*, because it often goes unnoticed, shielded from public knowledge by clever packaging.

Stealth garbage in particular and whole stealth Projects in general are the wave of the future. They will require heightened vigilance on the part of NIMBY activists.

See *BEHIND THE BERMS; UNWANTED MATERIALS COMPANY.; ENVIRONMENTAL RACISM.*

Don Phillips, "Out-of-State Garbage Is Paying the Freight: Shiny Cars Mask Trains' Controversial Cargo," *Washington Post*, Dec. 22, 1991.

STOPPING AT NOTHING

Though you can expect Entity to employ a sophisticated public relations effort to promote the Project, do not presume that there is not an ongoing parallel effort using much cruder methods. Employees, for example, have been asked to remove documents to keep them out of the hands of investigators; to rewrite environmental documents so that the findings seemed to be ambiguous; or to limit the circulation of sensitive documents so that higher officials could deny they had any knowledge of certain problems.

These are but a few examples among many more that appear regularly in court records and newspapers. They should serve as a reminder to not be naïve in expectations about business operations, especially when the stakes are high.

See *THE FISH AUTOPSY; TESTING, TESTING...; STOPPING AT NOTHING*

Martha M. Hamilton, "Fired Mobil Employee Wins $1.375 Million Judgment," *Washington Post*, Nov. 11, 1990.

STRANGE BEDFELLOWS DEPARTMENT

Allies can come from unexpected places. In Colorado, for example, plans for a giant hog farm were opposed by a coalition that included small farmers, the owner of an exclusive hunting lodge, animal rights activists, and the Coors beer family, among others.

Why should Georgia peanut farmers oppose paper pulp mill pollution?

Perhaps because the National Acid Rain Precipitation Assessment Program has estimated that high ozone levels in the atmosphere (partly from paper mills) cost three billion dollars in lost crop yields to farmers in a single year. Corn, soybeans, wheat and peanuts are among the crops most affected.

Companies which produce or import the rhodium and platinum used in auto emissions control equipment should benefit from and therefore support the new Clean Air Act. Railroad companies stand to benefit from transporting some of the cleaner western coal to power plants in the east.

See THE INSTITUTIONAL ENVIRONMENT; LOOKING FOR HELP IN ALL THE RIGHT PLACES.

William Booth, "Billionaires' Battle Lingers Over Colorado Hog Farm," *Washington Post*, Apr. 29, 1990; Jeff Nesmith, "Pollution taking toll on crops, institute says," (Cox News Service), *Austin American Statesman*, Sep. 9, 1988; Robert Reinhold, "Environmental Truce Brings Water to Rice Fields," *New York Times*, Dec. 12, 1992.

STUDIES AND MORE STUDIES

You are going to be dealing with many studies, so it may be useful to take a look at the different kinds of studies that you may encounter.

Studies may be done by individuals, consultant firms, or agencies. The people involved may or may not be associated with universities, research facilities, industry organizations, think tanks, or government agencies. You need to know who did the study, who paid them, whether the study was specifically requested (and if so, by whom), and whether or not there is an ongoing business or financial relationship between the persons requesting the study and the persons performing it.

It is rather common, for example, for a scientist who holds a faculty position at a university to conduct research partially or totally funded by a particular industry. The results of the study might then be made available to the industry, used as lecture material, and published in a scientific journal. Suffice it to say that a researcher whose life work depends on industry funding may not be the most reliable or objective source of information.

You also need to know the specific goals of the study. An Entity representative might claim that "the *ABC Study* found no evidence of discharge" from a particular facility. This may be true but not particularly relevant if measuring discharges was not one of the purposes of the study. Entity may not hesitate to distort and mislead in this way, so if a particular study is crucial to its case, you should be familiar enough with it to be able to counter such obvious tactics.

Depending on the subject, original research — research that requires actually gathering raw data — can be very time-consuming and expensive. In most cases, when a government agency or corporation commissions a study, it will not be asking for original research but for what is more correctly termed a 'literature review.'

The researcher, often more a compiler, will gather together all relevant literature (articles, studies, data on file, etc.) on the requested subject area. The literature will then be summarized and written up as a report, often with a conclusion reiterating major findings. The report thus produced will then be accepted by Entity and used to bolster claims that its proposed Project will be beneficial and benign.

There may be nothing new in reports based on quick literature reviews. Entity may not want to pay for, or see, the results of a piece of original research. It is expensive and risky to send someone out into a community and actually sample the water, test the air, check soil samples, collect medical records, or ask questions that generate unrehearsed and honest answers. Rarely are studies open-ended and exploratory; they have a specific goal which is usually to give Project supporters a favorable official-looking report to wave around.

In addition to its lack of original research, such a study may not be inclusive. It will select data and studies that tend to support the viewpoint of Project supporters. If recent published studies have questioned the rationale behind Entity's arguments, these studies may be either ignored, or dismissed as aberrant or atypical. I have never understood what is so compelling about hearing a three-piece-suited consultant label all negative studies as 'not representative' or 'not relevant,' but unless countered, the tactic seems to work all too well in both regulatory agencies and courts.

A standard literature review or literature search is often very easy to critique. This is because the actual study submitted is probably a generic study that has been customized to fit Entity's specific proposed Project. Furthermore, any site-specific data will have been furnished by Entity's staff. A staff that knows the process and controls the raw data is in an excellent position to influence, if not predetermine, the eventual conclusions.

Suppose, for example, that a particular consulting firm specializes in issues related to soil erosion. After a few years, it has done reports (literature reviews) on soil erosion and agriculture, highways, office buildings, strip mines, hills, beaches, cold climates, tropics, and most other aspects of the subject. It is by no means starting from scratch on each report. It takes its basic soil erosion study, removes anything that is inapplicable to Entity's Project, adjusts the variables for the particular soil types and conditions involved, adds on some site-specific maps, and generates predictable conclusions.

Your group's task is to locate the 'aberrant' and 'atypical' studies that have been left out and to find independent sources of information on the site in question. Previous studies conducted by others for different purposes and government reports based on routine data-gathering may include valuable data. Many impressive-sounding studies will actually prove to be hastily thrown-together documents that do not stand up even to the most cursory criticisms.

Often a consultant's report is little more than an Entity's attempt to have an already-made policy decision appear to be the result of a careful, independent study. Such reports will, among other things, use Entity's data base, conduct no field research, employ misleading averages, misrepresent existing conditions through omission and selection of data, and neglect to mention numerous regulatory loopholes of which Entity is well aware and intending to use. In addition, Entity will displace some of the responsibility for unpopular decisions on the consulting firm that makes a particular recommendation, supposedly based upon its independent analysis.

The displacement of responsibility in this manner is especially common when Entity is a government or quasi-government agency. Such agencies are at least indirectly subject to public pressure through elected officials who supervise the agency themselves or influence the appointment of those who do. With so much importance attached to the consultant's study, it is especially important for your group to dissect and critique it carefully and to become familiar with the unmentioned 'aberrant' research relevant to the Project.

See *PROFESSIONALISM AND YOU; A WORD ABOUT EXPERTS.*

'TAKINGS' AND THE FIFTH AMENDMENT: PROPERTY RIGHTS

Taking the Fifth is acquiring a whole new meaning in the realm of property rights law.

The Fifth Amendment of the U.S. Constitution states in part, "...nor shall private property be taken for public use, without just compensation." A *physical taking* of your land through the government's eminent domain (condemnation) powers (say, for an interstate highway or missile testing range) may be carried out only if the government pays you the fair market value of your condemned property. This is a fairly widely accepted and understood aspect of this Fifth Amendment clause.

In other cases, the government's taking may be less than complete. When the government puts a power line across your land, it 'takes' some of the land's value by restricting your use of it in some way. (You would not want children flying their kites there, for example, nor would your scenic campground be quite as successful.)

Recently, landowners have been claiming even further rights under this takings clause. In these recent cases, almost any government restriction or limitation on land use has been claimed as a taking — a *regulatory taking*. Those affected have demanded just compensation from the government for the loss in value.

The idea that government regulation amounts to a taking and thus requires compensation has opened the door to a wide variety of very cleverly argued claims. Compensation for lost value has been requested in cases where:

- zoning laws have limited the development of land;
- government-protected grizzly bears have killed cattle;
- protected wild animals have eaten part of the forage from grazing lands;
- the protection of spotted owls has made timber uncuttable.

The courts have not yet established clear guidelines governing such regulatory takings, but a number of interesting cases, such as the ones above, are winding their way through the courts.

Implications for NIMBY activists are not yet clear, but the new takings issue may aid NIMBY battles in some cases and hamper them in others. On the one hand, if regulatory takings are interpreted broadly and compensations are ample, the whole framework of regulatory law would be too expensive to maintain. The resulting collapse of the regulatory system would leave NIMBY activists with fewer and weaker legal pegs to hang their arguments on. On the other hand, NIMBY activists could conceivably use a very broad notion of regulatory takings to limit the government's ability to take land for Projects, essentially by making these lands unaffordable.

In the current legal context, most regulatory takings arguments would seem to limit the options now open to NIMBY activists. In order to bring in some other perspectives on the issue, consider the subject of takings as it applies to wetlands. This scenario is not confined to wetlands, however. It is readily applicable to a number of other issues, as well. In overview, seemingly reasonable steps too often result in a massive transfer of taxpayers' money to private fortunes. Viewing this phenomenon in the broader framework makes it possible to break the circularity of its argument.

The wetlands saga begins with the assertion that in order to accomplish certain things like safeguarding the shellfish and fishing industries, maintaining a safe and viable water table, or providing for a continued healthy tourist trade, wetlands must be protected. This is because the ecosystems that support the above concerns themselves depend on wetlands.

In order to protect and maintain the wetlands, some lands may have to be taken out of circulation, prohibited from being developed. If such lands are public, then such prohibition is relatively easy. If the lands are private, there are two options. One is the *physical taking* — purchasing the land through regular channels or by means of eminent domain. The second is the *regulatory taking* — leaving the land in private hands but placing heavy restrictions on what may be done with the property.

In either case, private landowners are going to want just compensation either for their land or for the lost value that they experience when new restrictions prevent them from developing or using the tract. Property owners may argue that they planned to develop the land as part of a condominium village for retirees or a golf course or that the purchase of comparable land elsewhere is now astronomically expensive.

Stated in this way, landowners' claims for compensation may seem just and reasonable. The flaw in this line of reasoning becomes evident, however, if such claims are placed in a broader context.

The purchase of the land was, among other things, an investment, and it should be evaluated as such. Investors who put their money in asbestos would have experienced a large drop in the value of their stock shares when public health regulations required cleanup of asbestos-related health hazards or compensation to workers for asbestos-caused diseases. Those who invested their money in nuclear power would have seen their investments suffer after federal law began requiring companies to be responsible for the actual costs associated with decommissioning plants and the safe disposal of radioactive waste materials. On a mundane level, anyone who buys a gas-guzzling car will be hard hit when gasoline prices skyrocket, whether the reason for such price increases is international tensions, environmental regulation, price manipulation, or tax increases.

The government is not held responsible for guaranteeing the value of these other investments when new laws or other external factors alter the social and political landscape in which they operate. Nor does the government guarantee the pension plans of workers whose retirement funds invested heavily in companies that subsequently went bankrupt while their top executives floated gently down to earth on golden parachutes. It is reasonable to ask why landed investments should be given special treatment, why the government should pay out compensation based on the imagined future profits of persons whose investment happened to take the form of land.

The issue has become clouded because of the special beliefs often associated with private property rights. The exercise of private property rights has always been encumbered by laws that range from the silly to the sensible. Your grass may not be longer than two inches, you cannot paint your house purple, you cannot abandon a car in your front yard, you cannot pour toxic chemicals in your lawn, you cannot open up a beauty parlor in your house, your mailbox must meet certain specifications, you must use a flush toilet connected to municipal sewer lines, you cannot cut your trees down and sell them for plywood, you cannot burn leaves, you cannot dam the creek that runs through your lands, you can water your lawn only on odd days, you cannot mine for copper without a permit, you cannot block your neighbor's solar collector, you cannot set up a private radio station, you cannot pile garbage in the yard, and so on. Not all laws governing the exercise of private property rights are good ones, but their very existence explodes the myth that rights to the use of private property are totally unencumbered.

Limitations on the use of private property have existed in one form or another since the dawn of humanity. They have been modified (not always for the better) as societies changed and our knowledge of how things work improved. Our understanding of ground water (aquifers) and bays and estuaries and wetlands has grown remarkably even in the last two decades. It is only natural that other social customs (including law in general and the notion of property rights in particular) will change in response to our deepened understanding — as has been happening since before humans started writing down rules.

New interpretations of the takings clause are reasonable and clever in the context of a pioneer's sense of property rights but shocking and revolutionary in terms of the more general regulation of everything from alcohol consumption to building codes that has gained widespread acceptance in our society.

The takings issue may be far from resolution, but it will certainly play an increasingly large role in NIMBY controversies of the future.

See *KEEP OUT; A ROSE IS A ROSE.*

Kirstin Downey, "A Conservative Supreme Court Addresses Property Rights; Environmentalists Worry About the Outcome of Three Test Cases, While Landowners are Heartened by Justices Now on the Bench," *Washington Post,* Feb. 16, 1992; Molly

Ivins, "On the Beach: Subsidized Stupidity," *Washington Post*, May 29, 1992; John Lancaster, "Lobby Gains Ground in Effort to Add 'Balance' to Wetland Laws, *Washington Post*, May 15, 1991; Warren Leary, "In Wetlands Debate, Acres and Dollars Hinge on Definitions," *New York Times*, Oct. 15, 1991; H. Jane Lehman, "The Changing Political Climate and Wetlands," *Washington Post*, Aug. 17. 1991; Lehman, Landowners Go to Court to Fight for Property Rights," *Washington Post*, Jan. 4, 1992; Lehman, "A Changing Tide on Wetlands Decisions," *Washington Post*, Jan 18, 1992; William Perry Pendley, "Unconstitutional 'Takings': No More 'Cheap' Environmental Votes," *New Mexico Stockman*, May 1992, p. 53; Keith Schneider, "Environmental Laws Provoke a Backlash: When the Bad Guy Is Seen as the One in the Green Hat," *Washington Post*, Feb. 16, 1992; Michael Weisskopf, "Wetlands Protection and the Struggle over Environmental Policy," *Washington Post*, Aug. 8, 1991; Florence Williams, "Landowners turn the Fifth into sharp-pointed sword," *High Country News*, Feb. 8, 1993, pp. 1-12.

THE TEMPEST IN THEIR TEAPOT

Just as crossword-puzzle makers argue about whether the clue *oreo* should refer to the Greek word for mountain or a cookie, Entity and Project personnel have a lot to argue about as well. Dive into their teapot and find out what is controversial for them. Their lawyers and accountants do not see things in the same way; nor do their engineers and salespeople, or their managers and planners.

These disagreements reflect Project weaknesses. By exploiting them you can both gain insights into internal rifts and learn about specific issues that cast doubt on the wisdom of going ahead with the Project. Such disagreements are often successfully concealed from most outsiders but seldom so well hidden that no signs show.

Any tiny sign of discord apparent in public is probably the sign of very deep discord within Entity. The surprising absence of an important person from a public meeting or the sudden resignation of a Project supporter can be a clue that an internal power struggle is underway. There is no need to emphasize that disgruntled former employees or managers forced out by internal politics can be excellent sources of information.

It is not always easy to recognize these kinds of disagreement. Considerable effort may in fact be expended to hide such spectacles or to deny their significance. But nothing blocks awareness of such dissension as completely as lack of alertness on your part to signs of it. Don't assume that Entity is monolithic and unstoppable. It is just as likely to be a fragile and fragmented coalition held together by greed and thirst for power. Make an effort to perceive and exploit the outward signs of inner conflicts.

See *THE HATFIELDS AND MCCOYS.*

TESTING, TESTING ...

Whether Entity is planning a facility or operating one, doing preliminary research for a license or renewing one, laboratory samples of one kind or another will be involved in some way. They may be water samples to show that the water somewhere is already dirty (the typical pre-construction sample) or that area water is remarkably clean (the kind usually taken after facility operations have already begun.) Or the samples may be taken to demonstrate that the soil is wet or erosive or that the air is contaminated or pristine.

The type of sample will depend on the kind of facility Entity is involved with, but you can expect that the samples will consistently demonstrate what Entity wants them to demonstrate.

There are lots of different tests, but there is no such thing as *the* test. There are many tests, all designed for different purposes, subject to different degrees of sensitivity, costing different amounts, producing immediate or delayed results, and requiring different handling, among other things. This is true whether you are testing for drugs in milk or heavy metals in power plant emissions.

Testing for a chemical is often not at all a straightforward matter, as the example of EDB illustrates. EDB (ethylene dibromide) was used as a fumigant for tree crops and grains, for waterproofing, and as a solvent. Widely used from 1948 until it was banned in 1983, EDB apparently can enter tiny micropores in the soil, where it is beyond the reach of water, microbes, and most standard residue-testing technology.

If recent studies are accurate, the usual methods for detecting EDB (and other) residues may be inadequate when they have found their way into micropores. Special tests must be used in order to detect much of the EDB in soil and water samples. Examples like this underscore the importance of knowing which tests are used and what their limitations are.

Testing abuse is rampant. Results that would never stand up in a court of law or regulatory hearing (where cross-examination is allowed) are often used in public relations campaigns. A few examples will illustrate. Entity will claim that test *A* showed no traces of chemical *X*. Entity may be a little hesitant to point out that test *A* was not designed to find chemical *X* unless it occurs in enormous quantities. Or, Entity will claim that testing using the most sensitive, expensive test available showed no traces of compound *Q*. It turns out that the sampling was done at a time, season, or hour when it was well-known that compound *Q* would not be present.

A little research into such testing will go a long way. Don't let yourself be bamboozled into not questioning test results because you are intimidated or confused. Whether you are facing a PR representative or an engineer with a long list of impressive credentials, do not hesitate to ask about the exact nature of the test results referred to, including the exact name of the test and the laboratory that performed it.

Sometimes testing procedures cross the line from merely misleading to actually dishonest. The easiest way to falsify lab test results is to lie about where the sample came from or get the samples from a 'magic barrel' from which results are always favorable. More subtle techniques are common, however. Just as athletes can mask the traces of certain drugs in their bodies by taking countermeasures (including counter-drugs), so can industry sanitize samples on their way to testing.

Many measurable characteristics (such as acidity and radioactivity, for example) are not stable. By carefully manipulating the timing of testing, altering the humidity, subjecting a sample to turbulence (jiggling), heat, cold, a change in altitude, or otherwise modifying its environment, the characteristics of a given sample may change in predictable ways. Samples can be shipped to a faraway lab instead of local labs so that, by the time they are tested, their content no longer reflects the original sampling conditions. Simply letting the samples age awhile before delivery to a nearby lab will achieve similar results.

In a real-life example which was reported in 1991, a coal company agreed to pay a substantial fine after its guilty plea to criminal charges that it had tampered with dust samples from its mines. These samples were used to assess the risk of black lung disease among mine workers. The Labor Department admitted that it had concluded from the doctored samples that the mines did comply with federal standards for coal dust exposure.

As part of the deal, the company admitted that one employee had violated company policy by tampering with the samples. In return, the company was given immunity from further legal actions for the tampering.

Perhaps things happened exactly as the bargain says they did, but this is also typical of how a guilty Entity will respond when caught in the act: it will claim that one or more employees were acting independently and against company policy. If the employees cannot prove that they were following unofficial company policy, they may be fired. If they have dangerous evidence, they may be bought off. In either case, the company keeps a good public face on the matter and admits no wrongdoing.

Entity cannot usually be prevented from using such techniques. But your group can request to be present during the handling of certain samples. You can also keep your ears open to whistleblowers within Entity who may want to tip you off to inappropriate handling. When the opportunity arises — in hearings, court appearances, or other public situations — do not hesitate to ask detailed and probing questions about sampling procedures.

Testing cannot be counted on to detect the results of human ingenuity. It would have been difficult to guess, for example, that mine operators were using Endust to keep coal dust from sticking to the filters, especially if you don't think of testing for Endust. Instead of trying to imagine what new methods of circumventing regulations have been developed, you might focus your efforts, as has the United Mine Workers, on improving enforcement. The UMW, for example, aware that the federal inspection system leaves much to be desired, has resolved to "take the dust sampling out of the hands of the mine operators."

Don't depend on testing to take the place of your own vigilance.

See *STOPPING AT NOTHING; THE FISH AUTOPSY; WHISTLEBLOWING IN THE WIND.*

Anon., "Experts Say Plants Used Spill as Cover to Dump Pollutants," (AP), *New York Times*, Feb. 22, 1988; Beth Hanson, "Spoiled Soil," *Amicus Journal*, Summer 1989, pp. 3-7; Frank Swoboda, "Peabody Coal Fined for Tampering," *Washington Post*, Jan. 18, 1991 and "Coal Mine Operators Altered Dust Samples: Labor Officials to Fine 800 Companies," *Washington Post*, Apr. 4, 1991.

THAT'S NOT OUR DEPARTMENT DEPARTMENT

There are loopholes and there are loopholes, but this is one of my favorites, thousands of acres wide. First, some background.

In the generally arid conditions of the West, strip mining can be a very dusty matter. With hundreds if not thousands of acres of land simultaneously disturbed and scores of huge piles of different kinds of dirt and minerals exposed to sun and wind, the air quality issue is a significant one.

Lignite strip mining has been pursued in Texas since the 1950s. Because of its low energy content, it is generally recognized that transporting lignite more than a few miles is not cost-effective. Therefore, a power plant which generates electricity from lignite needs to be located at or close to the mine site. Such an arrangement is called a mine-mouth plant.

In Texas (for reasons that are historically interesting but not relevant here), an agency called the Texas Railroad Commission (TRC) regulates strip mining operations, including lignite. The Texas Air Control Board (TACB) regulates air quality.

Opponents of a proposed mine-mouth lignite-fired power plant in Texas were eager to see the issue of mining dust addressed by a regulatory agency. But the TRC refused to deal with the issue, claiming that air quality wasn't their thing. The TACB did agree to regulate power plant emissions and dust from the lignite-handling equipment (conveyor belts and associated machinery at the plant itself), but it insisted that mining dust was part of the mine and should therefore be dealt with by the TRC as part of the mining operation. Neither claimed and neither accepted jurisdiction over the problem of controlling the mining dust.

Similar quirky loopholes exist among many federal and state laws and agencies. Try to stop them ahead of time and tighten them up so that less can slip through. If this is not possible, point them out for the public to see.

See *COMMON SENSE NEED NOT APPLY; GOVERNMENT REGULATORS WILL PROTECT YOU.*

TRIGGERS

As you read through Project descriptions and analyses, keep your eyes open for interesting patterns. An odd unexplained pattern may be the sign of a 'disarmed trigger.'

Suppose you find, for example, that a great number of ponds in a complex drainage system for the proposed Project are all sized under 20 acres (often 19 acres or 19-1/2). Or, suppose that individual buildings or facilities always contain fewer than 50 employees, but often 48 or 49. Or, that many requisitions or purchase orders total $990,000, or $889,500, or $997,300 but never exceed $1 million. These and other suspicious patterns in size, number, or cost are often the result of a combination of very careful planning plus intimate familiarity with applicable regulations.

They may have been designed to avoid setting off a regulatory trigger that would put into effect a whole cascade of additional regulations. Ponds over twenty acres in size may require the intervention and approval of another regulatory agency; facilities with over fifty employees present may be subject to much more stringent safety regulations; expenditures over a million dollars may have to be approved by a larger, more public board or commission. By keeping the proposed levels just under the next regulatory threshold, Entity may be able to avoid scrutiny, hearings, permit applications, delays, and possible legal actions.

So what, if it's apparently legal?

It is worth a second look. Plans change in response to public pressure, regulatory negotiating, more current technology, quietly introduced cost-cutting measures, and better data. They also change, often drastically, between the design phase and the construction phase of a Project. Variances,which are often granted quietly after the first publicity storm has abated, may essentially render immaterial many safeguards.

Regulatory triggers are created so that oversight can be maintained while excessive minutiae is avoided. If Entity is purposely segmenting its Project or misrepresenting large components as smaller ones in order to evade regulations, that tactic in itself may deserve legal action. It also raises questions about why Entity is so afraid to subject itself to the appropriate regulations as intended by the governing statutes or regulations.

See *YOU BUY THE BEER, I'LL BUY THE BUBBLES; GOVERNMENT REGULATORS WILL PROTECT YOU.*

TURNING THE HEAT UP

Saving money too often goes hand in hand with fouling the environment. Finding the connection, the causal link, between one and the other, however, is sometimes a bit indirect.

Some technology is still fairly transparent. Take the lamp you are reading this by. You can probably imagine how the electricity comes out of the wire and heats up a tiny filament in a light bulb, which glows to make light. But follow that same wire all the way back to the power plant where the electricity is generated and you'll find that it takes extremely complicated machinery to put into effect the simple principles of electricity generation.

Now, unless your electricity comes from solar, wind, hydroelectric, or nuclear power, the wire will eventually lead you to the combustion of some kind of fossil fuel in a furnace. Furnaces are an integral part of not only power plants but also various manufacturing plants, factories, chemical processing plants, industrial scale incinerators, and similar facilities. And it is to furnaces that our attention will turn briefly.

A furnace can be designed to burn a wide range of materials, but the wider the range, in general, the less efficient the furnace. A furnace operating at maximum efficiency, at the temperature it was designed for, will often also be burning cleaner, releasing fewer emissions. (It may also generate more solid waste or ash, but that's another matter, albeit an important one.)

Expect many Entities to lower the temperature of their furnaces during regular operations. Often, this saves them money, while increasing harmful air emissions. They will continue to claim that they are running the furnace according to specifications and are therefore meeting or exceeding regulations. Watch out for this tactic, and don't miss a chance to ask them about it in public, especially if they are under oath.

See *BURNING TOXIC WASTE.*

UNWANTED MATERIALS COMPANY

A large company (call it the Unwanted Materials Company, or UMC) that frequently deals with NIMBY issues offers NIMBY activists a preview of the shape of things to come. UMC's *modus operandi* is probably typical of the increasingly serious and sophisticated effort that will be made in the future to thwart NIMBY activism. The news is not good, but it's better to get a whiff ahead of time so as to be warned of the coming onslaught.

According to media reports, UMC has eighty lawyers, twenty-two Washington lobbyists, and a public market value of nineteen billion dollars, so it has the resources to be a formidable foe. At least two, well-known national environmental organizations have published special booklets focusing on the company. Reportedly, UMC has paid out over fifty million dollars in fines and settlements, an amount which has not prevented it from making handsome profits in the lucrative business of waste disposal.

Apparently in order to promote a green image, UMC has given over a million dollars to environmental and pro-nature groups, donated a portion of its fees to green causes, and planted trees and used recycled paper in an effort to appear environmentally sensitive. On the local political front, its staff spends long hours in efforts to win local supporters. When that fails, long, expensive, ruthless legal battles are carried out.

Mere familiarity with such corporate strategies does not provide sufficient means with which to defeat them. Your group must shadow every move and be prepared to re-interpret each one to a sometimes gullible public. The more closely you watch them, the better able you will be to anticipate and perhaps even to deflect the next moves. But remember that companies which pay three-million-dollar fines as a matter of course can also be quite persuasive in trying to buy off their opposition.

See *MANAGEMENT'S VIEW; A SPOONFUL OF SUGAR; WHICH SIDE ARE YOU ON?.*

Jeff Bailey, "Tough Target: Waste Disposal Giant, Often Under Attack, Seems to Gain from It," *Wall Street Journal*, May 1, 1991.

WE'D LIKE TO, BUT ...

During the long battle against lignite strip mining in two rural Texas counties, Project opponents repeatedly suggested that natural gas would be a good alternative fuel for electricity generation. Though natural gas prices (per unit of energy, or BTU) were higher at the time, natural gas-fired power plants were much cheaper to construct and did not involve risky and controversial strip mining operations. In time, even some of the directors of the electric utility company began mentioning the natural gas alternative at board meetings.

The staff of the electric utility, seemingly hell-bent on strip mining local lignite (a dirty coal with an energy content comparable at best to cow patties) refused to take the natural gas option seriously. One of their most frequently repeated reasons was that a mysterious 'Docket 600' prohibited the use of natural gas in power plants. They implied that they were forced to consider lignite because other options had been closed to them. This tough luck scenario was painted both at utility board meetings and at various public forums in the area prospectively to be affected.

Finally Project opponents got a chance to track down Docket 600. It did, in fact, order the phase-out of natural gas as a power plant fuel. However, it had been repealed in no uncertain terms a few years afterwards and had not been in effect at any time during the lignite controversy. A similar federal statute was still in effect, but variances (exceptions) had been liberally granted.

Entity backers can become zealously law-abiding when the law suits them, even it if is no longer in effect.

See DIFFERENT STROKES FOR DIFFERENT FOLKS; BE CONSISTENT.

WHAT GOES AROUND, COMES AROUND

Sometimes, it is difficult to convince people that the adverse effects of a Project will reach very far beyond local or Project boundaries. Somehow, long lectures about the web of life, the interconnected ecosystem, and interwoven ecological cycles just don't hit home the way specific examples do. For examples:

Tortoise Shell Glows in the Dark: Near the Savannah River nuclear weapons production facility on the Georgia-South Carolina border, deer, ducks, and collard greens all show traces of radiation; turtles absorb radioactive tritium, strontium, and cesium in their shells and flesh.

Organic Safety Vests: A fluorescent pink polar bear was found dead in Alaska. The cause of death was apparently ethylene glycol, an antifreeze. The bear's vivid coloration came from rhodamine-B, a pink dye used by an Alaskan oil company to mark runways.

Spicy Food, Hot Table Legs: Apparently a fly-by-night subcontractor disposed of radioactive wastes from a U.S. nuclear facility by taking them across the border and depositing them in a Mexican scrap heap. The scrap metal was then recycled into furniture parts, including table legs which found their way into Mexican restaurants in Austin, Texas.

See *ALL THE ANGLES; BEHIND THE BERMS.*

Matthew L. Wald, "Nature Helps to Spread Weapons Plants' Waste," *New York Times*, Dec. 10, 1988 and "Drilling Plan Points Up Questions on Oil and Wilderness in Alaska," *New York Times*, Apr. 23, 1989.

WHAT IS THAT FUNNY SMELL?

What funny smell? is probably the answer you will hear most frequently when you ask this question of local officials or company personnel. But never stop there. Chances are excellent that many people do know exactly what the smell is and that you have every right to know, too.

Some government bodies have written 'smell laws' with provisions for fines for illegal smells. At least one state (Colorado) now has state odor inspectors. A leading odor think tank is the University of Pennsylvania Smell and Taste Center, directed by Richard L. Doty.

The 1986 Emergency Planning and Community Right-to-Know Act can also help you track down a particular smell. Its Toxic Release Inventory provisions have made available a vast amount of information. Two reference books based on this inventory, *A Who's Who of American Toxic Air Polluters* and *A Who's Who of American Ozone Depleters* (both by Deborah Sheiman, David Doniger, and Lisa Dator) will be useful at the beginning of your search. One source used by bankers and realtors, among others, is Environmental Data Resources Inc. (EDRI), a Southport, Connecticut computer search company started by its chairman Peter L. Cashman. EDRI searches government records to evaluate properties in terms of possible environmental dangers.

Though such references will not replace research into specific permit provisions and conditions, they will give you a solid start. Some of the shortcomings of the toxic release inventory-reporting requirements are discussed in Keith Schneider's "For Communities: Knowledge of Polluters is Power". If you still believe that funny smells are unpleasant but not unhealthy, read through Michael H. Brown's *The Toxic Cloud*.

See INCENSE, PEPPERMINT.

Michael H. Brown, *The Toxic Cloud: The Poisoning of America's Air* (New York: Harper & Row, Publishers, 1987); Clive Burrow, "The Toxic Waste Detective Finds Many Eager Clients," New York Times, Oct. 4, 1992; Deborah A. Sheiman, "Who's Who: What You Don't Know Can Hurt You...And What You Can Do About It," *The Amicus Journal*, Summer 1990, pp. 19-21 (includes a list of the 'Top 50 Toxic Air Polluters' and how to find out more.); Sheiman, David Doniger, and Lisa Dator, *A Who's Who of American Ozone Depleters*, (Washington, DC: Natural Resources Defense Council, 1990) and *A Who's Who of American Toxic Air Polluters* (Washington DC: Natural Resources Defense Council, 1989); Keith Schneider, "For Communities, Knowledge of Polluters is Power," *New York Times*, Mar. 24, 1991; Robert Tomsho, "This Nose for Hire," *Wall Street Journal*, Jun. 11, 1992.

WHICH SIDE ARE YOU ON?

The public is accustomed to hearing large corporations toot their own horns. Chemical companies brag about helping save babies' lives while large oil companies make contributions to opera, classical music programs, and other highly visible forms of high culture. More recently, government agencies have begun making use of advertising and sophisticated public relations.

It may seem strange to see the federal Bureau of Land Management, perhaps one of the most unpopular government bureaucracies, taking to the airwaves to defend its policies and its very existence. But many government bodies, especially regulatory agencies, find themselves between a rock and a hard place. Regulated industries attack them for excessive red tape, over-regulation, and incompetence. Citizens groups and environmentalists attack them for lack of enforcement, numerous loopholes in regulations, and being too soft on the industries they monitor. So, these agencies are defending themselves in the same arena in which attacks are made: the media.

Industries and government agencies are not alone in resorting to public relations barrages to state their cases. Large consumer and environmental groups often use ongoing advertising campaigns as part of round-the-clock fundraising efforts.

So, we're surrounded. Corporations, government bodies, and consumer/environmental groups all shamelessly use the media to bolster their reputations and gain public support. This is part of a broad trend toward more public and more sophisticated debates.

Part of your NIMBY group's task is to make sure no one begins to think that any of these are neutral, objective, or have a corner on the truth. All of the above groups are interest groups, special interests in their own rights. Indeed, the possibility of confusion under these conditions makes it all the more important that your NIMBY group have a clear and non-simplistic public education program that answers all misleading claims, whatever their source.

See *MANAGEMENT'S VIEW; UNWANTED MATERIALS COMPANY.*

John Lancaster, "Marketing a Public Image: From Mail Delivery to Mining Law; Defensive Strategy Set at Land Management Bureau," *Washington Post*, Mar. 25, 1991.

WHISTLEBLOWING IN THE WIND

Whistleblowing is the term that is used when an insider *blows the whistle* or exposes practices that are illegal, fraudulent, unethical, or otherwise morally reprehensible. Usually the whistleblower is exposing practices that would have been very difficult for an outsider to detect or prove.

Whistleblowing is very difficult to carry off successfully, whatever the criteria of success may be. From the personal standpoint, it requires great courage. Anyone contemplating blowing the whistle should look ahead to trying times and expect difficulties with family, friends, and coworkers. The whistleblower is likely to lose his or her job and to find gaining similar employment elsewhere to be difficult. Years of legal proceedings lie ahead, with a rather low probability of happy resolution for the whistleblower. A whistleblower rarely escapes surveillance or harassment of some kind and is likely to be accused of being mentally unstable at some point in the process.

Whistleblowing is very much a process, usually a rather long one at that. No one should become a whistleblower with the false idea that all that they have to do is blow the whistle and then resume a normal life. The circuit from evidence-gathering, to exposure, through various hearings and proceedings, and back to normal is a long one after which many never really achieve the kind of normal day-to-day life that they had envisioned.

Probably the best advice is to get a good lawyer early on. This should be a trustworthy person who is sympathetic to your goals and is in no way connected to any part of the establishment that may want to see you silenced and made a fool of. (See below for some clues to whistleblower networks). Much if not all of your strategy should be worked out with your lawyer.

Documenting the practice that you want to expose is extremely important. Sometimes, obtaining or physically possessing the evidence that will prove your allegations is illegal. Work closely with your lawyer to resolve this difficulty. Keep in mind that the Entity on whom you are blowing the whistle may destroy or alter evidence at the first hint that a whistleblower may be about to go public.

Also keep in mind that others — co-workers, subordinates, supervisors, and anyone else in a position to know Entity's standard practices — may be bought off or otherwise silenced (even by blackmail or threats of job loss). You cannot assume that anyone in Entity will corroborate your claims, so your own documentation had better be good. Never leave any of your original evidence with any company or government official. If it is appropriate, leave copies, but guard your original evidence (of whatever sort) against any possibility of 'accidental' loss.

Many authorities — inside and outside of the organization —will discount or disbelieve your claims, even if your evidence is excellent. Some will honestly find it difficult to believe, others will not want to believe it because of the difficult situation it places them in, and still others may have a vested interest in insuring that it is kept quiet.

One of the most difficult aspects of whistleblowing is deciding who to blow the whistle to. If you start inside the organization (with an internal auditor or health inspector, for example), you can easily be fired or be set up to be accused of violations or infractions of which you are not actually guilty. Internal evidence will almost certainly be altered or destroyed.

If you don't start on the inside and follow regular channels, Entity staff will claim that they knew of no problems and would certainly have fixed any that they were aware of. Or, they will pick someone (possibly you) to be the fall guy and blame that individual for causing the problem, even if everyone knows that the transgression resulted from long standing if informal organizational policy.

Another approach is to take your allegations to a newspaper. Some people think that all a whistleblower has to do is show a few photocopied memos to a newspaper and then sit back and wait for a reporter to write up the story. It may sometimes work that way, but that certainly is not the usual result. Newspapers need strong evidence in order to protect themselves against legal action. In addition, they may have close ties with Entity or Project backers. Finally, they may actually leak the whistleblowing story back to Entity itself.

Neither government nor private business have exemplary records when it comes to the treatment of whistleblowers. One man who worked as a psychiatric social worker for the federal government found that he was expected to certify that former whistleblowers were too mentally unbalanced to continue their jobs — a certification that greatly assisted the government in firing them. Donald Soeken, the social worker in question, has since founded Integrity International to advise whistleblowers. A House of Representatives Government Operations subcommittee has set up an electronic message system called the Whistleblower's Bulletin Board. Any government fraud or waste may be reported, with anonymity supposedly assured, to its hotline number (202-225-5527).

Usually, whistleblowers pay a high personal price for their actions. But sometimes, they may even receive a financial reward. In some cases, citizens who assist in uncovering examples of environmental violations are entitled to a portion of fines recovered from the offender. There are efforts afoot to insure that such 'bounties' are in fact awarded. Watch for such a bill in the U.S. Congress under the name "Environmental Crime Act."

See *'BAD BOY' BILLS; BEHIND THE BERMS; THE CREDIBILITY GAP; ENVIRONMENTAL AUDITS; MANAGEMENT'S VIEW.*

Jack Anderson, "A Haven For Whistleblowers" *Parade*, Aug. 18, 1991; Timothy Egan, "Sometimes, the Disloyal Are Watched," *New York Times*, Oct. 27, 1991; Thomas W. Lippman, "2 Women at Rocky Flats Plant Tell

Of Intimidation, Safety Violations; Key Witnesses Say Their Role in Probe Led to Harassment on the Job," *Washington Post*, Dec. 28, 1991.

WITH A LITTLE HELP FROM YOUR FRIENDS

The president of the United States doesn't write his own speeches, so there is no reason for you to feel guilty about getting help with yours.

Many people are shy or nervous about speaking in public, say, at a public hearing. There are several easy ways of making it less uncomfortable to speak out. One is literally to read your speech. You can also read a speech written by someone else.

Probably someone in your group feels comfortable with language and can sit down and write up several speeches. These should be timed so that even a slow reader can get through them before the allotted time runs out. Each speech could be about a different chemical, a different emission, or a different aspect of the proposed Project. If the speech contains difficult words, be sure that the reader can pronounce them.

A simple list can also sometimes make an effective speech. One person might read a list of all the chemicals to be handled at the proposed facility. Another might read a list of all the possible kinds of accidents that could occur. A third could read a list of local people already on Entity's payroll as consultants, and so on.

Some of you might also want to read excerpts from newspapers, journals, or textbooks that are relevant to the Project. Reading a few paragraphs about the health effects of a certain compound from a medical textbook can be a very powerful statement. So can the quoted testimony of people who have suffered such effects.

Sometimes even silliness helps. Citizens in Austin, Texas spent over a decade trying to get out of their share of a nuclear power plant under construction. Over that period of time, innumerable hearings focused more and more on cost overruns and other hidden costs. At an appropriate time during each hearing, an enormous paper-mache 'nuclear dragon' would invade the room and gobble wads of fake dollars, always demanding more, more. The creature became an unforgettable symbol of the economics of nuclear power.

In short, be flexible about the kinds of presentations your group's members make at hearings and assist those who may be initially hesitant to speak out. Poems, lists, skits, songs, and quotes can really spice up a hearing by varying the pace. If your group earns the reputation of putting on a good show, the news media will be much more likely to cover your events.

A WORD ABOUT EXPERTS

Anyone who reads the newspapers knows that you can find an expert to testify to the soundness of almost any position on any issue. One says that the dilithium crystal plant is safe enough to house a day care center, and another advises you to wear a lead suit and gas mask if you get closer than ten miles. But the situation is even more confusing than this would suggest.

Experts don't do all this research as freelance brains. Instead, they are almost always affiliated with one or more institutions. Among these are universities, medical schools, consulting firms, research centers, and a variety of other so-called 'think tanks' and associations. To confuse things further, these latter organizations often choose names that sound neutral, or official, or governmental, or authoritative.

Faced with a multitude of well-credentialed experts with impressive-sounding affiliations and spouting widely divergent opinions, you should always keep two things firmly in mind. First, none of the experts is totally disinterested or objective. Second, that does not mean you cannot make an intelligent decision about what to believe.

Research costs money, and most good research costs lots of money. The questions or topics that have the most research committed to them are the best-funded ones. Government, industries, and business groups all fund research that will benefit them.

For this reason, we know a lot about the various insects that damage corn plants and the geological conditions that are associated with oil fields. We know much less about the effects of power lines and electromagnetic fields on health or the long-term effects of herbicides in ground water. The big research dollars have gone toward big-science, high-tech gizmos and solutions like improving our ability to incinerate wastes instead of examining incineration hazards or reducing wastes at their sources so they don't have to be incinerated in the first place.

All their research doesn't turn the experts into gods. In some cases, it can even do the opposite. As one physicist lamented,

> It is a sad fact that in recent years big businesses have often been guilty of prostituting science in an attempt to hide or distort the truth. They have capitalized on the layman's belief that the statements of scientists and doctors can always be accepted as impartial and proven scientific fact. But scientists are human beings, subject to personal bias like anyone else, and not always immune to personal profit. (Louise B. Young, *Power Over People*, p. 93)

If you find yourself (or, someone else) believing in the objectivity of a particular report or study, do some checking into the background of the author or authors or look into the history of any of dozens of funding organizations that sponsor research.

It is an eye-opening experience to glimpse the financial backing of official-sounding organizations. Prepare to have your eyes opened by Karen Rothmyer's "Citizen Scaife," or by Phillip Boffey's *The Brain Bank of America*, which documents corporate and governmental influence over National Academy of Sciences reports.

It is often wise to remind yourself that few issues of public policy can be reduced down to objective, technical issues. As Phillip Boffey reminds us, technological expertise goes only so far. "In almost all cases, an element of informal judgment is required," Boffey writes, "and what comes out strutting as 'objective' wisdom is actually the subjective opinion of those who prepared the advice."

Nor should we be surprised, given the way in which expertise is funded, that technical progress usually takes a direction favored by big institutions. Voiceless families, workers, consumers have been left outside the loop to be sustained perhaps by the faith that they will reap their benefits from these expert solutions sometime in the future. As if they have no right to be heard because they are not technologically gifted. As if social, economic, or political policies are none of their business.

Boffey's book provides brief histories of a few famous and controversial studies, background information on the research perspectives of certain special interest groups, and examples of the exercise of political influence on scientific questions. In the process, it offers a sort of walk-through tour of bias in supposedly 'objective' research. Another very sobering glimpse of science is offered by William Broad's and Nicholas Wade's *Betrayers of the Truth*. Both of these books are highly recommended.

Armed with insights from sources like these, you will be able to shop around through a variety of sometimes conflicting reports, check out the various claims made and points omitted, and formulate a well-informed and intelligent position on any given topic.

See *IF IT QUACKS LIKE A DUCK; PROFESSIONALISM AND YOU; STUDIES AND MORE STUDIES; BADGER HOLES; FRONTS.*

Louis Blumberg and Robert Gottlieb, "Garbage Wars: Citizens Take on the 'Experts,'" *The Nation*, May 28, 1990, pp. 742-744; Phillip M. Boffey, *The Brain Bank of America: An Inquiry Into the Politics of Science* (New York: McGraw Hill Book Co., 1975); William Broad and Nicholas Wade, *Betrayers of the Truth: Fraud and Deceit in the Halls of Science* (New York: Simon and Schuster, 1982); David Weir and Dan Noyes, *Raising Hell: How the Center for Investigative Reporting Gets the Story* (Reading, MA: Addison-Wesley Publishing Co., 1983); Louise B. Young, *Power Over People*, New York: Oxford University Press, 1973.

WORDS AND MORE WORDS

At public forums and in hearings, Entity representatives will make seemingly simple, transparent statements that are literally true but extremely misleading. The two examples below are taken from hearings to determine whether strip-mining lignite coal would compromise the surrounding aquifer (ground-water) system.

Project opponents were concerned that among other things, the water quality in two separate aquifer layers in the region around the mining operations would decline. During the hearings, these two geological formations were discussed extensively.

It was both obvious and important that the deeper aquifer, the Simsboro Sands, was a major aquifer in the area, and therefore, by definition, wet. But during expert testimony at a permit hearing, a consultant for Entity asserted that he had examined some one hundred core drills into this sandy layer and found no water. He further elaborated that these samples contained no evidence of moisture and were in fact "powder dry."

Finding that the aquifer was already dry would be convenient for Entity, which then would not have to concern itself, even nominally, with the problem of protecting the aquifer from damage. The attorney representing Project opponents saw through the charade, however, and forced the consultant to admit under cross-examination that he had others do the actual drilling and that he had not even looked at the core samples until they were completely dried out.

At another hearing related to the same strip mining Project, a consultant stated that mine operations would have no effect on wells in the Calvert Bluff, the aquifer layer just beneath the surface of the ground. Many people concluded from this that the Calvert Bluff as an aquifer would not be adversely affected by strip mining operations. But that's not what the consultant was claiming at all, though it was in Entity's interest to suggest it.

Again under cross-examination, the situation became clearer. At that time, there were few active wells in the Calvert Bluff and none very close to the mining area. Mining would therefore probably not affect those wells. However, the Calvert Bluff, as an aquifer could have been seriously degraded, along with the viability of future wells near the mining area.

Cleverly worded misleading statements like the two examples above are no different from disingenuous advertising claims. But sometimes they are less easy to spot when they are made by highly credentialed experts in official, solemn, regulatory proceedings.

See *THE FINE PRINT; INSTANT CLEANUP; A WORD ABOUT EXPERTS; TESTING, TESTING ...*

WOULD $100,000 MAKE A DIFFERENCE?

A New York Times story by Keith Schneider reported the following:

> Lured by lucrative grants, seven communities around the country have notified the Government that they are interested in becoming the site of a multi-billion-dollar warehouse to store thousands of tons of high-level nuclear wastes, the Department of Energy said today.
>
> Simply by applying to study the potential to build a nuclear waste installation, communities are eligible for up to $100,000 in grants from the Department of Energy. David Leroy, the United States Nuclear Waste Negotiator, said in an interview today that the communities were free to use the money almost any way they chose.
>
> Communities that decide to pursue the idea further are eligible for a second phase of study that could provide several million dollars in grants...

Incentives are increasingly a part of the NIMBY landscape. If Project opponents make arguments in terms of dollars only, they run the risk that Entity will say, "OK, here's the money." Health risks, tourism, and other quality-of-life issues are much less easy to answer with a fistful of bills.

See *MANAGEMENT'S VIEW; UNWANTED MATERIALS COMPANY.*

Eugene Meyer, "Trashman Woos a Md. County: Allegany Considers Multi-million-Dollar Landfill Offer," *Washington Post*, Dec. 26, 1992; Keith Schneider, "Grants Stir Interest in Nuclear Waste Site," *New York Times*, Jan. 9, 1992; Michael Weisskopf, "Even Cash for Trash Fails To Slow Landfill Backlash," *Washington Post*, Feb 28, 1992.

YOU BUY THE BEER, I'LL BUY THE BUBBLES: SEGMENTATION AS A TACTIC

The creativity that goes into evading laws is so astonishing that one has to admire it even while wishing that such efforts would be instead directed to finding cheap and effective ways to comply with laws.

One example of creative evasion is the unexpected and very profitable (for Entity) *segmentation* of the proposed Project. The explanation starts with money.

Money in any form — loans, grants, what-have-you — rarely comes with no strings attached. Many Projects are funded at least in part by state and/or federal funds, the use of which is contingent on certain conditions being adhered to.

Often, the conditions attached to federal funds are more stringent than those accompanying the granting of state funds. For example, the use of federal funds often means that an environmental impact statement (EIS) or at least an environmental assessment (EA) must be carried out. For Entity, this can mean delays, red tape, and opportunities for outsiders to find out more about the Project and to take steps to stop it or modify it.

If alternative financing can be arranged, Entity may pass up a chance to use federal funds because of the additional oversight and risks their use entails. But there are some even more clever means of getting around legal requirements associated with particular sources of funding. Two brief examples will suffice. Both are simplifications of actual cases in which the method was segmentation.

There was once a dam, funded from a variety of sources. One source gave money for flood control only; while another provided funds only for the generation of electricity. This was no problem: a joint accounting/engineering coup was accomplished when, for legal purposes, the bottom of the dam was paid for with the flood-control money, while the top portion was paid for with money for hydroelectric facilities.

In another case, a roadway was proposed to link two other highways. Funding for the roadway included both state and federal funds, and parts of the route proved very controversial. The fact that federal funds were involved meant that an *EIS* process would take place and the controversial parts of the road (especially a bridge over an environmentally sensitive waterway) would be subject to close scrutiny.

It did not quite happen that way. Entity re-arranged its plans, and announced that state funds would be used to build the controversial bridge while federal funds, with associated *EIS*, would be used for the less controversial balance of the roadway.

With both the dam and the road, the segmentation of a Project into convenient sections made it possible to sidestep troublesome regulations. Isn't segmentation with intent to avoid regulations against the law? In some cases, yes. But, like any law, its application is subject to interpretation, variation in enforcement, and politics.

See *TRIGGERS; A FOOT IN THE DOOR; THE INSTITUTIONAL ENVIRONMENT; ACCOUNTANTS' TRICKS.*

Robert A Caro., *The Path to Power: The Years of Lyndon Johnson* (NY: Alfred A. Knopf, 1982).

ADDITIONAL RESOURCES

All titles are listed under one of the following ten categories. If the content of the source is not clear from the title, or if a brief description would help the reader determine its relevance, I have included an explanatory note. Specific references noted in Parts I and II are only rarely repeated here.

- 1. Handbooks, Directories, Etc.
- 2. Getting Information
- 3. Lawyers and Law
- 4. Negotiations
- 5. Intimidation, Whistleblowing and Related Topics
- 6. Experts and Science
- 7. General Background
- 8. Newsletters and Organizations
- 9. Periodicals and Trade Journals
- 10. Newspaper Articles

1. Handbooks, Directories, Etc.

Bruce Anderson, *Ecologue: The Environmental Catalogue and Consumer's Guide for a Safe Earth* (New York: Prentice-Hall, 1990).

Jeff Belfiglio, Thomas Lippe, and Steve Franklin, *Hazardous Waste Disposal Sites: A Handbook for Public Input and Review* (Palo Alto: Stanford Environmental Law Society, 1981).

Kim Bobo, Jackie Kendall, and Steve Max, *Organizing for Social Change: A Manual for Activists in the 1990s* (Washington, DC: Seven Locks Press, 1991).

Written for professional activists but useful for others as well. Includes useful information on a number of topics. Brief discussions of passing legislation, setting up boycotts, organizing strikes, participating in demonstrations and hearings, using the media, fundraising, and petitions and letter campaigns. Includes a concise chapter on labor organizations, their structure and interests; a section on using courthouse records as information sources and researching corporations. Excellent guidelines concerning the legal and financial details of forming various kinds of organizations.

Shawn Brennan, Ed., *Consumer Sourcebook*, 7th. Edn. (Detroit: Gale Research, Inc. 1992-3).

Dwight F. Burlingame and Lamont J. Hulse, Eds., *Taking Fund Raising Seriously: Advancing the Profession and Practice of Raising Money* (San Francisco: Jossey-Bass Publishers, 1991).

Much more academic than how-to. Formal but informative.

1992 Earth Journal: Environmental Almanac and Resource Directory (Boulder, CO: Buzzworm Books, 1991).

Includes sections on the year in review, what you can do about issues from air pollution to wilderness, and useful statistics from around the world. Helpful hints for environmentally sound living and 'green' investing. Extensive lists of resources from books and magazines to software and organizations.

Citizen's Clearinghouse for Hazardous Wastes, *Leadership Handbook on Hazardous Waste* (Arlington, VA: CCHW, [P.O. Box 6806, Falls Church, VA 22040], 1983).

Community Care: A Guide to Local Environmental Action (Birmingham, MI: East Michigan Environmental Action Council, 1982).

Dumpsite Cleanups: A Citizen's Guide to the Superfund Program (Washington, DC: Environmental Defense Fund, 1984).

Joan Flanagan, *The Grass Roots Fundraising Book: How to Raise Money in Your Community*, (Chicago: The Swallow Press. 1977).

Well-organized, thorough, positive. Many good examples and details. Includes discussions of paperwork, records, and legal aspects. Excellent resource.

Wendy Gordon, *A Citizen's Handbook on Groundwater Protection*, (New York: Natural Resources Defense Council, 1984).

Mary Anne Guitar, *Property Power: How to Keep the Bulldozer, the Power Line, and the Highwaymen Away from Your Door* (Garden City, NY: Doubleday & Co., Inc. 1972).

Many examples of specific controversies, most involving the unsightly (ugly office buildings etc.) rather than the hazardous. Includes good (though dated) discussion about preserving land from development before it is already underway.

Bob Hall, Ed., *Environmental Politics: Lessons from the Grassroots* (Durham, NC: Institute for Southern Studies, 1989).

Sandra S. Hildreth, *The A to Z of Wall Street* (White Plains, NY: Longman Publishing Group, 1988).

J.D. Joseph, *How to Fight City Hall* (Chicago: Contemporary Books, Inc. 1983.)

Guidelines on dealing with the press and incorporating your group as a non-profit corporation with tax-exempt and non-tax-exempt options. Offers good basic explanations of what happens in a court of law, and an overview of using the Freedom of Information Act.

Si Kahn, *How People Get Power: Organizing Oppressed Communities for Action* (New York: McGraw Hill. 1970).

Based on Kahn's experience in the rural South and written for professional organizers. Special attention to problems related to or derived from the presence of outsiders in a community. Contains useful hints about analyzing county and community to come to an accurate and practical understanding of the local power structure. Clear discussions of specific actions that may be undertaken.

Si Kahn, *Organizing: A Guide for Grassroots Leaders* (New York: McGraw-Hill, 1982).

George Lakey and Martin Oppenheimer, *Manual for Direct Action* (Chicago: Quadrangle Books, 1965).

Anthony Mancuso, *How to Form a Nonprofit Corporation* (Berkeley: Nolo Press, 1990).

Andrew Owens Moore, *Making Polluters Pay: A Citizens' Guide to Legal Action and Organizing* (Washington, DC: Environmental Action Foundation, 1987).

Jon Naar, *Design for a Livable Planet: How You Can Clean Up the Environment* (New York: Harper and Row, 1990).

Includes brief but good discussion on forming and using a group and clear discussion of relevant laws. Chapters on garbage, toxic chemicals, water, air, acid rain, deforestation, global warming, radiation, renewable energy, environmental law, eco-action, and green lifestyles.

The Citizens' Toxics Protection Manual (Boston: National Campaign against Toxic Hazards, 1987).

Sheila Patterson, *Successful Community Fund Raising: A How-to Manual* (Ottawa, IL and Thornwood, NY: Caroline House Publishers, Inc., 1979).

Examples and specifics of fundraising.

Jeremy Rifkin, Ed., *The Green Lifestyle Handbook* (New York: Henry Holt & Co. 1990).

One of the best single references for getting information and organizing and fighting. Particularly see: Donald E. Davis, "A Bibliography for Community Organizers," and "Books to Read for the Global Future," both of which contain excellent bibliographies; Carol Grunewald, "The Activist Consumer's Weapon of Choice," (on boycotts); Andrew C. Kimbrell and Edward Lee Rogers. "The Environment, the Law, and You," which includes brief suggestions, a sample FOIA letter, a summary of how to use NEPA to require EIS's, specific summaries of some major environmental legislation and an excellent bibliography; and John O'Connor, "Grass Roots Organizing," which offers useful tips for the generic activist.

Fay Shapiro, Ed., *Oxbridge Directory of Newsletters 1990* (New York: Oxbridge Communications, Inc., 1990).

Among the newsletters listed are: Groundwater Newsletter, Livestock Marketing News, Turbomachinery Digest, Federal Lands, Slag Technical Bulletin, Regulatory Watchdog Service, Administrative Law News, Indoor Air Quality Update, Highway News, New Plants Report, Plumber's Friend.

Lee Staples, *Roots to Power: A Manual for Grassroots Organizing* (New York: Praeger Publishers, 1984).

Very useful. Includes valuable section on counter-tactics and several useful short articles. In particular, see: Will Collette, "Research for Organizing"; Meg Campbell, "Action Ideas", Mike Silver, "Before and After the Action," (which contains good examples of problems to avoid during confrontations or negotiations); Mark J. Splain, "Negotiations: Using a Weapon as a Way Out," which is the best seven pages I have seen anywhere on negotiations; Barbara Fultz Martinez & Roberta Weiner, "Guide to Public Relations"; and Mac McCreight, "Lawsuits for Leverage," which briefly summarizes how litigation can be used in conjunction with other methods.

Rachelle B. Warren and Donald I. Warren, *The Neighborhood Organizer's Handbook* (Notre Dame, IN: University of Notre Dame Press, 1977).

Steven Lewis Yaffee, *Prohibitive Policy: Implementing the Federal Endangered Species Act* (Cambridge: MIT Press, 1982).

How and why this act has and has not been implemented.

A. C. Lynn Zelmer, *Community Media Handbook*, Second Edn. (Metuchen, NJ and London: The Scarecrow Press, Inc. 1979).

Useful advice on gaining access to visual and print media at the local level. How to prepare short news releases, conduct and edit interviews, and organize community-based media.

2. Getting Information

James C. Brown, "Corporate Risks Stemming from the Community Right-to-Know Act of 1986." *Industrial Development*, vol. 157, no. 3, (May/June 1988) ,pp. 13-16.

Research For Action (Davis, CA: California Institute for Rural Studies [P.O. Box 530, Davis, CA 95616], n.d.).

Using the Freedom of Information Act: A Step by Step Guide, (Washington DC: American Civil Liberties Union, 1990).

Federal Regulatory Directory (Washington, DC: Congressional Quarterly, Inc.)

Herbert Edelhertz, *The Investigation of White Collar Crime: A Manual for Law Enforcement Agencies* (Washington, DC: U.S. Government Printing Office, 1977).

Toxic Release Inventory (Washington, DC: Environmental Protection Agency)

An annual database documenting toxic chemicals made, used, or released nationally. Available in most major libraries.

The Freedom of Information Act: A User's Guide (Washington, DC: Freedom of Information Act Clearinghouse, 1987).

Gale Research Inc. (Book Tower, Dept. 77748, Detroit, Michigan, 48277-0748) publishes a number of useful reference books, including: *Who's Who in Technology* (nearly 38,000 biographical profiles, within 46 technical disciplines, detailed areas of expertise, location, and employer); *Research Centers Directory* (10,000 research units in all fields, including research parks and technology transfer centers representing joint ventures between business, industry and universities); *Research Services Directory* (services, facilities, and expertise offered by more than 4,000 research and development companies in the U.S., including high technology research firms as well as those in management and marketing, clients, former company names, and databases maintained); *Consultants and Consulting Organizations Directory* (services offered, typical clients, 14,000 firms and individuals).

Thad Godish. *Air Quality* (Chelsea, MI: Lewis Publishers, Inc., 1985).

An excellent resource. Includes description of atmosphere and pollution sources, air circulation, dispersal patterns from industrial or power plant stacks; also includes information on health effects to humans, damage to crops, and other materials. Covers how sampling and modeling is done. Includes chapters on air pollution control regulations and indoor air pollution.

How to Research Your Local Bank (or Savings and Loan) (Washington, DC: Institute for Local Self-Reliance [1717 18th St., N.W., Washington DC 20009], 1976).

Dennis King, *Get the Facts on Anyone* (New York: Prentice-Hall, 1992).

"How to Read a Financial Statement." (New York: Merrill Lynch, Pierce, Fenner & Smith, Inc. [One Liberty Plaza, 165 Broadway, New York, NY 10006], 1973).

E. Willard Miller and Ruby M. Miller, *Environmental Hazards: Air Pollution* (Santa Barbara: ABC-CLIO, Inc. 1989).

Discusses the different types and sources of air pollution, the history of air pollution and acid rain, and legislation to control it. Helpful list of organizations; extensive, annotated bibliography.

Harry J. Murphy, *Where's What: Sources of Information for Federal Investigators* (New York: Warner Books, 1976).

Originally a CIA study.

Snigda Prakash, "Keeping Track of Environmental Rules: Mobil, Infodata Join Forces to Market EarthLaw Database System," *Washington Post/Washington Business*, Jan. 27, 1992.

Robert S. Sanoff and Laurie Burt, "Responding to a Superfund Information Request," *Industrial Development*, Vol. 156, No. 1, (Jan/Feb 1987), pp. 6-10.

Fred Setterberg, "Checking Out Facts at Oakland's Public Interest Library," *Writer's Digest*, Sep. 1991, pp. 64-5.

Deborah Sheiman, "Who's Who: What You Don't Know Can Hurt You..And What You Can Do About It," *The Amicus Journal*, Summer 1990, pp. 19-21.

Includes a list of the "Top 50 Toxic Air Polluters" and how to find out more.

Deborah A. Sheiman, David Doniger, and Lisa Dator, *A Who's Who of American Ozone Depleters* (Washington, DC: Natural Resources Defense Council, 1990)

Deborah A. Sheiman, David Doniger, and Lisa Dator, *A Who's Who of American Toxic Air Polluters* (Washington, DC: Natural Resources Defense Council, 1989).

Lee Stephenson, "Prying Open Corporations: Tighter Than Clams," *Business and Society Review*, No. 8, (Winter 1973-74), pp. 43-49.

Difficulties of and recommendations for evaluation and regulation.

Utility Information Digest (Washington, DC: Edison Electric Institute).

Washington Information Directory 1990-1991 (Washington, DC: Congressional Quarterly Inc., 1990).

Excellent resource. Information listed by category, including governmental and non-governmental organizations, with addresses. Also contains brief descriptions of the Freedom of Information Act and the Privacy Act.

How to Find Information about Companies (Washington, DC: Washington Researchers, 1979).

David Weir and Dan Noyes, *Raising Hell: How the Center for Investigative Reporting Gets the Story*. (Reading, MA: Addison-Wesley Publishing Co. 1983).

Reprints of eight investigative stories, each followed by the journalist's narration of how he or she got the story. Especially see: Karen Rothmyer, "Citizen Scaife" and Mark Dowie's "The Bechtel File". Also has excellent bibliography about locating possibly sensitive information.

"Welcome to the Federal Court" (U. S. Govt. Printing Office brochure no. 1989-0-251-831.) Distributed by the Federal Judicial Center, Dolly Madison House, 1520 H Street, NW, Washington, DC 20005.

Excellent explanation of the difference between federal and state courts and the various federal courts.

3. Lawyers And Law

Richard L. Abel, *American Lawyers* (New York: Oxford University Press, 1990).

Litigation under the Federal Freedom of Information Act and Privacy Act, 14th Edn. (Washington, DC American Civil Liberties Union Foundation, 1989).

Susan J. Bell, Comp., *Full Disclosure: Do You Really Want to Be a Lawyer?* (Princeton: Peterson's Guides, 1989).

Henry Campbell Black, *Black's Law Dictionary* (St. Paul: West Publishing Co. 1979).

User's Guide to Lawyers (Arlington, VA: Citizen's Clearinghouse for Hazardous Wastes, 1983).

Stephen Elias, *Legal Research: How to Find and Understand the Law*, 3rd rev. ed., (Berkeley: Nolo Press,1992).

Excellent introduction to law. Fairly formal but clear. Highly recommended.

Citizen Suits: An Analysis of Citizen Enforcement Action under EPA-Administered Statutes (Washington, DC: Environmental Law Institute, 1984).

Edward Felsenthal, "Lawyers Who Switch Sides Draw Ire With Big Checks." *Wall Street Journal*, Jul. 19, 1990.

Chris Goodrich, "A Problematic Profession." *The Nation*, Feb. 12, 1990, pp. 205-208.

Reviews four books about lawyers.

Cindy Hill, "Environmental Law: A Mixed Bag ... But Useful." *Wild Earth*, Spring 1991, pp. 46-49.

Thomas More Hoban and Richard Oliver Brooks, *Green Justice: The Environment and the Courts* (Boulder: Westview Press, 1987).

Rand Jack and Dana Crowley Jack, *Moral Vision and Professional Decisions: The Changing Values of Women and Men Lawyers* (New York: Cambridge University Press. 1990).

Lisa Jorgensen and Jeffrey Kimmel, *Environmental Citizen Suits: Confronting the Corporation* (Washington, DC: Bureau of National Affairs, 1988).

Lawrence E. Kaplan, "A Compendium of Hazardous Substance Laws and Issues Involving Real Estate," *Industrial Development*, Vol. 157 No. 1 (Jan/Feb 1988), pp. 13-21.

Samuel J. Kling, *The Complete Guide to Everyday Law*, 3rd. Edn. (Chicago: Follett Publishing Co. 1973).

Very useful.

Jonathan M. Moses, "Lawyer Given to Filing Shareholder Lawsuits Comes Under Scrutiny," *Wall St. Journal*, Oct. 28, 1992.

About shareholder activism.

Karen Orren, "Standing to Sue: Interest Group Conflict in the Federal Courts," *American Political Science Review*, 70 (Sep. 1976), pp. 723-41anan.

How to Use a Law Library (San Francisco: People's Law School [558 Capp St., San Francisco, CA 94110], 1976).

James Stokes, "Legal Aspects of Real Estate Transactions Involving Environmental Concerns," *Industrial Development*, Vol. 155, No. 5 (Sept/Oct 1986), pp. 10-14.

Robert V. Stover, *Making It and Breaking It: The Fate of Public Interest Commitment During Law School*, Howard S. Erlanger, Ed. (Champaign: University of Illinois. 1990).

4. Negotiations

Jim Britell, "Negotiate to Win," *Whole Earth Review*, Spring 1992.

Robert Cahn, *Footprints on the Planet: A Search for an Environmental Ethic* (New York: Universe Books, 1978).

Especially see Chapter 6 on negotiations concerning a molybdenum mine in Colorado and the aftermath.

Alan R. Chesler, "Negotiating the Environmental Issues in Real Estate Contracts," *Industrial Development*, Vol. 156, No. 3 (May/June 1987), pp. 19-22.

Includes discussion of environmental audits.

Herb Cohen, *You Can Negotiate Anything* (Secaucus, NJ: Lyle Stuart Inc., 1980).

Morton Yanow, "Mutual Agreement: Tactics For Negotiating," *Whole Earth Review*, Spring 1992.

5. Intimidation, Whistleblowing, And Related Topics

Penelope Canan and George W. Pring. "Strategic Lawsuits Against Public Participation," *Social Problems*, 35 (December 1988), pp. 506-19.

Ward Churchill and Jim Vander Wall, *Agents of Repression: The FBI's Secret Wars Against the Black Panther Party and the American Indian Movement* (Boston: South End Press, 1989).

Paul Duggan, "Bowie Woman Finds Activism May Carry $8 Million Price Tag: Some Say Contractor's Suit Against Development Foe Is Intimidation," *Washington Post*, June 24, 1991

Brian Glick, *War at Home: Covert Action Against U.S. Activists and What We Can Do About It* (Boston: South End Press, 1989).

About the FBI.

Diana R. Gordon, "Justice Watch: Can Sessions Tame the Bureau?" *The Nation*, Oct. 30, 1989, p. 488.

FBI surveillance of domestic organizations such as Southern Christian Leadership Conference and United Auto Workers.

Government Accountability Project, *Courage Without Martyrdom: A Survival Guide For Whistleblowers* (Washington, DC: Government Accountability Project [810 1st St. NE, Ste. 630, Washington, DC], n.d.).

About whistleblowing.

Joan Hamilton, "Blowing the Whistle Without Paying the Piper," *Business Week*, Jun. 3, 1991, pp. 138-9.

Timothy H. Ingram, "On Muckrakers and Whistle Blowers," *Business and Society Review*, No. 3 (Autumn 1972), pp. 21-30.

In-company underground papers, etc.

Associated Press, "Now Accepting Tip-Offs: The Whistleblowers Bulletin Board," *Washington Post*, Dec. 13, 1991.

Kenneth O'Reilly, *"Racial Matters": The FBI's Secret File on Black America, 1960-72* (New York: The Free Press/MacMillan, 1989).

Robert D. Richards, "Suing to Squelch: A New Way to Keep Activists Quiet," *Washington Post*, Aug. 6, 1992.

Robert J. Ringer, *Winning Through Intimidation* (New York: Funk & Wagnalls, 1975).

One man's view of how successful businesspeople operate. Examples from the world of real estate transactions.

Kirkpatrick Sale, "Silent Spring and After: The U.S. Green Movement Today," *The Nation*, Jul. 19, 1993, pp. 92-96.

Stephanie Simon, "Nader Suits Up To Strike Back Against 'Slapps'" *Wall St. Journal*, July 9, 1991.

Abigail Trafford, "Ivory Tower Whistle-Blowers: Researchers Who Allege Scientific Fraud Pay a Price" *Washington Post Health Magazine, March 26, 1991.*

"How to Deal With Intimidation" (Billings, Montana: Western Organization of Resource Councils, June, 1992).

Daniel Westman, *Whistleblowing: The Law of Retaliatory Discharge* (Washington, DC: BNA Books, 1991).

6. Experts And Science

Louis Blumberg and Robert Gottlieb, "Garbage Wars: Citizens Take on the 'Experts'," *The Nation*, May 28, 1990, pp. 742-744.

Brief, excellent glimpse at waste industry consultants and the revolving door between the industry, academia, and government. Discusses how this coziness affects quality and focus of related research. Mentions some useful alternative newsletters.

Phillip M. Boffey, *The Brain Bank of America: An Inquiry Into the Politics of Science*, Introduction by Ralph Nader (New York: McGraw Hill Book Co./Center for the Study of Responsive Law, 1975).

General background information and an episodic history of the National Academy of Sciences. Specific details and examples of reports or studies that have been influenced, rejected, not released, toned down, or otherwise modified for non-scientific reasons. Illustrates and discusses the revolving door and other links between government and corporations. Very helpful for understanding tricky wording, the framing of research questions, evaluating and critiquing technical studies.

William Broad and Nicholas Wade, *Betrayers of the Truth: Fraud and Deceit in the Halls of Science* (New York: Simon and Schuster, 1982).

Christopher Cerf and Victor Navasky, Eds., *The Experts Speak: The Definitive Compendium of Authoritative Misinformation). (New York: Pantheon Press, 1984).*

Barry Commoner, *Science and Survival* (New York: The Viking Press, 1963).

Barry Commoner, *The Closing Circle: Nature, Man, and Technology* (New York: Alfred A. Knopf, 1971).

Includes Commoner's famous four laws of ecology.

Frank Kuznik, "Fraud Busters," *The Washington Post Magazine*, Apr. 14, 1991.

How two men, known to some as the 'science police,' find out about, prove, and publicize fraud in health-related research.

Patrick Lagadec, *Major Technological Risk: An Assessment of Industrial Disasters* (New York: Pergamon Press. 1982).

Describes famous disasters and how they were handled, and provides brief history of disasters during last two centuries. Contains very blunt advice for proponents of unpopular projects on dodging questions, shifting attention, denying, reassuring, etc.)

George Miller and John Lawrence. "Muzzled Experts," *The Nation*, Feb. 26, 1990, p. 261.

Examples of experts forced by political pressure to alter findings.

Ralph Moss, *The Cancer Industry: Unraveling the Politics* (New York: Paragon House, 1989).

Farley Mowat, *Woman in the Mists: The Story of Dian Fossey and the Mountain Gorillas of Africa* (New York: Warner Books, 1988).

A glimpse into behind-the-scenes struggles in fundraising, research grants, and academic prestige. Highly recommended.

Charles Perrow, *Normal Accidents: Living With High-Risk Technologies* (New York: Basic Books, Inc. 1984).

Discussions of petrochemical plants, aircraft and airways, boats, dams, mines, lakes, space research, weapons, and DNA. Thorough notes and extensive bibliography.

Charles Perrow, "The Habit of Courting Disaster," *The Nation*, Oct. 11, 1986.

James Allen Smith, *The Idea Brokers: Think Tanks and the Rise of the New Policy Elite* (New York: The Free Press, 1991).

David Warsh, "Science Scandals Evidence of Trouble in Universities' Cloisters," *Washington Post*, Feb. 12, 1992.

Harriet Zuckerman, *Science Elite: Nobel Laureates in the United States* (New York: Free Press, 1979).

A sociology of Nobel Prizes.

7. General Background

anon., "Utility Challenges," *Corporate Examiner*, 3, No. 10, Oct 1974.

About a university study and pressure on a corporation to reduce a plant's harmful effects.

anon., "Siting of Hazardous Waste Landfills and Their Correlation with Racial and Economic Status of Surrounding Communities." (Washington, DC: General Accounting Office, June 1, 1983).

anon., "Why Your Radicals Zero in on Business," *Nation's Business*, July 1967, pp. 31-4.

Judd H. Alexander, *In Defense of Garbage*. (Westport, CT: Praeger. 1993).

Excellent details about waste-related issues.

Saul Alinsky, *Rules for Radicals: A Pragmatic Primer for Realistic Radicals* (New York: Vintage Books, 1972).

Leslie Allan, et al. *Paper Profits: Pollution in the Pulp and Paper Industry* (Cambridge: MIT Press, 1970).

Lawrence S. Bacow and James R. Milkey. "Overcoming Opposition to Hazardous Waste Facilities: The Massachusetts Approach," *Harvard Environmental Law Review*, Vol 6, No. 2 (1982), pp. 265-301.

Howard Ball, *Justice Downwind: America's Atomic Testing Program in the 1950's* (New York: Oxford University Press, 1986).

Bill Bishop, "The River Authority Lands a Deal — And Four Years Later, Throws It Back," *Texas Observer*, March 8, 1985, pp. 9-13.

Harry C. Boyte, *The Backyard Revolution: Understanding the New Citizen Movement* (Philadelphia: Temple University Press, 1980).

Denis J. Brion, *Essential Industry and the NIMBY Phenomenon* (New York: Quorum Books, 1991).

Dry, academic, somewhat sympathetic discussion of the NIMBY phenomenon, which recognizes that the phenomenon is more a symptom than a problem in itself. Critical discussion of the legal process and the judicial system.

Abraham J. Briloff, *Unaccountable Accounting* (New York: Harper & Row, 1972).

Paul Brodeur, *Currents of Death: Power Lines, Computer Terminals, and the Attempt to Cover Up Their Threat to Your Health* (New York: Simon & Schuster, 1990).

Paul Brodeur, "Annals of Radiation: Calamity on Meadow Street," *The New Yorker*, July 9, 1990, pp. 38-72.

Discusses the possible adverse health effects of electromagnetic fields (from power lines, electric substations, and other sources). Also illustrates how neighbors got together and struggled to discover possible health hazards in their environment.

David R. Brower, "The Politics of Environmental Compromise," *Earth First! The Radical Environmental Journal*, Brigid Edition, Feb. 2, 1990, pp. 26, 28.

Michael H. Brown, *The Toxic Cloud: The Poisoning of America's Air* (New York: Harper & Row, Publishers, 1987).

Largely anecdotal discussion of U.S. toxic chemicals and wind patterns.

Michael Brown, *Laying Waste: The Poisoning of America by Toxic Chemicals* (New York: Washington Square Press, 1981).

Phil Brown and Edwin J. Mikkelsen, *No Safe Place: Toxic Waste, Leukemia, and Community Action* (Berkeley: University of California Press, 1990).

Documents individual struggles to identify disease-causing toxic chemical releases and to obtain legal relief. Discusses obstacles to be overcome.

Robert D. Bullard, Ed., *Confronting Environmental Racism: Voices From the Grassroots* (Boston: South End Press, 1993).

Charles G. Burck, "The Intricate Politics of the Corporation," *Fortune*, Apr. 1975, pp. 109-112, 188-192.

Robert Cahn, *Footprints on the Planet: A Search for an Environmental Ethic* (New York: Universe Books, 1978).

Somewhat superficial, but useful example of negotiations concerning molybdenum mine in Colorado and its aftermath. Also discusses Nature Conservancy and other land trust options.

Frances Cairncross, *Costing the Earth* (Cambridge: Harvard Business School, 1992).

A mainstream analysis which looks at variety of less harmful industry practices. Also discusses government policies essentially subsidizing environmentally damaging practices.

Lynton K. Caldwell, *Citizens and the Environment: Case Studies in Popular Action.* (Bloomington: University of Indiana Press, 1978).

Jasper Carlton, "Of Politics, Extinctions, and Ecological Collapse," *Earth First! The Radical Environmental Journal*, Samhain Edition, Nov. 1, 1989.

Excellent update on current application and enforcement of the Endangered Species Act. Discussions of exemptions, loopholes, etc.

Jasper Carlton, "Hundreds of Species Going Extinct While Bush Administration Delays ESA Listings," *Earth First! The Radical Environmental Journal*, Eostar Edition, Mar. 20, 1990, Vol. X. No. IV.

Jasper Carlton, et al, "Killing Roads: A Citizens' Primer on the Effects & Removal of Roads," Insert in *Earth First! Journal*, May 1, 1990.

Rachel Carson, *Silent Spring* (Boston: Houghton Mifflin Co., 1962).

Still scary, compelling, and all too true.

Roger E. Celler, *The Challengers* (Washington, DC: Public Affairs Council, 1971).

Profiles 60 organizations "dedicated to changing the private sector in America." Updated in 1975, 1977.)

Alexander Cockburn, "Beat the Devil: Relatives and Close Friends of the Dead," *The Nation*, Feb. 26, 1990, p. 263.

Brief but clever example of analyzing statistics and finding contradictions, even while lacking outside, independent data.

Frank L. Cross and John L. Simons, Eds., *Industrial Plant Siting* (Westport, CT: Technomic Publishing Co., Inc. 1975).

Not current, but published after EPA laws of the early 1970s. Discusses social and environmental impacts, including community resistance and regulations. Offers insight into how siting decisions are made.

Cathy L. Dalcoff, "The State and Local Bond Rating Process," *Intergovernmental Perspectives*, Fall 1990, pp. 31-34.

Excellent summary of terms, ratings, current issues, possible trends, etc.

Michael Danielson, *The Politics of Exclusion* (New York: Columbia University Press, 1976).

Charles Darwin, *The Formation of Vegetable Mould, Through the Action of Worms* (London: John Murray, Albemarle Street, 1881).

Darwin's last work. Reminds us of need for humility and common sense in science.

Lee A. Deets, "Environmental Risk Management," *Industrial Development*, Mar/Apr. 1988, Vol. 157, No. 2, pp. 8-11.

Gary Delgado, *Organizing the Movement: The Roots and Growth of ACORN* (Philadelphia, PA: Temple University Press, 1986.)

Summaries and brief histories of organizing trends in U.S. Compares and contrasts origins and developments of various groups and movements, especially poor and ethnic minorities. Includes specific examples from campaigns.

Sara Diamond, "Free Market Environmentalism," *Z Magazine*, Dec. 1991, pp. 52-56.

Michael R. Edelstein, *Contaminated Communities: The Social and Psychological Impacts of Residential Toxic Exposure* (Boulder: Westview Press, 1988).

Robert Engler, "Portrait of an Oil Spill: How the System Fails," *The Nation*, Mar. 5, 1990, pp. 300-302.

Paul A. Erickson, *Environmental Impact Assessment: Principles and Applications* (New York: Academic Press, 1974).

Square and thorough.

Nicholas Freudenberg, *Not In Our Backyards! Community Action for Health and the Environment* (New York: Monthly Review Press, 1984).

Lois Marie Gibbs, *Love Canal: My Story* (Albany: State University of New York Press, 1982).

Marilyn Gittell, *Limits to Citizen Participation* (Beverly Hills: Sage Publications, 1980).

Bob Hall, Ed., *Environmental Politics: Lessons from the Grassroots* (Durham, NC: Institute for Southern Studies, 1989).

Charles F. Harding, "Company Politics in Plant Location." *Industrial Development*, Vol. 151, No. 5 (Sept/Oct. 1982), pp. 19-20.

Exceptionally useful and concise.

Tom Harris, "The Kesterson Syndrome: The federal irrigation projects that made the deserts bloom are now killing wildlife throughout the West," *The Amicus Journal*, Fall 1989, pp. 4-9.

Thomas More Hoban and Richard Oliver Brooks, *Green Justice: The Environment and the Courts* (Boulder: Westview Press, 1987).

Don Holmes, "The Southern Company: The Big Polluter," *Business and Society Review*, No. 14 (Summer 1975), pp. 14-20.

How an electric company really operated.

Robert Horvitz, "Inhabiting the Electromagnetic Environment," *Whole Earth Review*, Fall 1990, pp. 125-129.

Discusses other good references.

James C. Hoskins, "Environmental Considerations in the Disposal or Acquisition of Corporate Real Estate," *Industrial Development*, Vol. 156, No. 6 (Nov/Dec. 1987), pp. 1-6.

Includes legal references.

Gayle Hudgens, "Muons and megabucks: super collider - super bust?," *The Nation*, Mar. 19, 1990, p. 365.

Not-In-My-Backyard! Community Reaction to Locally Unwanted Land Use (Charlottesville: University of Virginia Institute for Environmental Negotiation, 1984).

Academic discussion of NIMBY phenomenon.

Stephen C. Jones, "Toxic Contamination and Liability: Precautionary Action and Post-Discovery Alternatives," *Industrial Development*, Vol. 156, No. 3 (Jul/Aug. 1987), pp. 4-7.

Eileen Kohl Kaufman, "Why the Paper Companies Cleaned Up," *Business and Society Review*, No. 6 (Summer 1973), pp. 51-55.

Charles Komanoff, et al., *The Price of Power: Electric Utilities and the Environment* (New York: Council on Economic Priorities, 1973).

Felicia Kornbluh, "Fight Harvard Fiercely," *The Nation*, Apr. 16, 1990. pp. 534-36.

Review of Trumpbour's How Harvard Rules.

Winona Laduke, "Practical Politics: White Earth," *Z Magazine*, Oct. 1990, pp. 39-40.

How recent private-property issues affecting Native Americans have been resolved.

Lisa Y. Lefferts, "Cows on Drugs?," *Nutrition Action Healthletter*, Apr. 1990, p. 8.

Steven D. Lydenberg, *Minding the Corporate Conscience 1978: Public Interest Groups and Corporate Social Accountability* (New York and San Francisco: Council on Economic Priorities. 1977).

Brian Maffly, "Open Meetings Law Goes to Court" *Texas Observer*, September 15, 1989.

Christopher Manes, *Green Rage: Radical Environmentalism and the Unmaking of Civilization* (Boston: Little, Brown & Co., 1990).

Reviews the practical and philosophical background of Earth First! and Deep Ecology. Discusses the validity of various strategies and tactics. Good discussion of professionalization and lawyerization among mainstream environmental groups during the late 1970s and 1980s.

Bruce S. Margolis, "Getting Started in Eminent Domain Valuations," Journal of Accountancy, Dec. 1990, pp. 63-71.

Good, introductory discussion about calculating prices in eminent domain evaluations. Covers a number of basic issues.

Steven J. Mastrovich, "An Overview of the Resource Conservation and Recovery Act," *Industrial Development*, Vol. 156, No. 6 (Sep/Oct. 1987), pp. 23-27.

George A. McAlmon, "The Corporate Boardroom: A Closed Circle," *Business and Society Review*, No. 12 (Winter 1974-75), pp. 65-71.

Good summary of structure, concentration of power, description of directors, etc.

Laton McCartney, *Friends in High Places: The Bechtel Story: The Most Secret Corporation and How It Engineered the World* (New York: Simon & Schuster, 1988).

Lee Metcalf and Vic Reinemer. *Overcharge* (New York: David McKay Co. Inc., 1967).

A basic though dated introduction to investor-owned utilities. Includes examples of regulatory tricks, especially during rate hearings. Guidelines for eliciting community support and step-by-step explanation of how investor-owned utility can take over a public power company. Often too uncritical, but offers good description of how large, powerful utility companies operate.

Gerald C. Meyers (with John Holusha), *When It Hits the Fan: Managing the Nine Crises of Business* (Boston: Houghton Mifflin Co., 1986).

Robert Cameron Mitchell and Richard T. Carson, "Siting of Hazardous Facilities: Property Rights, Protest and the Siting of Hazardous Waste Facilities," *The American Economic Review*, Vol. 76, No.2 May 1986), pp. 285-294.

Good, brief introduction.

David Morris and Karl Hess, *Neighborhood Power: The New Localism* (Boston, MA: Beacon Press, 1975).

Jane Anne Morris, "Board and Staff: An Ethnography of the Lower Colorado River Authority of Texas," (Ph.D. diss., University of Texas, 1987)

Ralph Nader, Mark Green, and Joel Seligman, *Taming the Giant Corporation* (New York: W. W. Norton & Co. 1976).

Excellent examination of corporate power in the U.S. and citizen's recourse. In particular, see Chapter V on "Corporate Secrecy vs. Corporate Disclosure."

Roderick Frazier Nash, *The Rights of Nature: A History of Environmental Ethics* (Madison: University of Wisconsin Press, 1989).

Wayne Owens, "Activists Must Learn to Sugar Coat the Bitter Pill," *Business and Society Review*, No. 71 Fall 1989), pp. 8-10.

Good, general, moderate, cautious, and concise discussion of activists' false assumptions.

Charles B. Perrow, *Organizational Analysis: A Sociological View* (Monterey, CA: Brooks/Cole Publishing Company. 1970).

Like the Thompson (James D., below) volume; a brief, excellent introduction to organizational behavior. Especially see chapters on "The Environment" and "Organizational Goals." Less academic than Thompson, Organizations In Action, cited below.

Charles B. Perrow, *The Radical Attack on Business* (New York: Harcourt Brace, Jovanovich, 1972).

Charles Piller, *The Fail-Safe Society: Community Defiance and the End of American Technological Optimism* (New York: HarperCollins, 1991).

Includes useful case studies and good though brief discussion of tradeoffs and conditions.

Frances Fox Piven and Richard A. Cloward, *Poor People's Movements: Why They Succeed, How They Fail* (New York: Pantheon Books, 1977).

Sidney Plotkin, *Keep Out: The Struggle for Land Use Control* (Berkeley: University of California Press, 1987).

Discussion of the meaning of "property rights" in the late twentieth century United States. Includes broad historical background and case studies. Highly recommended.

Richard Reynolds, Ed., *The Best of Mother Jones: Insights and Investigations from Our 1st Decade.* Deirdre English, *Exec. Ed.* (San Francisco: Foundation for National Progress, 1985).

Hart Schaefer, "Movement Mutterings: How to Deal with the Sierra Club." *Wild Earth*, Spring 1991, pp. 52-53.

Roger W. Schmenner, *Making Business Location Decisions* (Englewood Cliffs, N.J.: Prentice- Hall Inc. 1982).

S. Prakash Sethi, *Up Against the Corporate Wall* (Englewood Cliffs, N.J.: Prentice-Hall, 1971, 1974, 1977).

28 case studies about industry tactics. Especially see study of nuclear power plant in 1971 edition, which illustrates many typical industry maneuvers.

Jim Sibbison, "Going for Superfund Gold: Revolving Door at the E.P.A," *The Nation*, Nov. 6, 1989, p. 524.

How governmental cleanup dollars are bonanza for consulting firms and contractors in waste disposal industry.

Barry Sims, "Private Rights in Public Lands? The New 'Range War' Moves to a Familiar Battleground — the Courts," *The Workbook* (Southwest Research and Information Center [P.O. Box 4524, Albuquerque, NM 87106], Summer 1993).

Nathaniel N. Sperber and Otto Lerbinger, *Manager's Public Relations Handbook* (Reading, Mass.: Addison-Wesley Publishing Co. 1982).

Excellent introduction to public relations strategies and tactics used by managers and others. Especially useful for background into public relations and for insight into Entity behavior.

Robert Streeter, "Wilderness and Photography: The Killing Films." *Earth First! The Radical Environmental Journal*, Eostar Edition, Vol. X. No. IV (Mar. 20, 1990).

Use of chemicals in photography.

Bruce Stutz, "Environment: Cleaning Up," *The Atlantic*, October 1990, pp. 46-50.

Discusses the environmental cleanup business and citizen activities.

James D. Thompson, *Organizations in Action* (New York: McGraw Hill Co. 1967).

An excellent though academic overview of theories about how and why organizations work. Brief, concise, and clear. Discusses topics like how organizations buffer their contacts with the outside, control their external environment, re-

duce their uncertainties, and use co-optation. Contains excellent bibliography.

John Trumpbour, Ed., *How Harvard Rules: Reason in the Service of Empire* (Boston: South End Press. 1990).

Useful for adversary relationships with large, powerful universities.

David Vogel, "Corporations and the Left," *Socialist Review*, 20, No. 2 (Oct. 1974), pp. 45-66.

Milan Wall and Vicki Luther, *Six Myths about the Future of Small Towns* (The Heartland Center for Leadership Development [941 O St. Ste. 920, Lincoln, NE 68508], 1993).

Peter Wathern, Ed., *Environmental Impact Assessment: Theory and Practice* (London: Unwin Hymes, 1988).

Straightforward, mainstream analysis.

Elliott Weiss, "Proxy Voting on Social Issues: A Growth Industry," *Business and Society Review*, No. 11 (Autumn 1974), pp. 16-22.

William Worthy, *The Rape of Our Neighborhoods — And How Communities Are Resisting Take-overs by Colleges, Hospitals, Churches, Businesses and Public Agencies* (New York: Morrow, 1976).

Louise B. Young, *Power Over People* (New York: Oxford University Press. 1973).

How an Ohio community attempted to prevent an electric utility from erecting power lines, and what it learned along the way.

Margaret Hays Young and Mitch Friedman, "Legislative Corner: What the Big 10 [environmental groups] Don't Tell You," *Wild Earth*, Spring 1991, pp. 50-51.

8. Newsletters And Organizations

Acid Rain Foundation, Inc., 1410 Varsity Dr., Raleigh, NC 27606

American Rivers, 801 Pennsylvania Ave. SE, Ste. 400, Washington, DC 20003.

ATTRA News, Appropriate Technology Transfer for Rural Areas, Jim Lukens, Program Manager, P.O. Box 3657, Fayetteville, AR 72702.

Center for Investigative Reporting, 530 Howard St., 2nd Floor, San Francisco, CA 94105-3007.

Center for Policy Alternatives, 1875 Connecticut Ave. NW, Ste. 7110, Washington, DC 20009.

Center for Science in the Public Interest, 1875 Connecticut Ave. NW, No. 300, Washington, DC 20009.

Citizen Alert, Box 5391, Reno, NV, 89513.

A highly praised newsletter about the military.

Citizen's Clearinghouse for Hazardous Wastes, Inc., P.O. Box 6806, Falls Church, VA 22040.

*Publishes two newsletters, **Everyone's Backyard** and **Environmental Health Monthly**. CCHW also offers a number of very specific fact sheets on subjects like "Recycling Household Batteries" and "Pulp and Paper Mill Wastes", lists of toxic waste sites (by state), and numerous useful pamphlets, such as "Will a Health Survey Work for You?," "Users Guide to Experts," "Users Guide to Lawyers," "Should Your Group Incorporate?," "Best of Legal Corner," "Best of Organizing Toolbox," "200+ Questions about New Sites," "How to Deal With a Proposed Facility," "How to Deal With Trouble," "How to Raise & Manage Money," and "How to Win in Public Hearings."*

Citizens for Alternatives to Radioactive Dumping, 144 Harvard SE, Albuquerque, NM 87106.

Clean Water Action, 1320 18th St. NW, Washington, DC 20036.

The Radioactive Rag. Concerned Citizens for Nuclear Safety, 412 W. San Francisco St., Santa Fe, NM 87501.

The Corporate Examiner, Interfair Center on corporate Responsibility, 475 Riverside Dr., Rm. 566, New York, NY 10115.

Council on Economic Priorities, 30 Irving Pl., New York, NY 10003.

The Data Center, (464 19th St., Oakland, CA, 94612, 415/835-4692.)

Described as the nation's "leading public interest library."

Earth Island Institute, 300 Broadway, Ste. 28, San Francisco, CA 94133.

Endangered Species Update, University of Michigan, School of Natural Resources, Ann Arbor, MI 48109.

Endangered Species Technical Bulletin. Department of the Interior, U.S. Fish & Wildlife Service, 1849 C. St., NW, Washington, DC 20240.

Environmental Action, 6930 Carroll Ave., 6th Floor, Tacoma Park, MD 20912.

Environmental Defense Fund, 257 Park Ave. South, New York, NY 10010.

The Environmental Exchange, 1930 18th St. NW, No. 24, Washington, DC 20009.

Environmental Health Perspectives, U.S. Department of Health and Human Services, 200 Independence Ave. SW, Washington, DC 20201.

EPA Journal, Environmental Protection Agency, 401 M St. SW, Washington, DC 20460.

FOIA Update (Washington, DC: U.S. Department of Justice, Office of Information and Privacy, Constitution Ave. and Tenth St NW, Washington, DC 20530).

Forest Watch: The Citizens' Forestry Magazine, Cascade Holistic Economic Consultants, 3758 SE Milwaukee, Portland, OR 97202.

Freedom of Information Clearinghouse, P.O Box 19367, Washington, DC 20036.

Friends of the Earth, 218 D. St. SE, Washington, DC 20003.

Fully Informed Jury Association, National Headquarters, P.O. Box 59, Helmville, MT 59843 (800-835-5879).

Golob Oil Pollution Bulletin, Richard Golob, Publisher, World Information Systems, Box 535, Harvard Square Station, Cambridge, MA 02238.

Greens Clearinghouse, P.O. Box 30208, Kansas City, MO 64112.

The Greens/Green Party USA, P.O. Box 30208, Kansas City, MO 64112.

Ground Work, P. O. Box 14141, San Francisco, CA 94114.

Described as "a photo-newsmagazine covering community organizing, direct action, and other grassroots work." Includes many book reviews.

High Country News, High Country Foundation, P. O. Box 1090, Paonia, CO 81428.

Covers a wide range of issues including agriculture and ranching, forests and wildlife, energy and development, military issues of local importance, public lands, U.S. government agencies, Native American Issues, recreation, water issues, and legislation and advocacy groups.

Inside EPA, Washington Publishers, P.O. Box 7167, Ben Franklin Station, Washington, DC 20044.

Invaluable and detailed, but terribly expensive. State regulatory agencies may have copies you can look at.

Institute for Local Self-Reliance, 2425 18th St. NW, Washington, DC 20009-2096.

Produces concise fact sheets on different aspects of local self-reliance. Excellent for communities attempting to regain control of their futures.

Integrity International, Ste. 102, Dept. P, 6215 Greenbelt Rd., College Park, MD 20740.

On whistleblowing.

News for Investors, Investor Responsibility Research Center publication, 1755 Massachusetts Ave. NW, No. 600, Washington, DC 20036.

The Land trust Alliance, 900 17th St. NW, Washington, DC 20006-2596.

League of Conservation Voters, 1797 L St. NW, Washington, DC 20036.

National Association for the Advancement of Colored People, 4805 Mt. Hope Dr., Baltimore, MD 21215.

National Appropriate Technology Assistance Service, P.O. Box 2525, Butte, MT 50702-2525.

National Audubon Society, 950 Third Ave., New York, NY 10022.

National Center for Appropriate Technology, P.O. Box 3838, Butte, MT 59702-3838.

National Coalition Against the Misuse of Pesticides, 701 Edwards st. SW, Ste. 200, Washington, DC 20009.

National Coalition for Universities in the Public Interest, 1801 18th St. NW, Washington, DC 20009.

If Entity is a university, this organization will help with research.

National Environmental Coalition of Native Americans, 100 Watson Dr., No. N2, Yale, OK 74085.

National Lawyer's Guild, 55 6th Ave., New York, NY 10013.

National Renewable Energy Laboratory, 1617 Cole Blvd., Golden, CO 80401-3393.

National Resources Defense Council, 40 W. 20th St., New York, NY 10011.

National Toxics Campaign, 1168 Commonwealth Ave., Boston, MA 02134.

Native Americans for a Clean Environment, P.O. box 1671, Tahlequah, OK 74465.

The Nature Conservancy, 1815 N. Lynn St., Arlington, VA 22209.

Nuclear Information and Resource Service, 1424 16th St. NW, Ste. 601, Washington, DC 20036.

Public Citizen, 2000 P. St. NW, Ste. 610, Washington, DC 20036.

"Rachel's Hazardous Waste News." Peter Montague, Ed.. Environmental Research Foundation, Box 5036, Annapolis, MD 21403-7036.

Renew America, 1400 16th St. NW, Ste. 710, Washington, DC 20036

An environmental clearinghouse.

Rocky Mountain Institute, 1739 Snowmass Creek Rd., Snowmass, CO 81654.

Science for the People, Lisa Greber, Dir., 897 Main St., Cambridge, MA, 02139.

Southern Exposure, Institute for Southern Studies, Box 531, Durham, NC 27701-3163.

Sierra Club, 730 Polk St., San Francisco, CA 94109.

Southern Poverty Law Center, 400 Washington Ave., Montgomery, AL 36104.

Union of Concerned Scientists, 26 Church St., Cambridge, MA 02238.

United Church of Christ Commission for Racial Justice, 700 Prospect Ave. E., 7th Fl., Cleveland, OH 44115-1110.

Wilderness Society, 900 17th St., Washington, DC 20003.

Waste Not, Paul and Ellen Connett, eds., 82 Judson, Canton, NY 13617.

Includes information about incinerators.

The Workbook, Southwest Research and Information Center, P. O. Box 4524, Albuquerque, NM 87106.

A quarterly newsletter focussing on environmental and social change.

9. Periodicals and Trade Journals

Periodicals and trade journals are published by virtually every industry. They offer information, insights, and perspectives often available nowhere else, because they are written by insiders for insiders.

An example of a particularly useful journal is *Industrial Development* (which has, at different times, been titled *Industrial Development and Site Selection Handbook* and *Site Selection and Industrial Development*). This trade organ is international in scope, and it carries much advertising from states, localities, and energy companies promoting themselves to industry. Wide-ranging article discuss topics like hazardous substance disposal laws, corporate liability, requests for information on site acquisitions, site selection criteria and processes, and conflicts caused by endangerd species.

Among the other useful trade journals are: *The Appraisal Journal*; *Buildings*; *Business Insurance*; *The Business Lawyer*; *Case Research Journal*; *Chemical Marketing Reporter*; *Chemical Week*; *Chilton's Distribution*; *Coal*; *Construction Review*; *EP: Electrical Perspectives*; *Electric Power Monthly*; *Electrical World*; *ENR: Engineering News Record*; *The Facilities Construction and Management Magazine*; *Foundry Management and Technology*; *Industrial Engineering*; *Intergovernmental Perspective*; Iron *Age: The Management Magazine for Metal Producers*; *Journal of Accountancy*; *The Journal of Business Strategy*; *The Journal of Law and Economics*; and *The Transportation and Business Logistics Magazine*.

10. Newspaper Articles

anon., "Little of Superfund Settlements Go to Cleanup," (Associated Press), *New York Times*, Apr. 26, 1992.

Michael Abramowitz, "Chicago's 'Toxic Wasteland' Breeds Blue-Collar Environmentalism" *Washington Post*, Nov. 8, 1992.

William Claiborne, "Quebec Caught in Hydropower Clash; Environmental Dispute Jeopardizes Plan to Export Energy to U.S," *Washington Post*, Apr. 13, 1991; "Quebec, Indians Wage Public-Relations War: Crees Seek to Halt Hydroelectric Project," *Washington Post*, Nov. 28, 1991; "Duties Placed On Magnesium From Canada," *Washington Post*, Dec. 3, 1991.

Lynne Duke, "A Touch of Africa Makes a Last Stand; Resorts Threaten to Push Living Link Off South Carolina Island," *Washington Post*, Mar. 23, 1991; "Proliferating Boycotts Turn Buying Power Into Political Clout," *Washington Post*, Apr. 14, 1991.

John R. Emshwiller, "Don't Tell Mort Diamond You Can't Fight City Hall; Hot-Dog Hawker Proves Talk Is Cheap — and Effective — Against Regulators," *Wall Street Journal*, Mar. 12, 1991.

Barnaby J. Feder, "In the Clutches of the Superfund Mess," *New York Times*, Jun. 16, 1991.

Tim Golden, "Dump Bid Assailed Along Rio Grande," *New York Times*, Mar. 29, 1992.

Lauren Ina, "Sioux Debate Whether to Use 'Mother Earth' for Waste Dump," *Washington Post*, Aug. 24, 1991.

David Maraniss, "Fight Over Dump Unites Enemies in Texas Town," *Washington Post*, Jul. 27, 1991.

Bryan McKenzie, "Park's expansion in jeopardy as neighbors recollect legacy of lies." *Charlottesville* (Virginia) *Daily Progress*, Oct. 14, 1990.

Eugene L. Meyer, "Toxic Waste Incinerator Generates Activism," *Washington Post*, Sep. 23, 1991; "Trashman Woos a Md. County: Allegany Considers Multi-million-Dollar Landfill Offer," *Washington Post*, Dec. 26, 1991.

Robert B. Rackleff, "The Oozing of America: While Our Pipelines and Tank Farms Dribble, Congress Diddles," *Washington Post*, Sep. 15, 1991.

Megan Rosenfeld, "Shelters in a Storm; The Ward 3 Debate: Do the Homeless Make Good Neighbors?" *Washington Post*, Mar. 28, 1991.

Ronald Smothers, "Future in Mind, Choctaws Reject Plan for Landfill," *New York Times*, Apr. 21, 1991.

Mariflo Stephens, "When Issues Hit Home: LULUs, NIMBYs and Other Angles on Neighborhood Activism," *Washington Post*, Nov. 4, 1991.

Robert Tomsho, "Pollution Ploy: Big Corporations Hit By Superfund Cases Find Way to Share Bill; They Sue Small Businesses, Others That Put Garbage Into the Same Landfills," *Wall Street Journal*, Apr. 2, 1991.

How the Superfund Law of 1980 can be applied to waste-related NIMBY *issues.*

Sam Howe Verhovek, "Nuclear Dump Divides a Rural Town," *New York Times*, Jul. 12, 1991.

G. Pascal Zachary, "All the News? Many Journalists See A Growing Reluctance to Criticize Advertisers," *Wall Street Journal*, Feb. 6, 1992.

Focuses especially on newspapers and realtors.

Index

J

K

L

M

N